CLICK ON 3

Teacher´s Book

Virginia Evans - Neil O'Sullivan

Express Publishing

Contents

	TOPICS	VOCABULARY	GRAMMAR
UNIT 1 Busy Days (pp. 6 - 15)	work; routines; activities; animals	jobs; work routines; everyday & free-time activities; job qualities	present simple; present continuous; adverbs of frequency; relatives; relative clauses Phrasal verb: *LOOK*
EPISODE 1 The Adventures of Huckleberry Finn — How it All Started (pp. 16 - 17)			like – as
UNIT 2 What a Story! (pp. 18 - 27)	misfortunes; disasters; experiences	misfortunes; natural & man-made disasters; feelings	past simple; past continuous; linkers: *when, while, and, so, as, because* Phrasal verbs: *BREAK, BRING*
EPISODE 2 The Adventures of Huckleberry Finn — How Huck Was Murdered (pp. 28 - 29)			Time words; Possessive adjectives/pronouns; where
MODULE 1 SELF-ASSESSMENT (pp. 30 - 31)			
UNIT 3 On the Move (pp. 32 - 41)	our world; the weather holidays; accommodation	continents; countries; climate; types of holiday; holiday equipment; means of transport	present perfect; present perfect continuous (*yet, never, already, since, for, ever*); linkers: *although, even though, however* Phrasal verb: *GET*
EPISODE 3 The Adventures of Huckleberry Finn — Jackson's Island (pp. 42 - 43)			prepositions of movement
UNIT 4 Out and About (pp. 44 - 53)	town & country	accidents; holiday experiences; sights	comparatives; superlatives; past perfect; past perfect continuous Phrasal verb: *TURN*
EPISODE 4 The Adventures of Huckleberry Finn — Sarah Williams (pp. 54 - 55)			Clauses of Purpose
MODULE 2 SELF-ASSESSMENT (pp. 56 - 57)			
UNIT 5 Tasty Treats (pp. 58 - 67)	food & drink	types of food/drink; ways of cooking; taste; containers	countable-uncountable nouns; *will - going to*; reflexive pronouns Conditionals Type 0 & 1 Phrasal verb: *GIVE*
EPISODE 5 The Adventures of Huckleberry Finn — Down the Mississippi (pp. 68 - 69)			Result Clauses (so/such [a/an]... that)
UNIT 6 All Work and no Play (pp. 70 - 79)	the arts; clothes; entertainment	social life; music & mood; feelings & comments; clothes & accessories	infinitive; -ing form; modal verbs: *must(n't)*; *(don't) have to*; *can('t)*; *may*; *might* Phrasal verb: *SET*
EPISODE 6 The Adventures of Huckleberry Finn — Travelling with Royalty (pp. 80 - 81)			*must - can't* / tenses of the infinitive
MODULE 3 SELF-ASSESSMENT (pp. 82 - 83)			
UNIT 7 Nature's Warning (pp. 84 - 93)	the environment	environmental issues; the greenhouse effect; global warming; recycling	the passive Phrasal verbs: *CARRY, HOLD*
EPISODE 7 The Adventures of Huckleberry Finn — The Wilks Brothers (pp. 94 - 95)			*shall* (offers/suggestions); *will/would* (requests)
UNIT 8 One Good Turn Deserves Another (pp. 96 - 105)	public services; aches	public services; parts of the body; aches & pains; symptoms	question tags; short questions; reported speech (statements) Phrasal verbs: *MAKE, PUT*
EPISODE 8 The Adventures of Huckleberry Finn — Peter Wilks' Funeral (pp. 106 - 107)			could/was able to; used to
MODULE 4 SELF-ASSESSMENT (pp. 108 - 109)			
UNIT 9 A Healthy Mind in a Healthy Body (pp. 110 - 119)	education, sports	school subjects; educational system in England; games & sports; sports equipment; the time; days of the week	reported questions; reported orders; *too - enough* Phrasal verb: *TAKE*
EPISODE 9 The Adventures of Huckleberry Finn — Looking for Jim (pp. 120 - 121)			exclamations (*what - what a/an - how*)
UNIT 10 Our Changing World (pp. 122 - 131)	inventions; inventors; technology; ambitions; regrets	electronic machines; scientific instruments; appliances; future plans	Conditionals Type 2 & 3; wishes Phrasal verbs: *COME, RUN*
EPISODE 10 The Adventures of Huckleberry Finn — A Happy End (pp. 132 - 135)			so - neither/nor; both/neither - either - all/none
MODULE 5 SELF-ASSESSMENT (pp. 136 - 137)			

GRAMMAR REFERENCE SECTION   138
IRREGULAR VERBS   154
WORD LIST   155
RULES FOR PUNCTUATION   163

LISTENING PRACTICE & TAPESCRIPTS   164
SUGGESTED ANSWERS SECTION   168
WRITING PROJECTS – SUGGESTED ANSWERS 172
KEY – TEST BOOKLET   174

KEY – VIDEO ACTIVITY BOOK   180
AROUND THE ENGLISH-SPEAKING WORLD

READING	WRITING	LISTENING & SPEAKING	COMMUNICATION
It's a Dog's Life!	a discursive article: advantages & disadvantages of a job (project) a letter of reference	match speakers to routines; talking about people's/your routine; comparing jobs; taking notes Pron: word stress in compound nouns	registering with an unemployment office
Lost in the Jungle	a narrative essay (project) a letter to a friend describing a nasty experience	listening for gist; talking about past activities; narrating events Pron: intonation of apologies	giving apologies
Full Steam Ahead for the Trip of a Lifetime! (The Pride of Africa)	a letter of complaint (project) a letter to a friend about your recent news	listening to identify the correct picture; completing an advertisement; making decisions; talking about activities Pronunciation: silent letters	ordering room service
Poland - Portugal - Chile	a letter to a friend about your holidays (project) a letter to a friend recommending a gym	listening for specific information; past experiences; comparing places; expressing preferences Pron: intonation in questions of choice	booking a hotel room
Miracle Oil	a proposal (restaurant - supermarket) (project) an article about foods that cure	listening for specific information; making predictions; ordering from a menu Pronunciation: intonation in conditional sentences	complaining about food/service; booking a table at a restaurant
Living Statues	a letter to the editor (project) a film review	filling in an advertisement; evaluating films; describing costumes; making rules Pronunciation: rising intonation in polite requests	responding to invitations
Zoos: The Wildlife Time Capsule Greenhouse for the Future	an article providing solutions to a problem (project) a letter to a friend about changes in a place	listening for lexical items; making suggestions Pronunciation: sentence stress	giving advice
Helping Hands (OXFAM; VSO; Queen Elizabeth's Foundation for Disabled People)	a transactional letter asking for information (project) a letter to the editor suggesting types of voluntary work to help people in your town	listening for gist; giving advice Pronunciation: intonation in tag questions	registering as a volunteer
Bluewater Sports & Leisure Centre	an opinion essay (project) an article about your country's education system	listening for detail; filling in a table; expressing likes/dislikes; talking about educational system in your country Pronunciation: stressed syllables	buying tickets for a football match
People who Changed the World	a letter of application for a part-time job (project) an article about which objects you would put in a time capsule	positioning objects; describing your ideal house Pronunciation: intonation in conditionals	expressing regrets/opposite wishes

Published by Express Publishing

Liberty House, New Greenham Park, Newbury,
Berkshire RG19 6HW
Tel.: (0044) 1635 817 363
Fax: (0044) 1635 817 463
e-mail: inquiries@expresspublishing.co.uk
http://www.expresspublishing.co.uk

© Virginia Evans - Neil O'Sullivan, 2001

Design and Illustration © Express Publishing, 2001

First published August 2001
New edition 2004
Second impression 2007

Made in EU

ISBN 978-1-84558-126-8

Acknowledgements

Authors' Acknowledgements

We would like to thank all the staff at Express Publishing who have contributed their skills to producing this book. Thanks are
due in particular to: Megan Lawton (Editor in Chief), Stephanie Smith and Sean Todd (senior editors), Michael Sadler and
Andrew Wright (editorial assistants), Richard White (senior production controller), the Express design team, Onyx (recording
producer) and Rachel Robbins, Kevin Harris, David Smith, Erica Thompson, Kimberly Baker, Timothy Forster, Steven Gibbs,
Eric Simmons, Christine Little and Eric Taylor for their support and patience. We would also like to thank those institutions and
teachers who piloted the manuscript, and whose comments and feedback were invaluable in the production of the book.

The authors and publishers wish to thank the following, who have kindly given permission for the use of copyright material:

Officer Patrick Wyeth and K9 Kenzie, Alameda P.D. California, USA, for the article on p. 12; Thanks to Heike
Lindenberg of Rovos Rail Tours, P.O. Box 2837, Pretorial 0001, Gauteng, South Africa © Rovos Rail, The Pride of Africa,
for the articles on pp. 38, 39; taken from the Oxfam Web Site <http://www.oxfam.org.uk> reproduced with permission
of Oxfam Publishing, 274, Banbury Road, Oxford, OX2 7DZ for the article on p. 102; Voluntary Services Overseas,
317 Putney Bridge Road, London SW15 2PN, England, VSO is an international development charity that works through
volunteers. www.vso.org.uk © VSO, for the article on p. 102; © 2000 Queen Elizabeth's Foundation for Disabled
People. All rights reserved, for the article on p. 103.

Photograph Acknowledgements

Officer Patrick Wyeth for picture on p. 12; Heike Lindenberg of Rovos Rail Tours, for the pictures on p. 38; VSO for
pictures (1) © VSO/Jon Spaull, and (3) © VSO/Gary Parker p. 102; Oxfam for background logo and picture (2) Jenny
Matthews/Oxfam p. 102; Queen Elizabeth's Foundation for Disabled People for the picture on p. 103; © Reuters INKE
for pictures of Yuri Gagarin on p. 128 and Steve Jobs on p. 129.

Colour Illustrations: Nathan

Music Compositions & Arrangement by Ted and Taz © Express Publishing, 2001

Introduction to the Teacher

Click on 3 is a complete course for young learners studying English at pre-Intermediate level. It allows for flexibility of approach, which makes it suitable for classes of all kinds, including large or mixed ability classes.

The coursebook consists of five modules of two units each. Each unit is designed to be taught in four 50-minute lessons. The corresponding unit in the Workbook provides the option of an additional lesson. The coursebook also contains five Self-Assessment sections and an adventure story in ten episodes with accompanying language exercises. *Click on 3* and its components may be covered in a total of about 65 teaching hours.

Course Components

Student's Book

The Student's Book is the main component of the course. Each unit is based on a single theme and the topics covered are of general interest. All units follow the same basic structure (see **Elements of the Coursebook**).

Teacher's Book

This Teacher's Book contains Teacher's Notes, fully interleaved with the Student's Book. These provide step-by-step lesson plans and suggestions about how to present the material. Also included is a full Key to the exercises in the S's Book, tapescripts of the listening material as well as Key to Test Booklet and Video Activity Book.
Note: Writing Projects, Around the English-Speaking World and American English – British English Guide are presented in a separate supplement for the Students. Teachers will find the relevant sections at the back of the Teacher's book.

Workbook

The Workbook is divided into two parts. The first part consists of ten units corresponding to those in the S's Book. It contains exercises to revise, consolidate and extend Ss' learning through a variety of tasks. The second part, called **Click on Grammar**, summarises and revises the specific grammar items dealt with in each unit of the course and offers additional exercises. At the end of the book there are ten **Progress Tests**, one for each unit. A separate **Teacher's Key** reproduces the pages of the Workbook, overprinted with full answers to all exercises.

Test Booklet

The Test Booklet contains five tests, each in two equivalent versions to ensure result reliability, especially with larger classes. Ss sitting next to each other work on different tests, but are tested in the same language areas. The tests facilitate the assessment of Ss' progress and enable the teacher to pinpoint Ss' specific weaknesses. There is also an Exit Test which covers all the material learned at this level and can be used either as an effective assessment test or as a placement test for those planning to move on to the next level.

Class Audio CDs

The Class Audio CDs contain all the recorded material which accompanies the course. This includes the dialogues and texts in the Listening and Reading sections, as well as model dialogues, Pronunciation and the material for all listening tasks.

Student's Audio CD

The S's Audio CD contains the recorded dialogues and the main texts in the Listening and Reading sections of the S's Book for the purposes of homework and preparation, as well as the ten episodes of the story.

Elements of the Coursebook

Each unit contains the following sections:

Lead-in

- Assisted by pictures, Ss are introduced to the **vocabulary** and **grammar** of the unit.
- A **listen and repeat** drill presents everyday phrases and sentences which will be encountered in the dialogues that follow.

Listening and Reading

Each unit comprises two Listening and Reading texts.
- The first **Listening and Reading** text presents situational dialogues in a variety of everyday contexts. Students are made familiar with natural, everyday language.
- The second **Listening and Reading** text presents authentic, meaningful articles on cross-cultural topics.

In this way, Ss practise natural everyday communication. Skills such as reading for gist or for specific information are also practised, and vocabulary is seen in a functional and meaningful context.

Vocabulary

Vocabulary is practised through various types of exercises.
A particular feature of the book is the teaching of **collocations** and set expressions which help Ss to remember vocabulary items as part of set expressions.

Grammar

- The grammar items of each unit are presented by means of clear and concise theory boxes.
- **Grammar exercises and activities** reinforce Ss´ understanding of these items.

Listening tasks and Speaking practice

- Ss can develop their **listening skills** through a variety of tasks. These tasks employ the vocabulary and grammar practised in each unit, in this way reinforcing understanding of the language taught in the unit. There is also a Listening Practice Section at the back of the book to be done in conjunction with the Module Self-Assessment Sections.
- **Controlled speaking activities** have been carefully designed to allow Ss guided practice before leading them to **less structured speaking activities**.

Writing Projects

These provide visual and linguistic input for closely controlled **Writing Practice**. Ss are referred to the Writing Projects section of the Supplement by a **Project** in each unit. These should be discussed in class before being assigned as written homework. Suggested answers are provided at the end of the Teacher's Book.

Pronunciation

Pronunciation activities help Ss to recognise the sounds, intonation and rhythm of spoken English and to reproduce these correctly.

Communication

These sections provide practice in real-life communication. Standard expressions, functions and language structures associated with realistic situations are extensively practised.

Word Formation

These sections extend vocabulary learning by practising derivatives, prefixes/suffixes, compound nouns etc.

Reading texts

These texts practise specific reading skills (e.g. paragraphing, working with cloze texts, etc), while at the same time providing a model text for the writing tasks which follow.

Writing

The writing sections have been carefully designed to ensure that Ss systematically develop their writing skills.

- A **model text** is presented and thoroughly analysed, followed by guided practice of the language to be used.

- The final task is based on the model text and follows the detailed **plan** provided.
- All writing activities are based on realistic types and styles of writing such as letters, descriptions, stories and articles.

'What's in a word?'

This section at the end of each unit presents well-known quotations and proverbs related to the theme of the unit.

Adventure story

The story *The Adventures of Huckleberry Finn* is presented in comic strip format in ten episodes.

- Ss are invited to read for enjoyment.
- Each episode is followed by a variety of tasks, offering the opportunity for extra practice and consolidation.

Module Self-Assessment sections

These follow every second unit, and reinforce Ss´ understanding of the topics, vocabulary and structures that have been presented.

- The material has been designed to help Ss learn new language in the context of what they have already mastered, rather than in isolation.
- Each section concludes with an entertaining song which practises the language items presented in the preceding units.
- A marking scheme allows Ss to evaluate their progress and identify their weaknesses.

Grammar Reference section

- This section offers full explanations and revision of the grammar structures presented throughout the book.
- It can be used both in class and at home to reinforce the grammar being taught. The "Rules for Punctuation" section at the back of the book includes a full explanation of the rules in a clear and concise manner.

Around the English-Speaking World

- This section of the Supplement contains paired texts dealing with various aspects of countries and cultures worldwide associated with the English language. Suggested answers are provided at the end of the Teacher's Book.

American English – British English Guide

- This appendix outlines and highlights differences between the two main international varieties of English.

SUGGESTED TEACHING TECHNIQUES

A. Presenting new vocabulary

Much of the new vocabulary in *Click on 3* is presented through pictures; for instance, Ss are asked to **describe or discuss the pictures using listed words/prompts** *(see Ss' Book Unit 2, p. 18, Ex. 2)*.

Vocabulary is always presented in context, and emphasis is placed on **collocations** and set expressions, since memorising new words is easier if they are presented in lexical sets. *(see S's Book Unit 1, p. 13, Ex. 30)*

Further techniques that you may use to introduce new vocabulary include:

- **Miming.** Mime the word you want to introduce. For instance, to present the verb **sing**, pretend you are singing and ask Ss to guess the meaning of the word.
- **Synonyms, opposites, paraphrasing and giving definitions.** Examples:
  - present the word **store** by giving a synonym: "Store — shop."
  - present the word **sad** by giving its opposite: "Sad — not happy."
  - present the word **weekend** by paraphrasing it: "Weekend — Saturday and Sunday."
  - present the word **garage** by giving its definition: "Garage — the place next to the house where we put our car."
- **Example.** Examples give vocabulary a context, which makes understanding easier. For instance, introduce the words **city** and **town** by referring to a city and a town in the Ss' own country: "Rome is a city, but Parma is a town."
- **Visual prompts:** Show pictures, photographs or drawings to make understanding easier.
- **Use of dictionary:** Encourage Ss to try to explain the word, then check if they are correct by using their dictionaries. Ss should also use their dictionaries to find synonyms and antonyms of lexical items. Ss should refer to a monolingual dictionary wherever possible to help them extend their understanding of the target language.
- **Flashcards.** Flashcards made out of magazine or newspaper pictures, photographs, ready-made drawings and any other visual material may also serve as vocabulary teaching tools.
- **Use of L1.** In a monolingual class, you may explain vocabulary in the Ss' mother tongue, although this method should be employed in moderation.

The choice of technique depends on the type of word or expression. For example, you may find it easier to describe an action verb through miming, and not through a synonym or definition.

B. Choral and individual repetition

Repetition will ensure that Ss are confident with the sound and pronunciation of the lexical items and structures being taught.

- Always ask Ss to repeat chorally before you ask them to repeat individually. Repeating chorally will help Ss feel confident enough to then perform the task on their own.

C. Listening and Reading

You may ask Ss to read and listen for a variety of purposes:

- **Listening and reading for gist.** Ask Ss to read or listen to get the gist of the dialogue or text being dealt with. *See S's Book, Unit 3, p. 33, Ex. 4. Tell Ss that in order to complete this task successfully, they need not understand every single detail in the dialogues that follow — they need only understand enough of the general sense to match the speakers to the statements.*
- **Listening and reading for detail.** Ask Ss to read or listen for specific information. *See S's Book, Unit 3, p. 38, Ex. 27. Ss will have to listen for details such as specific words and numbers in the text and not for general information.*

D. Speaking

- Speaking activities immediately following the introduction of new material are usually **controlled**, allowing for guided practice. *See S's Book, Unit 1, p. 9, Ex. 12, where the task is essentially a substitution drill.*
- Ss are then led to progressively **less structured** speaking activities. *See S's Book, Unit 4, p. 46, Exs. 8-9, where Ss are given objectives but no prompts, and are asked to present their own ideas in discussion at an increasingly abstract level.*

E. Writing

All writing tasks in *Click on 3* have been carefully designed to closely guide Ss to produce a successful piece of writing.

- Always read the **model text** provided and deal with the tasks that follow in detail. Ss will then have acquired the necessary language to deal with the final writing task. *See S's Book, Unit 1, pp. 14-15, Exs. 36-39.*
- Make sure that Ss understand that they are writing for a **purpose**. Go through the writing task in detail so that Ss are fully aware of **why** they are writing and **who** they are writing to. *See S's Book, Unit 3, p. 41, Ex. 38. Ss are asked to write a letter of complaint to the hotel manager.*
- Make sure Ss follow the detailed **plan** they are provided with. *See S's Book, Unit 1, p. 15, Ex. 40.*
- It would be advisable to complete the task orally in class before assigning it as written homework. Ss will then feel more confident in their ability to produce a complete piece of writing on their own.

F. Projects

- When dealing with project work, Ss can find visual and linguistic input in the **Writing Projects** section of the Supplement.
- It is necessary to prepare Ss well in class before they attempt the writing task at home.

G. Assigning homework

It is strongly recommended that homework is regularly assigned and routinely checked. Independently of the **suggested homework** sections in the Teacher's Notes, you should feel free to assign tasks which will serve the specific needs of your class. When assigning writing tasks, prepare Ss as well as possible in advance. This will help them to avoid errors and get maximum benefit from the task.

Commonly assigned tasks include:

Dictation - Ss learn the spelling of particular words without memorising the text in which they appear;
Vocabulary - memorisation of the meaning of words and phrases;
Reading Aloud - assisted by the S's audio CD, Ss practise at home in preparation for reading aloud in class;
Project - after thorough classroom preparation, Ss complete the task in the Writing Projects section of the Supplement; and
Writing - after thorough preparation in class, Ss are asked to produce a complete piece of writing.

H. Correcting students' work

All learners make errors - they are part of the process of learning. The way you deal with errors depends on what the Ss are doing.

- **Oral accuracy work:**
  Correct Ss on the spot, either by providing the correct answer and allowing them to repeat it, or by indicating the error but allowing Ss to correct it. Alternatively, indicate the error and ask other Ss to provide the answer.
- **Oral fluency work:**
  Allow Ss to finish the task without interrupting, but make a note of the errors made and correct them afterwards.
- **Written work:**
  Do not over-correct; focus on errors that are directly relevant to the point of the exercise. When giving feedback you may write the most common errors on the board and get the class to attempt to correct them.

Remember that rewarding work and praising Ss is of great importance. Post good written work on a noticeboard in your classroom or school, or give 'reward' stickers. Praise effort as well as success.

I. Class organisation

- **Open pairs**
  The class focuses its attention on two Ss doing the set task together. Use this technique when you want your Ss to offer an example of how a task is done. *(See Unit 1, Ex. 12, p. 9.)*

- **Closed pairs**
  Pairs of Ss work together on a task or activity, while you move around offering assistance and suggestions. Explain the task clearly before beginning closed pairwork.

- **Stages of pairwork**
  - Put Ss in pairs.
  - Set the task and time limit.
  - Rehearse the task in open pairs.
  - In closed pairs, ask Ss to do the task.
  - Go round the class and help Ss where necessary.
  - Open pairs report back to the class.
- **Group work**
  Groups of three or more Ss work together on a task or activity. Class projects or role plays are most easily done in groups. Again, give Ss a solid understanding of the task in advance.
- **Rolling questions**
  Ss one after the other ask and answer questions, assisted by prompts. *(See Unit 8, Ex. 27a, p. 103.)*

J. Using the Student's Audio CD

- Dialogues and texts are recorded on the S's audio CD. Ss have the chance to listen to these recordings at home as many times as they want in order to improve their pronunciation and intonation.

  - S listens to the recording and follows the lines.
  - S listens to the recording with pauses after every sentence/exchange. S repeats as many times as necessary, trying to imitate the speaker's pronunciation and intonation.
  - S listens to the recording again. S reads aloud.

Abbreviations

Abbreviations used in the Student's Book and Teacher's Notes are as shown below:

T	Teacher
S(s)	Student(s)
HW	Homework
L1	Students' mother tongue
Ex.	Exercise
p(p).	Page(s)
e.g.	For example
i.e.	That is
etc	Et cetera
sb	Somebody
sth	Something

Moments in Life

◆ **Before you start …**

When did you start learning English?
How many hours do you do per week?
Why do you learn English?

◆ **Listen, read and talk about …**

Busy Days

UNIT 1

- jobs/job qualities
- job interviews
- work routines
- everyday & free-time activities

What a story!

UNIT 2

- misfortunes
- natural disasters
- accidents
- feelings

◆ **Learn how to ...**

- describe scenes
- narrate an event
- talk about routines & free-time activities
- talk about past activities
- register with unemployment office
- give apologies
- making a phonecall to arrange a job interview

◆ **Practise ...**

- present simple
- present continuous
- adverbs of frequency
- present continuous with a future meaning
- relatives
- defining/non-defining relative clauses
- as - like
- order of adjectives
- past simple
- past continuous
- time words
- possessive adjectives/pronouns
- linkers (when, while, and, so, as, because)

◆ **Phrasal verbs**

- look, break, bring

◆ **Write ...**

- a letter of reference
- a discursive article (advantages & disadvantages)
- a letter to a friend about a nasty experience
- a story

1 Busy Days

Lead-in

1 Use the prompts in the list to say what each person does at work.

- plant/flowers • represent people/court • look after/animals • sell/houses • teach/skiing • shoot/films

An estate agent sells houses.

2 Which of these jobs do you think:

- is part-time/full-time?
- requires an instructor's licence?
- requires experience?
- sounds exciting?
- requires a university degree?

- you can do indoors/outdoors?
- requires technical skills?
- requires creativity?
- is/isn't challenging?
- is hard/fun to do?
- is the best for you?

Being a pet sitter is a part-time job.

Listening and Reading

3 Listen and repeat, then close your books and try to remember as many sentences as possible.

- Is the job still available?
- Are you fully qualified?
- Have you got experience at all levels?

- Here's a job for me!
- I bet it's hard work.
- Shall I apply?
- It can't hurt to try!
- You are so lucky!
- That's a really fun job!

4 Listen and match the people to the jobs they do or want to do.

Dialogue 1   Steve   A   pet sitter
Dialogue 2   John   B   cameraman
Dialogue 3   Anne   C   ski instructor

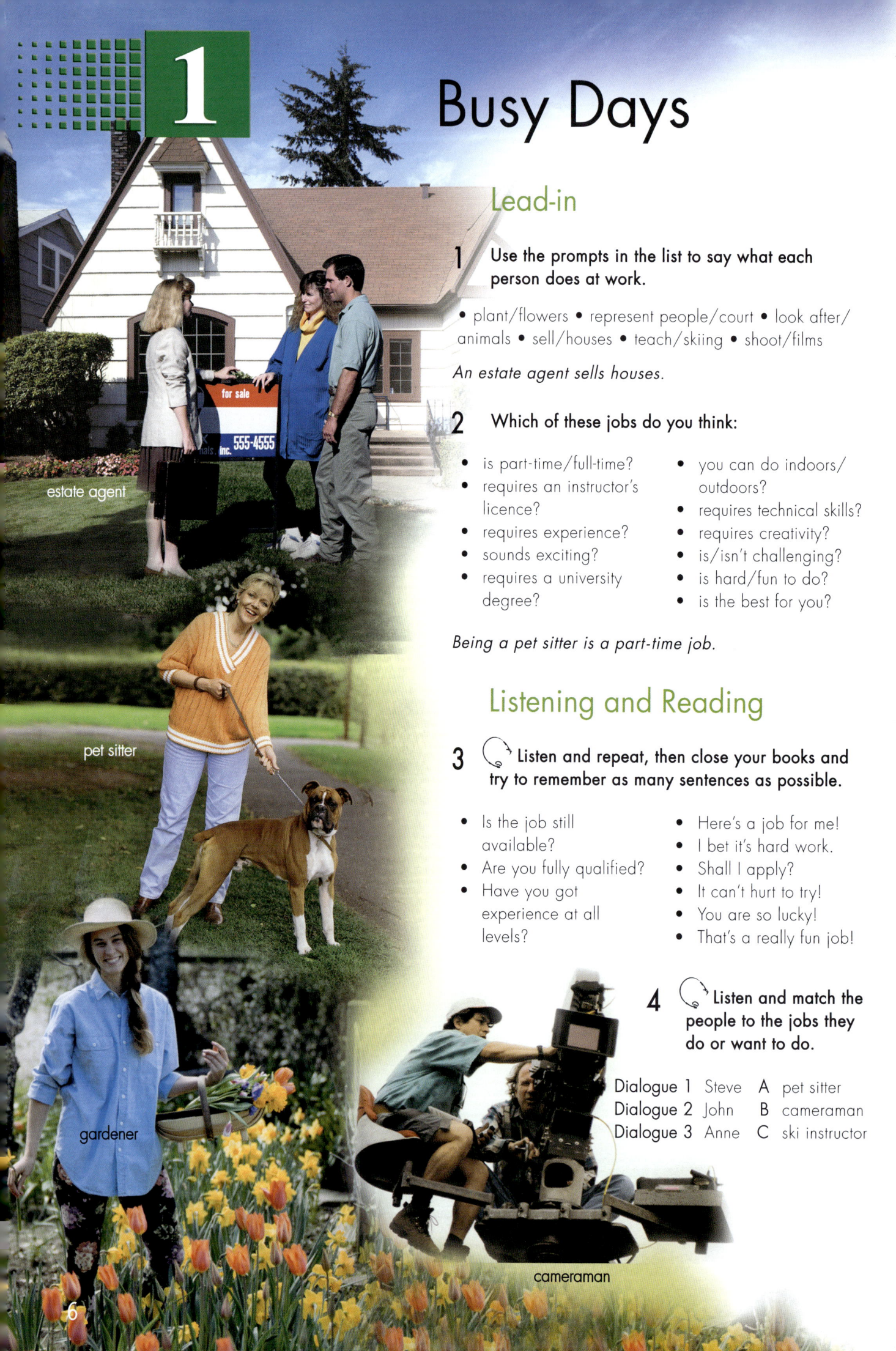

estate agent

pet sitter

gardener

cameraman

- **you can do outdoors:** estate agent/pet sitter/gardener/cameraman/ski instructor
- **requires technical skills:** cameraman
- **requires creativity:** gardener/cameraman
- **is challenging:** estate agent/cameraman/ski instructor/lawyer
- **isn't challenging:** pet sitter/gardener
- **is hard to do:** estate agent/cameraman/ski instructor/lawyer
- **is fun to do:** pet sitter/gardener/ski instructor
- Ss' own answers

Objectives

Vocabulary: jobs; personal qualities/skills; daily routines; free-time activities

Reading: reading for detailed understanding; multiple choice

Listening: listening for specific information; multiple matching

Speaking: talking about jobs/qualities; describing your daily routine; discussing your personality/daily routine/free-time activities; talking about activities; describing the daily routine of a police dog

Communication: registering with an employment agency

Pronunciation: stress in compound nouns

Grammar: present simple; present continuous; adverbs of frequency; relatives; relative clauses

Phrasal verbs: look

Word formation: forming nouns

Project: a reference

Writing: an essay giving the pros and cons of a job

Lesson 1 (pp. 6 - 7)

1 • Ask Ss to look at the pictures on pp. 6 & 7 and say how the title is associated with the pictures. *(The pictures show people at work.)* Read the job titles, then ask Ss to look at the pictures and describe each scene.
e.g. Where each of the people are; what they are doing; what their job is; etc
   • As an extension, Ss can describe the clothes each person is wearing.
e.g. The estate agent is wearing a purple skirt, a tailored jacket and flat shoes.
   • Ask Ss to read the prompts in Ex. 1 aloud. Elicit/Explain the meaning of any unknown words, then read out the example. Individual Ss do the exercise.

ANSWER KEY

A pet sitter looks after animals.
A gardener plants flowers.
A cameraman shoots films.
A ski instructor teaches skiing.
A lawyer represents people in court.

---

2 Read the prompts aloud and elicit/explain the meaning of any unknown words. Ask individual Ss to answer the questions.

SUGGESTED ANSWER KEY

- **is part-time:** pet sitter/gardener/ski instructor/cameraman/estate agent
- **is full-time:** estate agent/lawyer/gardener/cameraman
- **requires an instructor's licence:** ski instructor
- **requires experience:** estate agent/cameraman/ski instructor/lawyer
- **sounds exciting:** ski instructor/cameraman
- **requires a university degree:** lawyer
- **you can do indoors:** cameraman/lawyer/estate agent

---

3 • Play the recording. Ss listen and repeat, either chorally or individually.
   • Present these sentences by eliciting from Ss who the speaker of each sentence is and demonstrating how each sentence could be used.
e.g. **Is the job still available?** Ask Ss: *Who would say this: a person who is looking for a job or an employer? (A person who is looking for a job.)* Act out a short role play with a S:
   S: Is the job still available?
   T: Yes, it is. Would you like to apply? **OR** No, I'm sorry. We hired somebody this morning.
   Are you fully qualified? Ask Ss: *Who would say this: a person who is looking for a job or an employer? (An employer.)* Act out a short role play with a S:
   S: Are you fully qualified?
   T: Yes. I've got three A levels and a degree in English.   etc
   • Ss close their books. Ask individual Ss to say one of the sentences. Alternatively, Ss can form two teams and take turns to say sentences. The team which remembers the most sentences is the winner.
e.g. Team A S1: Is the job still available?
              T: Good! One point for Team A.   etc

4 Read the names (1-3) and jobs (A-C) aloud. Play the recording. Ss listen and match the people to the jobs.

ANSWER KEY

1 C   2 B   3 A

---

5   Read sentences 1 to 5 aloud. Allow Ss five minutes to read the dialogues silently and mark the sentences T (true) or F (false). Check Ss' answers. Ask Ss to correct the false statements.

ANSWER KEY

1   T
2   F (Steve usually instructs absolute beginners.)
3   T
4   F (John is interested in the job.)
5   F (Anne isn't going to accept the job offered by
*   Jason.)*

---

6   a) • Play the recording for Ex. 4 again. Ss listen and follow the lines, then Ss try to explain the meaning of the words in bold by giving examples, synonyms or opposites. Ss then make sentences using the words in bold.

e.g. I'm interested in the **position** of waiter. The manager is not **available** at the moment, etc

b) • Ss take roles and read out the dialogues.

Suggested Homework

1   **Vocabulary:** Exs 1 and 2 (p. 6)
2   **Reading aloud:** dialogues B, C (p. 7) (Point out that Ss practise *reading aloud* using the S's audio CD.)
3   **Dictation:** phrases/sentences from Ex. 3 (p. 6)
4   **Speaking:** Ss in pairs can act out dialogues similar to dialogue A (possible jobs: cameraman, doctor, teacher, shop assistant etc). Point out that Ss will need to amend their dialogues to match the new situations.

---

5   Read the dialogues A-C and mark sentences 1-5 T (true) or F (false).

1   Steve is looking for a new job.   ....
2   Steve usually instructs very good skiers.   ....
3   John probably has a university degree.   ....
4   John isn't interested in this job.   ....
5   Anne is going to accept the job offered by Jason.   ....

ski instructor

A   Steve: Hello. I'm calling about the **position** of ski instructor.
Laura: Oh good. What's your name, please?
Steve: It's Steve. Steve Philips. Is the job still **available**?
Laura: Oh yes. Are you fully qualified, Steve?
Steve: Yes. I got my **instructor's licence** two years ago.
Laura: I see. And have you got **experience** at all levels?
Steve: Well, I usually work with **absolute beginners**.
Laura: That's fine. Would you be able to come for an **interview** on Tuesday morning? Say, around 10 o'clock?
Steve: Of course.
Laura: Great. Just ask for Laura. See you then.
Steve: Thanks. Bye.

B   John: Oh, here's a job for me!
Paula: What's that?
John: A cameraman for the local TV channel.
Paula: Is that something you'd like to do?
John: Well, why not? It sounds exciting ...
Paula: Hmm, I bet it's hard work, too.
John: They want someone with a degree and good **technical skills**.
Paula: I expect there's more to it than that!
John: What do you think? Shall I **apply**?
Paula: Why not? It can't hurt to try!
John: OK, I will. Wish me luck!

lawyer

C   Jason: Hello, Anne. Is that your dog?
Anne: No. I'm just **looking after** him while his **owners** are away. It's my new job.
Jason: Your job?
Anne: Yeah. I'm a pet sitter.
Jason: You are so lucky! That sounds like a really fun job!
Anne: I know! It's perfect for me, because I love animals.
Jason: Listen, Anne. I'm going on holiday next week. Can you look after my pet python?
Anne: Erm ... I hate to **turn** work **down**, but I don't have much experience with reptiles. Sorry, Jason!

6   a) Read the dialogues again and explain the words in bold, then make sentences using them.

b) In pairs, read out the dialogues.

7

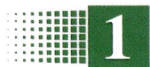
Vocabulary

● Jobs and Qualities

7 a) Match the prompts A-F to the pictures 1-6, then use the prompts to make sentences, as in the example.

A sells flowers
B designs buildings
C operates on people
D fits windows

E deals with guests in a hotel
F works underground

A miner is someone who works underground.

1 miner
2 florist
3 architect

4 glazier
6

5

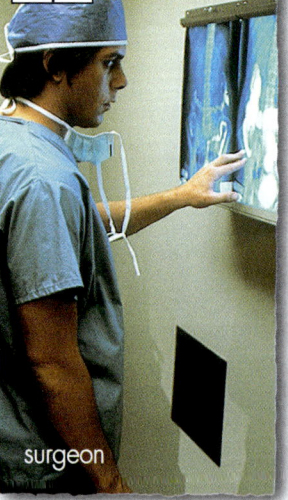

hotel receptionist
surgeon

Speaking

b) Which of the people above: work underground/outdoors/indoors? wear a uniform/special clothing for work? get a salary/wage? work shifts? are self-employed?

c) You are at a job interview for the position of part-time waiter. Ask for information on:
● wages ● working hours ● uniform
● experience required

8 a) Fill in the gaps with words from the list.

● brave ● dedicated ● creative ● courageous
● funny ● helpful ● careful

1 Florists have to be .... They make floral bouquets and arrangements.
2 Clowns need to be .... to make people laugh.
3 Hotel receptionists have to be .... because they have to help people and answer their questions.
4 You need to be .... to be a miner because it can be a dangerous job.
5 Policemen have to be .... because they often find themselves in dangerous situations.
6 Glaziers need to be .... because they have to handle glass.
7 You have to be .... to be a surgeon because it requires many years of study.

Speaking

b) Use the table below to make sentences, as in the example.

JOBS	QUALITIES	REASONS
politicians	brave	- give people information
teachers	confident	- make people believe in them
counsellors	patient	- help children to learn things
firefighters	persuasive	- listen to people's problems
		- perform in front of people
telephone operators	understanding	
actors	polite	- face dangerous situations

Politicians need to be persuasive because they have to make people believe in them.

c) Talk about more jobs you know and the qualities needed.

Lesson 2 (pp. 8 - 9)

* • Check Ss' HW (10').

7 a) • Read aloud the prompts and the jobs and elicit/explain the meaning of any unknown words. Allow Ss two minutes to match the prompts to the jobs. Check Ss' answers by asking individual Ss to read their answers aloud.
• Ss use their answers to make sentences about each job.

ANSWER KEY

1 F   2 A   3 B   4 D   5 E   6 C

*A miner is someone who works underground.
A florist is someone who sells flowers.
An architect is someone who designs buildings.
A glazier is someone who fits windows.
A hotel receptionist is someone who deals with guests in a hotel.
A surgeon is someone who operates on people.*

Game

Elicit from Ss various jobs and write them on the board. Choose a S to be the leader. He/She chooses a job from the board. Ss, in teams, try to guess what job the leader has chosen. Each correct guess gets one point. The team with the most points is the winner.

e.g.   Leader: (teacher)
Team A S1: Do you fit windows?
Leader: No, I don't.
Team B S1: Do you treat sick people?
Leader: No, I don't.
Team A S2: Do you teach students?
Leader: Yes, I do.
Team A S2: So you are a teacher.
Teacher: Correct. Team A gets 1 point.
Choose another S and continue the game.

b) • Read the questions aloud and elicit/explain the meaning of any unknown words. Ask individual Ss to answer the questions. Explain the difference between *wage* and *salary*.
salary: a fixed amount of money paid every year to an employee, usually paid monthly into a bank account
wage: a fixed amount of money paid, usually weekly in cash, to an employee (usually to manual/unskilled workers)

SUGGESTED ANSWER KEY

work underground: *miner*
work outdoors: *glazier/architect*
work indoors: *florist/hotel receptionist/surgeon/architect/glazier*
wear a uniform/special clothing for work: *hotel receptionist/surgeon/miner*
get a salary: *hotel receptionist/surgeon/architect*
get a wage: *miner/glazier/florist*
work shifts: *miner/receptionist/surgeon*
are self-employed: *florist/glazier*

• As an extension, Ss can talk about the jobs listed on the board.

c) Explain the task, then allow Ss two minutes to think of possible questions using the prompts. Check Ss' answers.

ANSWER KEY

• *What are the wages? What hours am I supposed to work?*
• *Do I have to wear a uniform?*
• *Is previous experience necessary for this position?*

8 a) • Read aloud the words in the list and the sentences and elicit/explain the meaning of any unknown words. Allow Ss three minutes to complete the sentences.
• Check Ss' answers by asking individual Ss to read the completed sentences aloud.

ANSWER KEY

*1 creative   5 courageous/brave
2 funny   6 careful
3 helpful   7 dedicated
4 brave/courageous*

b) • Read aloud the jobs/qualities/reasons in the table. Elicit/Explain the meaning of any unknown words. Help Ss to form sentences by asking them questions about the jobs in the table.
e.g. T: Which of these jobs requires someone to be brave?
S1: A firefighter.
T: Good. Why do firefighters need to be brave?
S2: Because they have to face dangerous situations. etc
• Ss make sentences about each job.

ANSWER KEY

*Teachers need to be **patient** because they have to **help children to learn things**.
Counsellors need to be **understanding** because they have to **listen to people's problems**.
Firefighters need to be **brave** because they have to **face dangerous situations**.
Telephone operators need to be **polite** because they have to **give people information**.
Actors need to be **confident** because they have to **perform in front of people**.*

c) Elicit various jobs and write them on the board. Ss work in pairs. Check Ss' answers by asking individual Ss to read out their sentences.

ANSWER KEY

• *Judges need to be **fair** to give all the evidence equal consideration.*
• *Painters need to be **creative** to come up with fresh ideas.*
• *Lifeguards need to be **brave** as they often find themselves in dangerous situations.*
• *Nurses need to be **caring** because they help sick people. etc*

9 • Explain the task to Ss. Read the jobs in the Ex. and elicit/explain the meaning of any unknown words.
  • Play the recording. Ss listen and match the speakers to their jobs. Check Ss' answers by asking individual Ss to read their answers aloud.

ANSWER KEY

Speaker A – 4   Speaker C – 1   Speaker E – 2
Speaker B – 5   Speaker D – 3

TAPESCRIPT

A: Well, I usually get up quite early, at about 7 am. I look through the papers and check the celebrity news on the Internet and I ring a few of my reliable sources to see if there are any interesting stories that I should know about. If there is any exciting news about a celebrity then I always call their agent to ask for a comment. I spend most of the morning on the phone, then I write my article in the afternoon and submit it to my editor. She's usually thrilled with what I come up with!

B: My routine varies depending on what jobs I've got on. I'm self-employed, so I get work through friends or through recommendations. On a working day, I get up at 6 in the morning because I like to get an early start. I prepare my equipment – brushes, ladders and so on – and drive to wherever it is that I'm working. I work all day, with a short break for lunch. When I get home I clean all the brushes, and myself, of course, and relax.

C: I've got quite a strange routine, really. I get up at 2 am and drive to the dairy to pick up my float. I deliver pints until eight or nine in the morning. When I've finished my rounds I go home, have breakfast and do a few jobs around the house. My working day is over before most people's have begun!

D: Well, if I'm doing a children's puppet show in the morning I get up at 8:30 am, load the scenery and the puppets onto the van and drive to the venue. I put up the set, do the performance and I often chat to the children afterwards to see what they liked or didn't like about the show. In the afternoons, I deal with any phone messages and correspondence and arrange bookings. After that, I spend some time in my workshop making puppets and scenery. I often perform shows in the evenings and especially at the weekends, so I'm always very busy.

E: As I don't have an actual boss I can alter my routine according to my mood, so I don't usually get up very early. I'm not a morning person, so I spend the first few hours of the day pottering around the flat before I get down to work. I work on different projects every day, for various newspapers and magazines. I usually do a bit of research, and then set about writing whatever it is I'm meant to write! It's a great job and I love being my own boss.

10 • Explain to Ss that some of the words in the table **can not** be used with the verbs they are listed with. Read aloud the words in the table and elicit/explain the meaning of any unknown words.
  • Allow Ss two minutes to look at the table and cross out the words which do not collocate with the verbs. Check Ss' answers by asking individual Ss to justify their answers.

ANSWER KEY

(do) some work	(have) a wash	(send) a fax
(take) the metro	(watch) the TV	(go to) the cinema
(ride) a bike	(have) a bath	(surf on) the net

  • Ss use the expressions to talk about their daily routines. This can be assigned as written HW.
    (Ss' own answers)

11 • Explain to/Elicit from Ss that a compound noun is a noun made up of two separate words (e.g. sky diving). Read aloud the words in the exercise and elicit/explain the meaning of any unknown words.
  • Allow Ss two minutes to match the words to make compound nouns. Ss then use the compound nouns to complete the sentences about themselves.

ANSWER KEY

1 c	3 e	5 a	7 f
2 d	4 b	6 g	

SUGGESTED ANSWER KEY

I really enjoy parachute jumping. / I don't mind bird-watching. / I hate stamp collecting. / I like horse riding. / I love sunbathing.

12 • Explain the task to Ss. Play the recording. Ss underline the correct activities.
  • Ss use their answers to ask and answer questions.

ANSWER KEY

1	ride a motorbike	3	vacuum the carpet
2	play table tennis	4	cut the grass

  • A: What is Sam's job?
    B: He's a lorry driver.
    A: What does he do?
    B: He drives lorries.
    A: What is he doing now?
    B: He's playing table tennis.   etc

TAPESCRIPT

David: Hi, I'm David. I'm 28 years old and I live in Newcastle. I'm a mechanic. It's a great job. (motorcycle revving)

Sam: Hello, my name's Sam. I'm 42 years old. I'm a lorry driver. I like to travel but I haven't got much time for my family. (sound of sb playing table tennis)

Sue: Hello, I'm Sue. I love animals and being outdoors, so I became a vet. I'm 25 years old. (sound of sb vacuuming the carpet)

Marie: Hi, my name's Marie. I'm 32 years old and I'm a waitress. I enjoy meeting lots of new people. I spend most of my free time looking after my garden. (sound of sb mowing lawn)

13 Read the prompts aloud and check Ss' understanding. Ss talk about themselves, in pairs. Check Ss' answers by asking individual pairs to report back to the class.
(Ss' own answers)

14 • Read sentences 1-7 aloud. Ask individual Ss to identify the tense used in each sentence.
  • Read aloud phrases a-g. Allow Ss two minutes to match the tenses in sentences 1-7 to their meanings (a-g). Check Ss' answers by asking individual Ss to read their answers aloud. Ss then make sentences of their own, explaining the meaning of the tense they use.

ANSWER KEY

1 b	present continuous		5 a	present simple
2 d	present simple		6 e	present continuous
3 f	present simple		7 g	present continuous
4 c	present continuous			

Suggested Homework

1 Vocabulary: Exs 7a & 7b and 8a & 8b (p. 8)
2 Dictation: Ex. 7a (p. 8)
3 Speaking: Ex. 10 (p. 9)
4 Writing: two short paragraphs about your daily routine and free-time activities

• Daily Routines

Listening

9   Listen to each person talking about their daily routine, and match the speakers to their jobs. There is one extra job which you do not need to use.

Speaker [A]   1 milkman
Speaker [B]   2 freelance writer
Speaker [C]   3 puppeteer
Speaker [D]   4 gossip columnist
Speaker [E]   5 housepainter
                6 tour guide

Speaking

10 Cross out the words which do not collocate with the verbs, then use the expressions to talk about your daily routine.

have	*a shower, a rest, breakfast, some work, a drink*
go	*to work/school, to bed, out to dinner, the metro, home*
catch	*the bus, the train, a taxi, a ferry, a bike*
do	*a wash, some paperwork, the housework*
answer	*the door, the phone, the TV, e-mails, letters*
make	*the bed, a bath, breakfast/lunch/dinner*
take	*a taxi, a fax, vitamins, a break, photographs*
watch	*TV, the news, the cinema, a video*
play	*computer games, board games, the radio, cards, records, golf, the net*

• Free-time Activities

11 Match the words to make compound nouns. Then, complete the sentences about yourself.

1 parachute   a surfing
2 bird   b skiing
3 stamp   c jumping
4 water   d watching
5 wind   e collecting
6 horse   f bathing
7 sun   g riding

I really enjoy ....
I don't mind ....
I hate ....
I like ....
I love ....

12   Listen and underline what each person is doing now, then ask and answer, as in the example.

1 David (mechanic) - ride a motorbike/drive a car
2 Sam (lorry driver) - play table tennis/wash the car
3 Sue (vet) - play a computer game/vacuum the carpet
4 Marie (waitress) - cut the grass/dig in the garden

A: *What's David's job?*
B: *He's a mechanic.*
A: *What does he do?*
B: *He repairs cars.*
A: *What is he doing now?*
B: *He's riding a motorbike.*

13 Talk with another student. Tell him/her:

• what your job is
• what kind of person you are
• what your daily routine is
• what you do in your free time

Grammar in Use

14 Identify the tenses in bold, then match the tenses to their meanings.

1 Claire **is staying** with her grandparents.   a habit/routine
2 She **lives** in Manchester.   b temporary situation
3 The film **starts** at 8:15.   c action happening now
4 They **are watching** TV.   d permanent states
5 He **goes** to the gym twice a week.   e fixed future arrangements
6 We **are going** on holiday next week.   f timetables
7 I**'m looking** for a new job at the moment.   g actions happening around the time of speaking

15 Put the verbs in brackets into the *present simple* or the *present continuous*.

1 .... (Alison/do) her homework now?
2 The Browns .... (live) in the house next door.
3 Mark .... (not/play) football every Saturday.
4 The train .... (leave) at half past two.
5 .... (you/go) to the party tonight?
6 We .... (work) a lot of extra hours these days.
7 .... (John/stay) with his grandparents for the weekend?
8 They .... (not/move) house next week.
9 .... (Sue/wash) her hair every day?
10 Carol .... (mend) her bike at the moment.

16 Complete the e-mail with the verbs in the list in the correct tense. Then, ask and answer questions, as in the example.

• serve • work • want • draw • live • share
• look • clean • paint • study • look forward

> Hi, Clare! I'm your new e-mail friend!
> My name is Neil Mitchell. I **1)** .... in York, in the north of England. I'm a student at York University. I **2)** .... Geography.
> At the moment, I **3)** .... in a restaurant. I **4)** .... meals three nights a week to earn some extra money.
> I **5)** .... a flat with two other students. We **6)** .... the flat at the moment, so it's a bit of a mess. We usually **7)** .... it on Sundays. I hate cleaning!
> When I graduate, I **8)** .... to work as a cartographer (that's someone who **9)** .... maps). I **10)** .... for jobs, because it's difficult to find work these days. Wish me luck!
> E-mail me soon. I **11)** .... to hearing from you.
> Neil

A: *Where does Neil live?*
B: *He lives in York.* etc

17 Listen and complete the telegram, then use the prompts to ask and answer questions.

> LEAVE FOR.....................7am—STOP—STAY
> BENELLI ....—STOP—MEET JOHN
> AND TOBY .... am
> — STOP — RETURN ....
> PM — STOP — JILL

1 Where/go?   4 When/meet/them?
2 Where/stay?   5 When/come back?
3 Who/meet?

A: *Where is Jill going?*
B: *She's going to ...*

• Adverbs of Frequency

18 Listen to Mr Harper talking to Paula Higgs and fill in the correct *adverbs of frequency*. When do we use adverbs of frequency? Where do we put them in a sentence?

1 Paula is .... late for work.
2 She .... leaves her computer on.
3 Her work is .... of a high standard.
4 She .... meets her deadlines.
5 She .... takes long lunch breaks.
6 She is .... polite and courteous.

• Project

Paula Higgs applied for a job in another company. The company's director, Mr James Smith, wrote to Mr Timothy Harper asking for a reference for Paula. Use the sentences in Ex. 18 to write the reference for Paula Higgs.

Speaking

19 How often do you:

• play football?
• go to the cinema?
• phone friends?
• travel abroad?
• treat sb to dinner?
• watch sport on TV?
• listen to the radio?
• read a newspaper?
• sleep late in the morning?
• forget to do your homework?

Lesson 3 (pp. 10 - 11)

* Check Ss' HW (10').

15 Allow Ss two minutes to do the exercise. Check Ss' answers on the board.

ANSWER KEY

1 Is Alison doing	6 are working
2 live	7 Is John staying
3 doesn't play	8 are not moving
4 leaves	9 Does Sue wash
5 Are you going	10 is mending

16 • Allow Ss two minutes to read the e-mail and fill in the verbs from the list in the correct tense. Check Ss' answers by asking individual Ss to read the e-mail aloud.

ANSWER KEY

1 live	7 clean
2 am studying	8 want
3 am working	9 draws
4 serve	10 am looking
5 share	11 am looking forward/
6 are painting	look forward

• Ss read the e-mail again. Elicit possible questions from Ss, then Ss, in pairs, ask and answer questions.

SUGGESTED ANSWER KEY

A: Where does Neil go to university?
B: He goes to York University.
A: What is he studying?
B: He is studying Geography. etc

17 • Ask Ss to look at the telegram and guess what type of word is missing from each gap. Explain the task, then play the recording twice. Ss listen and complete the telegram. Check Ss' answers orally.

• Ask Ss to look at the prompts. Read out the example. Ss, in pairs, ask and answer questions. Check Ss' answers, then choose pairs to report back to the class.

ANSWER KEY

LEAVE FOR ROME 7 AM – STOP – STAY BENELLI HOTEL
– STOP – MEET JOHN AND TOBY 10:30 AM – STOP –
RETURN FRIDAY PM – STOP – JILL

2 A: Where is she staying?
　 B: She's staying at the Benelli Hotel.
3 A: Who is she meeting?
　 B: She's meeting John and Toby.
4 A: When is she meeting them?
　 B: She's meeting them at 10:30 am.
5 A: When is she coming back?
　 B: She's coming back on Friday afternoon.

TAPESCRIPT

Jill: I must send John a telegram to tell him my plans, but I don't think I'll have time.
Claire: Don't worry. I'll send the telegram. Just tell me what you want to say.
Jill: Oh, thanks! Well, I need him to know that I'm leaving for Rome at 7 o'clock tomorrow morning.
Claire: ... leaving for Rome at 7 am ... OK, what else?
Jill: I'm staying at the Benelli Hotel.
Claire: Benelli Hotel. OK. Got it.

Jill: I'm meeting John and Toby at half past ten in the morning.
Claire: ... John and Toby ... 10:30 am ...OK.
Jill: And I'm coming back on Friday afternoon.
Claire: ... Friday ... right, I've got all that.
Jill: Oh, thanks, Claire, you're a lifesaver!

18 • Ask Ss to look at sentences 1-6. Explain the task, then play the recording twice. Ss listen and fill in the correct adverbs of frequency. Check Ss' answers by asking individual Ss to read the completed sentences aloud.

ANSWER KEY

1 usually	3 usually	5 often
2 sometimes	4 rarely	6 always

TAPESCRIPT

Mr H: Paula, could I have a word with you, please?
Paula: Of course, Mr Harper. Is anything the matter?
Mr H: Well, yes, as a matter of fact. I've noticed that you are usually late for work. This just isn't good enough, Paula.
Paula: Oh, I'm sorry, Mr Harper. It's just that I have trouble getting up in the mornings. I'll try harder.
Mr H: But that's not all, Paula. You sometimes leave your computer on, as well.
Paula: Oh, sorry ... I suppose I just forget.
Mr H: Also, I know that your work is usually of a high standard, but you rarely meet your deadlines. It takes you days to write a simple report ...
Paula: Well, reports are quite difficult...
Mr H: ... and I notice you often take very long lunch breaks, and return with bags of shopping ...
Paula: I won't do it again, Mr Harper.
Mr H: Paula, I have to be honest. It is only because of the fact that you are always polite and courteous to our customers that I am inclined to give you another chance.
Paula: Yes, Mr Harper.
Mr H: However, this is your final warning. Do you understand?
Paula: Yes, Mr Harper. I'll try to do better.

• Ask Ss to look at the completed sentences. Elicit from Ss when we use adverbs of frequency (to show how often something happens) and where we put them in a sentence (**before** the main verb e.g. *I always wear trousers to work*, but **after** an auxiliary or modal verb e.g. *I am always forgetting my briefcase*).

Project (p. 10)

• Explain that a reference is written by a person's employer to another employer commenting on the employee's work performance. Ask questions to check Ss' understanding.
e.g. Who is David Harper? (Paula's boss)
　　　Who is Mr Smith? (the director of another company)
　　　Is Paula a good employee? (No)
　　　Why not? (She is always late for work ... etc)
　　　How can you start the letter? (Dear Mr Smith, I am writing to ...)
　　　How can you end the letter? (Yours sincerely, Timothy Harper)

• Point out that Ss can use ideas of their own as well as their answers in Ex. 18 to write the reference. Do the exercise orally in class, then assign it as written HW.
See Writing Project 1 for the Answer Key.

19 Read aloud the prompts in the list. Ss, in pairs, ask and answer questions, using adverbs of frequency.
e.g. S1: How often do you play football?
　　　S2: I rarely play football. How often do you go to the cinema?
　　　S3: I usually go to the cinema once a week. etc
Check Ss' performance, then ask some pairs to report back to the class.

20 • Read sentences 1-4 aloud and ask individual Ss to identify the relative pronouns. Help Ss to complete the rules by eliciting the missing words from the Ss.
   • Drill your Ss. Say words. Ss say *who, which* or *whose* accordingly.
   Suggested word list: table, Mary, Tony's, the girls, bicycle, teacher, the doctor's, book etc
   e.g.   T: table
           S1: which
           T: Mary
           S2: who
           T: Tony's
           S3: whose etc

ANSWER KEY

• *We use **who/that** to describe people, **which/that** to describe things and **whose** to express possession.*

---

21 • Read aloud the sentences and explain the task. Allow Ss two minutes to complete the sentences.
   • Check Ss' answers by asking individual Ss to read the completed sentences aloud.

ANSWER KEY

1	which	6 whose
2	who	7 which
3	whose	8 whose
4	which	9 who
5	who	10 that

---

22 a) • Write the two examples on the board. Ask Ss to read the first sentence without the relative clause. Ask: *Which people? (We don't know.)* The meaning of the sentence is not clear if we omit the relative clause. Explain that the relative clause *(who park illegally)* is essential to the understanding of the main clause and therefore it cannot be omitted. This clause is called defining and is not put between commas.
   • Ask Ss to read the second sentence without the clause in commas. Ask: *Which people? (The ones next door.)* The meaning of the sentence is clear. Explain that the clause in commas is a non-defining relative clause. It only gives further information and if it is omitted it does not affect the meaning of the main clause. Explain that non-defining relative clauses are put in commas.
   • Read the theory box in their books.

b) Do items 1 and 2 with Ss. Allow Ss time to complete the task, then check Ss' answers round the class.

ANSWER KEY

1 , **which** I bought last week, *(ND)*
2 who *(D)*
3 , **who** is Canadian, *(ND)*
4 , **whose** grandparents live opposite me, *(ND)*
5 which *(D)*
6 whose *(D)*
7 who *(D)*

---

8 , **which** used to be my favourite, *(ND)*
9 , **who** works with my brother, *(ND)*
10 whose *(D)*

---

23 Ask Ss to look at the pictures. Read the picture prompts aloud. Then, read the prompts in the list and ask Ss to say which describe people/objects. Choose a S to read the example aloud. Then, Ss make sentences, as in the example.

ANSWER KEY

2 A hammer is a tool which we use to hit nails into wood.
3 A wetsuit is something we wear when we do water sports.
4 A firefighter is a person who puts out fires.
5 A computer is a machine which allows us to store information.
6 A vet is a person who treats sick animals.

---

24 • Explain the task. Allow Ss two minutes to make definitions.
   • Check Ss' answers by asking individual Ss to read their definitions aloud.

SUGGESTED ANSWER KEY

A florist is a person who makes floral arrangements and bouquets.
A newspaper is something which we read to find out the news.
A mechanic is someone who repairs cars.
Scissors are a tool which we use to cut paper, cloth etc.
An artist is a person who paints, draws or creates sculptures.
A comedian is a person who makes people laugh.
A journalist is a person who writes about the news.
A stamp is a small piece of paper which we stick on an envelope before we post it.
A mixer is a machine which we use to mix things together.
A ruler is a long piece of plastic, metal or wood which we use to draw straight lines or measure things with.

   • As an extension write words on the board. Ss, in teams, make definitions. Each correct sentence gets one point. The team with the most points is the winner.
   Suggested list: pen, nurse, doctor, cup, eraser, CD player, blackboard, politician, television, secretary etc

---

Suggested Homework

1 **Vocabulary:** Ex. 19 (p. 10) and Ex. 23 (p. 11)
2 **Reading aloud:** e-mail Ex. 16 (p. 10)
3 **Dictation:** sentences Ex. 23 (p. 11)
4 **Speaking:** Exs 17 & 19 (p. 10)
5 **Project:** (p. 10)

● Relatives - Relative Clauses

20 Read the sentences and underline the relative pronouns, then complete the rules.

1 Ann is the girl **who/that** is looking for you.
2 A hairdryer is a machine **which/that** is used for drying hair.
3 He's the man **whose** sister works as a nurse.
4 That's the man **who's** got a Ferrari.

● We use .... to describe people, ... to describe things and .... to express possession.

21 Underline the correct word.

1 A hose is something **which/whose** a firefighter uses to put out fires.
2 An architect is someone **who/which** designs buildings.
3 John is the boy **who's/whose** brother is in my class.
4 That's the house **which/who** was broken into last night.
5 Tara is the girl **which/who** is going to France this summer.
6 Simon is the man **who/whose** car is outside.
7 An axe is a tool **which/who** is used for chopping wood.
8 Mr Jones is the man **who's/whose** sister is on TV now.
9 Claire is the woman **whose/who** works in my office.
10 A vacuum cleaner is something **that/whose** is used for cleaning carpets.

22 a) In which sentence can we omit the relative clause?

1 People **who park illegally** are fined.
2 The people next door, **who own a Jaguar,** always park illegally.

● Defining relative clauses give essential information so we cannot omit them or put them in commas.
● Non-defining relative clauses give additional information, so we can omit them. We usually put them between commas.

b) Fill in the appropriate relative pronoun. Which clauses are defining (D)? Which are non-defining (ND)? Put commas where necessary.

1 My car .... I bought last week is second-hand.
2 The woman .... he is speaking to is my boss.
3 James .... is Canadian is a freelance writer.
4 Cindy .... grandparents live opposite me is moving to France.
5 The chair .... he is sitting on is an antique.
6 The band .... CD is playing now are very famous.
7 The people .... I met last night are doctors.
8 This blouse .... used to be my favourite is too small for me now.
9 Simon .... works with my brother is getting married.
10 The man .... daughter is on TV is an artist.

23 Look at the pictures and make sentences using *who* or *which* and the prompts below.

1 porter
2 hammer
3 wetsuit
4 firefighter
5 computer
6 vet

● something/wear/when we do water sports
● person/treat/sick animals
● machine/allow us/store information
● person/put out fires
● tool/use/hit nails into wood
● person/carry luggage

A porter is a person who carries luggage.

24 Give definitions for the following words using *who* or *which*.

● florist ● newspaper ● mechanic ● scissors ● artist
● comedian ● journalist ● stamp ● mixer ● ruler

11

Listening & Reading

25 What does each animal do at work? Choose from the list. You can use your own ideas.

- entertains the public
- finds criminals or evidence
- runs in races
- moves heavy objects
- carries people across the desert

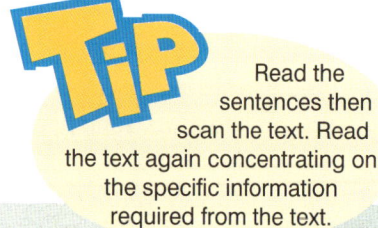

26 a) Look at the picture and the title and guess what the text is about. What do you think a police dog does? Discuss in pairs and decide.

 b) Listen and mark the prompts *Yes* or *No*.

1 finds lost children   .....
2 tracks down criminals .....
3 guards the house   .....
4 goes on patrol   .....
5 looks for evidence   .....
6 sniffs out food   .....
7 performs tricks   .....
8 retrieves lost things   .....
9 saves lives   .....
10 stops suspects from attacking his handler .....

27 Read the text and write *C* (correct) or *I* (incorrect) for questions 1 - 8, then explain the words in bold. Which sentences in the article best describe the picture?

Tip
Read the sentences then scan the text. Read the text again concentrating on the specific information required from the text.

It's a Dog's Life!

The Alameda Police Department in California is **proud** to have Kenzie **on the force**. He's a **real-life** super hero. Kenzie is not an **ordinary** police officer, though. He is a Police Service Dog (PSD) in the **canine unit** (K9).

As one of Alameda's K9s, Kenzie is a **fully-trained** police dog. He works **under cover of darkness**, using his **powers** of smell, hearing and night vision to **track down criminals**. He's a handsome German shepherd with dark tan fur and black markings on his head and neck. His **handler**, Patrick, tells us about a day in the life of a K9.

"Kenzie and I work the **night shift**," says Patrick. "Our working day starts at 5:00pm and ends at 3:00am. Kenzie sleeps in the same room as me because I like to know that he's sleeping and not playing! We get up at about midday and have our breakfast. Kenzie always has high-quality dry dog food and water. After breakfast, Kenzie has time to play with my other dog – another German shepherd – and enjoy his time off.

Before we go to work, Kenzie and I spend some time **training**. There is a lot of training and **testing** involved in being a K9, but Kenzie loves his work, so he **doesn't mind**. At 4:00pm, we leave the house and drive to the police station. Kenzie sits in the back of the car, which is actually a **mini kennel**. He waits in the car while I prepare for work, and then we **hit the streets**.

Kenzie is **on patrol** for ten hours. He knows that this is not a time for playing or sleeping so he **remains alert** at all times. Above all, his job is to protect me, but on **specialised assignments** he searches for criminals and looks for **evidence**, and he does all this very well. Kenzie's a real **professional**! He has a lot of experience in **sniffing out criminals** and is a great help in difficult situations. Kenzie even saved my life once when he stopped an **armed suspect** from attacking me. He's not only my hero but his work is of great **benefit** to me and to the police force in general.

When our shift is over, Kenzie and I return to the station, then we go home. Kenzie has his second meal at about 4:00am and after that we go straight to bed. We have the same routine every day, which is good. Like all dogs, Kenzie loves routine.

On our days off, Kenzie and I often travel together or do some training. We enjoy spending time together. Being a K9 handler requires a lot of **commitment**, but **it's well worth** it. I think of Kenzie as my friend as well as my partner, and I'm sure he feels the same way about me."

Lesson 4 (pp. 12 - 13)

* Check Ss' HW (10').

25 • Ask Ss to look at the pictures and identify the animals. Then, Ss try to guess what each animal does at work.
   • Ss look at the pictures and the prompts and make sentences about each animal.

ANSWER KEY

Horses run in races/pull carriages etc.
Dolphins entertain the public/perform tricks etc.
Dogs find criminals or evidence/help show the way to the blind etc.
Elephants move heavy objects/carry people etc.
Camels carry people across the desert/carry heavy objects etc.

   • Ss think of other animals and talk about what they can do at work.
   e.g. Rabbits perform tricks.

26 a) • Ss look at the picture and the title. Ask: *Is this an ordinary dog? (No, it's a police dog.) Where does it work? (In Alameda Police Department.) What do you think the text is about? (About what the dog does at work.)*
   • Read the phrases aloud and elicit/explain the meaning of any unknown words. Ss look at the prompts, then in closed pairs, discuss what a police dog does/doesn't do. Ask individual pairs to report back to the class.
   (Ss' own answers)

b) • Play the recording. Ss listen and check their answers by marking the prompts *Yes* or *No*.
   • Check Ss' answers by asking individual Ss to make sentences.
   e.g. S1: A police dog doesn't find lost children.
      S2: A police dog tracks down criminals. etc

ANSWER KEY

1 No	5 Yes	8 No
2 Yes	6 No	9 Yes
3 No	7 No	10 Yes
4 Yes		

27 • Read statements 1-8 on p. 13 aloud. Allow Ss about four minutes to read the text silently and write I or C. Check Ss' answers around the class.

ANSWER KEY

1 C	3 I	5 I	7 I
2 I	4 C	6 C	8 I

Sentence: Kenzie sits in the back of the car, which is actually a mini kennel. He waits in the car while I prepare for work, ...

• Help Ss to explain the words in bold by giving examples or synonyms, or using Ss' L1. Ss can look the words up in their dictionaries.
e.g. **ordinary:** typical
• Play the recording again. Ss listen and follow the lines, then individual Ss read aloud from the text.

Further practice

After Ss have done Ex. 27, ask them to visit:
http://www.lydiahiby.com/info.html
to collect information and write an article similar to that in Ex. 27 (p. 12).

28 Explain the task. Allow Ss two minutes to match the definitions to the words in the text. Check Ss' answers around the class.

ANSWER KEY

1	on patrol	5	fully-trained
2	specialised	6	benefit
	assignments	7	professional
3	under cover of	8	evidence
	darkness	9	commitment
4	on the force	10	armed

---

29 Write the headings on the board and elicit answers from Ss to complete the table. *(What does Kenzie do before work? What does he do at work? etc)* Ss copy the completed table into their notebooks, then use their notes to talk about Kenzie's daily routine. Point out that Ss should use appropriate linking words (first, then, after that, and, also, so etc)

SUGGESTED ANSWER KEY

- **Before work:** *get up at about midday; have breakfast; play with Patrick's other dog; spend some time training; go to police station; wait in car*
- **At work:** *be on patrol for ten hours; remain alert; protect Patrick; search for criminals; look for evidence*
- **After work:** *return to station; go home; have second meal; go to bed*
- **Free time:** *travel with Patrick; train; spend time with Patrick*

... he plays with Patrick's other dog. He spends some time training, then he and Patrick go to the police station. Kenzie waits in the car while Patrick gets ready for work.

At work, Kenzie is on patrol for ten hours. He remains alert and protects Patrick. Kenzie also searches for criminals and looks for evidence.

After work, Patrick and Kenzie return to the station, then they go home. Kenzie has his second meal and then he goes to bed.

In his free time, Kenzie travels with Patrick and trains. He enjoys spending time with Patrick.

---

30 • Allow Ss three minutes to fill in the correct word. Check Ss' answers round the class, then Ss make sentences.

ANSWER KEY

1 track; 2 armed; 3 fully; 4 specialised;
5 night; 6 instructor's; 7 university; 8 absolute;
9 super; 10 technical

---

31 • Allow Ss two to three minutes to fill in the correct preposition. Check Ss' answers around the class, then Ss make sentences.

ANSWER KEY

1 on 3 in 5 for 7 in   9 on 11 of 13 for
2 at 4 of 6 of 8 for 10 for 12 in 14 in

- As an extension, Ss make sentences using the phrases as they appear in the list.
  e.g. S1: Kenzie is **on patrol** for ten hours.
       S2: Steve has experience **at all levels** of teaching.
       etc

Vocabulary Revision Game

As an extension, Ss close their books and form two teams. Say words/phrases from the unit. Ss from each team take turns to make sentences with the words. Each correct sentence gets one point. The team with the most points is the winner.

e.g.   T: apply
        Team A S1: Did you **apply** for the job?
                T: Great! Team A gets 1 point. etc

Suggested words/phrases: apply, super hero, ordinary, professional, routine, evidence, of great benefit, remain alert, difficult situations, uniform, challenging, work shifts, technical skills, work experience, training, job interview, university degree

32 a) Read aloud the theory box and explain the task to Ss. Ss use their dictionaries to write the nouns. Check Ss' answers on the board.

ANSWER KEY

1	teacher	6	sailor	11	lawyer
2	builder	7	baker	12	beautician
3	waiter	8	conductor	13	artist
4	farmer	9	inspector	14	comedian
5	manager	10	dancer	15	politician

---

b) Read the questions aloud. Allow Ss two minutes to answer the questions, then check Ss' answers around the class.

ANSWER KEY

1 school – teaches children
2 building site – builds houses
3 restaurant – serves food
4 farm – grows crops/keeps animals
5 office – runs a company
6 boat/ship – sails to different places
7 bakery – makes bread and cakes
8 concert hall – conducts the orchestra
9 police station – investigates/solves crimes
10 theatre – dances/entertains people
11 court – argues legal cases
12 salon – makes people up/gives manicures
13 studio – paints/draws pictures
14 theatre/TV studio – makes people laugh
15 Houses of Parliament – makes laws

---

33 Read the table aloud and make sure Ss understand the meaning of each phrasal verb. Allow Ss two minutes to complete the sentences, then check Ss' answers. Ss can then make sentences of their own using the phrasal verbs. Ss should memorise these phrasal verbs.

ANSWER KEY

1 up, 2 through, 3 into, 4 after, 5 forward to,
6 for

(**Suggested Homework**)

1 **Vocabulary:** words in bold Ex. 27 (p. 12), Exs 30, 31 & 33 (p. 13)
2 **Reading aloud:** Ex. 27 (p. 12)
3 **Dictation:** any ten words from Vocabulary
4 **Speaking:** Ex. 29 (p. 13)

1 Kenzie works when most people are asleep. ....
2 Work starts at noon. ....
3 Kenzie has time for a nap during his shift. ....
4 Patrick thinks highly of Kenzie. ....
5 Kenzie eats three times a day. ....
6 Kenzie has got a varied work routine. ....
7 Kenzie sleeps in a kennel at night. ....
8 Patrick feels unhappy about his job. ....

28 **Find the words/phrases in bold which match the definitions below.**

1 moving around and checking the area
2 particular tasks
3 without being noticed because it is night
4 as a member of the police department
5 expert
6 assistance/help
7 one whose work is of a high standard
8 proof
9 devotion
10 carrying a weapon

Speaking

29 **Make notes under the headings, then talk about Kenzie's daily routine. Use:** *first, then, after, that, while.*

- Before work
- At work
- After work
- Free time

Kenzie gets up at about midday and has breakfast. Then ...

Vocabulary Practice

30 **Fill in the correct words from the list, then make sentences using the completed phrases.**

- fully • absolute • technical • instructor's
- night • specialised • super • armed • track
- university

1 to .... down
2 .... suspect
3 .... qualified
4 .... assignments
5 .... shift
6 .... licence
7 .... degree
8 .... beginners
9 .... hero
10 .... skills

31 **Fill in** *at, in, on, for, of,* **then make sentences using the phrases.**

1 .... patrol; 2 .... all levels; 3 a day .... the life of; 4 under cover .... darkness; 5 to look .... evidence; 6 years .... training; 7 to speak .... public; 8 to be late .... work; 9 .... the force; 10 to prepare .... work; 11 the position .... ski instructor; 12 to have experience .... doing sth; 13 to come .... an interview; 14 .... general

Word Formation

32 **a) Study the table, then write the nouns using your dictionary to help you.**

We can form nouns referring to people and jobs by adding -r, -er, or -or, -ist, -ian to the main verb or noun.
drive → driver, sing → singer, act → actor, type → typist, music → musician

1 teach	6 sail	11 law
2 build	7 bake	12 beauty
3 wait	8 conduct	13 art
4 farm	9 inspect	14 comedy
5 manage	10 dance	15 politics

b) Where does each person work? What do they do at work?

Phrasal Verbs

33 **Study the table, then complete the sentences.**

look after - to take care of; to keep sth healthy, safe or in good condition
look for - to search for
look forward to - to expect; to anticipate
look into - to find out about sth; to investigate
look through - to read (often quickly)
look up - to find a word in a dictionary/a phone number in a directory

1 Can I borrow your dictionary to look .... the meaning of this word?
2 He usually looks .... the newspaper while he is eating breakfast.
3 The police are looking .... the matter.
4 John is looking .... his neighbour's cat while she is abroad.
5 We are really looking .... the party on Saturday.
6 I can't find my wallet. Please help me look .... it.

Communication (registering with an employment agency)

34 Listen and complete the dialogue, then make similar dialogues using the prompts below.

A: Good afternoon. I'd like to 1) .... with this employment agency.
B: Certainly. What's your name, please?
A: It's **Robert Elliot**.
B: What kind of work can you do?
A: Well, **anything clerical**.
B: Great. What hours are you 2) .... to work?
A: I'd prefer to work **mornings**.
B: Thank you, **Mr Elliot**. Please 3) .... in this form.

- Jessica Blake/mainly managerial/from 9 to 5
- Stuart Huntley/mostly sales/in the evening

Pronunciation (stress in compound nouns)

35 Listen and underline the syllable of each word that is stressed. Listen again and repeat.

dog walker
taxi driver
estate agent
police officer

flight attendant
telephone operator
secret agent
newspaper editor

Writing (an essay about the pros and cons of a job)

When we write an essay giving the pros and cons of a topic, we usually write it in four paragraphs.
In the **introduction**, we state the topic. In the **main body** there are two paragraphs. In the **second paragraph**, we write the pros of the topic giving reasons/examples and in the **third paragraph**, we write the cons giving examples. In the **conclusion**, we summarise the topic and write our opinion. We use appropriate linking words to join our ideas (to list points: *first, second, furthermore, in addition*, etc; to show contrast: *on the other hand, however*, etc; to conclude: *all in all, to sum up, in conclusion*).

36 a) What do you think are the pros and cons of working as a flight attendant?

b) Read the essay and fill in the words from the list, then answer the questions.

- furthermore
- to begin with
- for example
- in addition
- however

THE PROS AND CONS OF WORKING AS A FLIGHT ATTENDANT

1 Some people see it as an ordinary job while others think it is an exciting and interesting career. Whatever your views, there is no doubt that working as a flight attendant is a demanding job with many advantages and disadvantages.

2 There are several arguments in favour of working as a flight attendant. 1) ...., it is a very exciting job because flight attendants are able to travel to lots of places. For instance, they could be in Spain one day and Iceland the next. 2) ...., it is an interesting job because flight attendants get to meet lots of different people from different countries every day.

3 3) ...., there are also a number of disadvantages to being a flight attendant. Firstly, it is a stressful job as flight attendants have a lot of responsibility. 4) ...., they must always be prepared to deal with any number of situations that may arise. 5) ...., it is a tiring job because they often have to work long and unsociable hours.

4 To conclude, I believe that, although being a flight attendant can be difficult at times, it is worth it. It is exciting to travel to lots of different places and meet lots of interesting people.

1 Which paragraph presents the advantages of working as a flight attendant?
2 Which paragraph presents the disadvantages of working as a flight attendant?
3 Which words/phrases are used: to list and add points? to introduce advantages? to introduce disadvantages? to show contrast? to give examples? to introduce the conclusion?
4 Which paragraph contains the writer's opinion?
5 What is a topic sentence? What topic sentences does the writer use?

Lesson 5 (pp. 14 - 15)

* Check Ss' HW (10').

34 • Ask Ss: *What is an employment agency? (An agency which finds jobs for people.)* Ss skim read the dialogue. Play the recording. Ss listen and fill in the missing words. Check Ss' answers.

ANSWER KEY

1 register   2 willing   3 fill

• Play the recording again. Ss listen and follow the lines, then Ss read the dialogue aloud in pairs.
• Read out the prompts and explain that Ss should replace the highlighted words in the dialogue with the prompts to make similar dialogues.
• Ss, in pairs, act out similar dialogues using the prompts. Check Ss' performance around the class.

ANSWER KEY

A: *Good afternoon. I'd like to register with this employment agency.*
B: *Certainly. What's your name, please?*
A: *It's **Jessica Blake/Stuart Huntley**.*
B: *What kind of work can you do?*
A: *Well, **mainly managerial/mostly sales**.*
B: *Great. What hours are you willing to work?*
A: *I'd prefer to work **from 9 to 5/in the evening**.*
B: *Thank you, **Ms Blake/Mr Huntley**. Please fill in this form.*

---

35 • Play the recording. Ss listen and underline the stressed syllable in each compound noun.
• Play the recording again. Ss listen and repeat individually.

ANSWER KEY

dog *walker*   **flight** *attendant*
taxi *driver*   **te**lephone *operator*
estate *agent*   **se**cret *agent*
police *officer*   **news**paper *editor*

Writing (p. 14)

• Explain what pros (good points) and cons (bad points, drawbacks) mean. Also explain that when we try to decide on a job, we need to take into consideration both pros and cons.
• Read the theory box aloud and elicit/explain the meaning of any unknown words.

36 a) • Read the question and brainstorm the topic. First, ask Ss what the good and bad points of working as a flight attendant are. Write Ss' answers on the board. Put the points you have brainstormed into the correct category - pros or cons.
Suggested list: work long hours (cons), have a lot of responsibility (cons), travel a lot (pros), earn good salary (pros), see new places (pros), rarely see their families (cons)   etc

b) • Read aloud the words in the list and elicit/explain their meaning. Allow Ss about four minutes to read the essay silently and fill in the words from the list. Check Ss' answers by asking Ss to read the essay aloud.
• Read the questions aloud and elicit/explain the meaning of any unknown words. Help Ss to answer the questions.

ANSWER KEY

1 To begin with   4 For example
2 In addition/Furthermore 5 Furthermore/In
3 However   addition

---

1 Paragraph 2
2 Paragraph 3
3 **to list and add points:** *to begin with; in addition; firstly; furthermore; and*
to introduce advantages: *There are several arguments in favour of ...;*
to introduce disadvantages: *However, there are also a number of disadvantages...*
to show contrast: *however*
to give examples: *for example*
to introduce the conclusion: *to conclude*
4 Paragraph 4
5 A topic sentence is the first sentence of a paragraph which introduces or summarises the main topic of the paragraph, to give readers an idea of what they are going to read.
The first sentences in each paragraph are the topic sentences.

1

c) • Write the headings on the board. Allow Ss time to read the essay again, then elicit answers from Ss to complete the table by asking questions.
e.g. What are the advantages of being a flight attendant? *(It's exciting.)* Why? *(Because they travel to lots of different places.)* Good. What else? etc

• Ss copy the table into their notebooks, then use their notes and appropriate linking words to talk about the pros and cons of working as a flight attendant. As an extension, Ss choose another job and think of its pros and cons.

SUGGESTED ANSWER KEY

Arguments for / Justification/Reasons
• *exciting:* travel to lots of different places
• *interesting:* meet lots of people from different countries
Arguments against / Justification/Reasons
• *stressful:* have a lot of responsibility
• *tiring:* have to work long and unsociable hours

There are many advantages to being a flight attendant. Firstly, it is an exciting job because they are able to travel to lots of different places. Secondly, being a flight attendant is interesting because they get to meet lots of people from different countries.
However, there are also several arguments against working as a flight attendant. To begin with, it is a stressful job because they have a lot of responsibility. In addition, it can be tiring because they have to work long and unsociable hours.

---

37 Allow Ss two minutes to read the sentences silently and underline the correct linking words/phrases. Check Ss' answers by asking individual Ss to read the sentences aloud.

ANSWER KEY: 1 Even though, 2 For instance, 3 argue that, 4 such as, 5 In addition, 6 Furthermore

---

38 a) Explain that a topic sentence is a sentence which starts a paragraph giving a summary of it. Explain the task, then Ss do the exercise. Check Ss' answers around the class.

ANSWER KEY

1 B To begin with, you are your own boss and can make your own rules. Secondly, it is rewarding, as you can do something which you really enjoy. Moreover, you can decide what hours to work and when to take a holiday.
2 ——
3 A First of all, you experience a different culture and broaden your mind. In addition, working abroad gives you the chance to learn a new language, which will improve your career prospects. Finally, you see interesting places and meet different people.

---

b) • Read aloud sentence 2 and elicit from Ss the disadvantages (as well as justifications/examples) of working from home. Write their answers on the board in note form.
• Ss copy the notes on the board into their notebooks. Allow Ss three to four minutes to expand their notes into a full paragraph using appropriate linking words.

SUGGESTED ANSWER KEY: Firstly, people who work from home may feel lonely, as they do not have the chance to socialise with people at work. Secondly, they may be unable to meet their deadlines, as they do not work to a steady timetable.

---

39 Explain the task, then Ss, in closed pairs, do the exercise. Check Ss' answers. Ss use the notes and linking words from Exs 37, 38 and 39 to talk about the pros and cons of being a doctor.

ANSWER KEY

Arguments for: 1 B   2 A
Arguments against: 1 A   2 B

There are several arguments in favour of being a doctor. First of all, it is a rewarding job, as doctors help sick and injured people to recover. Furthermore, doctors are rarely out of work as there is always a demand for people to treat the sick or injured.

However, there are also many disadvantages to working as a doctor. Firstly, it is a tiring job, because they work shifts and often work at night. In addition, working as a doctor can be depressing, as they often see people suffering.

---

40 Explain the task to Ss. Read out and explain the plan. Help Ss to complete the task orally, then assign it as written HW.

SUGGESTED ANSWER KEY

*   Some people see it as a difficult and stressful job while others think it is a rewarding and interesting career. Whatever your views, there is no doubt that working as a doctor is a demanding job with many advantages and disadvantages.*
*   There are several arguments in favour of being a doctor. First of all, it is a rewarding job, as doctors help sick and injured people to recover. Furthermore, doctors are rarely out of work, as there is always a demand for people to treat the sick and injured.*
*   However, there are also many disadvantages to working as a doctor. Firstly, it is a tiring job, because they work shifts and often work at night. In addition, being a doctor can be depressing, as they often see people suffering.*
*   To conclude, I believe that, although being a doctor can be difficult at times, it is worth it. It is rewarding to help people recover from sickness or injury.*

---

41 Read the sentences aloud and elicit/explain the meaning of any unknown words. Allow Ss time to read the sentences silently and try to guess what they mean. Ask/Help Ss to explain the meaning of each sentence.

SUGGESTED ANSWER KEY
• *If a lot of people help, a job will be easier to do.*
• *You can't work all the time. You need to take a break sometimes.*
• *Don't delay doing a job if you have time to do it now.*
• *Everyone has to work to earn a living.*
• *Work should make people happy not sad.*

(Suggested Homework)

1 **Vocabulary:** Ex. 36 (p. 14) and Ex. 37 (p. 15)
2 **Act out:** Ex. 34 (p. 14)
3 **Speaking:** Ex. 36c (p. 15)
4 **Writing:** Ex. 40 (p. 15)

(**Lesson 6**)

Workbook Unit 1
        Click on Grammar 1

c) Read the essay again and complete the table, then talk about the pros and cons using appropriate linking words.

Arguments for	Justification/Reasons
• exciting	• travel to lots of different places
•	•

Arguments against	Justification/Reasons
•	•
•	•

37 Underline the correct linking word/phrase.

1 **Even though/Nevertheless** working as a doctor is a rewarding job, it can be very tiring.
2 **For instance/Still**, people who communicate well with others usually succeed in managerial positions.
3 Some people **argue that/are against** job satisfaction is more important than financial reward.
4 Many jobs, **since/such as** teaching, require extensive training.
5 **In addition/In spite of**, personality plays an important role in finding the right job.
6 **Furthermore/Despite**, people who are willing to work overtime are more likely to get a promotion.

38 a) Read the topic sentences, then expand the notes into full paragraphs. Which topic sentence matches each paragraph?

1 Being self-employed has many advantages.
2 On the other hand, there are several disadvantages to working from home.
3 There are many arguments in favour of working abroad.

A First of all — experience a different culture — broaden your mind — in addition — learn a new language — improve career prospects — finally — see interesting places — meet different people

B To begin with — are your own boss — make own rules — secondly — rewarding — do something you really enjoy — moreover — decide what hours to work — when to take holiday

b) Now write a paragraph which matches the topic sentence which hasn't been used.

39 Match the arguments to the justifications/reasons, then talk about the pros and cons of working as a doctor. Suggest appropriate topic sentences.

Arguments for	Justification/Reasons
1 it's a rewarding job	A there is always a demand for people to treat the sick or injured
2 doctors are rarely out of work	B they help sick or injured people to recover

Arguments against	Justification/Reasons
1 it's a tiring job	A they work shifts and often work at night
2 it can be depressing	B they often see people suffering

40 Your teacher has asked you to write an essay about the pros and cons of working as a doctor. Use the notes in the table above and the plan below to write your essay. You can use the essay in Ex. 36 as a model.

Plan

Introduction
(Para 1) *general comment about the job*
Main Body
(Para 2) *advantages and justifications/reasons*
(Para 3) *disadvantages and justifications/ reasons*
Conclusion
(Para 4) *summary and your opinion*

41 Read the sentences. What do they mean?

What's in a word?

- Many hands make light work.
- All work and no play makes Jack a dull boy.
- Never put off till tomorrow what you can do today.
- If you don't work, you shan't eat.
- Work is a blessing not a curse.

THE ADVENTURES OF HUCKLEBERRY FINN

How It All Started

My name's Huckleberry Finn — but everyone just calls me "Huck" — and this is the story of my adventures. It all started with my best friend, Tom Sawyer … ①

Gold coins, Tom! We're rich!

We can ask Judge Thatcher to look after the money for us. ②

Here you are, boys — a dollar each, every day of your lives!

Thank you, Judge Thatcher. ③

Widow Douglas has got something to say, Huck …

Huck, no one has seen your father for a year …

… you live in the woods like a wild animal, and don't go to school … ④

You need a *real* home, Huck. I want you to come and live with me like my son. ⑤

A FEW MONTHS LATER …

Well, Huck — how is life at the widow's?

It's hard, Tom! Wearing smart clothes, going to school … and the widow's sister, Miss Watson, makes lots of rules. I like Jim, though — he's Miss Watson's slave. ⑥

Jim, I'm scared! My pap has come back!

But Huck, everyone says that your father's dead. ⑦

⑧ Well, everyone's wrong, then. See — that mark is from Pap's boot!

THAT NIGHT …

Pap! ⑨

You think you're better than me, don't you? Going to school, sleeping in a fancy bed … and people say you're rich!

Ow! Please, Pap — don't! ⑩

Pre-Reading Activities

1 **Fill in the gaps with words/expressions from the list.**

- After the Civil War
- At the age of 20
- as
- at the time
- a year later
- before long
- like
- When

Mark Twain's real name was Samuel Langhorne Clemens. Born in 1835 in Missouri, USA, he grew up in Hannibal, a small town on the Mississippi River. **1)** When his father died in 1847, Samuel left school to start work as a printer. **2)** At the age of 20, he began work on the Mississippi riverboats and became a riverboat pilot.

3) After the Civil War began in 1861, the riverboats stopped running, and Clemens tried many different jobs. He also started writing humorous stories for various newspapers, and **4)** before long he was well known as a writer. He wrote his first major book in 1869, and got married **5)** a year later. He published *Tom Sawyer* in 1876 and *Huckleberry Finn* in 1884. He was still famous and very popular, both in the USA and Europe, **6)** at the time of his death in 1910.

Huckleberry Finn is set in about 1845-1850 and begins in a small town just **7)** like Hannibal. In other words, Mark Twain was writing about the time and place of his own childhood. Many of the characters and events in the story are taken from his boyhood and his life **8)** as a riverboat pilot.

2 **Look at the pictures. Which show(s):**

1 Huck wearing a straw hat?   1
2 Tom and Huck at school, wearing smart clothes?   6
3 a footprint in the snow?   8
4 Huck's father, with dirty clothes and long hair?   4, 9, 10
5 Tom holding lots of gold coins?   2
6 a woman wearing black because her husband is dead?   4, 5
7 Huck walking with Miss Watson's slave, Jim?   7
8 Huck's father beating him?   10
9 Judge Thatcher's library?   3, 4, 5

Listening & Reading Activities

3 **Listen and write *Yes* or *No*.**

1 Huck's best friend is Tom Sawyer.   Yes
2 Huck lives with his father.   No
3 Widow Douglas wants Huck to live with her.   Yes
4 Everyone says Huck's father has come back.   No
5 Huck and his father are very happy to see each other.   No

4 **Read the episode on p. 16 and answer the questions using one to three words.**

1 How much money do Huck and Tom get every day? A dollar (each).
2 Where does Huck live at the start of the story? In the woods.
3 Who is Miss Watson? The widow's sister.
4 Who is Jim? Miss Watson's slave.

5 **Study the rules, then fill in *like* or *as*.**

> We use **like** to say what sb looks like.
>
> We use **as** to say what sb is like.
>
> *He works like a slave.* (He isn't a slave)
>
> *She works as a nurse.* (She is a nurse)
>
> ALSO: looks like, sounds like, feels like, be regarded as, known as

1 Huck started trembling like a leaf when he saw Pap.
2 Mr Thatcher works as a judge.
3 He is known as the best writer of his time.
4 The boys ran like the wind.
5 Sue looks like her sister.

6 **Listen to the episode again, then read it out.**

What a Story!

1 What do the pictures on pp. 18-19 show?

2 Look at the key words and say what was on last night's 9 o'clock news.

- earthquake - building collapsed
- robbery - robber was arrested
- burglary - burglar broke into a house
- plane crash - 50 people were injured
- car crash - car crashed into a tree

There was an earthquake. A building collapsed.

3 a) Listen to the sounds and put the sentences in the order you hear them.

3	*It* went off.		*It* crashed into a tree.
	He fired *it*.		*It* crash-landed.
	It collapsed.		

b) Match the pictures to the sentences. What does *it* in each sentence refer to?

3 — A The alarm went off.

c) Link the sentences below to the sentences in Ex. 3 using *when*.

1 The cashier was giving the robber the money when the robber fired a gun.
2 The ground was shaking ....
3 The driver was trying to avoid hitting the bus ....
4 The passengers were screaming ....
5 The burglar was trying to break into a house ....

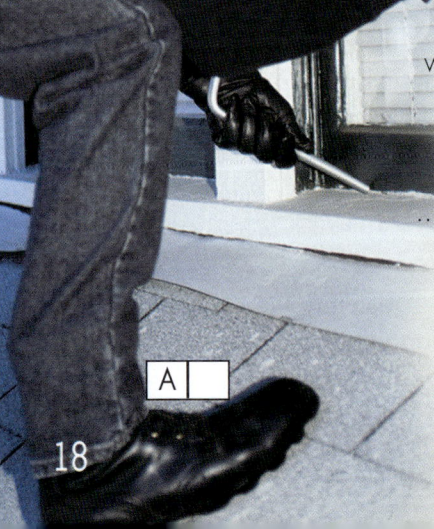

B

C

A

D

Objectives

Vocabulary: accidents and disasters; emergency equipment; crime; feelings and emotions; transport and travel
Reading: a story
Listening: listening to interpret feelings; listening for specific information
Speaking: summarising events; describing incidents; explaining the uses of emergency equipment; talking about past experiences
Communication: apologising
Pronunciation: intonation of apologies
Grammar: past simple; past continuous; linkers; adverbs of time
Phrasal verbs: break; bring
Word formation: forming adjectives
Project: a letter to a friend describing an unpleasant experience
Writing: a story

Lesson 1 (pp. 18 - 19)

1 • Ask Ss to look at the pictures on pp. 18-19 and say what each one shows.

SUGGESTED ANSWER KEY

A sb breaking into a house
B a robbery
C a plane crash
D a collapsed building
E a car crash

• As an extension Ss can say what was on last night's 9 o'clock news, giving details.
  e.g. There was a fashion show. Montanà presented the summer collection. There was a fire. Two buildings were completely destroyed.   etc

2 Read out the words/phrases in the list explaining any unknown words. Ss make sentences, as in the example.

ANSWER KEY

• There was a robbery. The robber was arrested.
• There was a burglary. The burglar broke into a house.
• There was a plane crash. Fifty people were injured.
• There was a car crash. The driver crashed into a tree.

3 a) Ask Ss to read sentences aloud one at a time. Elicit/Explain the meaning of any unknown words. Play the recording. Ss listen and number the sentences in the order they hear the sounds.

ANSWER KEY

3 It went off.   5 It crashed into a tree.
4 He fired it.   2 It crash-landed.
1 It collapsed.

b) Ask Ss to look at the pictures again and match them to the sentences. Then ask Ss to say what the pronoun **it** represents in each sentence.

ANSWER KEY

4 B He fired **the gun**.
2 C **The aeroplane** crash-landed.
1 D **The building** collapsed
5 E **The car** crashed into a tree.

c) • Explain the task. Read out the example, then Ss complete the task. Check Ss' answers around the class.

ANSWER KEY

1 The cashier was giving the robber the money when he fired the gun.
2 The ground was shaking when the building collapsed.
3 The driver was trying to avoid hitting the bus when the car crashed into a tree.
4 The passengers were screaming when the plane crash-landed.
5 The burglar was trying to break into the house when the alarm went off.

• Write sentence 1 on the board. Underline **was giving, fired**. Ask: *Which verb shows an action which was in progress? (was giving) What tense is it? (past continuous) Which verb shows that an action interrupted another action? (fired) What tense is it? (past simple)*
• Drill your Ss. Give prompts. Ss make sentences modelling the structure. *... when the lights went out.*
  Suggested prompts: read a magazine, listen to music, watch TV, have a bath, cook, make the beds, water the plants, do my homework   etc
  S1: I was reading a magazine when the lights went out.
  S2: I was listening to music when the lights went out. etc

4 • Play the recording. Ss listen and repeat, chorally or individually. Present each phrase/sentence by giving examples.

   e.g. **Oh my goodness!:** (Walk to the window and look outside. With a shocked expression say to Ss: *Oh my goodness! That man has crashed his car.*)

• Ss close their books. Individual Ss say a sentence from the list. This can be done as a game. See Unit 1 Ex. 3 p. 6(T).

5 Explain the task then play the recording, twice if necessary. Ss do the exercise. Check Ss' answers.

ANSWER KEY

1 ... it was coming in to land at Heathrow.
2 ... the cyclist pulled out of that side road.
3 ... I saw the man in front of me pull out a gun.

6 a) Read sentences 1 to 6 aloud. Allow Ss four minutes to read the dialogues and mark the questions Yes or No. Check Ss' answers, then help Ss explain the words in bold by giving a synonym, or example.

ANSWER KEY

1 No	3 Yes	5 Yes
2 Yes	4 No	6 No

b) Play the recording for Ex. 5 again. Ss listen and follow the lines, then read out the dialogues in pairs.

c) Allow Ss three minutes to read the dialogues again. Then for each one elicit the key words/phrases that describe each incident from Ss around the class. Write these on the board, then Ss copy these notes into their notebooks.

ANSWER KEY

Dialogue A:
plane crash – Heathrow – coming in to land – 150 people on board – many in hospital – fire brigade got everyone out – Boeing 727

Dialogue B:
accident – witness saw whole thing – blue car heading down road – cyclist pulled out of side road – driver swerved to other side of road – oncoming bus – swerved again – slammed on brakes – crashed into tree

Dialogue C:
Sarah – queue – pay for groceries – man in front – pull out gun – cashier – hand over money – fired gun – ran away – no one hurt – frightened – police – arrest robber

d) Ask individual Ss to use their notes to describe each incident.

SUGGESTED ANSWER KEY

Dialogue A:
... with 150 people on board. A lot of them are now in hospital but the fire brigade got everyone out of the Boeing 727.

Dialogue B:
There was a car accident. A witness saw the whole thing. A blue car was heading down the road when a cyclist pulled out of a side road in front of him. The driver swerved to the other side of the road into the path of an oncoming bus. He swerved again and slammed on his brakes but he crashed into a tree.

Dialogue C:
Sarah was in a queue waiting to pay for her groceries when the man in front of her pulled out a gun. He told the cashier to hand over the money but, when he was doing this, the robber fired the gun and ran away. No one was hurt but they were frightened. The police arrested the robber.

Suggested Homework

1 **Vocabulary:** words in Ex. 2 (p. 18), words in bold in dialogues A-C (p. 19), Ex. 4 (p. 19)
2 **Reading aloud:** dialogues A-C Ex. 5 (p. 19) (Point out that Ss practise *reading aloud* using the S's audio CD.)
3 **Dictation:** any ten of the words in Vocabulary with example/definition
4 **Writing:** any of the summaries in Ex. 6d (p. 19)

Listening and Reading

4 Listen and repeat, then close your books and try to remember as many sentences as possible.

- Oh, my goodness!
- That's terrible!
- Well, that's a relief.
- What caused it?
- Thank you for your cooperation.
- Was anyone hurt?
- Well, it's all over now.
- Just in time.
- Thankfully, no.

5 Listen and complete.

1 The plane crashed while …
2 The blue car was heading this way down the road when …
3 I was waiting in the queue to pay for my groceries when …

6 a) Read the dialogues and mark the sentences Yes or No, then explain the words in bold.

1 Fifty people were aboard the plane.
2 The witness saw the accident happen.
3 The driver could avoid hitting the cyclist.
4 The car crashed into a bus.
5 The robber was caught by the police.
6 Sarah was calm when she met Jane.

A

Jenny: Quick, Steve! Come and listen to this news report on the radio.
Steve: What is it? What happened?
Jenny: A plane crashed while it was coming in to land at Heathrow.
Steve: Oh my goodness! That's terrible! When did it happen?
Jenny: Just now!
Steve: Were there many people **on board**?
Jenny: About a hundred and fifty, I think. A lot of them are in hospital now, but the **fire brigade** got everyone out.
Steve: Well, that's a relief. What caused it?
Jenny: Ssh... Let's listen. They're telling us now.
Radio: For listeners just **tuning in**, a Boeing 727 … (fade)

B

Policeman: Can you tell me how the accident happened, sir?
Witness: Yes, I saw the whole thing. The blue car was heading this way down the road when the cyclist pulled out of that side road right in front of it.
Policeman: Was the car speeding?
Witness: No, but the driver had to act quickly to avoid hitting the cyclist. He **swerved** over to the other side of the road and into the path of an oncoming bus.
Policeman: I see. What happened next?
Witness: He swerved again, but he lost control of the vehicle. There was a loud **screeching** noise as he **slammed** on his brakes and then he crashed into that tree.
Policeman: Right. I don't think there'll be anything more at this point. I just need to take your full name and address for the **record**.
Witness: Okay. It's Tony Brown, 16 Bullpark Lane, Clevedon.
Policeman: That will be all for now, sir. Thank you for your **cooperation**.
Witness: You're welcome.

C

John: What's wrong? You look awful.
Sarah: I just witnessed a robbery.
John: Really? What happened?
Sarah: Well, I was waiting in the **queue** to **pay for my groceries** when I saw the man in front of me pull out a gun.
John: Oh no!
Sarah: Yes. He started **waving** the gun around and shouting at the **cashier** to hand over the money. While the cashier was giving him the money, he pressed the **alarm button**. The robber fired the gun and then ran away.
John: Was anyone hurt?
Sarah: Thankfully, no, and the police arrived just in time to arrest the robber.
John: What a frightening experience!
Sarah: Oh, tell me about it. **I'm still shaking**.
John: Well, it's all over now. Sit down and I'll make you a nice cup of tea.

b) Read out the dialogues in pairs.

c) Read the dialogues again and write down the words/phrases which describe each incident.

Speaking

d) Now use the words to give a brief summary of each incident.

A plane crashed at Heathrow. It was coming in to land …

E

19

Vocabulary

• Disasters and accidents

7 Underline the words in the headlines which are disasters/accidents. Which of these are natural disasters? Which are man-made?

A **Flood Washes Away Village!**

B **Explosion Kills 16**

C **Hurricane Destroys Coastline!**

D **Train Crash Wrecks Station**

E **Earthquake Shakes City!**

F **10-car Pile-up Closes Motorway**

8 **a)** Fill in the correct word, then match the sentences to the headlines in Ex. 7.

• crashed • derailed • drowned • blew
• shook • flames • burst • destroyed
• collapsed • tracks

1 Debris from the train crash was all over the ....
2 A woman .... when the River Avon burst its banks yesterday and flooded the village of Hampton-on-Avon.
3 Several buildings .... when an earthquake struck the town yesterday afternoon.
4 The coastline of Puerto Rico was .... last night when a hurricane swept through the area.
5 Several people were injured when the train .... and crashed into the station.
6 Ten vehicles .... into each other last night on the M25.
7 There was a sudden explosion and the entire building burst into ....
8 The winds were so strong that they .... away many rooftops.
9 The ground .... harder and harder during the earthquake.
10 Heavy rains caused the River Avon to .... its banks.

b) Close your books and say as many words as possible related to accidents or disasters.

Speaking

c) Imagine you have experienced/witnessed the disasters/accidents mentioned in Ex. 7? Talk about:
• what happened
• when/where it happened
• how you felt

9 Look at the pictures. Which of these do you need in case of an earthquake? a shipwreck? a fire? Ask and answer, as in the example.

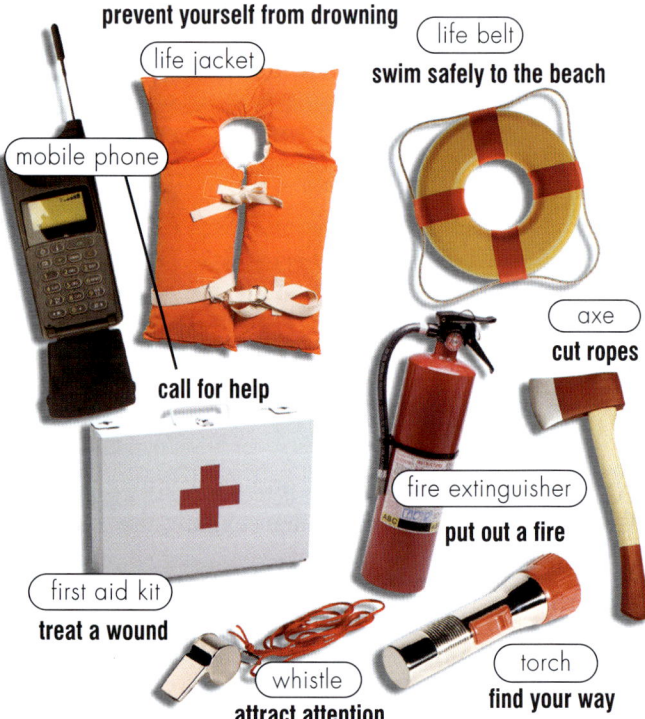

prevent yourself from drowning
life jacket
life belt
swim safely to the beach
mobile phone
axe
cut ropes
call for help
fire extinguisher
put out a fire
first aid kit
treat a wound
whistle
attract attention
torch
find your way

A: *What do you need in case of an earthquake?*
B: *You need a whistle.*
A: *Why?*
B: *To attract attention.*

• Feelings

Listening

10 Listen and match. What expressions do you use in your mother tongue to express the same feelings?

When I am surprised I say ...

1	G	Phew!	A	confused
2		Yuk!	B	amazed
3		Oh!	C	surprised
4		Wow!	D	disgusted
5		Huh?	E	uninterested
6		Mm...	F	interested
7		Really?	G	relieved

Lesson 2 (pp. 20 - 21)

* Check Ss' HW (10').

7   Present natural/manmade (caused by man). Read out the headlines one at a time. Elicit/Explain the meaning of any unknown words, then ask Ss to underline the correct words. Check Ss' answers, then ask individual Ss to identify which disasters are natural and which are man-made. Ss can add to the lists.

> **ANSWER KEY**
>
> A   Flood – natural
> B   Explosion – man-made
> C   Hurricane – natural
> D   Train crash – man-made
> E   Earthquake – natural
> F   Pile-up – man-made

8   a)   Explain the task. Ss do the exercise in closed pairs. Ss can look up any unknown words in their dictionaries. Check Ss' answers while Ss read out their completed sentences.

> **ANSWER KEY**
>
> 1   tracks (D)   6   crashed (F)
> 2   drowned (A)   7   flames (B)
> 3   collapsed (E)   8   blew (C)
> 4   destroyed (C)   9   shook (E)
> 5   derailed (D)   10 burst (A)

   b)   • Ss look at the sentences in Ex. 8a, then close their books and try to remember as many words as possible.

> **ANSWER KEY**
>
> **earthquake:** shook, debris, collapsed, struck, destroyed etc
> **flood:** river burst its banks, flooded, etc
> **hurricane:** swept the area, strong winds, blew away, roofs, etc

      • As an extension, Ss can write some more newspaper headlines related to disasters/accidents.

> **SUGGESTED ANSWER KEY**
>
> Earthquake kills 10
> Plane crashes
> Factory explosion damages village
> Volcano causes waves

   c)   Ss decide on a disaster/accident. Allow Ss two minutes to think of their answers. Individual Ss talk about the disaster/accident they chose.

> **SUGGESTED ANSWER KEY**
>
> Last summer I experienced an earthquake. I was in a small fishing village in Turkey on holiday. One afternoon, as I was swimming, the earth started shaking. A lot of houses collapsed. Some people were taken to hospital. I felt very scared.

9   Explain the task and read out the example. Then ask Ss to look at the pictures and do the exercise in closed pairs. Walk around the class and check Ss' answers, then ask individual pairs to report back to the class.

> **SUGGESTED ANSWER KEY**
>
> A: What do you need in case of fire?
> B: You need a fire extinguisher.
> A: Why?
> B: To put the fire out.
> A: What do you need in case of shipwreck?
> B: You need a life belt.
> A: Why?
> B: To swim safely to the beach.
> A: What do you need in case of fire?
> B: You need a mobile phone.
> A: Why?
> B: To call for help.
> A: What do you need in case of an earthquake?
> B: You need a torch.
> A: Why?
> B: To find your way.
> A: What do you need in case of shipwreck?
> B: You need a life jacket.
> A: Why?
> B: To prevent yourself from drowning.   etc

10   Explain the task. Play the recording twice. Ss listen and match. Check Ss' answers, then ask Ss around the class to give similar expressions in their L1.

> **ANSWER KEY**
>
> 2 D   3 C   4 B   5 A   6 E   7 F

TAPESCRIPT

1   A: I found your handbag in my car.
    B: **Phew**! I thought I'd lost it. (relieved)

2   A: Let's have some orange juice.
    B: **Yuk**! This is off! (disgusted)

3   A: Hi, Mom!
    B: **Oh**, I didn't expect to find you at home! (surprised)

4   A: This is a picture of a beach in Thailand.
    B: **Wow**! It's the most beautiful beach I've ever seen. (amazed)

5   A: This key should open the door.
    B: **Huh**? Which key? (confused)

6   A: ... and I tried another pair of shoes but they didn't fit me.
    B: **Mm**... did you? (uninterested)

7   A: There was a terrible plane crash near the north coast last night.
    B: **Really**? (interested)

11 a) Explain the task and elicit/explain the meaning of any unknown words. Play the recording twice. Ss listen and match. Check Ss' answers.

ANSWER KEY

1 F   2 D   3 B   4 C

TAPESCRIPT

1 **Jamie:** All I can remember is that we were walking along the top of this cliff when suddenly I slipped on the wet grass and fell over the edge. I don't know how I did it, but as I was falling I managed to grab onto this rock that was sticking out and stop myself. I was so afraid! I thought I was going to fall!

2 **Danny:** I didn't know what was happening at first. I didn't see him go over, I just heard him shouting for help. When I looked over the edge and saw him hanging there I froze! At first I didn't know what to do. Then, I shouted for Miss Bell and I climbed down the cliff and helped Jamie climb back up.

3 **Miss Bell:** To be honest, I thought the boys were playing a joke on me at first, but then I looked over the cliff and saw them both down there! I was really thankful to see them both still alive. I phoned for help on my mobile, but by that time Danny was on his way back up the cliff with Jamie. I didn't know whether to scold them or kiss them when they got back to the top!

4 **Ted Holmes:** Well, there wasn't really much for me to do when I arrived. Both Danny and Jamie were safe. They had a few cuts and bruises and so on, so I radioed for a helicopter to take them to hospital. I have to say, though, Danny is a very brave young man. We're all more than pleased with him — with both of them, in fact. By staying calm, they managed to get themselves out of a very sticky situation.

b) Explain the task, then read out the prompts and explain any unknown words. Ask Ss to match the adjectives to the situations. Read out the example, then Ss ask and answer in closed pairs. Walk around the class giving any necessary help. Then ask individual pairs to report back to the class.

SUGGESTED ANSWER KEY

A: Have you ever felt scared?
B: Yes, I have.
A: When was it?
B: When I heard a strange sound late at night.

A: Have you ever felt relieved?
B: Yes, I have.
A: When was it?
B: When my lost cat came home.

A: Have you ever felt shocked?
B: Yes, I have.
A: When was it?
B: When I had a car crash.

A: Have you ever felt proud?
B: Yes, I have.
A: When was it?
B: When I got a promotion.

A: Have you ever felt embarrassed?
B: Yes, I have.
A: When was it?
B: When I slipped on a banana skin.

---

12 Read out the example. Ask Ss to identify the tense forms. *(Each verb is in the past simple.)* Ask: *When did these actions take place? (They started and ended in the past.)* Ask: *Did these actions happen in order? (Yes, they happened one after the other.)* Read out the rest of the sentences (2-5) and the uses (a-e). Ss do the exercise. Check Ss' answers. Refer Ss to the Grammar Reference section for more details on the different uses of the past simple and past continuous.

ANSWER KEY

1 crashed (past simple) – overturned (past simple) – burst (past simple)
2 was washing (past continuous) – b
3 was working (past continuous) – called (past simple) – c
4 was laying (past continuous) – was polishing (past continuous) – a
5 was raining (past continuous) – was walking (past continuous) – e

---

13 Do item 1 with Ss. Allow Ss three minutes to do the exercise. Check Ss' answers by writing them on the board while Ss read the completed sentences aloud. Ask Ss to justify their answers.

ANSWER KEY

1 were driving	6 was cleaning, fell
2 left	7 was making, was reading
3 arrested	8 broke, was dusting
4 was walking, blew	9 took, got, turned off
5 didn't understand, said	10 did Mr Foster die

---

14 Explain the task, then Ss do the exercise. Check the order of the time adverbs, then individual Ss make sentences.

ANSWER KEY

1 yesterday morning	4 two days ago
2 yesterday afternoon	5 last week
3 last night	6 last summer

SUGGESTED ANSWER KEY

I didn't go to work yesterday morning.
I went to the park yesterday afternoon.
I slept late last night.
I ate snails two days ago.
I visited my grandparents last week.
I stayed on a farm last summer.

Suggested Homework

1 **Vocabulary:** Exs 8a & 10 (p. 20), Ex. 11 (p. 21)
2 **Dictation:** any ten words from Vocabulary
3 **Speaking:** Ex. 8b (p. 20)
4 **Writing:** Ex. 14 (p. 21)

---

11 a) Listen and match the people to the feelings.

1 ☐ Jamie	A	exhausted
2 ☐ Danny	B	relieved
3 ☐ Miss Bell	C	proud
4 ☐ Ted Holmes	D	shocked
	E	embarrassed
	F	scared

Speaking

b) Use the the adjectives in Exs. 10, 11 and the prompts below, as well as any ideas of your own, to ask and answer questions, as in the example.

• study all night • hear a strange sound late at night • my lost cat comes home • have car crash • travel all night • have very bad news • fall off a ladder • see earthquake on the news • pass exams • finish all my homework • get a promotion • slip on a banana skin • walk down a dark street • witness a train crash • spill coffee on my clothes at a party • win 1st prize in a contest • run in a marathon

A: *Have you ever felt exhausted?*
B: *Yes, I have.*
A: *When was it?*
B: *When I studied all night.*

Grammar

• Past Simple - Past Continuous

12 Study the sentences and identify the tense of the verbs in bold. Then match them to their use.

1 The lorry **crashed** into the tree, **overturned** and **burst** into flames. d
2 Eva **was** still **washing** her hair at 9:15 this morning.
3 Frank **was working** on a report when his boss **called** him into his office.

4 At 7 o'clock yesterday evening Mum **was laying** the table while Jane **was polishing** the silver.
5 It **was raining** heavily that September morning. Jim **was walking** quickly towards the bus-stop.

a actions happening at the same time in the past
b action happening at a certain time in the past
c action happening in the past when another action interrupted it
d actions which happened immediately one after the other in the past
e background information to a story

13 Put the verbs in brackets into the correct tense, *past simple* or *past continuous*.

1 They .... (drive) to the airport when the car broke down.
2 Can you give this to Sheila? She .... (leave) it in my office earlier.
3 The police .... (arrest) the thieves last night.
4 Bobby .... (walk) along the beach when a gust of wind .... (blow) his hat off.
5 "I .... (not/understand) a single word he .... (say). Did you?
6 Les .... (clean) the windows when he .... (fall) off the ladder.
7 Margaret .... (make) toast while Bob .... (read) the morning paper.
8 The maid .... (break) a valuable vase while she .... (dust).
9 He .... (take) his medicine, ... (get) into bed and .... (turn off) the light.
10 "When .... (Mr Foster/die)?" "Three years ago in a boating accident."

14 Put the time adverbs in the correct chronological order, then make true sentences about yourself using them.

• yesterday morning • two days ago
• yesterday afternoon • last week
• last summer • last night

I had dinner last night after the 9 o'clock news.

15 What were the people doing/wearing when the photograph was taken? Use the key words:

• drink • play • rollerblade • sit • walk • cross • cycle • talk • turn • read

A woman was walking her dog.

16 Make as many sentences as possible.

I was waiting for the bus	when my mobile rang.
	when I lost my keys.
	when I met a friend of mine.

1 wait for / bus   mobile / ring
2 cook lunch   lights / go out
3 do / shopping   someone steal / passport
4 watch / TV   slip on / banana skin
5 walk / park   meet / friend of mine
6 play / football   lose / keys

17 Ask and answer questions, as in the example.

1 What/happen/yesterday? There be/fire
2 Where/be/you? I/be/the living room
3 What/you do? I/read/a newspaper
4 How/you get out? Some firefighters/help me out
5 You know/how/fire start? My next door neighbour/fry fish/when oil/catch fire
6 How/you feel? I/feel scared but relieved

A: *What happened yesterday?*
B: *There was a fire.*

• Project

Use the notes in Ex. 17 to write a letter to a friend of yours describing your experience.

Speaking

18 Use the prompts to make true sentences about yourself in the present perfect or the past simple.

• go to the hairdresser • study hard
• go to the dentist • argue with my friend
• travel abroad • buy new clothes

• this month • yesterday • last week
• this week • last year • this year
• today • last month

I didn't go to the hairdresser last week.
I have been to the hairdresser this week.

19 Join the sentences using *when, while, and, so,* or *as/because.*

1	C	She was about to leave the office.
2		Jeff was watering the plants.
3		He had to go to work by taxi.
4		She looked upset.
5		They were about to light the barbecue.
6		Ali didn't have enough money.
7		The moon was shining.
8		The little boy was singing.
9		Rena can't babysit tonight.

A I lent him some.
B He missed the train.
C Her boss gave her a letter to type.
D Anne was mowing the lawn.
E She's got the flu.
F I asked her what was wrong.
G His father was playing the guitar.
H It began to rain.
I The stars were bright.

She was about to leave the office when her boss gave her a letter to type.

Lesson 3 (pp. 22 - 23)

* Check Ss' HW (10').

15 Ss look at the picture. Read out the example. Ss make sentences. Check Ss' answers.

ANSWER KEY

Two children **were rollerblading** on the pavement.
A man **was cycling** along the street.
Two women **were sitting** at a café. They **were drinking** coffee.
Children **were playing** football in the street.
A man **was reading** a newspaper at the café.
A man **was crossing** the street at the zebra crossing.
A car **was turning** the corner.
The women **were wearing** T-shirts, trousers and flat shoes.
The man on the bike **was wearing** a white T-shirt, brown shorts, socks and trainers.
The man who **was crossing** the road **was wearing** a brown and white T-shirt, brown trousers, a black belt and flat black shoes.
The children **were wearing** T-shirts, shorts and trainers.
One child **was wearing** an orange cap.

16 Explain the task. Ss in closed pairs do the exercise. Check Ss' answers orally in class.

ANSWER KEY

2 I was cooking lunch when **my mobile rang/the lights went out.**
3 I was doing my shopping when **my mobile rang/the lights went out/someone stole my passport/I slipped on a banana skin/I met my friend/I lost my keys.**
4 I was watching TV when **my mobile rang/the lights went out.**
5 I was walking in the park when **my mobile rang/ someone stole my passport/I slipped on a banana skin/I met my friend/I lost my keys.**
6 I was playing football when **my mobile rang/I slipped on a banana skin.**

17 Read out item 1 and explain the task. Ss, in open pairs, complete the exercise orally in class.

ANSWER KEY

2 A: Where were you?
  B: I was in the living room.
3 A: What were you doing?
  B: I was reading a newspaper.
4 A: How did you get out?
  B: Some firefighters helped me out.
5 A: Do you know how the fire started?
  B: My next door neighbour was frying fish when the oil caught fire.
6 A: How did you feel?
  B: I felt scared but relieved.

Project (p. 22)

Ss use the notes in Ex. 17 to describe what happened. Elicit how we start/end a letter to a friend (Dear + friend's first name/Yours (+ your first name), then Ss one after the other narrate the event. *(There was a fire yesterday. At the time I was in the living room. etc)* Elicit appropriate beginnings/endings to the letter, then assign the exercise as written HW. See Writing Project 2 for the Answer Key.

18 Explain the task. Point out that we can use the present perfect with this week/month etc when this period of time is not finished yet. Ss do the exercise orally in class.

SUGGESTED ANSWER KEY

I didn't study hard last year.
I have studied hard this year.
I didn't go to the dentist yesterday.
I've been to the dentist.
I didn't argue with my friend last month.
I have argued with my friend this month.
I didn't travel abroad last year.
I have travelled abroad this year.
I didn't buy new clothes last week.
I have bought new clothes this week.

19 Read out the sentences. Point out that **when, while, and, so,** and **as/because** are all conjunctions and we use them to link two clauses. Read out the example and allow Ss two minutes to complete the task. Help Ss where necessary. Check Ss' answers.

ANSWER KEY

2 D	4 F	6 A	8 G
3 B	5 H	7 I	9 E

2 Jeff was watering the plants **while** Anne was mowing the lawn.
3 He had to go to work by taxi **because** he missed the train.
4 She looked upset **so** I asked her what was wrong.
5 They were about to light the barbecue **when** it began to rain.
6 Ali didn't have enough money **so** I lent him some.
7 The moon was shining **and** the stars were bright.
8 The little boy was singing **while** his father was playing the guitar.
9 Rena can't babysit tonight **as/because** she's got the flu.

20 • Play the recording. Ss listen and say how the two people are related (e.g. two friends or relatives). Play the recording again. Ss listen and fill in the missing words. Check Ss' answers on the board, then Ss read out the dialogue.

• Ss, in open pairs, use the prompts to act out similar dialogues. Point out that Ss should replace the words in bold with the prompts.

ANSWER KEY

1 late   2 bus   3 get   4 forty   5 tea

A: Hi, **Janet**! Sorry I'm so late!
B: What happened? I was worried about you.
A: **My car broke down**.
B: Oh dear, how did you get here in the end?
A: **I had to phone for help. It took an hour to arrive!**
B: You must be tired, sit down and have a cup of tea!
A: Thanks! I'm exhausted.

A: Hi, **Mark**! Sorry I'm so late!
B: What happened? I was worried about you.
A: **The train drivers were on strike**.
B: Oh dear, how did you get here in the end?
A: **I had to catch two buses. It took me two hours longer!**
B: You must be tired, sit down and have a cup of tea!
A: Thanks! I'm exhausted.

A: Hi, **Mr Jones**! Sorry I'm so late!
B: What happened? I was worried about you.
A: **The traffic was terrible**.
B: Oh dear, how did you get here in the end?
A: **I had to park the car and walk. It took me over an hour!**
B: You must be tired, sit down and have a cup of tea!
A: Thanks! I'm exhausted.

---

21 Play the recording. Ss listen. Play the recording again with pauses. Ss repeat individually.

22 • Read out the table and explain the rules for forming opposites of adjectives when we add prefixes with a negative meaning.

• Read the sentences and elicit/explain the meaning of any unknown words. Ss complete the task. Check Ss' answers.

ANSWER KEY

1 insensitive	6 disloyal
2 irresponsible	7 displeased
3 discontented	8 impatient
4 unbelievable	9 unkind
5 immature	10 unforgettable

---

23 • Read out the table and explain the rules for the order of adjectives.

• Explain the task and read out the example. Ss do the exercise. Check Ss' answers by asking individual Ss to read out their sentences with the adjectives in the correct order.

ANSWER KEY

• beautiful, purple, straw
• small, rectangular, black, leather
• nice, multi-coloured, cotton

• As an extension, Ss describe objects in the classroom.
   e.g. It's a small green wooden desk.
      It's a big rectangular blackboard.   etc

• Ss can cut pictures from magazines, newspapers etc, stick them on to a piece of paper and write a short description of each as in Ex. 23.

(Suggested Homework)

1 **Vocabulary:** Ex. 16 (p. 22), Exs 22 & 23 (p. 23)
2 **Speaking:** Ex. 15 & 18 (p. 22), Ex. 20 (p. 23)
3 **Dictation:** any ten words from Vocabulary
4 **Writing:** project (p. 22)

Communication
(apologising)

20 🔊 Listen and say how the two people are related. Listen again and fill in the missing words. Then, in pairs, use the prompts to act out similar dialogues.

A: Hi, **Alex**! Sorry I'm so 1) ....!
B: What happened? I was worried about you.
A: I missed the 2) ....
B: Oh dear, how did you 3) .... here in the end?
A: I had to walk. It took me 4) .... minutes!
B: You must be tired, sit down and have a cup of 5) ....!
A: Thanks! I'm exhausted!

- Janet / car break down / phone for help / take an hour to arrive
- Mark / train drivers on strike / catch two buses / take two hours longer
- Mr Jones / traffic terrible / park car and walk / take over an hour

Pronunciation
(intonation of apologies)

21 🔊 Listen and repeat.

Sorry!	I'm so sorry.	I'm very sorry.
I'm sorry!	Sorry about that.	Look, I'm sorry. OK?

Word Formation

22 Read the table, then replace the words in bold with their opposites.

We can make adjectives negative by adding the prefixes **-dis**, **-in** or **-un**.
e.g.   loyal   –   **dis**loyal, active   –   **in**active, happy   –   **un**happy
Note: -in usually becomes **-il**, **-im** or **-ir** before letters -l, -m, -p and -r.
e.g.   legal – **il**legal, mature – **im**mature, patient – **im**patient, regular – **ir**regular

1 Jenny is so **sensitive**!   ....
2 Brian is a very **responsible** employee.   ....
3 Anna is very **contented** with her life.   ....

4 The girl's story was quite **believable**.   ....
5 Meg is very **mature** for her age.   ....
6 Ryan is very **loyal** to his family.   ....
7 My teacher was very **pleased** with my exam results.   ....
8 Paul is very **patient** with children.   ....
9 He is very **kind** to his colleagues.   ....
10 Our last holiday was **forgettable**.   ....

Order of adjectives

- There are two types of adjectives: **opinion adjectives** (beautiful, nice, etc) which describe what we think of someone/something, and **fact adjectives** (small, heavy, etc) which describe what someone or something really is. Opinion adjectives come before fact adjectives.
- When there are two or more fact adjectives before a noun they usually go in the order shown below.

	opinion	size	weight	shape	colour	material	
It's a	nice	small	light	round	red	plastic	ball.

---

23 Write the adjectives, as in the example.

- heavy • wooden • big • brown

It's a big, heavy, brown, wooden chest with a metal lock.

- straw • purple • beautiful

It's a .... hat with a blue ribbon.

- black • small • rectangular • leather

It's a .... handbag with a long strap.

- cotton • multi-coloured • nice

It's a pair of .... shorts.

23

Listening and Reading

24 Look at the pictures and the title. Where did the story take place? What time was it? Where did the boys go? What scared them? What was strange about the tiger? Can you guess the story?

25 Listen and put the pictures in the correct order. Listen again and circle the correct item.

1 The three friends were going to
   A India
   B a small village
2 As it got dark, the boys
   A lost their way
   B managed to get to the village
3 When they heard Abi's story the three friends felt
   A shocked
   B relieved

26 a) Read the story and fill in the sentences (A-E). There is one extra sentence that you do not need.

A We **screamed**, because we were sure it would kill us.
B The villagers were expecting us, but we were already four hours late.
C The 'tiger' stood up, and a young man took off the striped skin covering his head and shoulders.
D He ran towards us, pointing **desperately** at a large, dark shape moving through the trees.
E "Tiger!" he **whispered** urgently, pointing at a large, dark shape moving **silently** toward us through the trees.

b) Which is the climax event in the story?

A

C

D

Lost in the Jungle

The **shadows** were **growing** longer and the sky was getting dark as we walked through the **jungle.** My two friends and I felt hot and exhausted. We were heading for a small <u>village</u> in northern India. **1** B

As the last of the daylight disappeared, we began to feel very lost and afraid.

We tried to find our way to the village, but it was hard to tell which **path** we should follow in the **darkness.** All around us, strange **creatures** made terrifying noises as they woke up and began to **hunt** for food. We hoped they wouldn't want to eat us!

Then George, who was in front, stopped suddenly in his **tracks**. **2** We **froze** in horror. George was right. We could see the black stripes and shining yellow eyes of the most dangerous animal in the jungle. We **stared** at the tiger, too scared to move.

After a few seconds that felt like hours, there was the sound of branches breaking, and the tiger **leapt** at us, **roaring** loudly. **3**

Strangely, though, the tiger stopped – and then I noticed that it had six legs, two of them human!

4 "Hello!" he said, smiling **broadly**. "I'm Abi, from the village. When you didn't arrive, we were worried, so I came to look for you," he explained. "It's traditional for us to wear the tiger skin to **greet** new guests ... and I couldn't **resist** playing a trick on you! I hope you don't mind." **Recovering** from the shock, we began to laugh with **relief**.

We followed Abi to his village, where the villagers gave us a warm welcome. After a delicious meal we sat around the fire, listening to our new friend's **fascinating** stories about the *real* tigers in the jungle. It was a great end to a day full of adventure.

Lesson 4 (pp. 24 - 25)

* Check Ss' HW (10').

24 Elicit/Explain the meaning of any unknown words, then Ss
do the exercise.

SUGGESTED ANSWER KEY

*The story took place in the jungle. It was early evening.
The boys were going to a village to meet someone. A
tiger scared them. It wasn't a real tiger. It was a man
in a tiger's skin.
I think the story is about some young men's experience
in the jungle.*

25 Explain the task. Play the recording. Ss put the pictures in
the correct order. Check Ss' answers. Ss read questions 1
to 3. Play the recording again. Ss listen and do the
exercise. Check Ss' answers.

ANSWER KEY

Pictures: *A 4*   *C 1*   *E 5*
              B 6   *D 2*   *F 3*

              1 B   *2 A*   *3 B*

26 a) Explain the task. Read the tip aloud. Ss read out
sentences A to E. Do item 1 with Ss. Allow Ss five
minutes to do the exercise. Check Ss' answers.

ANSWER KEY

2 E   *3 A*   *4 C*

b) Explain that the climax event is the most dramatic event
in the story. Ss discuss to find which event this is.

ANSWER KEY

The moment the tiger leapt at them roaring loudly.

Further practice

After Ss have done Ex. 26, ask them to visit:
http://www.qtm.net/~geibdan/newse/bud.htm/   OR
http://www.parascope.com/en/bermuda1.htm
read the information, then think of a story of their own which
took place there.

c) Ss explain the words in bold by giving examples or looking the words up in their dictionaries.

d) • Allow Ss two to three minutes to read the story again and underline the adjectives. Check Ss' answers, then ask individual Ss around the class to suggest opposites. Point out that where appropriate Ss should suggest adjectives that use prefixes with a negative meaning as learnt in the word formation section.

ANSWER KEY

(growing) longer ≠ shorter • (sky) dark ≠ light • (felt) hot ≠ cold • (felt) exhausted ≠ energetic • small ≠ big • afraid ≠ brave • hard ≠ easy • strange (creatures) ≠ normal • terrifying (noises) ≠ calming/comforting • large (shape) ≠ small • dark (shape) ≠ light • right ≠ wrong • black ≠ white • shining ≠ dull • dangerous (creature) ≠ harmless • scared ≠ unafraid • (were) sure ≠ unsure • (them) human ≠ inhuman • young (man) ≠ old • (were) worried ≠ calm • (It's) traditional ≠ untraditional • new (guests) ≠ old • warm (welcome) ≠ cool • delicious (meal) ≠ awful/disgusting • fascinating (stories) ≠ boring • real (tigers) ≠ fake • great (end) ≠ awful

---

• Ss own answers. *I liked the story a lot because it had an unexpected ending.*

27 a) Explain the task. Point out that Ss must skim the text to pick out the correct adverbs. Check Ss' answers, then ask individual Ss to read out their sentences.

ANSWER KEY

1 broadly   3 urgently   5 suddenly
2 silently   4 loudly

SUGGESTED ANSWER KEY

1 She smiled broadly when she read the note.
2 The burglar moved silently around the house.
3 She cried urgently to the firefighter to save her.
4 "Please be quiet," shouted the teacher loudly.
5 A dog ran out suddenly into the path of an oncoming car.

---

b) • Elicit the correct answers from Ss.
• If necessary, drill your Ss. Give adjectives and ask Ss to say the relevant adverb. Check Ss' spelling on the board.
Suggested adjective list: fearful, fast, fortunate, sleepy, hopeless, impatient, early, etc
e.g. T: fearful
     S1: fearfully
     T: fast
     S2: fast   etc
Refer Ss to the Grammar Reference section for more details.

ANSWER KEY

We usually form adverbs by adding -ly to the adjective. Adverbs usually describe verbs.

---

28 a) Explain the task, then individual Ss use the plot outline and the pictures to retell the story. Assign the summary as written HW.

SUGGESTED ANSWER KEY

6 The tiger leapt at them, roaring loudly.
3 They began to feel very lost and afraid.

---

4 *Suddenly George stopped. "Tiger!" he whispered.*
1 *The boys were heading for a small village.*
2 *They were already four hours late.*
5 *They stared at the tiger, too scared to move.*
9 *It was a great end to a day full of adventure.*
7 *They noticed the tiger had six legs, two of them human.*
8 *Recovering from the shock, they began to laugh.*

The sky was getting darker as the boys walked through the jungle. They were heading for a small village but they were already four hours late. They began to feel lost and afraid.

Suddenly, George stopped. "Tiger!" he whispered. The boys stared at the tiger, too scared to move. Then, the tiger leapt at them, roaring loudly. The boys screamed!

When the tiger stopped, the boys noticed the tiger had six legs, two of them human. The tiger stood up and they saw it was a young man. He took off the tiger suit and said, "Hello". Recovering from the shock, they began to laugh.

That night, they ate a delicious meal and listened to stories about real tigers. It was a great end to a day full of adventure.

b) Explain the task, then Ss work in groups of four. They take the roles of the four characters in the story and act out the story.
e.g. George: It's really scary here.
     Tony: Yes. I think we've lost our way.
     Jim: What can we do now?
George: Ssh! Listen. There is something behind the bushes. etc.

29 • Read out the table. Ss do the exercise. Check Ss' answer.

ANSWER KEY

1 up   3 up   5 into
2 down   4 (a)round   6 up

• As an extension, Ss make sentences using the phrasal verbs in the table. Ss should memorise the table.

30 Allow Ss two minutes to fill in the words. Check Ss' answers, then ask Ss to make sentences using the completed phrases. Each correct sentence gets 1 point.
e.g. Team A S1: The brakes made a horrible screeching noise.
     Team B S1: Have you ever witnessed a robbery?
Ss should memorise these phrases.

ANSWER KEY

1 screeching   6 follow   11 fire
2 witness   7 side   12 shining
3 find   8 full   13 warm
4 news   9 greet   14 get
5 alarm   10 play

Suggested Homework

1 **Vocabulary:** words in bold in text Ex. 26a (p. 24), Exs 29 & 30 (p. 25)
2 **Dictation:** any ten words from Vocabulary giving example/synonym
3 **Speaking:** Ex. 28 (p. 25)
4 **Writing:** short summary of the story using prompts in Ex. 28 (p. 25)

Tip

Read the text for gist, then read the sentences quickly. Re-read the gapped text more carefully and underline in the text words such as time markers, adverbs, names etc which will help you do the task. Finally, check the completed text with sentences filled in to see if it flows and makes sense.

c) Explain the words in bold.

d) Underline the adjectives in the story. Suggest opposites. How did you like the story?

27 a) Read the story again and fill in the appropriate adverbs, then make sentences using them.

1 to smile ....   4 to roar ....
2 to move ....   5 to stop ....
3 to whisper ....

b) How do we usually form adverbs? What do they describe?

---

28 a) Put the sentences in order, then use the pictures to tell the class the story. Use *when, then, first, after that, finally.*

- [ ] The tiger leapt at them, roaring loudly.
- [ ] They began to feel very lost and afraid.
- [ ] Suddenly George stopped. "Tiger!" he whispered.
- [ ] The boys were heading for a small village.
- [ ] They stared at the tiger, too scared to move.
- [ ] They were already four hours late.
- [ ] It was a great end to a day full of adventure.
- [ ] They noticed the tiger had six legs, two of them human.
- [ ] Recovering from the shock, they began to laugh.

b) Read the story again, then take roles and act it out.

Phrasal Verbs

29 Study the table, then fill in the correct particle.

> **break down** - 1) to stop working (train, car etc), 2) to lose control of feelings (in tears etc)
> **break into sth/break in** - to enter by force
> **break up** - 1) to finish school at the end of term, 2) to end a relationship
> **bring about** - to make sth happen
> **bring (a)round** - 1) to help sb regain consciousness, 2) to persuade sb to change their ideas or do sth
> **bring up** - 1) to raise a child (usu.), 2) to mention a subject

1 James Parker was brought .... by his grandparents.
2 My car broke .... in the middle of the road.
3 The Beatles broke .... in 1970.
4 I'm trying to bring her ....to my point of view.
5 Thieves broke .... Natlay's Bank yesterday.
6 Schools break ....in June for the summer.

Vocabulary Practice

30 Fill in the correct words, then make sentences.

- get • news • side • screeching • find
- full • witness • alarm • shining • warm
- follow • greet • fire • play

1 .... noise   8 .... name
2 to .... a robbery   9 to .... a guest
3 to .... our way   10 to .... a trick
4 .... report   11 to .... a gun
5 .... button   12 .... eyes
6 to .... a path   13 .... welcome
7 .... road   14 to .... dark

25

31 Fill in: *from, over, for, about, in, at, of, on, into*, **then make sentences using the phrases.**

1 .... board; 2 to swerve .... to the other side .... the road; 3 to lose control .... sth; 4 to slam .... his brakes; 5 to crash .... a tree; 6 to wait .... the queue; 7 to pay .... sth; 8 to shout .... sb; 9 .... the darkness; 10 to freeze .... horror; 11 to stare .... sth; 12 to head .... somewhere; 13 to recover .... the shock; 14 fascinating stories .... tigers

32 **While you were abroad on holiday, you witnessed a car accident. Tell your friend:**

- where and when the accident took place
- who was involved
- how it happened
- what the consequences were

33 **Underline the correct word.**

1 Several passengers **died/killed** in the plane crash.
2 Can I **borrow/lend** some money from you?
3 Laura **missed/lost** the last bus so she took a taxi.
4 Jimmy was really **ashamed/embarrassed** about cheating on his test.
5 He is **nervous/angry** about flying, so he takes the train.

Writing (a story)

To write a story we first decide on the type of story, the plot and the main characters. Our story can be a comedy, a spy story, a thriller, an adventure story, a detective story, a fairy tale, etc.

In the **first paragraph,** we write when and where the event happened, who the people in the story were, what the weather was like and what happened first.

In the **main body,** we describe the events in the order they happened. One of the events should be the climax event. We can use *so, because, and, also* etc to join our sentences or ideas.

In the **last paragraph,** we write what happened in the end and how the people in the story felt.

We can use a variety of adjectives or adverbs to make our story more interesting. We normally use past tenses in stories.

34 **Replace the words in bold with words in the list, then suggest other synonyms.**

- terrible • tiny • lovely • extremely • well-behaved

1 It was a **nice** May afternoon.
2 The room was **small** but clean.
3 The weather was **bad**.
4 Emma grew into a **good** but lively child.
5 They were all **very** happy.

We can start or end a story by:
- asking a rhetorical question (i.e. a question which requires no answer) e.g. *Why did we have to go through so much suffering?*
- addressing the reader directly e.g. *Are you afraid of spiders?*
- referring to moods/feelings e.g. *Ivan was cold, wet and miserable by the time he reached the finishing line.*
- using direct speech e.g. *"I can't wait to go," said Anne.*

NOTE: We can also start a story by describing a person or a place.
e.g. *"I looked at the sweet elderly lady trying to remember who she was. Her round face, white curly hair and friendly blue eyes were familiar to me."* (person)
"I parked the car, got out and locked the door. I looked at Mrs Aston's house. It was a small stone cottage with a colourful garden. I felt relaxed as I walked along the path toward the wooden front door." (place)

35 **Match the beginnings and endings. Which techniques did the writer use in each extract?**

A The hot Peruvian sun was burning Professor Bingham's bare head as he studied the map of the Andes. He was hot and tired but excited. He knew he was close to finding the hidden city in the mountains of Peru.

B What would you do if a tigress looked at you sadly through the bars of a cage? I couldn't forget that question as Ran, my guide, and I set off to release Tara back into the wild.

1 Breathless but excited, the Professor stood among the ruins of the ancient city. "This is it!" he said. "It wasn't just a legend after all!"

2 As Tara disappeared into the jungle, Ran and I felt relieved. Tara was going to be safe in her new home. She was back where she truly belonged at last.

26

Lesson 5 (pp. 26 - 27)

* Check Ss' HW (10').

31 Allow Ss two minutes to fill in the prepositions. Check Ss' answers, then ask Ss to make sentences using the completed phrases.

   e.g. S1: I **waited in a queue** for an hour at the bank today.

   S2: Stop **shouting at me**. It's not my fault.   etc

   Ss should memorise these phrases.

   ANSWER KEY

1	on	6	in	11	at
2	over, off	7	for	12	for
3	of	8	at	13	from
4	on	9	in	14	about
5	into	10	in		

32 Explain the task, then allow Ss three minutes to do the exercise. Ask individual Ss to describe the accident in class, then assign it as written HW.

   SUGGESTED ANSWER KEY

   The accident happened on a country lane, near York.
   The car was speeding round the bend.
   The driver was tired from the long drive.
   I saw it heading towards me.
   The road was slippery.
   I started to panic.
   The driver saw me at the last minute.
   He had to act quickly to avoid hitting me.
   He swerved over to the other side of the road.
   He almost hit an oncoming vehicle.
   He lost control of the car.
   I cried out in fright.
   There was a loud screeching noise.
   The car crashed into a tree.
   I was amazed that no one was hurt.
   The driver was very lucky.
   He had slammed on the brakes just in time.
   He was relieved that only his car was damaged.

33 • Explain the task, then allow Ss two minutes to do the exercise. Check Ss' answers while Ss read out their sentences.

   • As an extension, ask Ss to make sentences using the words which were not underlined. Help Ss where necessary.

   e.g. S1: Three people were **killed** in the accident.

   S2: I can **lend** you this book when I've finished reading it. It's really good.

   ANSWER KEY

1	died	3	missed	5	nervous
2	borrow	4	ashamed		

Writing (a story) (p. 26)

Read out the theory box. Refer Ss to the story on p. 24 and ask questions to check that Ss understand the theory.

   e.g. T: What type of story is it?
   S1: An adventure story.
   T: Who is/are the main character(s)?
   S2: Three friends.
   T: Where did it happen?
   S3: In the jungle in India.   etc

34 Read the sentences aloud and elicit/explain the meaning of any unknown words. Allow Ss two minutes to do the exercise, then check Ss' answers around the class. Then, read out words from the list and ask individual Ss to give a synonym.

   e.g. T: terrible
   S1: awful   etc

   ANSWER KEY

1	lovely	3	terrible	5	extremely
2	tiny	4	well-behaved		

35 Present the writing tip. Explain the task, then Ss do the exercise. Help Ss if necessary.

   ANSWER KEY

   A – 1 → referring to moods/feelings
   B – 2 → addressing the reader directly

36 Ask Ss to read out the extracts. Ss then do the exercise. Help Ss if necessary. Check Ss' answers by asking individual Ss to read their rewritten paragraphs aloud.

> **SUGGESTED ANSWER KEY**
>
> Who would expect a holiday to end in disaster? Ben was so excited that he couldn't sleep, so he got up early. He couldn't stop thinking about the long journey ahead of him. He was really looking forward to driving across the country to spend the holidays with his parents. He was so eager to leave that he didn't notice that the weather forecast said it was going to snow.
>
> Exhausted but happy, Ben arrived at his parents' house two days later. He had lost everything, even his car and his suitcase, but he didn't care. He was exhausted but happy to be alive and with his parents at last.

37 Explain the task. Ss look at the pictures and the title. Explain any unknown words in the list, then Ss make sentences for the pictures.

> **SUGGESTED ANSWER KEY**
>
> S1: Jason was standing on the deck. (pict. 1)
> S2: Black clouds were gathering in the sky. (pict. 1)
> S3: Tony radioed for help. (pict. 4) etc

38 Elicit possible endings from Ss around the class. Play the recording. Ss listen and check.

> **ANSWER KEY**
>
> They are rescued by the coastguard.

TAPESCRIPT

It was a warm afternoon last summer and Jason and his friends were on a sailing holiday in the Mediterranean.

Jason was standing on the deck of his boat and looking anxiously up at the sky. The weather was usually nice at this time of the year, but now black clouds were gathering. Although it was early afternoon, it was already very dark. "It looks like we're in for a storm," he said to his friends, Paul and Tony. "We'd better get ready."

Before they knew it, they were in the middle of the storm. Lightning flashed and thunder rolled across the sky. Soon the boat was rocking from side to side and huge waves were crashing around it. They were all very scared. Tony realised that they were in danger and quickly radioed for help. Just then a bolt of lightning struck the boat and the mast burst into flames. They all began to panic. "We're going to sink!" they cried.

Paul told the boys to get into the life raft. "We can't save the boat," he said, "but we can save ourselves." They threw the life raft into the water and jumped in after it. As they climbed aboard, they wondered what would happen now. They watched as their burning boat sank slowly into the sea.

Suddenly they heard the sound of a boat over the roar of the storm. They shouted and waved and the boat drew closer to them. It was the coastguard. They were relieved that their adventure was over at last. They all agreed to plan a safer holiday next time.

39 Allow Ss two minutes to do the exercise. Check Ss' answers. Ask individual Ss to retell the story. The climax event – the most dramatic event – is the moment they have to leave their boat because of the fire.

> **ANSWER KEY**
>
> A 4   D 6   G 3
> B 1   E 2   H 5
> C 9   F 7   I 8

40 Explain the task and the plan, then ask questions to make sure Ss can do the exercise.

e.g.   T: Where did the story take place?
       S1: In the Mediterranean Sea.
       T: When did it happen?
       S2: Last summer.
       T: Who were the main characters in the story?
       S3: Jason and his two friends, Paul and Tony.
       T: What happened in the beginning?
       S4: Jason and his friends were on a sailing holiday when they found themselves in the middle of a storm.   etc

> **SUGGESTED ANSWER KEY**
>
> It was a warm afternoon last summer and Jason and his friends, Paul and Tony, were on a sailing holiday in the Mediterranean. Jason was standing on the deck looking anxiously up at the sky. Black clouds were gathering in the sky and a storm was coming.
>
> Before they knew it, they were in the middle of the storm. Soon the boat was rocking from side to side and huge waves were crashing around it. Tony realised they were in danger and quickly radioed for help.
>
> Just then, a bolt of lightning struck the boat and the mast burst into flames. Paul told the boys to get into the life raft. They threw it into the sea and jumped in after it. As they climbed aboard, they wondered what would happen next. The boat was on fire and they watched it sinking.
>
> Suddenly, they heard the sound of a boat. They shouted and waved and the boat came closer. It was the coastguard. They were relieved that their adventure was over at last.

41 Read the sentences aloud. Elicit answers around the class.

> **SUGGESTED ANSWER KEY**
>
> - Everything ends sometime, even nice things.
> - A picture can give a lot of information, often much more than can be given in words.
> - It doesn't matter if we experience difficulties or danger, as long as everything turns out all right in the end.

> **Suggested Homework**
>
> 1 Vocabulary: Ex. 31 (p. 26) and Ex. 37 (p. 27)
> 2 Speaking: Ex. 32 (p. 26)
> 3 Writing: Ex. 40 (p. 27)

> **Lesson 6**

Workbook Unit 2
   Click on Grammar 2

36 Read the following beginning and ending, then rewrite them applying one or more of the techniques mentioned above.

> Ben got up early because he had a long journey ahead of him. He was driving across the country to spend the holidays with his parents. The weather forecast said it was going to snow.

> Two days later Ben arrived at his parents' house without his car or his suitcase. He was very tired. His parents were pleased to see him. Ben was happy, too.

37 A popular magazine is holding a short story competition entitled *"A Storm at Sea"* and you have decided to enter. Use the words in the list to make sentences which match the pictures.

- huge waves were crashing • in danger
- bolt of lightning struck the boat • sailing holiday
- black clouds were gathering • lightning flashed • sink slowly
- stand on the deck • storm • thunder rolled across the sky
- life raft • boat was rocking from side to side • were scared
- radioed for help • mast • burst into flames

Tony   Paul   Jason

A Storm at Sea

38 The last picture of the story is missing. What do you think happened in the end? Listen and check if your guesses were correct. Now draw the last picture of the story.

39 Put the sentences in order, then retell the story. Which is the climax event in the story?

A [ ] The boat was rocking from side to side.
B [1] Jason was standing on the deck of the boat.
C [ ] They heard the sound of a boat.
D [ ] A bolt of lightning struck the boat.
E [ ] Black clouds were gathering.
F [ ] The mast burst into flames.
G [ ] Lightning flashed.
H [ ] Tony radioed for help.
I [ ] They jumped into the life raft.

40 Now write your story. Write 120-150 words. Use your answers from Exs. 37-39 as well as the plan below. You can use the story in Ex. 26 as a model.

Plan

Introduction
(Para 1)   *who, when, where, what happened*

Main Body
(Paras 2-3)   *events in the order they happened*

Conclusion
(Para 4)   *end the story, people's feelings/ comments*

41 Read the sentences. What do they mean?

What's in a word?

- All good things must come to an end.
- Every picture tells a story.
- All's well that ends well.

THE ADVENTURES OF
HUCKLEBERRY FINN

How Huck Was Murdered

Huck is living with Widow Douglas — but now his father (Pap) has come back.

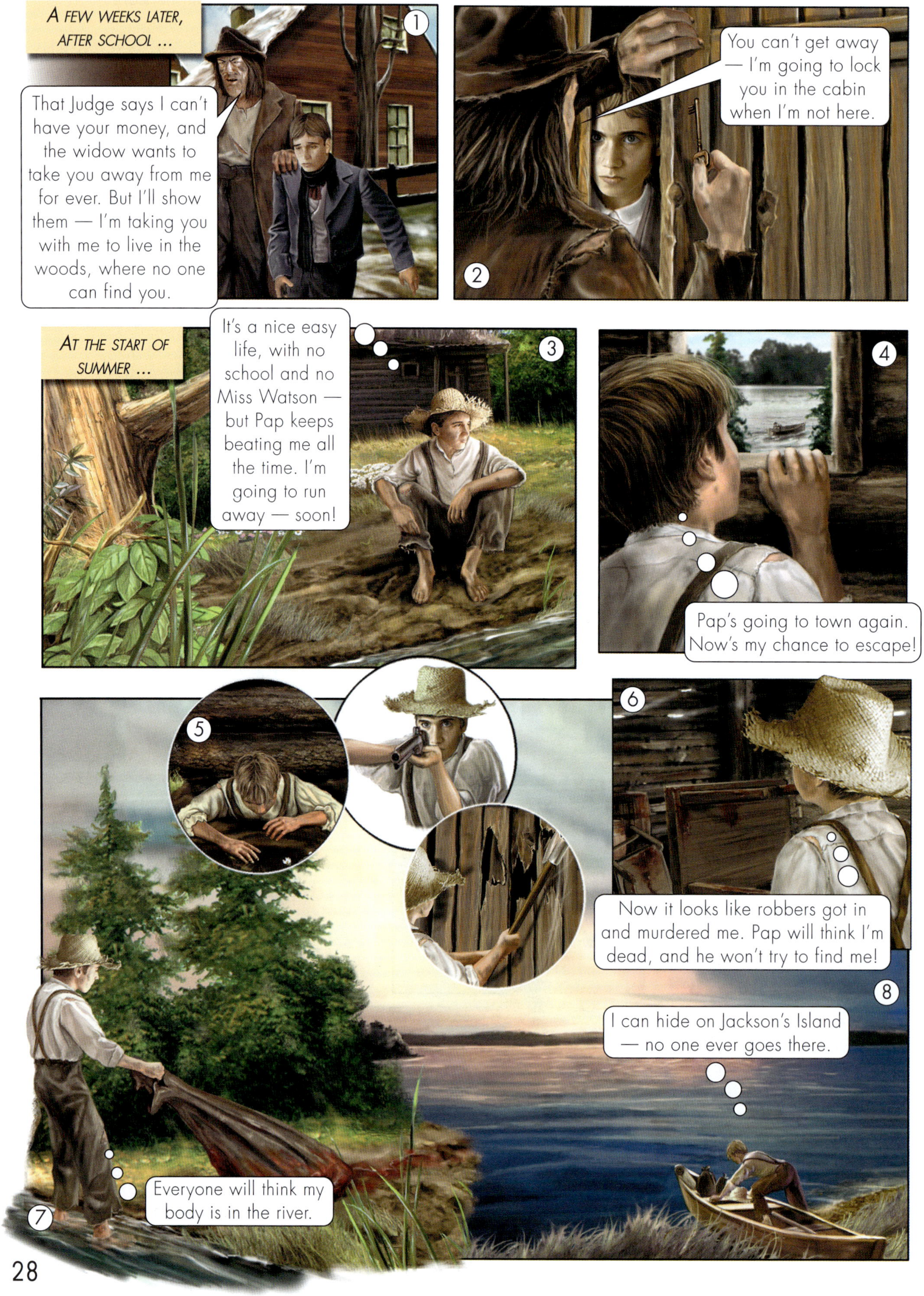

Pre-Reading Activities

1 Look at the pictures on p. 28 and circle the correct answer.

1 Where does Pap take Huck?
  (a) to the woods   b to an island
2 Where does Pap lock Huck?
  a on a boat   **(b)** in a cabin
3 What does Huck use to break the door?
  a an oar   **(b)** an axe

Listening & Reading Activities

2 Listen and mark the sentences T (true) or F (false).

1 Huck lives with Judge Thatcher. F
2 Pap keeps beating Huck. T
3 Robbers murder Pap. F
4 Huck hides on Jackson's Island. T

3 Read the episode on p. 28 and replace the words in bold with the correct name from the list.

  • Huck • Judge Thatcher • Pap • Miss Watson

1 **He** doesn't give Pap Huck's money. Judge Thatcher
2 Huck's life is nice and easy without **her**. Miss Watson
3 **He** keeps beating Huck. Pap
4 **He** wants to escape. Huck
5 **He** will hide on an island. Huck

Grammar

  • Time words

4 a) Read the examples. Which one is wrong?

a I'll do it when I come back.
(b) I'll do it when I will come back.
c Can you tell me when you will come back?

b) Look at sentences a and c. Why do we use the future after *when* in c? When is a question word.

5 Fill in the correct tense.

1 I'm not sure when the guests will arrive (arrive).
2 He'll join us when he is (be) ready.
3 Do you know when they will come back (come back)?
4 His father will be angry when he finds (find) him missing.
5 She will call us when she gets (get) to the airport.
6 Can you tell me when John will finish (finish) work?

  • Possessive Adjectives/Possessive Pronouns

6 Underline the correct word.

1 I can't tell <u>him</u>/his the truth.
2 This is Jennifer/<u>Jennifer's</u> boat.
3 We don't know where **their**/<u>they</u> are.
4 Do you like <u>our</u>/us new house?
5 Is this <u>her</u>/hers latest novel?
6 I don't know **their**/them names.
7 How is you/<u>your</u> family these days?
8 That car is **my**/<u>mine</u>. It's very old.
9 This house isn't **our**/<u>ours</u>. We live in a flat.
10 "Is that bag **yours**/your?" "No, it's him/<u>his</u>."

  • Where (question word/relative pronoun)

7 a) Study the examples. In which sentence do we use *where* as a relative pronoun?

a Where is Jenny?
(b) That's the cabin where Huck is.

b) Join the sentences using *where*.

1 That's the island. Huck will hide there.
  That's the island where Huck will hide.
2 That's the office. She works there.
  That's the office where she works.
3 Here's the house. We live here.
  Here's the house where we live.
4 This is the hotel. He is staying here.
  This is the hotel where he is staying.
5 That's the place. I'll go to college there.
  That's the place where I'll go to college.

8 Listen to the episode again, then take roles and read it aloud.

9 a) Join the sentences using *who, which, where.*

• The Judge is the man. He has got Huck's money.
  The Judge is the man who has got Huck's money.
• Pap is the man. He wants Huck's money.
  Pap is the man who wants Huck's money.
• Pap is the man. He takes Huck away.
  Pap is the man who takes Huck away.
• The cabin is the place. Pap keeps Huck there.
  The cabin is the place where Pap keeps Huck.
• Pap is the man. He beats Huck.
  Pap is the man who beats Huck.
• An axe is the thing. Huck uses it to escape.
  An axe is the thing which Huck uses to escape.
• Jackson's Island is the place. Huck can hide there.
  Jackson's Island is the place where Huck can hide.

b) Use the sentences to re-tell the story. (As an extension Ss can write the summary of the episode.)

Vocabulary & Grammar

1 Fill in the correct word.

1 Do you think I should apply for this job?
2 Being a lawyer requires a university degree.
3 "What are you looking for?" "My watch."
4 Policemen can work night shifts.
5 The river burst its banks and flooded the area.
6 Are you interested in a part-time or full-time job?
7 Joan broke down when she heard about the terrible accident.
8 The doorbell is ringing. Can you please answer the door?
9 The driver lost control of the vehicle and crashed into a tree.
10 Mr Perkins works as a teacher in our school.
11 John takes/catches the 7:45 train to work.
12 The policemen interviewed everyone who witnessed the accident.
13 Where were you when the earthquake started?
14 A porter is a person who carries luggage.
15 She was walking when it started raining.
16 Have you got experience at all levels?
17 John is always late for work.
18 Does Ben start work at 9:00 every day?
19 That's the man whose son lives in Brazil.
20 The police were on patrol all night.
21 A lot of jobs, such as teaching, require extensive training.
22 Where did they go on holiday last year?
23 The police use dogs to track down criminals.
24 Jane was sleeping while Tony was reading.
25 John is working in the garden at the moment.
26 It was a frightening experience. I'm still shaking.
27 The car burst into flames.
28 The train drivers are on strike.
29 They both gave us a warm welcome.
30 Mary couldn't find her way in the dark room.

(30 marks)

2 Circle the correct item.

1 The train .... soon after it left the station.
   A tracked   B slammed   C swerved **D** derailed
2 Steve works with .... beginners.
   A fully-trained   C experienced
   B absolute   D good
3 She left the building an hour ....
   A last   B then   C before   **D** ago
4 Fifty people were on .... when the plane crashed.
   A track   B air   C deck   **D** board
5 The boat was .... from side to side.
   A rocking   B waving   C sinking   D crashing
6 Paul never .... to work.
   A walking   B walk   C is walking   **D** walks
7 John froze in .... when he saw the tiger.
   A fright   B shock   **C** horror   D panic
8 Is Ann .... living in Manchester?
   A then   **B** still   C yet   D already
9 They were .... to see their son was OK.
   A relieved   B interested   C exhausted   D proud
10 She passed out but we .... her round.
   A brought   B took   C looked   D came

(20 marks)

Communication

3 In pairs use the prompts to act out the dialogue.

A	B
Hello! / I speak / Bob?	Who / call?
It / be / Steve	hang on / second?
OK	Sorry / Bob / go out
I / call back?	Sure / you want / leave / message?
No / that / be OK / call later	
Bye	Bye

(See Suggested Answers section)   *(20 marks)*

Reading

4 Read the story and fill in the missing sentences from the list. There is one sentence which you do not need to use.

Air Adventure

Kate felt very excited as she climbed the steps and boarded the plane. It was the first time she had ever travelled alone and she was looking forward to the adventure. **1** | **B** |

She found her seat and made herself comfortable. She felt a little nervous when the air hostesses told the passengers what to do in an emergency, but once the plane had taken off, she soon forgot her worries. She gazed out of the window in amazement as the English countryside grew smaller and smaller beneath her. **2** | **E** | She closed her eyes and, before long, she was fast asleep.

Suddenly, a loud roaring noise woke her. She opened her eyes and looked around in panic. **3** | **F** | They looked scared, but they spoke calmly to the passengers and told everyone not to be afraid. "What's happening?" Kate asked. "There's a small problem with one of the engines," replied one of the air hostesses. "It's nothing to worry about."

Nevertheless, Kate was worried. The roaring sound grew louder and louder and the plane began to rock from side to side. Some of the passengers screamed. **4** | **A** | Kate fastened her seatbelt and gripped the edge of her seat tightly as the plane went down.

The plane hit the earth with a loud bump and raced along the ground. Kate saw trees and plants rush past her window. **5** | **D** | Everyone was relieved that the worst was over. Kate smiled as she got onto the bus which would take her to the nearest airport. "Travelling alone really is an adventure!" she thought.

A Then, the pilot announced that they would have to make an emergency landing.

B She was going to visit her aunt and uncle in Spain.

C Kate smiled and went back to sleep.

D When the plane finally stopped, the passengers cheered.

E Soon, the plane was high above the clouds and Kate felt relaxed and happy.

F The air hostesses were walking down the aisle.

(15 marks)

Units 1 - 2

Writing (a narrative)

5 Use the notes to write a short story entitled *"A train accident"* (120-180 words). Use the notes below as well as your own ideas.

Plan

(See Suggested Answers section)

Introduction
(Para 1) *early Friday afternoon – train station – Tony Smith – look forward to visiting brother in Leeds*

Main Body
(Para 2) *Tony sit – comfortable carriage – half an hour later – hear loud explosion – train stop – people cough crawl towards door*
(Para 3) *bang from outside – door break open – firefighters help people out*

Conclusion
(Para 4) *Tony shocked but happy – safe at last!*

(15 marks)

(Total = 100 marks)

 Let's sing!

6 Listen and fill in. Listen again and sing.

Bad luck Blues

I feel bad this morning
I should 1) stay in bed
I've got a frown on my face
And an ache in my head
I've got the blues
And there is nothing I can do.

I bought a new house
It 2) cost thousands of pounds
But an earthquake
3) shook
My home down to the ground
I've got the blues,
And there is nothing I can do.

I worked in the garden
Planting flowers all day
But a big bad hurricane
4) blew them all away

I've got the blues
And there is nothing I can do.

I had a new sports car
It was painted gold
But I 5) crashed it into a telephone pole
I've got the blues
And there is nothing I can do.

I feel bad this morning
It's a mystery
Why all this bad luck
Is 6) following me
I've got the blues.
And there is nothing I can do.

I've got the bad luck blues
And there is nothing I can do.

31(T)

Going places

◆ **Before you start ...**

What qualities does a teacher need to be successful?
What do you do in your free time?
Which jobs do you consider dangerous? Why?
Have you ever been involved in an accident? How
did you feel? Describe it.

◆ **Listen, read and talk about ...**

On the Move

UNIT 3

- continents, countries & climates
- types of holidays & holiday equipment
- means of transport
- accommodation

Out & About

UNIT 4

- scenery & sights
- holiday experiences
- town & the countryside

Module 2
Units 3-4

◆ **Learn how to ...**

- make decisions
- talk about climates/weather conditions
- describe past experiences
- order sth from room service
- complain about sth
- make suggestions
- compare places
- book a hotel room/cruise
- describe a place

◆ **Practise ...**

- present perfect (simple & continuous)
- comparatives/superlatives
- past perfect (simple & continuous)
- clauses of purpose
- prepositions of place/time

◆ **Phrasal verbs**

- get, turn

◆ **Write ...**

- a letter to a friend about recent changes
- a formal letter of complaint
- a letter to a friend giving specific information
- a letter to a friend describing a place you have visited

3 On the Move

A Tom

Lead-in

1 a) Look at the title. What does it mean? How is it related to the pictures?

b) Use the prompts to make sentences about the pictures.

1 car break down
2 stop for a break
3 reach the top of a cliff
4 find a taxi at last
5 miss his flight

Tom's car has broken down.

B Eric
C John
D Leo

2 Match the sentences (a-e) to the prompts (1-5) in Ex. 1, then make full sentences, as in the example.

a [2] He's been cycling for two hours.
b [ ] He's been waiting for the breakdown service for an hour.
c [ ] She's been looking for one for ages.
d [ ] He's been waiting for the next flight for two hours.
e [ ] He's been hiking since 10 o'clock this morning.

a-2 John has stopped for a break. He's been cycling for two hours.

Listening and Reading

3 Listen and repeat, then close your books and try to remember as many sentences as possible.

- How long have you been in Ireland?
- I've never been there myself.
- Would you like a lift, then?
- I thought you'd never ask.
- They must have got stuck in traffic.
- Have you got any idea how long they'll be?
- Here they are.
- What's going on?
- Have you missed your flight?

Objectives

Vocabulary: continents; countries; climate; types of holidays; holiday equipment; means of transport
Reading: multiple matching; multiple choice
Listening: listening for specific information; understanding meaning
Speaking: talking about personal experiences; describing climate; talking about a journey
Communication: room service
Pronunciation: silent letters
Grammar: present perfect; present perfect continuous; linkers
Phrasal verb: get
Word Formation: forming adjectives
Project: a letter to a friend talking about recent changes
Writing: a formal letter of complaint

Lesson 1 (pp. 32 - 33)

1 a)
- Read aloud the title. Ask Ss what it means. *(Travelling from one place to another.)*
- Elicit from Ss how the title of the unit is related to the pictures by asking questions.
  e.g. T: Is Eric on the move?
  S1: Yes.
  T: Where is he?
  S2: At the airport.
  T: How is he travelling?
  S3: By plane.   etc

b)
- Ask Ss to look at the pictures and read the prompts 1-5 silently. Ask: *What's happened to Tom?* Answer: *His car has broken down.* Elicit from Ss the tense and when it is used (present perfect – used for actions which happened at some time in the past and have a visible result in the present). Drill Ss. Say verbs from the *Irregular Verbs section.* Ss say the corresponding past participle.
  e.g. T: find
  S1: found
  T: catch
  S2: caught
  T: see
  S3: seen   etc
- Ss do the exercise.

ANSWER KEY

B Eric has missed his flight.
C John has stopped for a break.
D Leo has reached the top of a cliff.
E Ellie has found a taxi at last.

2
- Read out sentences (a-e) and elicit/explain any unknown vocabulary by giving/asking for examples, using synonyms, opposites, etc.
  e.g. **breakdown service:** a service sb calls to ask for help when their car breaks down

- Ask Ss to look at the verb form. Write the first sentence on the board. Explain that the verb is in the present perfect continuous form. Elicit from Ss how this tense is formed (**have + been + verb-ing**). Explain that this tense is used to describe an action which started in the past and continues up to the present giving emphasis to duration, usually with *for/since.*
  Drill your Ss. Write the following prompts on the board. Ss expand them into full sentences using the present perfect continuous.
  Suggested prompts: he/learn English/three years *(He has been learning English for three years.)*; I/live here/six months now *(I've been living here for six months now.)*; she/type letters/three hours *(She has been typing letters for three hours.)*   etc
- Ss do the exercise, then make sentences.

ANSWER KEY

b 1 Tom's car has broken down. He's been waiting for the breakdown service for an hour.
c 4 Ellie has found a taxi at last. She's been looking for one for ages.
d 5 Eric has missed his flight. He's been waiting for the next flight for two hours.
e 3 Leo has reached the top of a cliff. He's been hiking since 10 o'clock this morning.

3
- Play the recording with pauses between each sentence. Ss listen and repeat individually. Present these sentences by giving examples. Alternatively, Ss can give examples.
  e.g. **How long have you been in Ireland?** (Pretend that you are on holiday in Ireland for two weeks when you meet a friend who's there on holiday too. You say: *I've been here for two weeks. How long have you been in Ireland?)*   etc
- Ask Ss to look at the sentences for about a minute. Then Ss close their books and do the exercise. Alternatively, this can be done as a game.
  See Unit 1 Ex. 3 p. 6(T) for instructions.
  e.g. S1: I thought you'd never ask.
  S2: Here they are.   etc

4 Explain the task then play the recording. Ss listen and circle. Check Ss' answers.

> **ANSWER KEY**
>
> 1 a   2 b   3 a

5 a) Allow Ss four minutes to read the dialogues silently and answer the questions. Check Ss' answers.

> **ANSWER KEY**
>
> 1 L   2 T, E   3 E   4 L

b) Ss use their dictionaries to find synonyms for the highlighted words. Check Ss' answers by asking individual Ss to read them aloud.

> **SUGGESTED ANSWER KEY**
>
> **fantastic:** wonderful
> **turned up:** arrived
> **shortly:** soon
> **set off:** left
> **vehicle:** car
> **stuck:** trapped

c) • Help Ss explain the words in bold by giving examples/synonyms/opposites or by miming.
> e.g. **take a month off:** have a month's break from work
> **hitchhike:** get free lifts from passing vehicles
> etc

• As an extension, Ss can ask and answer comprehension questions.
> e.g. S1: How long has Leo been in Ireland?
> S2: For almost a month. Has he been to Galway yet?
> S3: No, he hasn't. What is Galway like?
> S4: It's a fantastic place. Where is Leo going now?
> S5: To Cork. Why ...?   etc

d) • Play the recording for Ex. 4. Ss listen and follow the lines, then take roles and read the dialogues aloud.

(Suggested Homework)

1 **Vocabulary:** Ex. 3 (p. 32), words in bold in dialogues (p. 33)
2 **Reading aloud:** dialogues A-C Ex. 5a (p. 33) (Point out that Ss practise *reading aloud* using the S's audio CD.)
3 **Dictation:** any ten of the words from Vocabulary with example/definition
4 **Speaking:** Ex. 2 (p. 39)

4 Listen and choose the correct topic for each dialogue.

1 Dialogue A
  a hiking holiday   b coach holiday
2 Dialogue B
  a car accident   b breakdown
3 Dialogue C
  a missed flight   b cancelled flight

5 a) Read the dialogues (A-C) and answer the questions (1-4). Write *L* (for Leo), *T* (for Tom) or *E* (for Eric).

Who ...
1 has been travelling for four weeks? ....
2 has been waiting for sth for some time? ....
3 has missed sth? ....
4 has been having a nice time? ....

A
Jerry: So, how long have you been in Ireland, Leo?
Leo: I've been here for almost a month, now. There's so much to see.
Jerry: You're right, there. It would take you years to see everything. Have you been to Galway, yet?
Leo: Yes. It's a fantastic place. I'm on my way to Cork, now. I hear it's great there, too.
Jerry: That's what they say. I've never been there myself and I've lived in Ireland all my life.
Leo: Perhaps you should **take a month off** and do some travelling as well.
Jerry: Perhaps I should! I expect hiking's very tiring, **though**.
Leo: It is **a bit**. Sometimes I **hitchhike**. That way, I get the **chance** to have a rest.
Jerry: Oh. Would you like a lift, then?
Leo: I thought you'd never ask!

B
Lyn: Hello. Bradford Road Rescue. Can I help you?
Tom: My name's Tom Barker. I called your **breakdown service** over an hour ago and no one's turned up yet.
Lyn: I'm sorry. They must have got stuck in traffic.
Tom: Have you got any idea how long they'll be?
Lyn: They should be with you shortly.
Tom: They've **definitely** set off then?

Lyn: Oh, yes. Don't worry. Just stay with your vehicle and someone will be with you soon.
Tom: OK. Is there anything else I need to do?
Lyn: Just turn on your **hazard lights** and put your **warning triangle** on the road, please.
Tom: I've already done that. Oh, wait! I think I can see the **truck** now. Yes, here they are! Thank you. Bye.

C
Eric: Hello, Paula. It's Eric.
Paula: What's going on? Are you in Brussels already?
Eric: No, I'm still in New York, stuck at the airport.
Paula: Oh no. Have you missed your flight?
Eric: Yes and I've been waiting for two hours for the next one, but there haven't been any **announcements** yet.
Paula: I see. Well, why don't you check the **departure times** on the **screens**?
Eric: I've done that, but it doesn't say it's been **delayed** or anything.
Paula: Why don't you ask if there is an **alternative route via** Paris or get on the waiting list for another flight?
Eric: Good idea. I'll do that. Thanks.

b) Find synonyms for the highlighted words in your dictionary.

c) Explain the words in bold. Choose any five to make sentences.

d) Read the dialogues aloud.

E Ellie

33

Vocabulary

- ## Continents, Countries and Climates

6 a) Match the cities to the continents, then say where each city is.

Cairo is in Africa.

Cairo
Sydney
Seattle
Anchorage
Bangkok
Brasilia
Rome
Helsinki

Asia
North America
Europe
Africa
South America
Antarctica
Australia

b) Use the colour code to describe the climate of each city in Ex. 6a.

 Tropical wet — always hot and humid with heavy rain

 Tropical dry — always hot with heavy rain in the wet season and less rain in the dry season

 Desert — very hot days and cool to cold nights; little rain

 Mediterranean — hot, dry summers; winters are mild and wet

 Humid subtropical — warm to hot summers and cool winters with some rain all year

 Humid oceanic — warm summers and cool winters with some rain all year

 Humid continental — mild summers and cold winters with some rain all year

Arctic — short cool summers and long very cold winters with snow and ice

Cairo has a desert climate. It has very hot days and cool to cold nights with little rain.

Speaking

c) What is the climate like in your city/town?

34

- ## Types of holidays

7 Match the types of holidays to the types of transport, then make sentences.

1	safari	a	aeroplane/coach
2	sailing	b	yacht
3	cycling	c	bike
4	cruise	d	jeep
5	package	e	ship

When you go on a safari holiday, you travel by jeep/in a jeep.

- ## Holiday Equipment

8 a) Make sentences, as in the example.

cool box   helmet   rucksack

- protect our skin from the sun
- carry our clothes and equipment in
- keep food and drinks cool
- find our way
- prevent us from drowning
- see things clearly from a distance
- keep insects away
- help us see and breathe underwater
- protect our head if we fall off our bike
- carry our money safely

mask & snorkel

compass

binoculars   money belt   life jacket

We use a cool box to keep food and drinks cool.

Speaking

b) Emily is going on a cycling holiday and Scott is going on a safari holiday. Which of the items in Ex. 8a do you think Emily/Scott should pack? Use the phrases to ask and answer, as in the example.

A: *I think Emily should pack sun screen.*

B: *I agree. She needs sun screen to protect her skin from the sun. What about a rucksack?*

A: *Sure. She needs a rucksack to ...   etc*

Lesson 2 (pp. 34 - 35)

* Check Ss' HW (10').

6 a) • Explain the task, then Ss do the exercise. Check Ss' answers.

> **ANSWER KEY**
>
> - *Sydney is in Australia.*
> - *Seattle is in North America.*
> - *Anchorage is in North America.*
> - *Bangkok is in Asia.*
> - *Brasilia is in South America.*
> - *Rome is in Europe.*
> - *Helsinki is in Europe.*

- As an extension, Ss can name other cities which are in the six continents. Explain that there are no cities in Antarctica.
  Alternatively, divide the class into two teams. Say names of countries/cities. Ss, in teams, give the corresponding continent. Each correct answer gets 1 point. The team with the most points is the winner.
  Suggested list: (countries) Kenya, Thailand, Austria, India, Japan, Nepal, The Czech Republic, Jordan, Egypt, Argentina, Uruguay, etc
  (cities) Ankara, Warsaw, Athens, Lisbon, Tokyo, Seoul, Dublin, Kingston, Amman, Tripoli, etc
  e.g. T: Kenya
  Team A S1: Africa
  T: Thailand
  Team B S1: Asia   etc

b) • Explain that the words in colour are climates. Choose Ss to read the characteristics of each one. Explain/ Elicit any unknown vocabulary by giving examples/ definitions/opposites/synonyms, etc.

> **ANSWER KEY**
>
> *Sydney has a humid subtropical climate. It has warm to hot summers and cool winters with some rain all year.*
> *Seattle has a humid oceanic climate. It has warm summers and cool winters with some rain all year.*
> *Anchorage has an arctic climate. It has short cool summers and long cold winters with snow and ice.*
> *Bangkok has a tropical wet climate. It is always hot and humid with heavy rain.*
> *Brasilia has a tropical dry climate. It is always hot with heavy rain in the wet season and less rain in the dry season.*
> *Rome has a Mediterranean climate. It has hot, dry summers and mild, wet winters.*
> *Helsinki has a humid continental climate. It has mild summers and cold winters with some rain all year.*

c) Ask individual Ss to describe the climate in their city/town.

> **SUGGESTED ANSWER KEY**
>
> *My town has a Mediterranean climate. It has very hot, dry summers and mild winters.*

7 • Ask Ss to quickly read the listed words. Elicit what sb can do if he goes on one of the holidays mentioned.

e.g. safari (You can see lions and tigers. etc)
sailing (You can travel round the islands. etc)

- Ss do the exercise. Check Ss' answers, then Ss make sentences. Focus Ss' attention on the use of prepositions with means of transport.

> **ANSWER KEY**
>
> 1 d   2 b   3 c   4 e   5 a
> *When you go on a sailing holiday, you travel by yacht/ on a yacht.*
> *When you go on a cycling holiday, you travel by bike.*
> *When you go on a cruise, you travel by ship/on a ship.*
> *When you go on a package holiday, you travel by plane/by coach/on a plane/in a coach.*

8 a) Explain the task. Ss do the exercise in closed pairs. Check Ss' answers.

> **ANSWER KEY**
>
> - *We use/wear a helmet to protect our head if we fall off our bike.*
> - *We use sun screen to protect our skin from the sun.*
> - *We use a compass to find our way.*
> - *We use insect repellent to keep insects away.*
> - *We use binoculars to see things clearly from a distance.*
> - *We use a money belt to carry our money safely.*
> - *We use/wear a life jacket to prevent us from drowning.*
> - *We use a mask and snorkel to help us see and breathe underwater.*
> - *We use a rucksack to carry our clothes and equipment in.*

b) Explain the task, then Ss do the exercise in closed pairs. Go round the class and check Ss' answers, then ask some pairs to report back to the class.

> **SUGGESTED ANSWER KEY**
>
> A: ... carry her clothes and equipment in. I think she should also pack some insect repellent.
> B: I agree. She needs it to keep insects away. I believe she should also pack a compass.
> A: Yes. She needs a compass to find her way. Anything else?
> B: Yes, I think she should pack a money belt.
> A: I agree. She needs a money belt to carry her money safely. She also needs a helmet.
> B: Sure. She needs a helmet to protect her head if she falls off her bike. ... etc
>
> A: I think Scott should pack some sun screen.
> B: I agree. He needs sun screen to protect his skin from the sun. What about a compass?
> A: Sure. He needs it to find his way. I think he should also pack some insect repellent.
> B: Good idea. He needs it to keep insects away. What about a cool box?
> A: Yes, of course. He needs a cool box to keep food and drinks cool. ... etc

9 • Explain the task. Do each item with Ss, explaining/ eliciting any unknown vocabulary if necessary. Alternatively, Ss can do the exercise on their own, checking any unknown vocabulary in their dictionaries. e.g. **guesthouse:** small hotel   etc

ANSWER KEY: accommodation: beach — places to eat: confectioner's — sightseeing: shopping centre — shopping: library — entertainment: supermarket

1 I usually stay in youth hostels because they are quite cheap.
2 I usually eat at small restaurants. I sometimes eat at fast food restaurants. I never eat at expensive restaurants.
3 In the mornings, I go sightseeing. I enjoy visiting museums and art galleries. Sometimes I go shopping in antique shops or department stores. In the evenings, I usually go to the theatre, to a concert or to a bistro. I enjoy shopping. I usually buy souvenirs.

10 a) Explain to Ss that they are going to listen to some people talking about their holiday. Ask Ss to read the information in the table. Play the recording. Ss listen and fill in the missing words. Check Ss' answers, then individual Ss talk about each person's holiday.

ANSWER KEY: Means of transport: **coach**; Accommodation: **hotel**; Weather: **cold**; Activities: **cycling**, **swimming**; Comments: **fantastic**

• ... She stayed in a tent for a week. The weather was wet. She went walking and cycling. It was an exhausting holiday.
• Pete and Ann went to Jamaica by aeroplane. They stayed in a 5-star hotel for two weeks. The weather was warm. They went swimming and scuba diving. It was an exciting holiday.
• Tony went to Austria by coach. He stayed in a chalet for a week. The weather was cold. He went skiing and sledging. It was a fantastic holiday.

TAPESCRIPT

Carol: I usually go to Blackpool for my holidays, but this year my friend persuaded me to go on a tour of the Lake District with him for a week. We went on our bikes and stayed in a tent for a week. It was really cramped, so I couldn't sleep properly. We spent every single day walking and cycling, even when it was pouring with rain, which was most days! We cooked all our meals on a campfire - they weren't too bad but I missed my home comforts. I've decided not to go camping again. It was an exhausting trip!

Pete: We've just got back from a holiday in Jamaica. We got a special deal: return flight and luxurious accommodation in a 5-star hotel for 2 weeks for only £1,200. The hotel was just a stone's throw from the beach and the weather was lovely and warm. We went swimming in the sea every day, and we spent a lot of time scuba diving, too. The best part of the holiday was when we went to a moonlight beach party. We stayed until the sun came up! We would definitely go to Jamaica again. It was such an exciting place, so lively!

Tony: I've just got back from a winter holiday in Austria. I went by coach and stayed in a chalet for a week. The chalet was basic but very comfortable. The weather was nice and cold and there was plenty of snow so I did lots of skiing. I even tried sledging, which was great fun. I really enjoyed myself the whole time. There was never a dull moment. It was a fantastic holiday.

b) Explain the task. Ss, one after the other, ask and answer.

ANSWER KEY
S3: ... Where did she stay?
S4: In a tent. How long did she stay there?   etc

11 a) Ss work in pairs. Explain that one S should pretend they want to go on a cruise, while the other should pretend they want to go on a package holiday. Check Ss' performance around the class, then ask individual pairs to report back to the class.

SUGGESTED ANSWER KEY

A: I want to go on a cruise this year. I think it would be really exciting to sail to different places.
B: I don't know. We won't have much time for sightseeing because the ship won't stay in one place for very long. Also, I get seasick.
A: There are lots of things to do on the ship, though. I'm sure we won't get bored.
B: I don't like being at sea. I don't think we can afford a cruise.
A: In that case, why don't we go on a package holiday instead.

b)

SUGGESTED ANSWER KEY: I last went on holiday to Spain. I stayed there for two weeks. The weather was warm. I went sightseeing and shopping. I also went swimming and scuba diving. I had a really nice time, especially in the evenings when we went out for dinner and tried traditional dishes.

12 Explain the task. Play the recording. Ss listen and tick accordingly. Check Ss' answers.

ANSWER KEY   1 C, 2 B, 3 A, 4 C, 5 C

TAPESCRIPT
1 Where does the man want to put the pool?
Man: I want to build an outdoor swimming pool.
Woman: Where – in the back garden?
Man: No, it's too small.
Woman: Well you can't put it at the front!
Man: I'm thinking of building it at the side of the house, actually.
Woman: Good idea!
2 What does Sheila need to buy?
James: So, have you bought what you need for your holiday?
Sheila: No, I still need a few things. Have you got a rucksack I can borrow?
James: Sure. I can lend you one.
Sheila: Thanks. I also need a torch and a sunshade.
James: I haven't got a sunshade, but I can find you a torch if you want me to.
Sheila: That would be great. Thanks.
3 Which holiday do they decide to go on?
Man: I think we should spend our holiday at sea.
Woman: OK. I didn't really fancy a cycling holiday anyway.
Man: How about sailing our own boat around the Greek islands?
Woman: That sounds lovely, but it would be very hard work.
Man: You're right! Let's go by ship and relax on the deck.
4 What is the weather like in Florida?
Man: Hello.
Woman: Hi, it's me. I just thought I'd give you a quick ring and tell you what a great time I'm having.
Man: That's nice of you. What's the weather like in Florida? It's snowing here.
Woman: Oh, it's nice and sunny here, although it's a little windy.
Man: Perfect weather for sightseeing, then?
Woman: Yes, it is.
5 What time did Peter leave?
Man: Have you seen Peter?
Woman: He's already left for the airport.
Man: But it's only quarter to twelve. I thought his flight wasn't until quarter past two.
Woman: You're right, but he left at quarter past nine because he wanted to go to the office first.
Man: Oh, I see.

Suggested Homework

1 Vocabulary: Exs 6b & 8a (p. 34), Ex. 9 (p. 35)
2 Dictation: any ten words from Vocabulary
3 Speaking: Exs 6b & 8b (p. 34), Ex. 11a (p. 35)
4 Writing: Ss can choose five cities, each in a different continent and write about their climate.

9 Underline the odd word out. Then, answer the questions.

accommodation: caravan, chalet, 5-star hotel, beach, guesthouse, youth hostel, tent, B & B

places to eat: café, confectioner's, fast food restaurant, picnic area, bistro, restaurant

sightseeing: museum, art gallery, castle, palace, shopping centre

shopping: bookshop, antique shop, jeweller's, library, department store, market

entertainment: theatre, cinema, opera, theme park, supermarket, concert

1 Which type of accommodation do you usually stay in? Why?

2 Where do you usually/sometimes/never eat while on holiday?

3 How do you spend your days/evenings while on holiday? Do you like shopping? What do you usually buy?

Listening

10 a) Listen and complete the table, then talk about each person, as in the example.

Name:	Carol	Pete & Ann	Tony
Destination:	Lake District	Jamaica	Austria
Means of transport:	bike	aeroplane	....
Accommodation:	tent	5-star	chalet
Length of stay:	1 week	2 weeks	1 week
Weather:	rainy	warm	....
Activities:	walking	................., scuba diving	skiing, sledging
Comments:	exhausting	exciting	....

Carol has just come back from the Lake District. etc

b) Use the table in Ex. 10 to ask and answer, as in the example.

S1: *Where did Carol go?*

S2: *She went to the Lake District. How did she...? etc*

Speaking

11 a) You and your friend have decided to go on holiday together. You want to go on a cruise but your friend wants to try a package holiday. Persuade your friend to come on a cruise with you.

- tell him/her that you want to go on a cruise and give a reason
- disagree with the arguments presented by your friend and give your own arguments
- suggest a solution

b) Where did you last go on holiday? How long did you stay there? What did you do there? What was the weather like? Did you enjoy yourself?

Listening

12 Listen and tick (✔) the correct picture.

1 Where does the man want to put the pool?

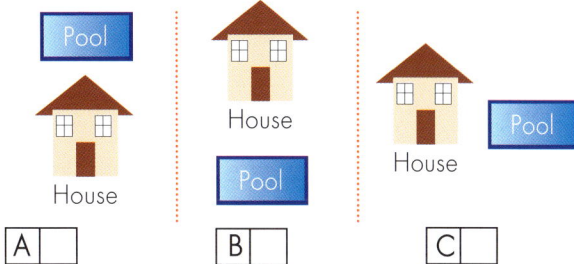

A ☐   B ☐   C ☐

2 What does Sheila need to buy?

A ☐   B ☐   C ☐

3 Which holiday do they decide to go on?

A ☐   B ☐   C ☐

4 What is the weather like in Florida?

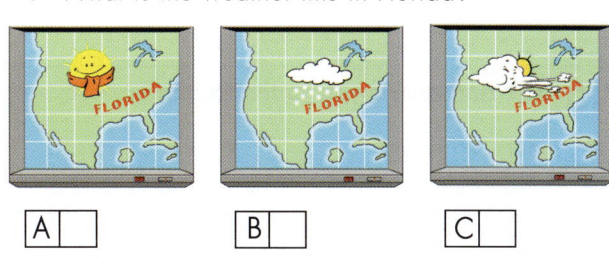

A ☐   B ☐   C ☐

5 What time did Peter leave?

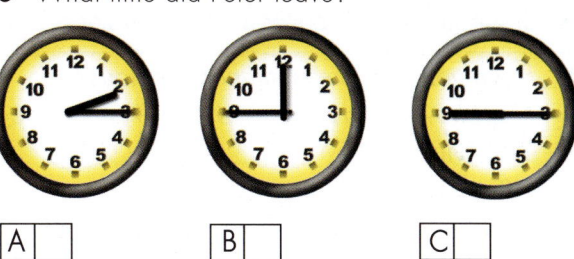

A ☐   B ☐   C ☐

Grammar

• **Present perfect** (have + past participle)

13 Match the tenses in bold to their use.

1		Ann **has lost** ten kilos.
2		I've **been** to Italy. Have you?
3		We **have been** friends for ten years.
4		She is sad. She **has failed** her test.

a   an action which began in the past and continues up to the present

b   an action which has finished recently having a visible result in the present

c   experience (unstated time in the past)

d   recent changes/recent happenings

14 **a)** Look at the past participles below. Which are the same as in the past simple?

lost	risen	spoken
failed	given	said
flown	heard	spilt
kept	broken	taken
done	seen	burnt
won	missed	written

b) Choose time expressions from the box and make five sentences about yourself using the *present perfect*.

Time expressions used with the present perfect: how long, for, since, already, yet, just, ever, never, so far, recently, lately

I have lost two kilos so far.

Speaking

15 Ask and answer, as in the example.

- meet sb famous
- break your leg
- see a tiger
- eat snails
- go bungee jumping
- go up in a hot-air balloon
- win a prize
- sing in public
- call sb names
- climb a tree
- lock yourself out
- try water-skiing

A: *Have you ever met somebody famous?*
B: *No, I haven't. Have you ever broken your leg?*
A: *Yes, I have.*
B: *When was that?*
A: *Five months ago. Have you ever ...?   etc*

16 Tom has bought a cottage for his summer holidays. Use the prompts to make sentences about what he has already done or hasn't done yet, then describe the picture using *there is/there are*.

- hang/curtains ✗
- unpack/boxes ✔
- buy/new furniture ✔
- clean/windows ✔
- tidy/garden ✗
- paint/walls ✔
- lay/carpets ✗
- meet/neighbours ✗
- scrub/floors ✔
- mend/fence ✗

Tom hasn't hung the curtains yet.
Tom has already unpacked the boxes.

• **Project**

Use the ideas in Ex. 16 to write the letter Tom sent to his friend Jim.

17 Complete the sentences, as in the example.

1   Carol can't see very well. She has lost her glasses.
2   Sue is very happy. She .... her exams.
3   Mike is very rich. He .... the lottery.
4   Simon is late for work. He .... the bus.
5   Mark isn't here. He.............................. the dog for a walk.
6   Janet can't walk. She .... her leg.
7   Alice .... her coffee. Her carpet is ruined.
8   Tony's kitchen is full of smoke. He .... his dinner.

18 Complete the questions, as in the example.

1   A: *Have you ever flown in a plane?*
    B: No, I haven't. I'm afraid of flying.
2   A: ....?
    B: Yes, I have. I had a cat when I was a child.
3   A: ....?
    B: No, he hasn't. He's never been to Spain.
4   A: ....?
    B: Yes, we have. We stayed at a hotel last summer.
5   A: ....?
    B: Yes, she has. She slept in a tent last May.
6   A: ....?
    B: Yes, I have. I love concerts.

Lesson 3 (pp. 36 - 37)

* Check Ss' HW (10').

13 • Allow Ss two minutes to do the exercise. Check Ss' answers.

ANSWER KEY

1 b	2 c	3 a	4 d

• Revise the form and basic use of the present perfect. Write the names of various countries on the board. Invite Ss to ask you questions to find out which places you have been to. Tick (✔) the countries accordingly.
Suggested list: Austria, Poland, the USA, Argentina, Turkey, India, etc
e.g. S1: Have you ever been to Austria?
     T: No, I haven't.
    S2: Have you ever been to Poland?
     T: Yes, I have. (Tick Poland.) etc
When Ss have asked about all the countries, say: *I've been to Poland. I went there last summer.* Write the two sentences on the board and elicit the difference between the two tenses (present perfect – unstated time in the past; past simple – stated time in the past). Write a time phrase next to each country you have visited to show when you went there (e.g. the USA – two years ago, etc). Invite Ss to make sentences about you (e.g. Mr Parker has been to the USA. He went there two years ago. etc).
• Ss use the information on the board to ask and answer, as in the example.
e.g. S1: Has Mr Parker been to Austria?
    S2: No, he hasn't. Has he been to Poland?
    S3: Yes, he has. When did he go there?
    S4: Last summer. Has he been to ...? etc

14 a) Allow Ss a minute to do the exercise. Check Ss' answers.

ANSWER KEY

lost, failed, kept, won, heard, missed, said, spilt, burnt

b) • Go through the time expressions table. Elicit their meaning from Ss. Drill your Ss. Say phrases. Ss, in teams, add *since* or *for*.
Suggested list: 1991, three hours, in March, last week, a week, etc
e.g.   T: 1991
    Team A S1: since 1991
          T: three hours
    Team B S1: for three hours etc
• Explain the task. Practise structures with Ss asking individual Ss to make sentences using each of the expressions. Ss, then make five sentences about themselves in writing. Check Ss' sentences round the class, then individual Ss read out their sentences.

SUGGESTED ANSWER KEY

*I've travelled abroad twice **since** 1987.*
*I haven't given Pat the letter **yet**.*

---

*I've **never** been to Scotland.*
*I haven't played tennis **recently**.*
*I've **already** done my homework.*

15 Read out the prompts and explain any unknown vocabulary. Choose two Ss to read out the example. Ss then do the exercise in closed pairs. Check Ss' performance, then ask some pairs to report back to the class.

SUGGESTED ANSWER KEY

A: ... seen a tiger?
B: No, I haven't. Have you ever eaten snails?
A: Yes, I have.
B: When was that?
A: Last Saturday. Have you ever gone/been bungee jumping?
B: No, I haven't. Have you ever gone/been up in a hot-air balloon?
A: No, I haven't. Have you ever ... ? etc

16 • Read out the prompts and elicit any unknown vocabulary by miming, or giving synonyms, opposites or examples.
e.g. **hang curtains** (mime the action of hanging curtains)
• Ss do the exercise. Check Ss' answers then Ss describe the picture (*There are two armchairs with cushions on them. etc*)

ANSWER KEY

Tom has already bought new furniture.
Tom has already cleaned the windows.
Tom hasn't tidied the garden yet.
Tom has already painted the walls.
Tom hasn't laid the carpets yet.
Tom hasn't met his neighbours yet.
Tom has already scrubbed the floors.
Tom hasn't mended the fence yet.

Project (p. 36)

Explain the task. Elicit beginning/ending of the letter. Ss do the exercise orally in class, then assign it as written HW.
See Writing Project No. 3 – Suggested Answers section at the back of the book.

17 Read out the example and explain the task. Ask Ss to quickly read sentences 1-8 for any unknown words. Ss, in closed pairs, complete the sentences with the correct verb in the present perfect. Check Ss' answers.

ANSWER KEY

2 has passed	5 has taken	7 has spilt
3 has won	6 has broken	8 has burnt
4 has missed		

18 Read out the example, then allow Ss three minutes to do the exercise in closed pairs. Check Ss' answers by asking individual Ss to read out their answers.

ANSWER KEY

2 Have you ever had a cat?
3 Has he ever been to Spain?
4 Have you ever stayed at a hotel?
5 Has she ever slept in a tent?
6 Have you ever been to a concert?

19 Read out the sentences. Ask Ss to match the tenses in bold to their use. Refer Ss to the Grammar Reference Section for a more detailed analysis. Drill your Ss. Write prompts on the board. Ss make sentences in the present perfect continuous.
Suggested prompts: do/homework, clean/house, repair/fence, fix/bike, write/invitations, talk/on/phone, etc.
e.g. S1: He has been doing his homework all morning.
      S2: He has been cleaning the house since lunch-time. etc
Ss then give examples of their own.

ANSWER KEY

1 b   2 a

Suggested sentences:
She has been working since 9 o'clock this morning.
I can smell cigarettes. Someone has been smoking in here.

---

20 • Explain the task, then read out prompts a-f and elicit the meaning of any unknown vocabulary.
   • Play the recording. Ss listen and do the exercise, then make sentences.

ANSWER KEY

2 a Bob has been chopping wood since 10 o'clock this morning.
3 f Lucy has been playing the piano since 10 o'clock this morning.
4 e Steve has been mowing the lawn since 10 o'clock this morning.
5 c Tim and Ted have been feeding the chickens since 10 o'clock this morning.
6 b Sandra has been doing the washing-up since 10 o'clock this morning.

• As an extension, you can mime actions. Ss, in teams, try to guess what you are doing and make sentences using the present perfect continuous.
   Suggested list: mop the floor, dust the furniture, sleep, cook, read, dance, listen to music
   e.g.   T: (mime mopping the floor)
      Team A S1: He has been mopping the floor since 10 o'clock this morning.   etc

21 Ss work in closed pairs to do the exercise. Check Ss' answers. Any answer is acceptable provided it is grammatically correct and makes sense in the context.

SUGGESTED ANSWER KEY

2 ... has been studying/working/cleaning the house/ etc since ...
3 ... have been walking/dancing/etc for ...
4 ... has been taking driving lessons for ...
5 ... has been playing/taking piano lessons for ...
6 ... have been waiting for ...
7 ... has been living here since ...
8 ... have been watching it since ...
9 ... has been revising/studying for ...
10 ... has been sunbathing since ...

---

22 Ss do the exercise in closed pairs. Check Ss' answers in class while individual Ss read out their completed sentences.

ANSWER KEY

1 has Sam been learning   5 have ever seen
2 Has Anne visited   6 have been cleaning
3 haven't finished   7 hasn't given
4 have been waiting,   8 Has James travelled
   have you been

---

23 Explain the task. Ss make their own sentences.

SUGGESTED ANSWER KEY

I've just finished cooking.
It's the best film I've ever seen.
I've never been to Japan.
I've typed three letters so far.
I've been studying Italian since last January.
I've been tidying my room for the last two hours.
I've recently been to a rock concert.
I haven't been to the opera lately.
I haven't done the washing-up yet.

---

24 • Play the recording. Ss listen and do the exercise. Check Ss' answers.
   • Play the recording again. Ss listen and repeat individually.

ANSWER KEY

answer   half   farm
foreign   honest   wrestle
climb   walk   wrong

(Suggested Homework)

1 **Vocabulary:** Exs 14 & 15 (p. 36), Ex. 20 (p. 37)
2 **Dictation:** any ten words from Vocabulary
3 **Speaking:** Ex. 15 (p. 36)
4 **Writing:** Project (p. 36)

• Present perfect continuous

(have/has been + verb -ing)

19 Match the tenses in bold to their use, then give an example for each use.

| 1 | | He **has been typing** letters all morning. |
| 2 | | My hairbrush is broken. Who **has been using** it? |

a expressing anger, annoyance or irritation

b an action which started in the past and continues up to the present giving emphasis to duration

20 Listen to the sounds and match the people to the actions. Then make sentences, as in the example.

1	d	Sally		a	chop wood
2		Bob		b	do the washing-up
3		Lucy		c	feed chickens
4		Steve		d	type letters
5		Tim and Ted		e	mow the lawn
6		Sandra		f	play the piano

Sally has been typing letters since 10 o'clock this morning.

21 Complete the sentences, as in the example. Use *for* or *since*.

1 Mary can play the flute very well. She has been taking lessons for five years.

2 John is tired. He .... 5 o'clock this morning.

3 My feet hurt. I .... three hours.

4 Mark .... two months and he still can't drive.

5 Stuart is a good pianist. He .... ten years.

6 Where is the bus? We .... half an hour.

7 He isn't new to the neighbourhood. He .... last September.

8 Turn that TV off. You .... this morning.

9 He is bound to pass the exam. He .... four weeks.

10 Kate is sunburnt. She .... this morning.

22 Put the verbs in brackets into the *present perfect* or the *present perfect continuous*.

1 How long .... (Sam/learn) German?

2 .... (Anne/visit) her grandparents recently?

3 We .... (not/finish) our homework yet.

4 I .... (wait) for you since 10 o'clock this morning. Where .... (you/be)?

5 It's the most beautiful garden we .... (ever/see).

6 You .... (clean) the house for hours. Why don't you have a rest?

7 She .... (not/give) a copy of the report to the manager yet.

8 .... (James/travel) all over the world?

23 Make true sentences about yourself using the *present perfect* or *present perfect continuous* and the adverbs in the list, as in the example.

• already • just • ever • never • so far • since • for • recently • lately • yet

I've already done the washing-up.

Pronunciation (silent letters)

24 Listen and underline the consonants which are not heard. Listen again and repeat.

answer	half	farm
foreign	honest	wrestle
climb	walk	wrong

Communication

• Room service

25 a) Listen and fill in the missing words then, in pairs, read out the dialogue.

A: Room service, how can I 1) .... you?
B: Hello, I'd 2) .... to order **lunch**, please.
A: Certainly. Which room are you 3) ....?
B: **Room 207**.
A: And what would you like to order?
B: A **tuna salad and a bottle of water**, please.
A: Right. And what 4) ....
would you like it sent to your room?
B: Erm ... at **1 o'clock**.
A: OK. That's fine. Will 5) .... be all?
B: Yes, thank you. Goodbye.

b) Use the prompts to act out similar dialogues.

• breakfast for tomorrow morning/Room 659/continental breakfast/8:30
• dinner/Room 372/chef's salad and fried chicken with rice/6:45

Listening & Reading

26 Which picture shows: a steam train at the station? a dining car? a lounge car? an observation car? a waiter? waterfalls? Which country do the pictures show? How do you know?

27 Listen and fill in the advertisement.

THE PRIDE OF AFRICA
The most luxurious train in the world

All Aboard for a Steam Safari

Take the trip of a lifetime aboard the Pride of Africa - one of the world's most luxurious hotel 1) ....
Cape Town to Dar es Salaam, 29 June - 11 July from $5,250

● **12-day tour includes:**
- 5-day safari in Kruger Park Game Reserve
- visit to the diamond town of Kimberley
- visit to the capital city of Pretoria
- trip to Victoria Falls

● **The Pride of Africa train offers:**
- Royal/Deluxe Suites
- accommodation for up to 2) ....
  passengers
- delicious food prepared by first-rate 3) ....
- observation car

● **Price includes:**
- all meals
- unlimited drinks
- 24-hour room service
- laundry service
(Also available on board: doctor,
4)
...................................,
historian)

● **Activities available:**
- golf
- visit to a crocodile
5) ....
- rafting trip
- trip through the rainforest
- visit to a craft village
- evening of traditional tribal
6) ....

● Sightseeing tours, excursions, tour 7) ...., game park entrance fees and safari drives are also included in the price.

For more information and a full itinerary visit our website: www.rovos.co.za

Lesson 4 (pp. 38 - 39)

* Check Ss' HW (10').

25 a) • Elicit from Ss what room service is by asking appropriate questions.

   e.g. Where could you ask for room service: on a ship? at a hotel?
   What things does room service offer: meals? snacks? drinks?

   • Ask Ss to read the dialogue quickly. Play the recording. Ss listen and fill in the missing words. Check Ss' answers by asking them to read the completed dialogue aloud.

ANSWER KEY

1 help	3 in	5 that
2 like	4 time	

   • Play the recording again. Ss listen and follow the lines, then read the dialogue aloud in pairs.

b) Ss, in pairs, act out similar dialogues using the prompts. Check Ss' performance around the class.

ANSWER KEY

A: Room service, how can I help you?
B: Hello, I'd like to order **breakfast for tomorrow morning**, please.
A: Certainly. Which room are you in?
B: **Room 659.**
A: And what would you like to order?
B: A **continental breakfast,** please.
A: Right. And what time would you like it sent to your room?
B: Erm ... at **8:30.**
A: OK. That's fine. Will that be all?
B: Yes, thank you. Goodbye.

A: Room service, how can I help you?
B: Hello, I'd like to order **dinner**, please.
A: Certainly. Which room are you in?
B: **Room 372.**
A: And what would you like to order?
B: A **chef's salad and fried chicken with rice,** please.
A: Right. And what time would you like it sent to your room?
B: Erm ... at **6:45.**
A: OK. That's fine. Will that be all?
B: Yes, thank you. Goodbye.

26 • Ask Ss to look at the pictures and try to guess how they are related to the title of the advertisement in Ex. 27.
   • Ss look at the pictures more closely and, in pairs, identify what each one shows. Check Ss' answers.

ANSWER KEY

a steam train at the station: pict. 1
a dining car: pict 5
a lounge car: pict. 4
an observation car: pict. 2
a waiter: pict. 3
waterfalls: pict. 6

The pictures show Africa. I know because there are waterfalls in Africa and because the waiter is African. Also, in the advertisement it says "The Pride of Africa".

27 • Read out the advertisement and explain any unknown vocabulary by giving examples, definitions, synonyms or opposites.
   • Play the recording twice if necessary. Ss do the exercise. Check Ss' answers.

ANSWER KEY

1 trains	4 hairdresser	6 dancing
2 72	5 farm	7 guides
3 chefs		

   • As an extension, Ss use the completed advertisement to ask and answer comprehension questions.
   e.g. S1: How long does the trip last?
   S2: From 29 June to 11 July. How much does it cost?
   S3: £5,250 minimum. What does the tour include? etc

28 • Explain the task. Point out that Ss should read the headings first, then skim the text to get the gist. Ss read each paragraph again trying to find the key words which match the headings.
   • Read out the headings, then choose a S to read the first paragraph aloud. Read the tip aloud and focus Ss' attention on the underlined words in both the paragraph and the matching heading. (dream - ever wanted, come true - now you can do all this). Explain that Ss should underline the words in each paragraph related to the heading.
   • Allow Ss three to four minutes to complete the task. Check Ss' answers. Ss then explain the words in bold by giving examples, synonyms or opposites. Ss can look up the words in their dictionaries.
      e.g. **spectacular:** fantastic, great

ANSWER KEY

2 B   journey – trip, to remember – unforgettable
3 D   lap of luxury – elegant accommodation/ splendour/Royal, Deluxe suites/first - rate chefs
4 A   spoilt for choice – plenty of opportunities/wide variety of activities/ choose
5 E   an offer - with much to offer, you can't refuse - not to be missed

29 • Allow Ss two minutes to complete the phrases. Check Ss' answers round the class. Ss memorise these phrases.
   • Ss then use the phrases to persuade each other to go on a trip on the Pride of Africa.

ANSWER KEY

1 luxurious	5 en-suite	9 unlimited
2 wonderful	6 delicious	10 24-hour
3 elegant	7 first-rate	11 laundry
4 private	8 breathtaking	12 wide

SUGGESTED ANSWER KEY

   You should go on a trip on the Pride of Africa. It is a **luxurious hotel train** with **elegant accommodation**. The suites have a **private lounge** and **en-suite facilities**. The Pride of Africa offers **24-hour room service** and a **laundry service**. You can enjoy **unlimited drinks** and **delicious food** prepared by **first-rate chefs**.
   During your **wonderful twelve-day journey**, you can take part in a **wide variety of activities** or simply relax and enjoy the **breathtaking scenery**. A steam safari on the Pride of Africa is not to be missed.

30 Ss use the highlighted words from the text to complete the exercise. Check Ss' answers by asking individual Ss to read their answers aloud.

ANSWER KEY

1 spacious	5 comfortable
2 most	6 wonderful
3 delicious	7 natural
4 better	8 beautiful

31 Allow Ss two minutes to fill in the correct preposition. Check Ss' answers round the class, then Ss make sentences Ss should memorise these phrases.

ANSWER KEY

1 at	4 on	7 on
2 on	5 on	8 over
3 on	6 in	9 to

32 • Write the headings on the board. Allow Ss two minutes to read the advertisement and article again, then elicit information from Ss by asking questions.
      e.g. What is the Pride of Africa? (It's a luxurious hotel train.) etc
   • Write Ss' answers on the board in note form, under the correct headings. Ss copy the notes into their notebooks, then use the notes to talk about the Pride of Africa.

SUGGESTED ANSWER KEY

   • *What The Pride of Africa is:* luxurious hotel train
   • *Where the train takes you:* twelve – day journey across Africa – from Cape Town to Dar es Salaam – Kimberley – Pretoria – Victoria Falls
   • *What the train itself offers:* Royal/Deluxe suites – accommodation for up to 72 passengers – delicious food prepared by firstrate chefs – observation car – 24-hour room service – laundry service – services of doctor, hairdresser, historian
   • *What activities you can take part in during the journey:* 5-day safari in Kruger Park Game Reserve – flight over Victoria Falls – play golf – visit crocodile farm – rafting trip – trip through rainforest – visit to a craft village – evening of traditional tribal dancing
   • *What the price includes:* all meals – unlimited drinks – 24-hour room service – laundry service – services of doctor, hairdresser and historian – sightseeing tours – excursions – tour guides – game park entrance fees – safari drives

   The Pride of Africa is a luxurious hotel train. It takes you on a twelve-day journey across Africa from Cape Town to Dar es Salaam stopping at Kimberley, Pretoria and Victoria Falls on the way. The train itself offers elegant accommodation for up to 72 people in Royal or Deluxe suites. It has delicious food prepared by first-rate chefs and passengers can admire the breathtaking scenery from the observation car.
   There is a wide variety of activities to take part in during the journey. You can go on a 5-day safari in Kruger Park Game Reserve, play golf, visit a crocodile farm, go on a rafting trip or a trip through the rainforest, visit a craft village or enjoy an evening of traditional tribal dancing.
   The price includes all meals and unlimited drinks, as well as 24-hour room service, a laundry service plus the services of a doctor, hairdresser and historian. It also includes sightseeing tours, excursions, tour guides, game park entrance fees and safari drives.

Suggested Homework

1 **Vocabulary:** words in bold Ex. 28 (p. 39), Exs 30-32 (p. 39)
2 **Dictation:** any ten words from Vocabulary
3 **Speaking:** Ex. 29 (p. 39)
4 **Act out:** Ex. 25a (p. 38)
5 **Writing:** a short summary using notes in Ex. 32 (p. 39)

28 Read the text and label the paragraphs with the correct headings. One heading does not match. Then, explain the words in bold.

    A Spoilt for choice
    B A Journey to remember
    C A dream come true
    D In the lap of luxury
    E An offer you can't refuse
    F A natural wonder

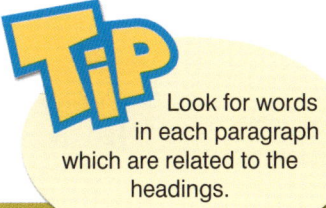

Tip Look for words in each paragraph which are related to the headings.

Full Steam Ahead for the Trip of a Lifetime!

1   C

Have you ever wanted to stay in a luxurious hotel, travel on a **beautiful** *steam train, visit one of the* **natural** *wonders of the world or go on an African safari? Well, now you can do all this and more on board the Pride of Africa.*

2

The Pride of Africa is one of the world's **most** *luxurious hotel trains. It takes you on a* **wonderful** *twelve-day journey across Africa, following in the* **footsteps** *of such great* **explorers** *as Livingstone and Stanley. This unforgettable trip from Cape Town to Dar es Salaam is one of many on offer and includes a five-day safari in Kruger Park Game Reserve. It stops at beautiful sites along the way, including the diamond town of Kimberley, the capital city of Pretoria and the* **spectacular** *Victoria Falls.*

3

The train itself offers **elegant** *accommodation that has been perfectly restored to its 1930's* **splendour**. *There are four Royal Suites and thirty-two Deluxe Suites to accommodate up to 72 passengers. The Royal Suites are elegant and have a private* **lounge** *and* **en-suite** *facilities. The Deluxe Suites are* **comfortable** *and* **spacious** *as well as* **stylish**. *Passengers can also enjoy* **delicious** *food prepared by first-rate chefs in the dining car, and admire and photograph the* **breathtaking** *scenery from the observation car. All meals,* **unlimited** *drinks, 24-hour room service and a laundry service are included in the price. Also available to guests are the* **services** *of a doctor, a hairdresser and a historian.*

4

During the journey there are plenty of opportunities to take part in a wide variety of activities. You can choose to play a round of golf, go on a visit to a crocodile farm, go on a rafting trip, take a trip through the rainforest and even take a flight over Victoria Falls. Alternatively, you can simply relax, take photographs and enjoy the scenery and wildlife. Cultural events along the way include a visit to a **craft** *village and an evening of* **traditional** *tribal dancing. The cost of all sightseeing tours,* **excursions**, *tour guides,* **game park** *entrance fees and safari drives is included in the price.*

5

With so much to offer, a steam safari on the Pride of Africa is really not to be missed. What **better** *way to experience the heart of Africa and the golden age of rail travel? So* **all aboard** *and* **full steam** *ahead for the holiday of a lifetime!*

3

Vocabulary Practice

29 Fill in the adjectives from the text. Then, use the completed phrases to persuade someone to go on a trip on the Pride of Africa.

1 .... hotel train; 2 .... twelve-day journey; 3 .... accommodation; 4 .... lounge; 5 .... facilities; 6 .... food; 7 .... chefs; 8 .... scenery; 9 .... drinks; 10 .... room service; 11 .... service; 12 .... variety of activities

30 Fill in the highlighted opposites from the text.

1 cramped ≠ ....
2 least ≠ ....
3 disgusting ≠ ....
4 worse ≠ ....
5 uncomfortable ≠ ....
6 terrible ≠ ....
7 artificial ≠ ....
8 ugly ≠ ....

31 Fill in *in, on, at, to, over,* then make sentences.

1 stuck .... the airport; 2 .... my own; 3 to get .... the waiting list; 4 to travel .... a train, 5 to be .... offer; 6 to take part .... activities; 7 to go .... a rafting trip; 8 to take a flight .... Victoria Falls; 9 available .... guests

Speaking

32 Make notes under the headings, then talk about the Pride of Africa.

• what the Pride of Africa is
• where the train takes you
• what the train itself offers
• what activities you can take part in during the journey
• what the price includes

Word Formation

33 Study the table then write the adjective derived from the noun or verb. Use the adjectives to make sentences.

> **Forming adjectives**
>
> We can add *-able*, *-al*, *-ary*, *-ful*, *-ible*, *-ical*, *-ive*, *-less*, *-ous*, *-ar*, or *-y* to form adjectives from nouns and verbs.

1 fame – ....
2 terror – ....
3 impress – ....
4 tradition – ....
5 taste – ....
6 colour ....
7 imagine ....
8 comfort ....
9 point ....
10 spectacle ....

Phrasal Verbs

34 Study the table, then underline the correct particle in the sentences below.

> **get away** - 1) to depart, 2) to escape from danger
> **get away with** - to do sth wrong without punishment
> **get by** - to manage
> **get on (with)** - to start or continue doing sth
> **get over** - to recover from an illness/injury
> **get up** - to rise from bed

1 Mark is looking for another job. He can't get **by/over** on the money he earns.
2 Stop talking and get **on/away** with your work!
3 Poor Mr Jackson doesn't seem to be getting **away/over** his back injury.
4 Brian managed to get **up/away** from the fire and call the fire brigade.
5 The careless driver got **away/over** with paying a fine.

Writing (a letter of complaint)

> When we write a letter of complaint, we usually write five paragraphs. In the **first paragraph**, we state the complaint, saying what has happened and where/when the incident took place. In the **second and third paragraphs**, we write our complaints, giving examples or reasons. We write a new paragraph for each complaint. We use *firstly, secondly, to start with, to make matters worse, furthermore*, etc to link our complaints. In the **last paragraph**, we ask for some kind of compensation, e.g. an apology, a refund, a replacement, etc.
>
> We can use a mild tone to sound more polite or a stronger tone when we are extremely upset or annoyed. However, we must never sound rude.

35 a) Read the letter and fill in the gaps with words from the list.

- in addition • firstly • as well as • however
- to make matters worse

Dear Sir/Madam,

▶1 I am writing to complain about the terrible service provided by your airline when I travelled with you on flight B2452 to Rome last Thursday.

▶2 1) ...., although the flight was delayed for over two hours, passengers were given no explanation for the delay and we were not even offered a drink.

▶3 2) ...., when we finally boarded the plane, the staff were most unhelpful and refused to respond to the call button. One member of the cabin crew actually spilt coffee on my jacket. 3) ...., he made no effort to clean it up or to apologise.

▶4 4) ...., when we reached our destination, one of my suitcases was open and some of my clothes were missing.

▶5 As you can imagine, I was extremely upset and angry about the whole experience. I expect a full refund on my ticket as compensation for the missing items, 5) .... a written apology from the airline. I hope to hear from you at your earliest convenience.

Yours faithfully,

Ian Webb

Ian Webb

b) Answer the questions.

1 Why does the writer start the letter with *Dear Sir/Madam*?
2 What are the writer's complaints? What examples/ reasons does he give?
3 What action does he expect the airline to take? In which paragraph does he mention this? How does he sound? Is it a mild or a strong complaint?

36 Which sentences are beginnings/endings? What tone (mild or strong) has the writer used in each?

1 I would appreciate it if the missing parts could be sent to me as soon as possible.
2 I am writing to express my disgust at the quality of service offered by your restaurant.
3 I demand an immediate refund, or I shall be forced to take legal action.
4 I was disappointed by the hi-fi I recently purchased from your company.

Lesson 5 (pp. 40-41)

* Check Ss' HW (10').

33 Go through the table, then Ss do the exercise. Check Ss' answers on the board. Ss then make sentences using the adjectives.

e.g. Big Ben is a famous **tourist** attraction.

> **ANSWER KEY**
>
> | | | | |
> |---|---|---|---|
> | 1 | famous | 6 | colourful |
> | 2 | terrible | 7 | imaginary |
> | 3 | impressive | 8 | comfortable |
> | 4 | traditional | 9 | pointless |
> | 5 | tasty | 10 | spectacular |

34 • Read out the table and check Ss' understanding of each phrasal verb. Ss then do the exercise. Check Ss' answers. Ss should memorise the table.

> **ANSWER KEY**
>
> 1 by   2 on   3 over   4 away   5 away

• As an extension, Ss close their books. Read out definitions listed in the table. Ss, in teams, say the relevant phrasal verb. Each correct answer gets 1 point. The team with the most points is the winner.

e.g.   T: depart
    Team A S1: get away
               T: rise from bed
    Team B S1: get up

Writing (p. 40)

Elicit from Ss why sb would write a letter of complaint (*wrongly delivered item; terrible service at restaurant/hotel; faulty items; etc*) and what he would ask for (*refund; apology; etc*). Read out the theory box explaining any unknown words.

35 a) Allow Ss two minutes to read the letter silently and fill in the words. Check Ss' answers.

> **ANSWER KEY**
>
> | | | | |
> |---|---|---|---|
> | 1 | Firstly | 4 | To make matters |
> | 2 | In addition | | worse |
> | 3 | However | 5 | as well as |

b) Ask Ss to re-read the letter and underline words and phrases which describe how the writer feels. Draw Ss' attention to phrases that show that this is a 'strong' complaint.

> **ANSWER KEY**
>
> 1 Because he doesn't know the name of the person he is writing to
> 2 • flight delayed for two hours →
>   passengers given no explanation
>   not even offered a drink
>   • staff unhelpful, no response to call button →
>   member of cabin crew spilt coffee/no effort
>   to clean it up or apologise
>   • one of his suitcases open – clothes missing
> 3 The writer expects a full refund on his ticket as compensation for the missing clothes, as well as a written apology. para 5
>   – angry/upset
>   – strong/complaint
>   para 1: ... terrible service ...
>   para 2: ... not even offered a drink ...
>   para 3: ... most unhelpful; ... actually spilt ...
>   para 5: ... I was extremely upset and angry ...; I
>   expect ...

36 Allow Ss two minutes to do the exercise. Check Ss' answers, asking them to justify their choice. Ask Ss to underline examples of mild/strong language in the sentences. Point out that Ss should memorise these sentences.

> **ANSWER KEY**
>
> 1 ending; mild (would appreciate, if, could be sent, as soon as possible)
> 2 beginning; strong (disgust)
> 3 ending; strong (demand, immediate refund, forced, take legal action)
> 4 beginning; mild (disappointed)

40(T)

37 a)
- Read out the example. Focus Ss' attention on the sentence structures in the example (*Although/Even though* + clause used at the beginning of the sentence − *However* used after the main sentence at the beginning of the clause of concession, followed by a comma).
- Allow Ss two minutes to do the exercise. Check Ss' answers.

SUGGESTED ANSWER KEY

2 – *Although/Even though the watch was brand-new, it stopped working after two hours.*
   – *The watch was brand-new. However, it stopped working after two hours.*
3 – *Although/Even though he booked a single room, the hotel charged him for a double.*
   – *He booked a single room. However, the hotel charged him for a double.*
4 – *Although/Even though the staff were at fault, they didn't apologise.*
   – *The staff were at fault. However, they didn't apologise.*
5 – *Although/Even though she paid for three chairs, the company only delivered two.*
   – *She paid for three chairs. However, the company only delivered two.*
6 – *Although/Even though the brochure claimed the hotel was on the beach, it was twenty-five minutes' walk away.*
   – *The brochure claimed the hotel was on the beach. However, it was twenty-five minutes' walk away.*
7 – *Although/Even though the glass was dirty, the waiter refused to replace it.*
   – *The glass was dirty. However, the waiter refused to replace it.*
8 – *Although/Even though we booked in advance, the hotel had no record of our reservation.*
   – *We booked in advance. However, the hotel had no record of our reservation.*

b) Ss work in closed pairs. Help them where necessary, then ask some Ss to report back to the class.

SUGGESTED ANSWER KEY

1 *(Beg.) I am writing to complain about the terrible service offered by your restaurant which I visited last Monday evening.*
2 *(End.) I demand a written apology from you.* etc

38 Read out the rubric. Allow Ss two minutes to read the table and match the complaints to the examples/reasons. Check Ss' answers, then Ss make full sentences.

ANSWER KEY

2 c *There was a lack of facilities. Although there was a pool advertised in the brochure, it was closed for repairs during our stay.*
3 a *There was a lack of staff. We needed help with our luggage. However, there was no porter.*

39
- Read out the plan, then ask questions to check Ss' understanding.
   e.g. T: What will your complaint be about?
   S1: Bad service, lack of facilities and lack of staff at a hotel.
   T: Where was that?
   S2: At the Seaside Hotel.
   T: When were you there?
   S3: On 27th and 28th June *(any dates are acceptable provided Ss say two consecutive dates).*
   T: What is the first complaint?
   S4: Unreliable room service.
   T: What example can you give?
   S5: We ordered two simple dishes. However, they took over an hour to arrive and were cold.   etc
- After you have discussed this in class, assign the task as written HW.

ANSWER KEY

Dear Sir/Madam,

   I am writing to complain about the terrible service and lack of facilities provided by the Seaside Hotel when I stayed there with my wife on 27th and 28th June.
   Firstly, the room service was extremely unreliable. We ordered two simple meals. However, they took over an hour to arrive and were cold.
   In addition, I was very disappointed with the lack of facilities. Even though there was a pool advertised in the brochure, it was closed for repairs during our stay.
   Finally, although we needed help with our luggage, there was no porter available. Our luggage was quite heavy and was difficult for us to carry up and down the stairs.
   As you can imagine, I was extremely disappointed with the whole experience. I would like an apology, as well as a refund of part of the cost of the hotel room. I look forward to your immediate reply.

Yours faithfully,
Martin Johnson
Martin Johnson

40 Read out each sentence and help Ss explain them by giving examples.

SUGGESTED ANSWER KEY

- *No matter where you go, you will never find anywhere as good as your home.*
- *The more you travel, the more you learn.*
- *If you don't hurry, you will reach your destination faster.*
- *If you keep moving, you will never develop any attachments to the place you have visited.*

Suggested Homework

1 **Vocabulary:** Exs 33, 34 & 36 (p. 40)
2 **Dictation:** Ex. 34 (p. 40)
3 **Writing:** Ex. 39 (p. 41)

Lesson 6

Workbook Unit 3
Click on Grammar 3

37 **a)** Join the sentences with: *although*, *even though*, *however*, **as in the examples.**

1 I ordered a vegetarian lasagne. There was meat in it.
Even though/Although I ordered a vegetarian lasagne, there was meat in it.
I ordered a vegetarian lasagne. However, there was meat in it.

2 The watch was brand-new. It stopped working after two hours.

3 He booked a single room. The hotel charged him for a double.

4 The staff were at fault. They did not apologise.

5 She paid for three chairs. The company only delivered two.

6 The brochure claimed the hotel was on the beach. The beach was twenty-five minutes' walk away.

7 The glass was dirty. The waiter refused to replace it.

8 We booked in advance. The hotel had no record of our reservation.

b) Write beginnings/ endings for three of the above situations.

38 Study the rubric, then match the following complaints to their examples/reasons and make full sentences using appropriate linking words.

> You recently spent two days at the Seaside Hotel. Unfortunately, you had problems with the room service, the staff and the facilities at the hotel. Write a letter of complaint to the hotel manager, explaining the reasons for your complaints and saying what you expect the hotel to do (120 -150 words).

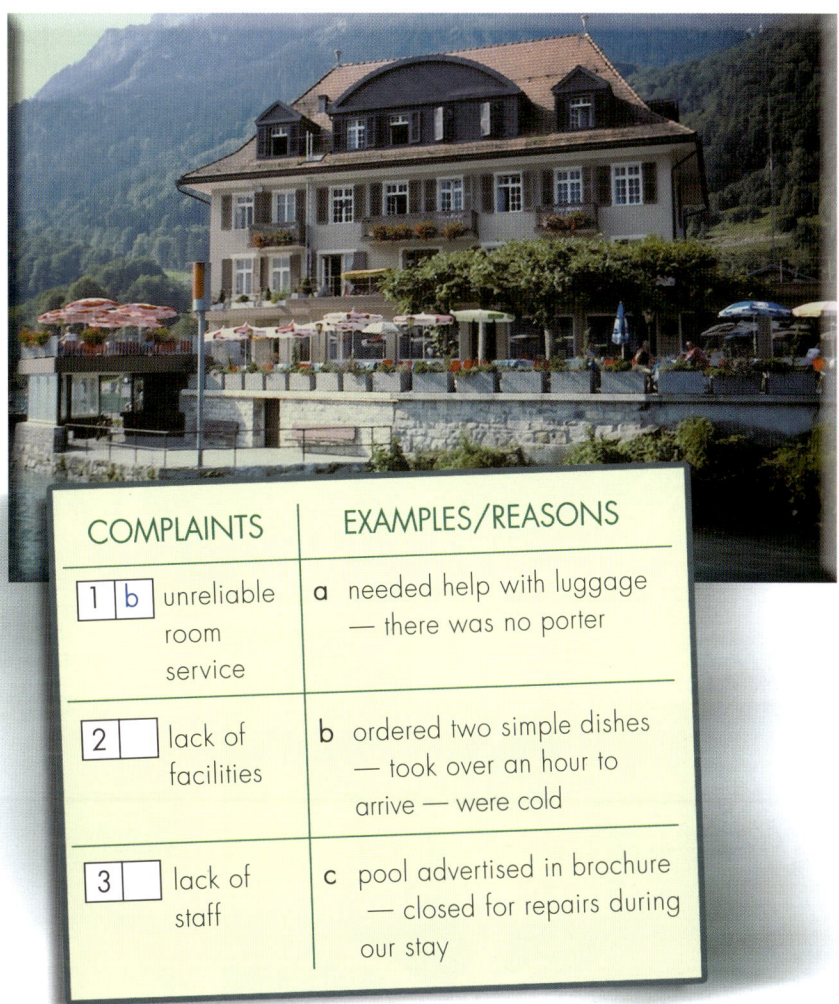

COMPLAINTS	EXAMPLES/REASONS
1 b unreliable room service	a needed help with luggage — there was no porter
2 lack of facilities	b ordered two simple dishes — took over an hour to arrive — were cold
3 lack of staff	c pool advertised in brochure — closed for repairs during our stay

The room service was extremely unreliable. We ordered two simple dishes. However, they took over an hour to arrive and were cold.

39 Use the ideas in Ex. 38 as well as the plan below to write your letter. You can use the letter in Ex. 35 as a model.

Plan

Introduction
(Para 1)   *state complaint and details (where/when/what)*
Main Body
(Para 2)   *1st complaint & example/reason*
(Para 3)   *2nd complaint & example/reason*
(Para 4)   *3rd complaint & example/reason*
Conclusion
(Para 5)   *action you expect to be taken*

40 Read the sentences. What do they mean?

What's in a word?

- East, west, home's best.
- Travel broadens the mind.
- The longest way round is the shortest way home.
- A rolling stone gathers no moss.

THE ADVENTURES OF
HUCKLEBERRY FINN

Jackson's Island

Huck has run away from his father and is hiding on Jackson's Island.

1. I don't think we'll ever find poor Huck's body, Tom …

My plan's working — they all think I'm dead!

THE NEXT DAY …

2. Jim!

Master Huck's ghost!

3. I'm not dead, Jim! I ran away from Pap, that's all. What are *you* doing here?

Well, Huck … I — ran away, too!

Ran away?! But — you're a *slave*, Jim!

4. I know, Huck … but Miss Watson wants to sell me — in New Orleans! I can't go so far away from my wife and children!

Jim and Huck made camp and lived on Jackson's Island together. They often found things floating down the river …

5. Look — I've got us a raft!

Well done, Huck! She's a beauty!

6. A whole house! Let's get in through the window!

Nobody will recognise you in this dress we found — but why do you want to go to town?

7. There are all sorts of clothes … and tools … and — what's that, Jim?

It's a dead man, Huck. Don't look!

8. To get the latest news, Jim.

Pre-Reading Activities

1 **Read the text, and fill in the gaps with verbs from the list.**

- hunt • bought • offered • worked
- continued • take • escape • involved

Huck's adventures 1) take place during a time when slavery was legal in the Southern States of America. This 2) involved the buying and selling of people.

Rich landowners 3) bought slaves from Africa to work on their plantations. The men worked in the fields picking cotton and the women 4) worked as cooks, maids and housekeepers in their owners' mansions.

Slaves were often badly treated and separated from their families. Many slaves ran away to try to find their families or to 5) escape to the North where they could be free. The plantation owners usually 6) offered a big reward for the return of a runaway slave, so some people would 7) hunt them down like animals.

Slavery ended after the American Civil War (1861-1865). Nevertheless, the after-effects of slavery 8) continued well into the twentieth century.

2 **Look at the pictures. Which shows:**

1 Huck in a girl's dress and bonnet? 8
2 a whole house floating down the river? 6, 7
3 Huck standing on a raft? 5
4 Huck with a rifle in his hands? 2

Listening & Reading Activities

3 **Listen and mark the sentences T (true) or F (false).**

1 They all think Huck is alive.   F
2 Miss Watson wants to sell Jim.   T
3 Jim and Huck live on Jackson's Island. T
4 Jim wants to go to town.   F

4 **Read the episode on p. 42 and choose the correct answer, A or B, to each question.**

1 Why is Jim afraid when he sees Huck?
  (A) He thinks Huck is a ghost.
  B He thinks Huck is going to shoot him.

2 Why did Jim run away?
  A Miss Watson is going to New Orleans.
  (B) Miss Watson wants to sell him.
3 When Jim says, "She's a beauty!" (picture 5), what does he mean?
  A Miss Watson is a beautiful woman.
  (B) It's a very nice raft.
4 Why does Huck want to go to town?
  A So nobody will recognise him.
  (B) To find out what is happening.

Grammar

- Prepositions

5 **Underline the correct word in bold. Which of the prepositions in bold are prepositions of place/movement?**

Huck got 1) out/away of the cabin and went 2) at/to Jackson's Island. He saw Widow Douglas and Tom 3) on/with a boat, looking for his body.

While Huck was walking 4) through/around the island, he saw Jim sleeping 5) along/on the ground. Jim thought Huck was a ghost. Jim had run away from Miss Watson because she wanted to sell him 6) in/at New Orleans.

Jim and Huck made camp and lived 7) on/at the island. They often found things floating 8) over/down the river. Once, a whole house floated 9) past/across the island! They got 10) in/on 11) from/through the window, and Huck found some clothes. There was also a dead man 12) inside/beside the house, but Jim told Huck not to look at the body.

Later, Huck put on a dress he found, so he could go 13) to/in town to get the latest news.

6 **Listen to the episode again, then read it aloud.**

Speaking

7 **Use the key words to re-tell the episode.**

- run away • dead man • ghost • sell Jim
- camp on Jackson's island • found a house
- all sorts of clothes and tools
- nobody would recognise him • latest news

8 **What do you think will happen to Huck while he is in town?**   (Ss' own answers)

Out and About

Lead-in

1 Look at the pictures of York and New York. Use these adjectives to compare the two cities.

- crowded/quiet
- polluted/clean
- big/small
- noisy/peaceful
- old/modern
- dangerous/safe
- busy/calm
- exciting/boring

New York is more crowded than York, **whereas/ while** *York is quieter than New York.*

2 Compare the two cities to the place where you live, as in the examples below.

My town isn't **as polluted as** *New York/York.*
My town is **less crowded than** *New York.*
My town is **much bigger than** *York.*
My town is **the most attractive** *place* **of** *the three.*

Listening & Reading

3 Listen and repeat, then close your books and try to remember as many sentences as possible.

- How's that?
- Sounds great!
- Never mind.
- You'll never guess.
- Go on then, tell me!
- You're joking!
- There's only one problem with that.
- I haven't seen you for ages.
- You lucky thing.
- What was it like?
- Not in the least.

4 Listen and write who said each of the sentences below; Kate, Tony or Louise?

1 "She had just sat down at a café when she noticed Julia Roberts was sitting at the next table."
2 "When I got there I realised I had forgotten to take my camera."
3 "The airline had left my luggage in London, so it didn't turn up until three days after I had arrived there."

5 a) Read the dialogues (A-C) and answer the questions, then explain the words in bold.

1 Who forgot to take something on holiday?
2 Who liked the people he met?
3 Who met someone famous while on holiday?
4 What was Tony's problem?

b) Find synonyms for the highlighted words.

44

Objectives

Vocabulary: scenery; sights; town; countryside; holiday experiences; misfortunes
Reading: multiple matching; matching prompts to elements in the text
Listening: listening for specific information; filling in a table; listen and match; listening for interpretation
Speaking: suggesting activities; comparing places; giving reasons
Communication: booking a hotel room
Pronunciation: intonation in questions of choice
Grammar: comparatives/superlatives; past perfect/past perfect continuous
Word formation: word combinations
Phrasal verbs: turn
Project: a letter to a friend giving information
Writing: a letter to a friend describing a visit to a place

Lesson 1 (pp. 44 - 45)

1 • Ask Ss to look at the pictures and say where each town is (New York – America; York – England). Ask Ss if they know how the two cities are related.
History: New York was discovered by Henry Hudson on 3rd September, 1609. He sailed into the harbour while he was on a mission to India on behalf of the Dutch West India Company. Its first settlers were Dutch. They named the place New Amsterdam. On 8th September, 1664, a fleet sent by the Duke of York seized the city. The English changed the name to New York, in honour of the Duke of York.
• Read out the prompts, then the example. Ask Ss to underline *more crowded than*, then identify the grammar form (comparative). It is assumed that Ss at this level are familiar with the structure. Quickly revise comparative forms using the adjectives listed. Write the comparatives on the board and elicit spelling rules.
e.g. noisy – noisier; clean – cleaner etc
• Ss make sentences comparing the two cities.

ANSWER KEY

York is quieter than New York.
New York is more polluted than York
York is cleaner than New York.
New York is bigger than York.
York is smaller than New York.   etc

2 • Explain the task. Read out the examples. Focus Ss' attention on the comparative/superlative forms used in the example.
(not) as + adj + as (used to say that two people, animals etc are/aren't similar)
more/less + adj + than (used to say that two people, animals etc aren't similar)
much + comparative degree + than (emphatic comparative)
the + superlative + of/in (comparing one person/place/thing/etc with more than one of the same kind)
• Quickly revise superlative forms. Say adjectives from those listed in Ex. 1. Ss say the appropriate superlative form. Write them on the board to elicit theory.
e.g. crowded – the most crowded of
clean – the cleanest of
noisy – the noisiest of etc

• Ss make sentences. Any sentence is acceptable provided it is grammatically correct.

ANSWER KEY

My town isn't as crowded as New York.
My town is much quieter than York.
My town is the most peaceful place of the three.
My town is busier than York.
My town is less noisy than New York.   etc

3 • Play the recording. Ss listen and repeat individually. Present these sentences by giving examples, miming etc.
e.g. **Sounds great!** Ask a S: *Where did you go on holiday? (Rome.) What did you do there? (I went sightseeing, shopping, etc.)* Say: **Sounds great!** etc
• Ask Ss to look at the sentences for one minute, then close their books and try to remember as many sentences as possible. This can be done as a competition game. Divide the class into two teams. The teams, in turn, say sentences. Each correct sentence gets 1 point. The team with the most points is the winner.
e.g. Team A S1: Sounds great!
Team B S1: You lucky thing.   etc

4 • Explain the task. Ss read sentences 1-3 silently. Play the recording. Ss do the exercise. Check Ss' answers.

ANSWER KEY

1 Louise   2 Kate   3 Tony

• Read out sentence No 1. Ask Ss to underline **had just sat down** and **noticed**. Ask which of the two actions happened first *(had just sat down)*. Explain that this verb form is the past perfect and is used to describe an action which happened before another one in the past. Elicit the form from Ss (had + past participle). Quickly drill your Ss. Say verbs in the infinitive form. Ss say the relevant past perfect form.
e.g. T: play
S1: had played
T: swim
S2: had swum
T: write
S3: had written   etc

5 a) Allow Ss two to three minutes to read the dialogues silently and answer the questions. Check Ss' answers, then Ss explain the words by giving examples, synonyms or opposites. Ss can look up the words in their dictionaries.
e.g. **definitely:** absolutely   etc

ANSWER KEY

1 Kate   2 Tony   3 Paula
4 The airline left his luggage in London (it turned up three days after he had arrived in China.)

b) Ss look up the words in the dictionaries, and suggest synonyms. Check Ss' answers.

SUGGESTED ANSWER KEY

are back: return
allowed: permitted
realised: understood
Never mind: That's OK
have to: must
go on: continue
you're joking: you're saying something I find hard to believe
lucky thing: lucky person
turn up: appear
in the least: at all

c) • Play the recording for Ex 4 again. Ss listen and follow the lines, then take roles and in pairs, read out the dialogues.

• As an extension, Ss ask and answer rolling questions based on the dialogues.

e.g. S1: Did Kate have a nice time?
S2: Yes, she did. Where did she go?
S3: To York. Did she like it?
S4: Yes, she did.   etc

Suggested Homework

1 **Vocabulary:** words in Exs 1 & 3 (p. 44), words in bold Ex. 5a (p. 44)
2 **Speaking:** Exs 1 & 2 (p. 44)
3 **Dictation:** any six sentences from Ex. 3 (p. 44)
4 **Reading aloud:** dialogues A-C Ex. 5a (p. 45)
5 **Writing:** six sentences from Ex. 2 (p. 44)

A

Amy: Kate! You're back! Did you have a good time?

Kate: Yes, thanks. York is so beautiful!

Amy: Were you able to relax, then?

Kate: Oh, **definitely**. It's much quieter and cleaner than London.

Amy: How's that?

Kate: Well, for one thing, cars aren't **allowed** in the **city centre** during the day so there's less noise and pollution.

Amy: That's great! What did you do there?

Kate: I visited the museums and did some shopping. The **antique shops** in The Shambles are fantastic.

Amy: Sounds great!

Kate: Yes, except when I got there I realised I had forgotten to take my camera, so I don't have any photos to show you.

Amy: Never mind. You'll just have to go again, won't you?

B

Mike: Louise, is that a postcard from Paula?

Louise: Yes, and listen to this. You'll never **guess** what happened while she was on holiday in New York.

Mike: Go on then, tell me!

Louise: She had just sat down at a café when she **noticed** Julia Roberts was sitting at the next table.

Mike: You're joking!

Louise: No, it's true. She got her **autograph** and took a picture of her.

Mike: Perhaps we should go to New York and take some photos of famous people too.

Louise: Hmm. There's only one problem with that.

Mike: What do you mean?

Louise: The tickets are far too expensive!

C

Pat: Hello, Tony! I haven't seen you for ages!

Tony: Hi, Pat. Yes, I've been away. I've been on a trip to China.

Pat: China? You lucky thing! What was it like?

Tony: Well, all the cities I visited were very crowded, but the people were really friendly.

Pat: So, did you have a great time?

Tony: Oh, yes. It's the most amazing place I've ever been to. The only problem was the **airline** had left my **luggage** in London, so it didn't **turn up** until three days after I had arrived there. I had to buy some clothes and a few other things.

Pat: Oh dear. It didn't **spoil** your trip, did it?

Tony: Not in the least.

c) In pairs, read out the dialogues.

YORK

45

Vocabulary

• Scenery & Sights

6 Which of the following would you find in a town; in the countryside; both?

countryside   town

• fields • factories • department stores • car parks
• libraries • suburbs • nightclubs • museums
• cottages • fashion houses • shopping centres
• hospitals • woods • restaurants• cinemas
• offices • banks • police stations
• universities • colleges • schools • 5-star hotels
• squares • beaches • rivers • lakes

You can find fields in the countryside.

7 Match the adjectives to the nouns, then use them to describe the place you live.

1 narrow, quiet, congested, deserted   a beaches
2 picturesque, tiny, old-fashioned, attractive   b streets
3 sandy, clean, crowded, isolated   c cottages
4 huge, attractive, multi-storey, tall   d restaurants
5 expensive, popular, local, traditional   e buildings
6 well-kept, huge, quiet, clean   f parks
7 important, noisy, modern, pretty, large   g village
8 unspoilt, picturesque, peaceful, boring   h town

Elham is a picturesque village with quiet, deserted streets and old-fashioned cottages.

Speaking

8 A friend of yours is visiting your town for the first time on a two-day business trip. He will have a few hours free each afternoon. Suggest:

– places he should visit
– shops where he can buy presents for his family
– food he should try

9 Look at the pictures in Ex. 6. In pairs, discuss:

– the best place for a family to live
– the pros & cons of living in either place

Listening

• Holiday Experiences

10 a) Listen and match the people to their holiday problems.

People		Problems
1	Jane	A lose passport
2	Peter	B airline cancel flight
3	Jennifer	C get food poisoning
4	the Smiths	D lose credit card
5	Ronald	E be seasick
		F get sunburn
		G get on the wrong bus

b) Complete the sentences, as in the example.

1 Jane had to borrow some money because she had lost her credit card.
2 Peter had to stay overnight at a hotel because ....
3 Jennifer had to spend her holiday in her hotel room because ....
4 The Smiths' daughter had to drive more than 300km to pick them up because ....
5 Ronald couldn't eat or drink anything because ....

c) Have you ever experienced any of these problems while on holiday? Talk about them.

11 a) Where would you hear the following? Listen and underline the correct word.

1 aeroplane – hotel
2 train station – airport
3 bus station – train station
4 hotel – shop
5 department store – library
6 aeroplane – train

b) Look at the words. Listen again and circle the words/phrases heard. Make sentences using the words.

booking
a single, a double or a twin
seat belt   take-off
flight   customers   has been delayed   credit card
single or return
first or economy   platform 6
black or white

Lesson 2 (pp. 46 - 47)

* Check Ss' HW (10').

6 Explain the task. Ss, in closed pairs, look through the list of words and do the exercise. Check Ss' answers. Ss also say what you can do/buy etc in each place.

> **ANSWER KEY:** T (town), C (countryside), B (both)
> fields C, factories T, department stores T, car parks T, libraries B, suburbs T, nightclubs T, museums T, cottages C, fashion houses T, shopping centres T, hospitals T, woods C, restaurants B, cinemas T, offices T, banks T, police stations B, universities T, colleges T, schools B, 5-star hotels T, squares B, beaches B, rivers B, lakes B

7 Explain the task, then Ss, in closed pairs, do the exercise. Check Ss' answers, then explain any unknown vocabulary by giving examples, synonyms or opposites. (e.g. **congested:** with lots of traffic). Ss then describe their town.

> **ANSWER KEY:** a 3, b 1, c 2, d 5, e 4,
> f 6, g 8, h 7

> **SUGGESTED ANSWER KEY:** I live in York. It is a pretty town, with quiet narrow streets and attractive buildings. There are lots of clean parks and traditional restaurants there.

8 Explain the task. Write useful phrases on the board (see phrases in bold below). Allow Ss two minutes to prepare their suggestions. Check Ss' answers.

> **SUGGESTED ANSWER KEY:** You **should** visit the Jorvik Viking Centre to see what York was like when Vikings lived there. **Don't miss a visit** to the Castle Museum to see the fascinating exhibitions. You **can** walk around The Shambles and look at the many antique shops or the souvenir shops. You **should** pay a visit to one of the many restaurants, where you can try the traditional English dish of roast beef and Yorkshire pudding.

9 Explain the task. Write useful phrases on the board (see phrases in bold below), then Ss work in closed pairs. Check Ss' answers, then ask some pairs to report back to the class.

> **SUGGESTED ANSWER KEY**
>
> A: **I think** that the best place for a family to live is the town.
> B: **Really? I believe** the best place for a family is the countryside.
> A: **I agree, but on the other hand** there aren't any shopping centres or cinemas, **so** they would get bored. There are lots of things to do in the town.
> B: **That's true, but** there are lots of parks in the countryside where children can play safely, and there are no busy streets.
> A: **You're right.** The countryside is the best place for a family to live. etc
>
> ---
>
> A: **I think** that the pros of living in the countryside are that it is beautiful and peaceful. You are living in a natural environment.
> B: **Yes, and furthermore**, the air is clean **because** it is not polluted by traffic or factories. **However**, there are no restaurants, cinemas or shopping centres, so there isn't much to do.   etc

10 a) Explain the task. Point out that only five problems will be heard. Ask Ss to read out the prompts. Elicit/Explain the meaning of any unknown words by giving examples, synonyms or opposites. Play the recording. Ss do the exercise. Check Ss' answers.

> **ANSWER KEY:** 1 D, 2 B, 3 F, 4 G, 5 E

TAPESCRIPT

Speaker 1:
female I was on holiday last year in Paris, when I ran into Mrs Melville, my old French teacher, at the Louvre. She'd helped me so much when I was at school that I really wanted to do something to repay her, so I invited her to lunch. We went to a really wonderful restaurant and I told her to order whatever she wanted - that it was my treat. It was great talking about old times, and the food was brilliant. Then, the bill came, and I opened my bag to get out my credit card. But I couldn't find it. I searched everywhere, but it was nowhere to be found. I didn't even have enough cash to pay the bill. So, in the end I had to borrow money from Mrs Melville. I was so embarrassed. I got her address, of course, and paid her back as soon as I could, but that's not the point, is it?

Speaker 2:
male A couple of years ago I was on my way back from San Francisco. Everything was wonderful until I got to the airport to come home. The airlines had cancelled all flights back to Europe due to bad weather. We waited in the departure lounge for hours. It was incredibly crowded and, of course, everyone had lots of luggage. But all we could do was sit and wait. Finally, we were all put on buses and taken to nearby hotels for the night. The next day we went to the airport again and luckily we only had to wait a couple of hours before we got put on a flight home.

Speaker 3:
female I went to a beach resort for the first time a few years back. It was beautiful – the longest beaches I'd ever seen, lined with palms. On the first day I found the perfect location on the beach. I put on my suntan oil, lay back - and fell asleep. I woke up hours later, alone on the beach, and red all over. I had the worst sunburn of my life and I had to spend my ten-day holiday in my hotel room, covered in cream. Then, to make matters worse, I started peeling as soon as I arrived back home. I went back to work with a red peeling face. What a nightmare!

Speaker 4:
male Last year, we decided to visit our daughter. She was living in Spain at the time, wasn't she, dear? Now, we wanted to surprise her so we made all the arrangements ourselves. The flight arrived in Madrid on time and then we had to catch a bus to Valladolid. As soon as we got off the bus we called our daughter so that she could come and pick us up. It was only then that we realised we'd taken the wrong bus - we were in Valdepeñas, not Valladolid! Our daughter did come and pick us up, but she had to drive more than 300km to get us! Much longer than we had planned!

Speaker 5:
male I had a terrible year, so I decided to treat myself to a cruise. I chose the most luxurious one I could afford - a tropical island hop. What I didn't take into consideration was that it was the rainy season. The seas were really rough, it rained almost constantly and I got seasick. I spent most of my time either in bed or in the bathroom. I couldn't eat or drink anything except barley water. So much for the gourmet food! What a waste!

b) Allow Ss two minutes to complete the sentences. Check Ss' answers.

> **ANSWER KEY:** 2 ... the airline had cancelled his flight;
> 3 ... she had got sunburn; 4 ... they had got on the wrong bus; 5 ... he had got seasick

c) Ss' own answer

11 a) Explain the task. Play the recording. Ss listen and underline. Check Ss' answers.

> **ANSWER KEY:** 1 hotel, 2 airport, 3 train station, 4 hotel, 5 department store, 6 aeroplane

b) Play the recording. Ss listen and circle, then make sentences.

TAPESCRIPT

1 I'm afraid I don't have any booking under that name, sir.
2 This is an announcement for all passengers waiting to board British Airways Flight 207 to Mexico. This flight has been delayed until further notice. Please check the monitors for further information. We apologise for any inconvenience this may cause.
3 The Express train for Brighton is now boarding at Platform 6. Platform 6 for the Express train to Brighton.
4 Would you like a single, a double or a twin?
5 We would like to remind all customers of today's book sale on the third floor. There are plenty of special offers, so don't miss out!
6 Please fasten your seat belt during take-off. All passengers are advised to keep their seat belts fastened for the duration of the flight.

> **ANSWER KEY: Words to be circled:** booking, a single, a double or a twin, seat belt, has been delayed, flight, platform 6, take-off, customers

Suggested sentences: When you stay at a hotel you have to **make a booking**. Please, fasten your **seat belt**.   etc

12 a) Explain the key, then read out the example. Ss use the table to make sentences using **very, quite** and **not very**.

> **SUGGESTED ANSWER KEY**
>
> *Mexico City is not very expensive, but it's very big and noisy.*   *etc*

b) Go through the examples with Ss, then Ss talk about the cities. Refer Ss to the Grammar Reference section for more details.

> **ANSWER KEY**
>
> 1 *We form the comparative form of adjectives by adding* **-er/-ier** *to short adjectives or* **more** *to longer adjectives. We form the superlative form by adding* **-est/-iest** *to short adjectives or* **the most** *to longer adjectives.*
> 2 *We use* **than** *in the comparative and the ...* **of/in** *in the superlative.*
> 3 *Much*
> 4 *as ... as*
> 5 *Less*

- Ss go through the table of irregular forms. As an extension, ask Ss to close their books then, in teams, say the comparative/superlative forms of various adjectives. Each correct answer gets 1 point. The team with the most points is the winner.
  Suggested list of adjs: good, noisy, old, healthy, delicious, hot, funny, clever, little, bad, sunny, warm, expensive, comfortable, far, much   etc
  e.g.   T: good
     Team A S1: better – best
             T: noisy
     Team B S1: noisier – noisiest etc

- **Optional Activity**
  Prepare cards of 6 famous people (3 men, 3 women) from magazines, newspapers etc. Stick them on the board. Give/Elicit a list of adjectives for Ss to use. Ss make sentences comparing these people.
  Suggested list: old, young, tall, short, good-looking, beautiful, handsome, pretty, serious, friendly, smart, slim, thick/thin/long/short/dark/light hair   etc
      e.g. Tom Cruise is younger than Harrison Ford.
             Tom Cruise isn't as tall as Harrison Ford.
             Harrison Ford is the most handsome of the three.   etc

13 Explain the task. Ss do the exercise. Check Ss' answers on the board.

> **ANSWER KEY**
>
> 1 the hottest   5 more expensive
> 2 the fastest   6 the tastiest
> 3 smaller   7 more intelligent,
> 4 the funniest   the most intelligent

14 Go through the table with Ss. Play the recording. Ss listen and do the exercise. Check Ss' answers, then Ss make sentences using comparative/superlative forms.

> **ANSWER KEY**
>
> | | Tony's Gym | The Health & Fitness Centre | Universal Health Club |
> |---|---|---|---|
> | Membership fee (per month) | £30 | £85 | £100 |
> | No. of Members | 438 | 1000 | 321 |
> | Facilities | ★★ | ★★★ | ★★★★ |
> | Opening Hours | 8am - 7pm | 10am - 10pm | 9am - 7pm |
> | Equipment | 2 years old | 1 year old | 6 months old |

TAPESCRIPT

Announcer 1: Join Tony's Gym today and pay a special membership fee of only £30 a month! 438 members can't be wrong! Tony's Gym has a good range of facilities and we're open every day from 8am until 7pm. All our equipment is no more than two years old, so everything is in great condition. Get yourself in great condition, too! Call Tony's Gym on 0700 263549 today!

Announcer 2: The Health and Fitness Centre in Winkley Square is the perfect place for you to get into shape. With a membership fee of just £85 a month, you can join our 1,000 members and get fit in style. Our facilities are very good, with a variety of machines and equipment. The Health and Fitness Centre is open from 10am until 10pm every day. All our equipment is only one year old and ready for you to use. Visit us today and find out why the Health and Fitness Centre is the best choice in town.

Announcer 3: Universal Health Club is now open in Church Street, with a membership of just £100 a month. We already have 321 members, so join now and find out why the Universal Health Club is so popular! Is it our excellent facilities, or our long opening hours? We're open from 9am to 7pm daily, so you can work out at a time that suits you. Try out all our new equipment – it's only six months old! Call the Universal Health Club now on 0802 679134.

> **SUGGESTED ANSWER KEY**
>
> *Tony's Gym doesn't have as many members as The Health and Fitness Centre.*
> *Tony's Gym is open longer than Universal Health Club.*
> *Universal Health Club has the newest equipment of all three.*
> *Tony's Gym hasn't got as good facilities as Universal Health Club.*
> *Universal Health Club has got the most members of the three.   etc*

Project (p. 47)

Explain the task. Elicit how a letter to a friend starts/ends. Elicit useful sentences to begin/finish off the letter and write them on the board.
e.g. **(Beg.)** Hi! How are you? / Sorry, I didn't write to you earlier but ...
     (End.) That's all, I guess. / I hope this will help you decide. etc
Ask: *Which of the three gyms is the most expensive? (Universal Health Club.) Which is the cheapest of all? (Tony's Gym.)* Ss then make sentences comparing the three gyms.
After Ss have done the exercise orally in class, then assign it as written HW. See Writing Project 4 for the Answer Key.

> **Suggested Homework**
>
> 1 **Vocabulary:** Exs 6, 7 & 11b (p. 46)
> 2 **Dictation:** any ten words from Vocabulary with example or definition
> 3 **Speaking:** Exs 8 & 9 (p. 46), Ex. 14 (p. 47)
> 4 **Project:** (p. 47)

• Past Perfect Continuous

19 Compare the sentences below. Which sentence puts emphasis on the duration of an action? What tense has been used?

a) Ann **had typed** four letters when her boss entered the office.

b) Ann **had been typing** letters for four hours that morning when her boss entered the office.

Affirmative	I/you/he/etc had been typing …
Negative	I/you/he/etc hadn't been typing …
Interrogative	Had I/you/he/etc been typing?
Short Answers	Yes, I/you/he etc had. No, I/you/he etc hadn't.

Time expressions used with the past perfect continuous: **for, since, how long, before, until,** etc

20 Put the verbs in the list into the *past perfect continuous*.

• walk • talk • save • play • work • wait

1 Helen .... on the phone for an hour when her father told her to hurry up.

2 John was very tired. He .... hard all day.

3 Sarah was fed up. She .... for the bus for an hour.

4 Tom .... rugby all afternoon and he was covered in mud.

5 Laura .... for an hour before she realised she was going in the wrong direction.

6 Terry .... his money all summer so he could buy a new bicycle.

Listening

21 Listen and underline the correct phrase, then ask and answer, as in the example.

John:	cut wood / <u>wash the car</u>
Anne:	listen to music / do the vacuuming
Simon:	ride his bike / play football
Bob & Emily:	play tennis / swim
Sally:	water the plants / type letters

A: *Had John been cutting wood all morning?*

B: *No, he hadn't. He had been washing the car.*

22 Complete the sentences, as in the example.

1 Jane was exhausted because she had been working hard all day.

2 Peter was angry because .... with his brother all morning.

3 Diana was sleepy because .... TV all night.

4 Jenny's feet hurt because .... for hours.

5 Paul's shoes were muddy because .... football in the park.

Communication
(booking a hotel room)

23 a) Listen and fill in, then in pairs read out the dialogue.

A: Good morning, **Crown Hotel**.

B: Yes, good morning. I'd like to book a **room**, please.

A: Certainly, **Sir**. When for?

B: 1) .... July for **two nights**.

A: That's fine. Would you like a single or a double **room**?

B: 2) ...., please.

A: Could I take your name, please?

B: Yes, it's **John Black**. How 3) .... does the **room** cost?

A: It's 4) .... a night including **breakfast**.

B: Great! Do I have to pay **a deposit**?

A: **No, not at all.** You pay **when you check 5)** ....

B: Right then. Thank you very much.

A: Thank you, **Mr Black**.

b) Use the prompts to act out a similar dialogue.

• Norten's Travel • Mediterranean cruise
• Madam • 21st August • two weeks • cabin
• Vicky White • cruise • £1,650 • person
• all meals • in advance • Yes, you do.
• a month before

c) Close your books and try to remember four questions a receptionist would ask when you book a room.

Pronunciation (intonation in questions of choice)

24 Listen and repeat.

• Which is the deepest ocean in the world, the Atlantic, the Pacific or the Indian?

• Which river is longer, the Amazon or the Nile?

• Which is the fastest animal in the world, the zebra or the cheetah?

Listening & Reading

25 Look at the articles. Where do you think you could read them? Which of these countries would you most like to visit? Why?

Tip Read the questions, then scan the articles and try to find words which match the questions.

A | POLAND

Whether you are interested in culture or countryside, Poland has something for you. With a long, fascinating history and rich traditions, it certainly won't leave you bored.

Warsaw is the capital city and the **cultural centre** of Poland. Here you can visit the Royal Castle and Lazienki Park, as well as many museums and theatres. Don't miss the Royal Route, a line of streets filled with grand palaces, ancient monuments, elegant shops, art galleries, and traditional restaurants and cafés. An evening of theatre, opera or ballet at the National Theatre or a performance of **exquisite** classical music from the Warsaw Philharmonic will be an unforgettable experience.

Those who want to relax and spend some time by the sea should visit one of Poland's many **health resorts** in Pomerania. Nearby Warmia is the perfect place to relax by a beautiful lake or walk through a green forest. You can also go horse riding, whitewater rafting or take a trip up into the mountains.

With so much unspoiled countryside, and so many impressive sights, any visit to Poland is sure to be the experience of a lifetime!

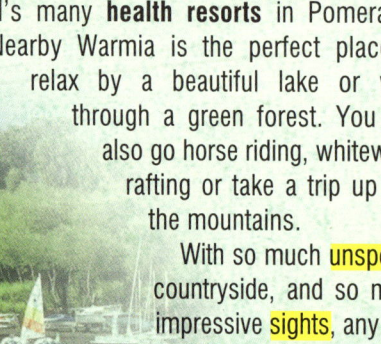

26 Listen and match.

1	Poland	a	rent mopeds
2	Portugal	b	visit health resorts
3	Chile	c	buy colourful rugs

27 a) Read the three articles. Then, for questions 1-10, choose from A-C. The articles may be used more than once.

Which article(s) mention(s):

- a volcano
- beaches
- luxurious hotels
- a national dish
- a castle
- cobbled streets
- grand palaces

1	C

2		3	
4		5	
6			
7		8	
9			
10			

b) Which words in the texts are similar in your language?

c) Read the texts in Ex. 25 again and explain the words in bold. Then, suggest an appropriate title for the three articles.

d) Find synonyms for the highlighted words.

Vocabulary Practice

28 Fill in the correct word from the list, then make sentences using the completed phrases.

- ancient • cobbled • trendy • green
- beach • suit • winding • dry • outdoor
- ethnic

1	.... shops	6	.... streets
2	.... resorts	7	.... monuments
3	.... every taste	8	.... restaurants
4	.... rivers	9	.... desert
5	.... cafés	10	.... forest

Lesson 4 (pp. 50 - 51)

* Check Ss' HW (10').

25 Ss look at the articles, then answer the questions.

SUGGESTED ANSWER KEY

Travel magazine.
I'd like to visit Chile.
Because I'd like to see the Andes.
You could probably read them in a travel brochure.

26 Ss read the prompts. Play the recording for Ss to listen and do the exercise. Check Ss' answers.

ANSWER KEY

1 b   2 a   3 c

27 a) • Explain the task. Point out that Ss should read the questions first, then quickly scan the articles trying to find the words which are in questions 1-10. Ss can underline these words so that they can easily find the answers to the questions.
 • Do question 1 with Ss, then allow them three minutes to do the exercise. Check Ss' answers.

ANSWER KEY

2 B ⎫ in any order   7 A ⎫ in any order
3 C ⎭   8 B ⎭
4 B ⎫ in any order   9 B
5 C ⎭   10 A
6 C

b) Ss' own answers

c) • Ss explain the words in bold by giving synonyms, opposites or examples. Help Ss where necessary.
 • Then Ss, in closed pairs, think of an appropriate title for the three articles.

SUGGESTED ANSWER KEY

 • Countries to visit
 • Holiday destinations

d) Ss look up the words in their dictionaries. Check Ss' answers.

SUGGESTED ANSWER KEY

elegant: stylish   facilities: amenities
performance: concert   out and about: around
unspoiled: perfect   delicious: tasty
sights: things to see

Further practice

After Ss have done Ex. 27, ask them to visit:
http://cityguide.lycos.com/southamerica/south_sam/ARGBuenos Aires.htm   OR
http://www.civi/a.com/brasilia/bsb_aug/htm
and write an article similar to the ones in Ex. 27.

28 • Allow Ss two minutes to fill in the words. Check Ss' answers, then ask Ss to make sentences. This exercise can be treated as a competition game. Ss, in teams, make sentences. Each correct sentence gets 1 point. The team with the most points is the winner.

ANSWER KEY

1 trendy   6 cobbled
2 beach   7 ancient
3 suit   8 ethnic
4 winding   9 dry
5 outdoor   10 green

 • **Competition Game:** As an extension write the following phrases on the board. Ss, in teams, make sentences. Each correct answer gets 1 point. The team with the most points is the winner.
 Suggested phrases: enchanting countryside, perfect blend, luxurious hotel, outdoor cafés, ethnic restaurants, suit every taste, health resorts, rich traditions, city centre, holiday destination, etc
 e.g. Team A S1: Portugal has got enchanting countryside.
       Team B S1: Poland is the perfect blend of the modern and the traditional.

4

29 Allow Ss two minutes to fill in the prepositions. Check Ss' answers, then ask Ss to make sentences. Ss should memorise these phrases. This exercise can be treated as a competition/game. Ss, in teams, make sentences. Each correct sentence gets 1 point. The team with the most points is the winner.

ANSWER KEY

1	in	5	with	8	in
2	on	6	on	9	on
3	of	7	in	10	in
4	of				

30 • Ss, in teams, make sentences using the phrases. Each correct sentence gets 1 point. The team with the most points is the winner.
    e.g. Team A S1: There are lots of **ancient monuments** in Poland.
    Team B S1: There are **elegant shops** in Warsaw where you can buy high quality things. etc

   • Ss are allowed two to three minutes to prepare their monologues about their country. Check Ss' answers orally in class.

SUGGESTED ANSWER KEY

I come from Argentina. It is a very beautiful country. The countryside is full of impressive sights from long winding rivers to beautiful sandy beaches like Mar del Plata, a popular tourist resort. There are spectacular high mountains as well as wide grasslands and beautiful lakes. If you visit Argentina, you will be amazed by the unspoiled countryside.
Our capital city, Buenos Aires, has wide tree-lined avenues full of trendy shops and large luxurious hotels. You shouldn't miss a visit to one of our museums, art galleries or theatres at night. You can also visit a traditional restaurant before you take a walk along the banks of the Rio de la Plata. Argentina is a truly beautiful country.

31 Explain the task. Ss do the exercises, then make sentences as in the example.

ANSWER KEY

1	cheap shop	4	shallow river
2	deserted beach	5	dreadful sight
3	noisy restaurant		

It was the most deserted beach I've even been to.
It was the noisiest restaurant I've ever eaten at.
It was the shallowest river I've ever swum in.
It was the most dreadful sight I've ever seen.

32 Read out the rule and example. Ss do the exercise. Check Ss' answers.

ANSWER KEY

1	a two-week cruise	3	a ten-minute ride
2	a five-star hotel	4	a candle-lit dinner

(Suggested Homework)

1 **Vocabulary:** Ex. 28 (p. 50) and Exs 29 & 31 (p. 51), words in bold in articles (pp. 50-51)
2 **Dictation:** any ten words from Vocabulary with example or definition
3 **Speaking:** Ex. 28 (p. 51)
4 **Writing:** seven sentences about your country using the phrases in Ex. 30 (p. 51)

51(T)

B PORTUGAL

Portugal is one of Europe's most fascinating countries, with fantastic beach resorts, beautiful towns and cities and **enchanting** countryside. It is the perfect **blend** of the traditional and modern and has something to offer every traveller.

The Algarve, in the south of Portugal, is where you will find the most popular tourist resorts, such as Lagos. It has **superb** beaches and luxurious hotels, as well as facilities for renting **mopeds**, bicycles and even horses, so you can get out and about and enjoy the wonderful scenery.

Lisbon, the capital of Portugal, is one of the oldest capitals in Europe, with a fascinating mixture of beautiful building **styles**. The lower part of the city contains the busy new town, with its **trendy** shops and outdoor cafés. The old town, Alfamar, with its **cobbled** streets, narrow **alleys** and colourful buildings, rests on the upper level. This is where all the restaurants and nightclubs can be found. Don't forget to visit the castle, which offers a wonderful view over the city and the Rio Tejo.

Whichever part of Portugal you choose to visit, one thing is certain. You will have an **unforgettable** holiday.

C CHILE

Chile, home of the Andes Mountains and the Atacama Desert, is a wonderful place for a holiday. With an amazing range of scenery, from dry desert to green forests and **winding** rivers to sandy beaches, it is a holiday destination to suit all tastes and pockets.

For the perfect adventure holiday, Pucon, a small town at the foot of Volcano Villarrica in Chile's Lake District, is the place to go. You can go rafting, water-skiing or boating on the Trancura River. If you are in good shape, climb to the **snow-capped** top of Volcano Villarrica and enjoy the **panoramic** beauty of the Andes. You can also try horse riding or fishing, or simply relax in the **hot springs** that surround the Bio-Bio River.

For the perfect **city break**, go to Santiago, Chile's capital. Here you will find luxurious hotels, shopping centres, museums, theatres and fun parks. You can eat at a variety of **ethnic** restaurants and try foods from around the world. Be sure to try the national dish, *empanada*. It's delicious! You can buy colourful **rugs** and beautiful jewellery in the large shopping centres and traditional markets which are open daily.

Chile is a magical country with something to **suit** every **taste**. You're sure to have the time of your life there.

---

29 Fill in: *on, of, in, with*, then make sentences using the phrases.

1 .... the city centre; 2 to go .... a trip; 3 to have the time .... your life; 4 to take a picture .... sb/sth; 5 filled .... sth; 6 .... the upper level; 7 to be interested .... sth; 8 to be .... good shape; 9 .... holiday; 10 .... the south of

30 Use the phrases to make sentences about each country. Then, use some of the phrases to talk about your country.

Poland: • cultural centre • elegant shops • traditional restaurants • unspoiled countryside • impressive sights • unforgettable experience

Portugal: • most fascinating countries • perfect blend • trendy shops • cobbled streets • narrow alleys

Chile: • amazing range of scenery • dry desert • green forests • winding rivers • sandy beaches • snow-capped volcano • colourful rugs • shopping centres

31 Fill in the opposites of the words in bold, then make sentences as in the example.

• noisy • shallow • deserted • cheap • dreadful

1 **expensive** shop ≠ ....; 2 **crowded** beach ≠ ....; 3 **quiet** restaurant ≠ ....; 4 **deep** river ≠ ....; 5 **impressive** sight ≠ ....

It was the cheapest shop I've ever been in.

Word Formation
(compound nouns)

32 Study the theory box, then make phrases.

> To form compound nouns we can put a compound adjective (i.e. two words joined together with a hyphen) in front of a noun. The noun is always singular.
> e.g. *a trip that takes two hours → a two-hour trip*

1 a cruise that takes two weeks ....
2 a hotel that has five stars ....
3 a ride that lasts ten minutes ....
4 a dinner that is lit by candles ....

Phrasal Verbs

33 Read the table, then fill in the correct particle.

> **turn back** - to stop and return the way you came
> **turn down** - 1) to refuse a request or an offer, 2) to reduce the amount of sound or heat
> **turn into** - to change and become something else
> **turn off** - to stop (TV, heater, light etc) working
> **turn on** - to start (TV, heater, light etc) working
> **turn out** - 1) to prove to be sth, 2) to appear, be present
> **turn up** - 1) to arrive somewhere, 2) to increase the amount of sound or heat

1 Peter finally turned .... at the meeting over an hour late.
2 Sarah was sure that things would turn .... fine.
3 As the weather was getting worse, they decided to turn ....
4 Can you please turn that music ....? I can't hear what Jim is saying.
5 Martha was offered a better job, but she turned it ....
6 He parked the car in the garage and turned .... the engine.
7 Turn .... the TV. There is a film on that I want to watch.
8 Jim turned .... to be an efficient worker.

Writing (a letter to a friend about a visit to a place)

When we write a letter to a friend about a short visit to a place we usually write four paragraphs. We start with Dear and our friend's first name. In the **first paragraph**, we write our opening remarks and state the place we visited, the length of our stay and where we stayed. In the **second paragraph**, we write what the place is like. In the **third paragraph** we write what we did/saw there and what happened to us there. In the **last paragraph**, we write our closing remarks.

We normally use present tenses to describe the place and past tenses to describe what we did there. We use short forms and a variety of descriptive adjectives. We end our letter with Yours,/Love,/Kisses, etc and our first name.

34 Read the letter and correct the mistakes. Write *S* (for spelling), *G* (for grammar) or *WO* (for word order). Then, underline the topic sentences, and suggest other appropriate ones.

Dear Jim,

week's - G

Sorry I haven't written for a while, but I've just got back from a weeks holiday in Buenos Aires. We stayed in one of the city's best hotels on the Plaza de Mayo, right in the hurt of the city. It was ideal to sightseeing and shoping.

Buenos Aires is an amazing place. It's the larger city in the Argentina, very modern and exciting, but relaxing and cultured at the same time. Did you knew it has the world's widest street?

There's plenty to do there, too. We spent more of our time shopping and visiting the main sights, like the 'Casa Rosada' – it is one of the more beautiful buildings I've ever seen! Unfortunately, I had a mishap on the last day. While I was shopping, my passport I lost. As you can imagine, I was realy upset, but when I went to police station to report it, some kind person already had handed it in. What relief!

Well, all my news is that. Hope you are OK. See you soon.

Yours sincerely,
Barry

1 Who is writing the letter?
2 Who is going to read the letter?
3 Does the writer use any short forms or a variety of adjectives? Why?
4 Is it a formal or informal letter?
5 What other endings can you think of?

Lesson 5 (pp. 52-53)

33 Read out the table explaining any unknown words to Ss. Ss, then do the exercise. Check Ss' answers. Ss should memorise the meanings.

> **ANSWER KEY**
>
> | | | | | | | | |
> |---|---|---|---|---|---|---|---|
> | 1 | up | 3 | back | 5 | down | 7 | on |
> | 2 | out | 4 | down | 6 | off | 8 | out |

Writing (p. 52)

Read out the theory table, and explain any unknown words to Ss. Explain that in such pieces of writing we use contracted forms. e.g. *I'm, Here's, We've* etc and a chatty, friendly tone.

34 • Allow Ss two minutes to read the article and do the exercise. Check Ss' answers.

> **ANSWER KEY**
>
> week's – G
>
> Dear Jim,
>
> Sorry I haven't written for a while, but I've just got back from a weeks holiday in Buenos Aires. We stayed in one of the city's best hotels on the Plaza de Mayo, right in the hurt of the city. It was ideal to sightseeing and shoping — *shopping – S* — for – G — heart – S
>
> no the – G — Buenos Aires is an amazing place. It's the larger city in the Argentina, very modern and exciting, but relaxing and cultured at the same time. Did you knew it has the world's widest street? — largest – G — know – G
>
> There's plenty to do there, too. We spent more of our time shopping and visiting the main sights, like the 'Casa Rosada' – it is one of the more beautiful buildings I've ever seen! Unfortunately, I had a mishap on the last day. While I was shopping, my passport I lost. As you can imagine I was realy upset, but when I went to the police station to report it, some kind person already had handed it in. What relief! — most – G — most – G — I lost my passport – WO — had already handed – WO — What a relief! – G
>
> really – S
>
> Well, all my news is that Hope you are OK. See you soon. — that's all my news – WO
>
> Yours sincerely,
> Barry — sincerely not needed, wrong register
>
> **Topic sentences:**
>
> **Para 1:** Sorry I haven't written ... Buenos Aires.
> Suggested: Hi! How are you?
>
> **Para 2:** Buenos Aires is an amazing place.
> Suggested: Buenos Aires is fantastic.
>
> **Para 3:** There's plenty to do there, too.
> Suggested: You can never feel bored there.
>
> **Para 4:** Well, that's all my news.
> Suggested: Do drop me a line.

• Ss answer the questions.

> **ANSWER KEY**
>
> 1 Barry.
> 2 Jim.
> 3 Yes, he does, because he is describing a place he has recently visited.
> Para 1 – ... I haven't ...; ... I've ... .
> Para 2 – It's ... .
> Para 3 – There's ...; ... it's ...; ... I've ... .
> Para 4 – ... that's ... .
> 4 It is an informal letter and he is writing to a friend.
> 5 Suggested: That's all for now. Do drop me a line. See you soon.

35 Explain the task, then Ss, in closed pairs, do the exercise. Check Ss' answers.

> **ANSWER KEY**
>
> | | | | |
> |---|---|---|---|
> | 1 | I (ending) | 7 | F (beginning) |
> | 2 | F (beginning) | 8 | I (beginning) |
> | 3 | F (ending) | 9 | F (ending) |
> | 4 | F (beginning) | 10 | I (ending) |
> | 5 | I (beginning) | 11 | F (beginning) |
> | 6 | I (ending) | 12 | I (ending) |

36
- Elicit from Ss possible reasons for writing a letter to a friend (congratulate sb on sth, asking for advice etc)
  e.g. Ask: *Imagine your friend had passed his exams. What letter would you write? (A letter congratulating him.)*   etc
- Read out the situation in item 1. Choose a S to read out the example. Ss, in closed pairs, write possible beginnings/endings. Check Ss' answers round the class, then ask some Ss to report back to the class.

> **SUGGESTED ANSWER KEY**
>
> 2 *opening*
>   *Hi, I hope you're well. I know you're a sailor. Could you give me a bit of advice about what to take on a sailing trip?*
>   *closing*
>   *Well, I must go now. Thanks for everything. I really know nothing about sailing.*
>
> 3 *opening*
>   *Hi, how's everything? John just told me you got your driving licence. Congratulations!*
>   *closing*
>   *Well, that's all for now. Once again, well done.*
>
> 4 *opening*
>   *Thanks for the invitation, it sounds like fun. Unfortunately, I won't be able to come.*
>   *closing*
>   *I'm really disappointed I can't come. I hope you all have a great time!*

37 a) Ss read the message and answer the questions.

> **ANSWER KEY**
>
> *In Budapest.*
> *For 5 days.*
> *At a Hotel in Belvaros.*
> *He wants his father to deposit £200 in his bank account.*

b) Explain that when we write a message we do not write full sentences. Instead, we write the most important information sb would need to understand our message. Elicit from Ss what points we need to include in our message *(when, where exactly)*. Ss, in pairs, write their messages. Check Ss' answers.

> **SUGGESTED ANSWER KEY**
>
> *Hi from Budapest. I'm in Belvaros Hotel. Meet me here on Tuesday. Tony*

38 Ss read the advertisement and answer the questions.

> **ANSWER KEY**
>
> *In Hungary you can see the Royal Palace and the Museum of Fine Arts. You can relax at traditional coffee houses and take a riverboat tour at night.*

39 Read out the plan. Ask questions.
  e.g. T: Where was Edward?
    S1: In Budapest.
       T: How long did he stay there?
    S2: Five days.
       T: Where did he stay?
    S3: At a nice hotel in Belvaros.   etc
Ss do the exercise orally in class, then it is assigned as written HW.

> **SUGGESTED ANSWER KEY**
>
> *Dear John,*
>   *Sorry I haven't written in a while, but I've been away on holiday. I just got back from five days in Budapest. I'd been planning it for ages.*
>   *Budapest is fantastic. I managed to get a room at a nice hotel in Belvaros. It was a beautiful Art Nouveau hotel. Budapest really is an amazing place. It's the centre of Hungary's culture and industry, very modern and exciting, but relaxing and traditional at the same time.*
>   *There's plenty to do there, too. I saw most of the sights, like the Royal Palace and the Museum of Fine Arts. They were two of the most interesting places I've ever been to. I relaxed at traditional coffee houses and I even went on a riverboat tour at night. It was fantastic! Unfortunately, I forgot my credit card. As you can imagine, I was really upset, but I sent a text message to my father and asked him to put £200 in my account. He did, and everything turned out well in the end!*
>   *Well, that's all my news. Hope you are OK. See you soon.*
> *Yours,*
> *Edward*

40 Read the sentences aloud and talk about their meanings.

> **ANSWER KEY**
>
> - *Something will always go wrong.*
> - *If something starts well, then it will probably end well.*
> - *When you visit a place you should follow the laws and customs of that place.*

(Suggested Homework)

1 **Vocabulary:** Ex. 34 (p. 52)
2 **Speaking:** Ex. 38 (p. 53)
3 **Writing:** Ex. 39 (p. 53)

(Lesson 6)

Workbook Unit 4
    Click on Grammar 4

35 Mark the phrases as *F* (for formal) or *I* (for informal). Which are beginnings? Which are endings?

1 Well, I must go now.
2 I am writing to complain about the poor quality of service …
3 I look forward to meeting you at your earliest convenience …
4 I'm writing to invite you to a …
5 Just a quick note to tell you …
6 Do drop me a line.
7 I am writing to apply for …
8 I can't tell you how sorry I was …
9 Thank you for taking the time to read this letter.
10 Well, that's all for now.
11 With reference to your advertisement in Monday's …
12 Let me know soon!

36 Suggest opening and closing remarks for the letters below, as in the example.

1 invite a friend to a fancy dress party
2 ask a friend for advice on what to take with you on a sailing trip
3 congratulate a friend on getting his driving licence
4 apologise to a friend for not being able to go to his fancy dress party

1 *opening*
   Hi, how's everything? I'm having a fancy dress party next Saturday and I hope you can come.

   closing
   Well, that's all for now. Let me know soon. I hope I'll see you on Saturday.

37 a) Read the text message Edward sent to his father on his mobile phone, then answer the questions.

• Where is Edward? • How long is he staying there?
• Where is he staying? • Why is he sending the text message?

b) Write a similar message to your friend asking him to meet you in Budapest.

HI FROM BUDAPEST I'M HERE 5 DAYS
NICE HOTEL IN BELVAROS FORGOT
CREDIT CARD PLEASE DEPOSIT £200 IN
MY ACCOUNT THANKS EDWARD

38 Look at the advertisement and talk about the place. Say where it is and what you can do and see there.

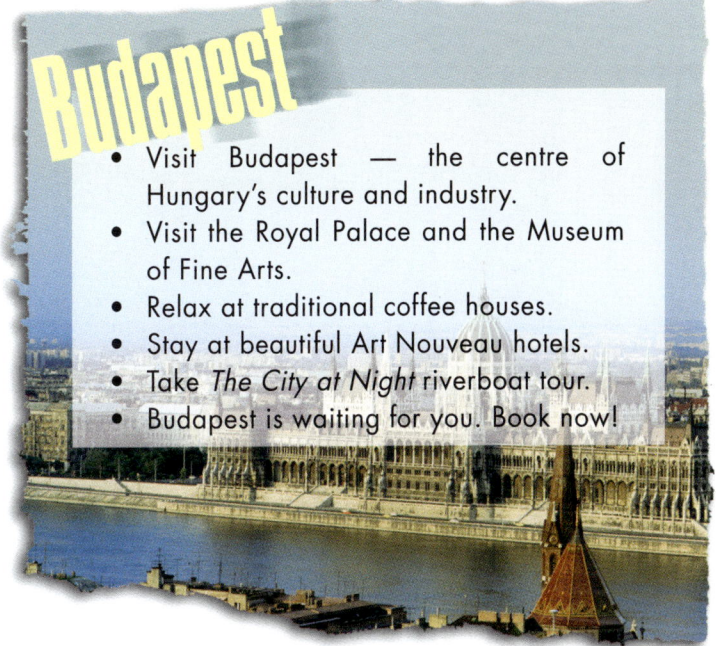

Budapest

• Visit Budapest — the centre of Hungary's culture and industry.
• Visit the Royal Palace and the Museum of Fine Arts.
• Relax at traditional coffee houses.
• Stay at beautiful Art Nouveau hotels.
• Take *The City at Night* riverboat tour.
• Budapest is waiting for you. Book now!

39 Edward is back in London. Use the information in Exs 37 and 38 as well as the plan below, to write the letter he sent to his friend John describing his holiday and what happened to him. (120-180 words). You can use the letter in Ex. 34 as a model.

Plan

Dear John,

Introduction
(Para 1) *opening remarks*
         - state place (where did he stay?)
         - length of stay (how long did he stay?)

Main Body
(Para 2) *What is the place like?*
(Para 3) *What did he do there?*
         What happened to him there?

Conclusion
(Para 4) *closing remarks*
Yours,
Edward

40 Read the sentences. What do they mean?

What's in a word?

• If anything can go wrong, it will.
• A good beginning makes a good ending.
• When in Rome, do as the Romans do.

THE ADVENTURES OF HUCKLEBERRY FINN

Sarah Williams

Huck goes to town to get the latest news. He dresses up as a girl so that nobody will recognise him.

1 This woman is new in town — she's never met me.

2 I'm Hu — er, Sarah, um, Sarah Williams.

I'm Mrs Loftus. Come in and sit down, Sarah.

3 Did you hear about Huck Finn's murder?

Yes! And Miss Watson's slave ran away the same day. They say he's the murderer. There's a $300 reward for catching him …

4 … and I think I know where he is — Jackson's Island! My husband's going there at midnight with a gun.

5 I *knew* you weren't a girl! What's your *real* name, boy?

It's George, George Peters. I have to go now, ma'am …

6 I'll have to hurry — it's almost midnight!

Well, Huck, here we go — off down the mighty Mississippi River!

7 Jim! Wake up! We've got to go — right now!

8

54

Pre-Reading Activities

1 Look at the pictures, read the questions and choose the correct answer, A, B or C.

1 What is the woman (Mrs Loftus) doing when Huck knocks on the door in picture 1?
A cooking   (B) knitting   C watching TV

2 What is Huck doing in picture 3?
(A) holding Mrs Loftus' wool
B making a scarf
C washing his hands

3 How does Huck feel in picture 4?
A hungry   B bored   (C) afraid

4 Mrs Loftus is angry in picture 5 because …
A Huck's bonnet falls off.
(B) she can see Huck isn't a girl.
C Huck isn't looking at her.

Listening & Reading Activities

2 Listen and mark the sentences as *T* (true) or *F* (false), then correct the false sentences.

1 The woman is new in town. T
2 People say that Miss Watson's slave is a murderer. T
3 There is a $300 reward for catching Huck. F
4 Jim is asleep when Huck gets to the island. T
5 Huck and Jim set off down the Missouri River. F

3 Read the episode on p. 54 and answer the questions.

1 Why does Huck decide to ask Mrs Loftus for news, instead of asking someone else?
Because she is new in town and doesn't know him.
2 What happened the same day that Huck was "murdered"?
Miss Watson's slave ran away.
3 Why is Mrs Loftus' husband going to Jackson's Island?
To catch Miss Watson's slave and get the reward.
4 Why do Huck and Jim have to leave the island quickly?
Because they don't want Mrs Loftus' husband to catch Jim.
5 What time is it when Jim and Huck leave the island?
It's almost midnight.

Grammar

- Clauses of Purpose

4 a) Study the table and examples, then complete the sentences with *to*, *so that* or *in case*.

> **Clauses of Purpose** explain why someone does/ should do something.
> - **to - infinitive** (infinitive of purpose)
>   *I'll go/I went/etc to town **to buy** some new clothes.*
> - **so that + subject + can/will** (present or future reference)
>   *Please **turn out** the light **so that I can** go to sleep.*
>   **so that + subject + could/would** (past reference)
>   *I **turned out** the light **so that I could** go to sleep.*
> - **in case + present tense** (present or future reference)
>   *Don't go near the dog, **in case** it bites you.*
>   **in case + past tense** (past reference)
>   *He didn't go near the dog, **in case** it bit him.*

1 Take an umbrella in case it rains.
2 He wanted to save money so that he could go on a skiing holiday next winter.
3 He gave me his telephone number in case I needed to call him later.
4 Please take your muddy boots off so that you don't leave marks on the clean floor.
5 In my country, students have to pass a difficult exam to get into university.

b) Look at the pictures 1, 6, 7 and 8 on p. 54 and make sentences using *to*, *so that* or *in case*.
(See Suggested Answers section)

Huck went to Mrs Loftus to get the latest news.

5 Read the summary and fill in *to*, *so that* or *in case*.

Huck goes to town 1) to get the latest news. He dresses up as a girl 2) so that nobody will recognise him. He sees a woman who is new in town and he knocks on her door. He tells her his name is Sarah Williams.

She tells him that people think Jim murdered Huck and there is a $300 reward for catching him. Her husband is going to Jackson's Island at midnight 3) to catch Jim.

Huck hurries back to the island 4) so that he can warn Jim in time and they leave quickly 5) in case the woman's husband arrives.

6 Listen to the episode again, then read it aloud.

55(T)

Vocabulary & Grammar

1 Fill in the correct word.

1 Jane lost her credit card while on holiday.
2 You must fasten your seat belt before take off.
3 When she called, Laura had already left.
4 By the time they got home, Steve had finished cooking.
5 Good morning. I'd like to book/reserve a room for two nights, please.
6 Helen was tired. She had been typing letters all morning.
7 Take an umbrella in case it rains.
8 There are a lot of shopping malls which are open daily.
9 Why don't you get on the waiting list for another flight?
10 Tokyo is one of the most expensive cities in the world.
11 "Have you seen her?"
"No, she hasn't got up yet."
12 My house is much bigger than yours.
13 The Smiths aren't here. They have gone to Italy.
14 Cairo has a desert climate with hot days and cold nights.
15 We haven't seen her since March.
16 Check if there is an alternative route via Paris.
17 If you are interested in culture, Poland is the best place for you.
18 Why don't you take a few days off?
19 Jane is going to be late. She missed the bus.
20 Put on some insect repellent to keep the insects away.
21 The services of a doctor are available to guests.
22 You can take part in lots of activities during your stay there.
23 Your trip will be the experience of a lifetime.
24 She offered to help but he turned her down.
25 Room service, how can I help you, sir?
26 This is the trendiest shop I've ever been in.
27 If you are in good shape, go on a mountain climbing excursion.
28 "How long have you been studying Chinese?"
"Two years."
29 Sally is still in Paris, stuck at the airport.
30 They went on a safari holiday in a jeep.

(30 marks)

2 Circle the correct item.

1 Don't do it; you won't get .... with it.
A up   B away   C over   D round
2 The trip .... a visit to a safari park.
A offers   B includes   C lets   D allows
3 One can admire the .... view from the top of the mountain.
A breathtaking   C traditional
B natural   D ethnic
4 .... the waiter was at fault, he didn't even apologise.
A Although   B Even   C However   D Despite
5 The .... river passes through the picturesque countryside.
A congested   B winding   C bending   D deserted
6 *Empanada* is one of Chile's national ....
A food   B plates   C tastes   D dishes
7 The car broke down, so he had to turn on his .... lights.
A warning   C departure
B breakdown   D hazard
8 Peter is .... taller than John.
A less   B more   C much   D as
9 He hasn't called ....
A since   B yet   C already   D still
10 You can walk its .... streets and narrow alleys to reach the castle.
A local   B traditional   C elegant   D cobbled

(20 marks)

Communication

3 Fill in the missing questions.

A: *Good morning, madam*?
B: I'd like to book a room, please.
A: 1) How long would you like it for?
B: A week.
A: 2) Would that be a single or a double?
B: A single, please. 3) How much will it cost?
A: That's £480, breakfast included.
B: 4) Can I pay by credit card, please?
A: Certainly. Which credit card?
B: Visa. Here you are.
A: Thank you. Could you fill in this card, please?

(20 marks)

Reading

4 Read the article and mark the sentences *T* (true) or *F* (false).

THE MAGIC OF INDIA

Have you been having trouble deciding whether to go on a beach or a city holiday? The best solution is to combine the two and go to India.

Why not begin your holiday in New Delhi, the nation's busy capital? As a first-time visitor, you can expect to be shocked by your first impressions of this fascinating city. The noisy mixture of car horns and street sellers loudly advertising their goods, as well as the sight of street children begging at the traffic lights, often puts tourists off. However, there is much more to New Delhi than this.

New Delhi is rich in historic sights. One of the most famous of these is the Red Fort, where you can visit the bazaar at the entrance and gaze at the beautiful red sandstone architecture of the fort itself. Another building which you certainly shouldn't miss is the Rashtrapati Bhavan. This presidential home with 340 rooms is surrounded by acres of attractive gardens. If you want a break from sightseeing, the best thing you can do is visit Connaught Place. In this shopping centre, you can buy beautiful clothes in the many boutiques or have a delicious meal in one of the restaurants.

When you have tired yourself out exploring New Delhi, you can spend the second half of your holiday in Goa. Don't forget to head for Palolem Beach, as this is the ideal spot for enjoying the spectacular Goan sunset. The beach is on a quiet island, so you will be guaranteed a peaceful and relaxing time. If you want to check out the local wildlife, there are a number of sanctuaries around the resort. Visit the Bondla Sanctuary and see lions and snakes. You can even have an elephant ride!

India's major cities and beach resorts offer many truly magical experiences. Travel to India and enjoy a holiday with a difference.

1   A lot of companies film advertisements in New Delhi.   F
2   There are a lot of old buildings in New Delhi.   T
3   The bazaar outside the Red Fort is made of sandstone.   F
4   Rashtrapati Bhaven has 340 acres of gardens.   F
5   Connaught Place is the best place for sightseeing.   F
6   Palolem Beach is the perfect place to get a tan.   T
7   You can get close to wild animals in Goa.   T

(15 marks)

Writing (a letter of complaint)

5 *You went on a Pacific Island Cruise from 4 August to 18 August. Unfortunately the cabin was very small, there was no bathroom in the cabin, and the meals were disappointing. Use the plan to write a letter of complaint. (120-180 words)*

> ### Plan   (See Suggested Answers section)
>
> *Dear Sir/Madam,*
> **Introduction**
> (Para 1) *writing to complain – cruise – 4-18 August*
> **Main body**
> (Para 2) *cabin small – no space for suitcase*
> (Para 3) *no bathroom – share with 4 other cabins*
> (Para 4) *meals – food not fresh – tasteless*
> **Conclusion**
> (Para 5) *expect – apology – refund*
> *Yours faithfully,*

(15 marks)

(Total = 100 marks)

 Let's sing!

6 🔊 Listen and fill in. Listen again and sing.

Travel

Get on a boat; get on a plane;
Get in your car or get on a train
Travel to a place where you've never been
And see things you've never seen

I've been to Italy twice so 1) far
I flew there and then hired a car
I 2) drove around and saw the sights
And ate pasta every 3) night

I've 4) never been to the USA
But my friend went there for a 5) holiday.
He went to Washington and New York too –
That's something I would 6) love to do.

Jamaica's a great place to 7) go
I went last 8) year, so I should know.
I lay on the sand by the clear blue 9) sea
under a swaying palm 10) tree.

Time for Fun

◆ **Before you start ...**

Where do you prefer to live: town or country? Why?

What is the weather like in your country?

Can you describe a nasty experience you had while on holiday?

Which places should a tourist visit in your town?

◆ **Listen, read and talk about ...**

Tasty Treats

UNIT 5

- foods & drink
- vitamins & minerals
- ways of cooking
- containers

Module 3
Units 5-6

All Work and no Play ...

UNIT 6

- the arts
- music & mood
- clothes & accessories
- entertainment
- jobs

◆ **Learn how to ...**

- order food
- decide on a menu
- book a table
- complain about food
- comment on films
- describe clothes
- make suggestions

◆ **Practise ...**

- will - going to
- zero & first conditionals
- countable & uncountable nouns
- some/any/a lot of/much/many/ (a) few/(a) little
- reflexive pronouns
- result clauses
- infinitive
- -ing form
- modals
- must - can't (logical assumptions)

◆ **Phrasal verbs**

- give
- set

◆ **Write ...**

- an article giving information
- a report
- a film review
- a letter to the editor

5 Tasty Treats

Lead-in

1 **a)** Which of these words are similar in your language? Which of the following can/can't you see?

- corn • milk • oil • courgettes • bread • garlic • sardines • eggs • chocolates
- mushrooms • rice • cauliflower • pulses • meat • pineapple • pasta • broccoli
- turkey • yogurt • bananas • peanuts • aubergine • asparagus • kiwi fruit • cashews
- grapes • lemon • strawberries • almonds • melon • mango • blueberries • beans
- watermelon • oranges • apples • steak • lamb • prawns • haddock • parsley
- cheesecake • honey • mustard • salmon • chocolate cake • cucumber • shellfish

I can see corn in picture 4.

b) Mention as many drinks as possible. e.g. water, coke, lemonade etc. What do you like or don't like? How often do you eat or drink these everyday? quite often? never? sometimes? very often? Talk about your favourite dish.

2 **a)** Match the food groups (a-g) below to the sections (1-8) of the food pyramid.

a	fruit	**e**	carbohydrates
b	meat, fish & poultry	**f**	beans, nuts &
c	vegetables		seeds
d	fats & sugars	**g**	dairy products

b) Which group(s) contain foods that are high in: vitamins? protein? fibre? calories? iron? calcium?

Fruit is high in vitamins.

Listening & Reading

3 Listen and repeat, then close your books and try to remember as many sentences as possible.

- Are you ready to order?
- I'll have that, please.
- How would you like it cooked?
- Medium rare.
- That's nice of you.
- What's on the menu?
- Got any ideas?
- You can't go wrong with that!
- Leave it to me.
- I've got that covered.

4 Listen and match the dialogues to the topics.

Dialogue A	deciding on a menu
Dialogue B	choosing from a menu
Dialogue C	cooking disaster

Objectives

Vocabulary: food; drink; ways of cooking; eating habits; containers
Reading: multiple choice; multiple matching
Listening: listening for specific information; multiple matching
Speaking: talking about the benefits of vitamins and minerals; talking about food abroad; talking about places to eat food in your country; making predictions/plans
Communication: booking a table; complaining about food
Pronunciation: intonation in conditional sentences
Grammar: countable/uncountable nouns; will/going to; zero and 1st conditional; reflexive pronouns
Phrasal verb: give
Word formation: verb opposites
Project: an article about foods that cure
Writing: a report suggesting ways to make a supermarket more popular with customers

Lesson 1 (pp. 58 - 59)

1 a) • Read out the title and ask Ss what they think it means. *(Nice things to eat.)* Ask Ss what their idea of a tasty treat is *(chocolate, ice cream, etc)*.
   • Read aloud the words in the list, one at a time, and ask Ss which they can see in the pictures.
   e.g. T: corn. Can you see corn?
   S1: Yes.
   T: Where?
   S1: Pict. 4
   T: Very good. Milk. Can you see milk? etc

ANSWER KEY

corn (4)	pineapple (6)	almonds (7)
milk (2)	pasta (5)	melon (6)
oil (1)	broccoli (8)	blueberries (6)
bread (4)	turkey (3)	beans (7)
garlic (8)	bananas (6)	watermelon (6)
sardines (3)	peanuts (7)	steak (3)
eggs (2)	aubergine (8)	lamb (3)
chocolates (1)	kiwi fruit (6)	chocolate cake
mushrooms (8)	grapes (6)	(1)
cauliflower (8)	strawberries (6)	cucumber (8)
meat (3)	pulses (7)	parsley (3)

   • Ask Ss which of the words are similar in Ss' own language.
   Ss' own answers

b) Ss' own answers

SUGGESTED ANSWER KEY

fruit juice, tea, coffee, milk etc

2 a) Read aloud the food groups and elicit/explain the meaning of any unknown words. Help Ss to match the food groups to the sections of the food pyramid.

ANSWER KEY

a 6	c 8	e 4,5	g 2
b 3	d 1	f 7	

b) Read aloud the question and elicit/explain the meaning of the listed words. Help Ss to answer the questions.
   vitamins: substances one needs to remain healthy
   protein: substance found in meat, eggs and milk
   fibre: consists of parts of plants & seeds that one's body cannot digest. It helps make food pass quickly through one's body.
   calories: units used to measure the energy value of food
   iron: mineral which is found in food e.g. lentils, spinach, etc and helps maintain healthy blood cells
   calcium: mineral which promotes growth of healthy bones and teeth

ANSWER KEY

Vegetables are high in vitamins.
Dairy products, meat, fish and poultry are high in protein.
Vegetables are high in fibre.
Fats & sugars, dairy products and pasta are high in calories.
Meat, fish, poultry and vegetables are high in iron.
Dairy products are high in calcium.

3 • Play the recording. Ss listen and repeat individually. Elicit/Explain what each sentence means by giving examples or synonyms or by miming. Ss should memorise these sentences.
   e.g. **Are you ready to order?** Pretend to be a waiter. Walk to a S's desk and say: *Are you ready to order?*
   • Ss look at the sentences, then close their books and try to remember as many sentences as possible. Alternatively this can be done as a game. Ss, in teams, say sentences. Each correct sentence gets one point. The team with the most points is the winner.

4 Play the recording. Ss do the task. Check Ss' answers.

ANSWER KEY

Dialogue A	choosing from a menu
Dialogue B	cooking disaster
Dialogue C	deciding on a menu

5 a) • Read out questions 1 to 5. Allow Ss three minutes to read the dialogues silently and do the exercise. Check Ss' answers.

ANSWER KEY

1 Because she can't eat spicy food.
2 Because it's Tom's favourite.
3 Because the fish is burning.
4 She can't decide what to cook.
5 Because one of the guests is a vegetarian.

   • Ss explain the words in bold by giving examples, synonyms or opposites. Help Ss where necessary.
      e.g. **Specials:** special meals which are available but which are not on the menu.

b) • Play the recording for Ex. 4 again. Ss listen and follow the lines, then take roles and read out the dialogues.
   • Explain to Ss they are to write an invitation to one of the situations presented in dialogues B and C e.g. a dinner party. Point out that Ss should use polite, informal language in their invitations as they are addressed to friends. Do the exercise orally in class, then assign it as written HW. (Approx. 50 words)

SUGGESTED ANSWER KEY

Dear Julie,
   Just a short note to invite you to dinner on Saturday night at 8:30.
   It's Tom's birthday on Saturday and I'm having a small dinner party. Just a few close friends.
   Hope you can make it.
                                          Lauren

(Suggested Homework)

1 **Vocabulary:** Exs 1 & 3 (p. 58), words in bold in dialogues A-C (p. 59)
2 **Dictation:** any six sentences from Ex. 3 (p.58)
3 **Reading aloud:** dialogues A-C (Point out that Ss practise *reading aloud* using the S's audio CD.)
4 **Speaking:** Exs 1 & 2 (p. 58)
5 **Writing:** invitations (Ex. 5b T's book)

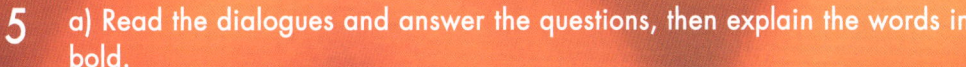

5 a) Read the dialogues and answer the questions, then explain the words in bold.

1 Why doesn't Martha want the steak?
2 Why has Lauren decided on a chocolate cake?
3 Why is Lauren in a panic?
4 What is Joyce's problem?
5 Why can't Joyce serve chicken for the main course?

A Waiter: Are you ready to order?
Martha: I'm not sure. Can you tell me what today's **specials** are, please?
Waiter: Certainly, madam. Today we have **salmon bake** cooked in a **creamy** mushroom **sauce** with **flaked** almonds on top.
Martha: Ooh, that sounds lovely!
Waiter: Then there's **sirloin steak** with a **spicy** tomato and pepper sauce.
Martha: Oh, I'm afraid I can't eat anything spicy.
Waiter: Well, we also have **roast lamb** served with a honey and **mustard** sauce.
Martha: Oh yes. I'll have that, please.
Waiter: And for you, sir?
Tom: I'll have the steak, please.
Waiter: How would you like it cooked?
Tom: Medium rare. No, **on second thoughts**, I think **I'd rather have** it **well done**.
Waiter: Right. Thank you.

B Brian: Mmm! Something smells good! What's cooking, Lauren?
Lauren: I'm cooking a special meal for Tom's birthday.
Brian: That's nice of you. What's on the **menu**?
Lauren: I'm making fish and **roast** potatoes.
Brian: Sounds delicious. What's for **dessert**?
Lauren: I'm going to make a chocolate cake. It's his favourite.
Brian: Yum! ... What's that smell, Lauren?
Lauren: Oh no, the fish is burning! Turn the **cooker** off, quick!

C Ron: So, Joyce. Are we **all set for the dinner party** on Saturday, then?
Joyce: Not quite. I haven't decided on the menu yet. It's difficult to choose **dishes** that everyone will like. Got any ideas?
Ron: What about prawn cocktail for starters? Most people like that.
Joyce: Yes, but Gordon's **allergic** to prawns.
Ron: Oh dear. Well how about a nice vegetable soup? You can't go wrong with that!
Joyce: Right, and the main course is a problem.
Ron: Well, most people like chicken, don't they?
Joyce: Yes, except Sarah is a vegetarian.
Ron: Does she like pasta? I could make **vegetable lasagne** with a **rich** cheese sauce.
Joyce: That would be great. Are you sure you can **manage** that?
Ron: Leave it to me. Now, what about dessert?
Joyce: I've got that **covered**. I'm making my special **cherry cheesecake**.
Ron: Great! I can't wait!

b) Now, in pairs, read out the dialogues.

Vocabulary

- Food and Drink

6 Study the table and identify the foods, then use the information to make sentences, as in the example.

Vitamins	Foods	Benefits
A		is good for our eyes
B complex		helps our bodies process the foods we eat
C		is good for our bones and teeth
D		helps our bones to grow properly
E		keeps our skin healthy

Minerals	Foods	Benefits
iron		maintains healthy blood cells
calcium		promotes growth of healthy bones and teeth
potassium		is good for our muscles and nerves
sodium		helps to keep the right amount of water in our bodies
zinc		helps our bodies process carbon dioxide

We can find vitamin A in fish, butter, carrots and broccoli. Vitamin A is good for our eyes.

- Methods of cooking & preparation

7 Fill in: *diced, fried, sliced, mashed, boiled, grilled, grated, scrambled.*

1 The Smiths often eat scrambled eggs for breakfast.
2 I don't want to put on weight, so I usually eat .... fish or chicken.
3 You need some .... cheese to put on the pizza.
4 Use .... bread to make the sandwiches.
5 You need lots of .... fruit to make a fruit salad.
6 Shepherd's Pie is a traditional British dish made from mince and .... potato.
7 Chips are .... food.
8 Grilled fish and .... vegetables is a low-fat meal.

8 Match the foods/drinks to the questions, then, in pairs, talk as in the example.

- a glass of water • a cup of coffee
- some potatoes • a steak • some fish
- some sugar • some bread

1 Brown or white? ....
2 Still or sparkling? ....
3 Black or white? ....
4 One lump or two? ....
5 Fresh or frozen? ....
6 Medium, rare or well done? ....
7 Roast or boiled? ....

SA: *I'd like some bread, please.*
SB: *Brown or white?*
SA: *I'd like brown, please.* etc.

Vocabulary Practice

29 Fill in the correct word from the list, then make sentences using the completed phrases.

- rich • sirloin • main • take • dinner
- stomach • cooking • lower • treat • squeaky
- oil-rich • heart • healing • nutritional

1	.... steak	8	.... sauce
2	.... party	9	to .... the risk
3	.... course	10	to .... notice
4	an .... diet	11	.... doors
5	.... disease	12	.... effect
6	.... oil	13	.... disorders
7	.... benefits	14	to .... wounds

30 Fill in: *on, with, in, of, to,* then make sentences using the completed phrases.

1 to link sth .... sth else; 2 .... the menu;
3 cooked .... a sauce; 4 ready .... order;
5 served .... sth; 6 .... second thoughts;
7 to decide .... sth; 8 to lower the risk .... sth;
9 to be allergic .... sth; 10 to have an effect
.... sth; 11 .... top of this

Listening

31 You will hear a conversation between Tom and Ann about an evening out. Listen and tick (✔) Yes or No.

	Yes	No
1 Ann felt the meal was expensive.	☐	☐
2 The service was excellent.	☐	☐
3 Tom had a pizza.	☐	☐
4 Tom and Ann's table was next to the kitchen.	☐	☐
5 The knives and forks weren't clean.	☐	☐
6 Tom and Ann had booked a table.	☐	☐

Word Formation
(verb opposites)

32 Study the table, then fill in the opposites. Finally, make sentences using the words.

We use **dis-, mis-, un-,** to form verb opposites.

e.g.   like → **dis**like, understand → **mis**understand,
        cover → **un**cover

1	behave	5	dress ....
2	use	6	respect ....
3	obey	7	fasten ....
4	agree	8	please ....

Communication

- **booking a table**

33 Listen and fill in the missing words then, in pairs, read out the dialogue.

A: Good evening, Mario's restaurant. How can I 1) .... you?

B: Hello. I'd like to 2) .... a table for tomorrow night, please.

A: Of course. What 3) ...., please?

B: Brown.

A: How many 4) .... is the booking for?

B: Three.

A: That's fine. And what 5) .... would you like to eat?

B: At 8:00.

A: I'm terribly sorry. We have no 6) .... tables until 8:30.

B: Oh, well, 8:30 is 7) ....

A: Wonderful. We look 8) .... to seeing you tomorrow night.

B: Thank you. Goodbye.

- **complaining about food**

34 a) Listen and fill in the correct word.

A: Excuse me, waiter.

B: Yes, sir. What seems to be the 1) ....?

A: This 2) .... is overcooked.

B: I'm terribly 3) ...., sir. I'll replace it at once.

A: Actually, I think I'd rather 4) .... something else.

B: Of course, sir. What would you 5) ....?

A: I'll have the 6) .... in mushroom sauce.

B: Certainly.

b) In pairs, use the prompts to act out similar dialogues.

- vegetable soup (cold) • omelette
- roast chicken (undercooked) • sirloin steak

Pronunciation (intonation in conditional sentences)

35 Listen and repeat.

If you see Pam, ask her to phone me.

If I go to London, I'll visit Mike.

If it rains, we'll stay at home.

If you're hungry, I'll make you a sandwich.

Phrasal Verbs

36 Study the table, then fill in the correct particle.

> **give away** - 1) to reveal sth, 2) to give sth for free
> **give in** - to surrender
> **give off** - to produce (heat, smell, fumes, sound, etc)
> **give out** - 1) to hand out, 2) to stop working
> **give up** - to stop doing sth

1 Cindy's parents finally gave .... and allowed her to have a puppy.
2 The drains are giving .... a horrible smell.
3 I can't forgive him for giving .... my secret.
4 The engine gave .... halfway through their journey.
5 You should give .... smoking. It's bad for your health.

Writing (a report)

A report is a formal piece of writing. We write it for someone in authority (e.g. our boss, the local council, etc). A report contains facts only and presents suggestions for future actions. To write a report, we start with an **introduction** where we write the purpose of our report. In the **main body**, we write a paragraph for each topic. In each paragraph we may write the good points and state the problem. We also make our suggestions to solve the problem. We write suitable subheadings for each paragraph. In the **conclusion**, we summarise our points and make our recommendations or suggestions.

37 Read the report and fill in the correct subheadings, then answer the questions.

• Facilities • Purpose • Conclusion
• Decor • Menu

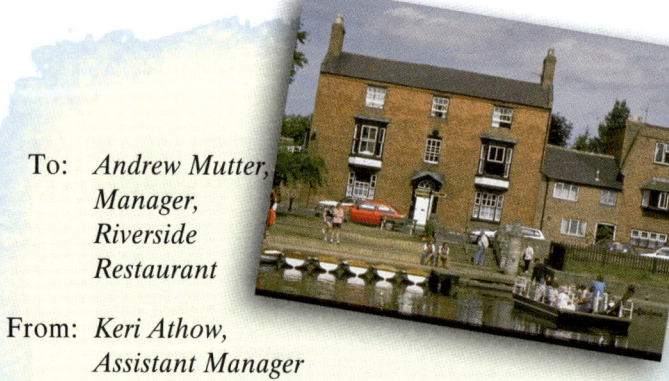

To: *Andrew Mutter, Manager, Riverside Restaurant*

From: *Keri Athow, Assistant Manager*

Date: 25th June, 20 ......

Subject: **Attracting customers to Riverside**

A) ....

The purpose of this report is to suggest ways to attract more customers to Riverside Restaurant.

B) ....

Most of the meals at Riverside contain meat and are **therefore** unsuitable for vegetarians. As many people are vegetarians these days, we should offer a wider variety of dishes. We should **also** provide a children's menu **in order to** encourage more families to eat at Riverside.

C) ....

At present, the interior of Riverside is rather dark **and** old-fashioned. We should decorate the restaurant in brighter colours. If the restaurant looks modern and cheerful, people will be more likely to visit it.

D) ....

Although Riverside's current facilities are adequate, we could improve them. For example, a play area and high chairs would attract families with small children. **Furthermore**, a separate area with popular background music would attract young people. Finally, parking facilities also need improving.

E) ....

In conclusion, I think that Riverside restaurant will attract more customers if it has a more varied menu, modern decor and better facilities.

1 Who is going to read the report?
2 What is the reason for writing the report? In which paragraph is it mentioned? What are the topics of each paragraph?
3 What are the writer's suggestions?
4 Look at the words in bold. Which express: addition? contrast? effect? purpose? (See Grammar Reference Section)

Lesson 5 (pp. 66 - 67)

* Check Ss' HW (10').

35 Play the recording. Ss listen and repeat, first chorally, then individually.

36 Read out the table, then Ss do the exercise. Check Ss' answers. Ss should memorise the theory table.

> **ANSWER KEY**
>
> 1 in   2 off   3 away   4 out   5 up

Writing (p. 66)

- Ask Ss to look at the text in Ex. 37. Explain that this is a report. Ask Ss to comment on its layout. *(It starts with To/From and the full name and title of the person who writes the report and the person the report is addressed to. After that is the date, then the subject (i.e. what the report is about). There are headings before each paragraph.)* Ask: Why do you think someone would write a report? *(To make suggestions; to evaluate sth; to comment on sth; etc)*
- Read out the theory table.

37 Allow Ss three minutes to read the report silently and fill in the subheadings. Check Ss' answers, then help Ss answer questions 1 to 4.

> **ANSWER KEY**
>
> A Purpose   C Decor   E Conclusion
> B Menu   D Facilities
>
> 1 Andrew Mutter. The manager of Riverside Restaurant.
> 2 To attract more customers to the restaurant. It is stated in para A.
> 3 • offer a wider variety of meals/provide a children's menu
>   • decorate the restaurant in brighter colours
>   • provide a play area and high chairs
>   • create a separate area with popular background music
>   • improve parking facilities
> 4 addition: also, and, furthermore
>   contrast: although
>   effect: therefore
>   purpose: in order to

38 Explain the task. Allow Ss two minutes to do the exercise. Check Ss' answers.

> **ANSWER KEY**
>
> | | |
> |---|---|
> | 2 Therefore | 5 On the other hand |
> | 3 In addition | 6 Alternatively |
> | 4 Although | |

39
- Explain that in reports we use rather formal language and we avoid using colloquial, everyday English. Ask Ss to read the extract, then replace the words in bold.
- Check Ss' answers.

> **ANSWER KEY**
>
> | | |
> |---|---|
> | 1 excellent | 5 therefore |
> | 2 affordable | 6 One solution is |
> | 3 However | 7 In addition |
> | 4 fashionable | |

40 Explain the task. Allow Ss two minutes to read the table silently and do the exercise. Check Ss' answers.

> **ANSWER KEY**
>
> | | | | |
> |---|---|---|---|
> | 1 d | 2 b | 3 c | 4 a |
>
> See Suggested Answer Key for Ex. 41 for answers.

41 Go through the plan. Discuss the points Ss will include in their reports.

T: Who is the report addressed to?
S1: Full name of person, manager Fergy's Supermarket.
S2: Our full name, e.g. Richard Harris, title e.g. Assistant Manager
T: What is the purpose of the report?
S3: How to make Fergy's more attractive to customers.
T: What information will you include in the first paragraph and what sub-heading will you use?
S4: The reason for writing the report; the best sub-heading is purpose.
T: What will your next paragraph be about?
S5: Prices.
T: What will you write?
S6: That prices are not very competitive. Therefore, we should offer lower prices to customers as well as special offers and money-off coupons. etc

Help Ss to do the task orally in class, then assign it as written HW.

> **SUGGESTED ANSWER KEY**
>
> To: Dennis Huntley, Manager, Fergy's supermarket.
> From: Richard Harris, Assistant Manager.
> Date: 15th May, 20...
> Subject: Attracting customers to Fergy's supermarket
>
> **Purpose**
> The purpose of this report is to suggest ways to make Fergy's supermarket more popular with customers.

> **Prices**
> At present, the prices at Fergy's supermarket are not very competitive. We should offer lower prices, special offers and money-off coupons in order to attract more customers.
> **Service**
> The service at Fergy's supermarket is quite slow. Therefore, many customers spend a long time queuing at the checkout. If we increase the number of checkouts, customers will not have to wait so long to be served.
> **Products**
> The range of products at Fergy's supermarket is not very broad. We should definitely offer a wider range of products in order to be more popular with customers.
> **Opening Hours**
> Although Fergy's supermarket is open every day, the opening hours are quite restricted. One solution is to open earlier in the morning and close later at night.
> **Conclusion**
> In conclusion, it is my opinion that Fergy's Supermarket will attract more customers if it has lower prices, better service, a wider range of products and longer opening hours.

42 Ask individual Ss to read the sentences aloud and try to explain their meanings. Help Ss if necessary.

> **SUGGESTED ANSWER KEY**
>
> - Only by putting something to the test can you be sure it works.
> - You can't always have everything the way you want it.
> - If too many people work on the same project, things will go wrong.
> - What is good for one person may be bad for another.
> - Take advantage of a good opportunity while you can as it may not last.

> (Suggested Homework)
>
> 1 Vocabulary: Ex. 36 (p. 66)
> 2 Speaking: Ex. 40 (p. 67)
> 3 Writing: Ex. 41 (p. 67)

(Lesson 6)

Workbook Unit 5
Click on Grammar 5

38 Fill in: *however, in addition, therefore, on the other hand, alternatively, although.*

1 Prices at Morton's supermarket are very reasonable. However, there are no special offers on popular products.

2 The staff at Comfrey's department store are not very well-trained. ...., they are rarely able to help the customers.

3 The supermarket offers a wide range of products. ...., they can order any product on request.

4 .... the store is bright and spacious, the displays are not well-organised.

5 The meals at Harper's are of a very high quality. ...., there is little choice for vegetarians.

6 In order to attract more customers, we could offer a childcare service. ...., we could provide a children's play area.

39 Replace the words in bold with the ones below to make the extract read like a report.

- affordable • however • one solution is to
- excellent • in addition • fashionable • therefore

Becky's restaurant offers 1) **really good** food at 2) **cheap** prices. 3) **But,** the restaurant is not very 4) **nice** and, 5) **so,** it does not attract young people. 6) **What we should do is** decorate the restaurant in bright colours. 7) **Also,** we should play modern music to appeal to younger customers.

40 Match the problems points to the suggestions below, using appropriate linking words.

Problems	Suggestions
1 prices are not very competitive	a open earlier in the morning and close later at night
2 range of products is not very broad	b offer a wider range of products
3 service is quite slow	c increase the number of checkouts
4 opening hours are restricted	d offer lower prices, special offers and money-off coupons

41 *Your manager has asked you to write a report about Fergy's supermarket suggesting ways to make it more popular with customers.* Write your report in 120-180 words. Use ideas from Exs. 38-40, the following subheadings and the plan below as well as the report in Ex. 37 as a model.

Purpose   Opening
Prices   Hours
Service   Conclusion
Products

Plan

To:
From:
Date:
Subject:
Introduction
(Para 1)   *state the purpose of your report*
Main Body
(Paras 2-4) *state each point under suitable subheadings, then offer suggestions/recommendations*
Conclusion
(Para 5)   *summarise your points/ problems and your recommendations*

42 Read the sentences. What do they mean?

What's in a word?

- The proof of the pudding is in the eating.
- You can't have your cake and eat it.
- Too many cooks spoil the broth.
- One man's meat is another man's poison.
- Make hay while the sun shines.

THE ADVENTURES OF HUCKLEBERRY FINN

Down the Mississippi

Huck and Jim leave Jackson's Island and set off down the Mississippi on their raft.

1

What are we going to do now, Jim?

Well, Huck, we can float all the way down to Cairo, where the Ohio River joins the Mississippi ...

2

When we reach Cairo, we'll sell the raft, and go up the Ohio on a steamboat to the Free States!

I'll be a free man, Huck! Then I'll help my family get free, too ...

3

We'd better hide during the day, and only travel at night.

I don't mind, Jim. It's so pretty, with the stars, and the towns all lit up.

One night there was a thick fog ...

Jim! Where are you?!

Over here, Huck!

4

IN THE MORNING ...

5

Jim!

Huck! I thought I was never going to see you again!

THE NEXT NIGHT ...

We're looking for some runaway slaves. Who's on your raft, boy?

Ma and Pa and Mary Anne, sir. They're awfully sick. I'm taking them down to Cairo.

6

7

Let's go — we don't want to get sick too! And Cairo is *that* way, boy — *up* the river!

It's all right, Jim — they've gone now.

That was clever, Huck — but what are we going to do now? We went past Cairo in the fog last night!

8

9

That steamboat hasn't seen us!

It's going to hit us, Huck! JUMP!

Pre-Reading Activities

1 Look at the map, then read and fill in words from the list.

- Cairo
- Northern
- Ohio
- on
- south

Northern (Free) States
Southern (Slave) States

Huck and Jim set off down the Mississippi, going 1) south. In the Southern states, Jim might be caught as a runaway slave, but in the 2) Northern states, where there is no slavery, he would be a free man.

The 3) Ohio River joins the Mississippi at a town called 4) Cairo. If they go up the Ohio towards New York 5) on a steamboat, Jim can get to safety and freedom.

2 a) Look at the pictures on p. 68. Which shows:

1 a boat and a raft? 6, 7
2 towns lit up? 1, 3
3 Jim imagining the future? 2
4 a small steamboat? 9
5 thick fog? 4

b) Guess the story through the pictures.

Listening & Reading Activities

3 Listen and correct the words in bold.

1 "When we reach Cairo, we'll sell the ~~boat~~." raft
2 "We only travel at ~~noon~~." night
3 "We are looking for ~~two~~ runaway slaves." some
4 "We went past Cairo in the fog ~~yesterday morning~~." last night

4 Read the episode on p. 68 and answer the questions.

(See Suggested Answers section)

1 What do Huck and Jim plan to do when they reach Cairo?
2 What will Jim do if he gets to the Free States?
3 Why do Huck and Jim have to hide during the day?
4 Why does Huck tell a lie about having a sick family on the raft?
5 When did they go past Cairo? Why didn't they stop there?
6 Why do Huck and Jim jump off the raft into the river?

Grammar

- Result Clauses

5 Study the grammar box, then rewrite the sentences, using result clauses with *so* or *such (a)*, as in the example.

> Result Clauses explain what happens as a result of something else.
> - so + adjective/adverb (that) …
>   *It was **very pretty**. As a result, Huck liked travelling at night.*
>   *> It was **so pretty (that)** Huck liked travelling at night.*
> - such (a/an) + adjective + noun (that) …
>   *It was **a very foggy night**. As a result, they went past Cairo.*
>   *> It was **such a foggy night (that)** they went past Cairo.*

(See Suggested Answers section)

1 It was very hot. We decided to go swimming.
   *It was **so hot that** we decided to go swimming.*
2 They are very nice people, so everybody likes them.
3 It was a very noisy party. The neighbours complained.
4 It was very dark. The steamboat didn't see their raft.
5 The news was very good. We could hardly believe it.

6 Make sentences using the words in the list.

- so late • so much fog • such nice weather • such a long way
- such a clever boy • so tired • so little money

(See Suggested Answers section)

7 Listen to the episode again, then read it aloud.

8 Fill in *the* where necessary, then number the events in the correct order. Retell the story using past tenses.

☐1 —Huck and —Jim start floating down the Mississippi towards Cairo.
☐5 The next night, two men stop the raft, looking for runaway slaves.
☐8 Huck and Jim jump off the raft just before a steamboat hits it.
☐2 From — Cairo, Jim plans to go up the Ohio River to the Free States.
☐7 Huck and Jim realise they have gone past Cairo without seeing it in the fog.
☐6 Huck says his —family is sick, and the men leave quickly.
☐4 Huck is in his canoe and can't find Jim and the raft in the fog.
☐3 They decide to travel at —night and hide during the day.

69(T)

6 All Work and no Play..

Lead-in

1 a) Look at the pictures. Which forms of entertainment do/don't you enjoy? What sort of person are you: a cinema goer/ a sports fan/ a culture buff/ a TV addict/ a bookworm/ a loner or a sociable person?

b) In pairs make dialogues.

invitations/suggestions

- Do you fancy ...?
- Why don't we ...?
- How about ...?
- Would you like to ...?

- Shall we ...?
- Let's go to ... .
- Are you doing anything ...?

accepting

- I'd love to ...
- Great idea!
- Yes. That would be nice.
- Brilliant idea!

refusing

- I'm afraid I can't, I have to ...
- I don't really like ... How about ... instead
- I'm really sorry, but I'm busy
- I'd love to but ...

A: Are you doing anything tomorrow?
B: No, nothing special.
A: Shall we go to the football match, then?
B: No, I don't really like football. Let's go to the circus.
A: Brilliant idea!

2 Match the words to the places in pictures, then use them to make sentences, as in the example.

- safety net • sculptures • marine park
- acrobat • conductor • band • players
- paintings • referee • screens • audience
- orchestra • musicians • half-time • singer
- whale trainer • guide • visitors • pool
- spectators • exhibits • lighting
- tightrope • instruments

The safety net will catch the acrobat if he falls.

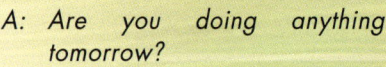
1 art gallery

2 marine park

3 orchestral performance

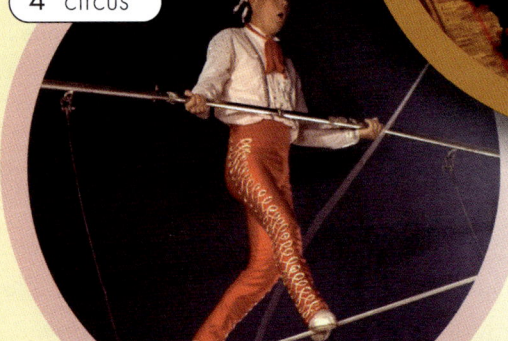
4 circus

5 rock concert

Objectives

Vocabulary: arts; entertainment; occupations; music & mood; clothes & accessories; comments & feelings; rules
Reading: multiple choice; reading for detailed understanding
Listening: filling in missing information; completing tables; listening for specific information
Speaking: commenting on films; performances etc; describing costumes; commenting on jobs
Communication: making suggestions
Pronunciation: rising intonation in polite requests
Grammar: infinitive/-ing form; modal verbs (must - mustn't; have to - don't have to; can - can't), -ing/-ed participles
Phrasal verbs: set
Word formation: forming nouns from verbs
Project: film review
Writing: a letter to the editor

Lesson 1 (pp. 70 - 71)

1 a) • Read out the title. Explain that it is part of a proverb "All work and no play makes Jack a dull boy". Ask Ss to interpret the proverb. (We all need a break in our work routine or else we soon become boring.)
    • Ask Ss to look at the pictures on pp. 70-71 and say which they do/don't enjoy. Ss then answer the questions. Elicit from/Explain to Ss what the words mean.
    cinema goer: sb who goes to the cinema
    sports fan: sb who likes sports
    culture buff: sb who enjoys going to cultural events e.g. opera, ballet etc
    TV addict: sb who watches a lot of TV
    bookworm: sb who reads a lot
    loner: sb who prefers to be alone

SUGGESTED ANSWER KEY

I'm a cinema goer.
I love going to the cinema and watching films.
I quite enjoy watching videos, too.
I really like going to museums, and I don't mind going to art galleries, so I suppose I'm a culture buff, too.
I don't like sports very much, though.

b) Go through the prompts, then choose two Ss to read the example aloud. Ss, in closed pairs, act out similar dialogues. Check Ss' answers. Choose some pairs to report back to the class.

SUGGESTED ANSWER KEY

A: Are you doing anything, tonight?
B: No, nothing special.
A: Shall we go to an orchestral performance?
B: No, I don't really like classical music. How about a rock concert instead?
A: Great idea!

2 Read out the list of words one by one. Ss can look up any unknown words in their dictionaries. Ss match them to the pictures, then make sentences.

SUGGESTED ANSWER KEY

Pict. 1: paintings; visitors; exhibits; guide; sculptures
Pict. 2: spectators; whale trainer; pool; marine park
Pict. 3: conductor; orchestra; musicians; audience; instruments
Pict. 4: acrobat; safety net; tightrope
Pict. 5: singer; band; musicians; audience; instruments; lighting; screens
Pict. 6: referee; spectators; players; half-time

There are many sculptures in the art gallery.
You can see whales performing in a marine park.
The acrobat is on the tightrope now.
The conductor is in front of the orchestra.
The band is on stage.
There are many beautiful paintings here.
The referee watches the game carefully.
You can see the band on the screens.
The audience claps and cheers.
The orchestra is very famous.
The musicians are ready to perform.
The players went off the field at half-time.
I think the lead singer is fantastic.
You can see the whale trainer feed the whale.
The guide explains the exhibits in the art gallery.
The visitors are crowding around the painting.
The whales perform in the pool every day.
All the spectators cheered when they scored a goal.
You mustn't touch the exhibits.
The lighting is very bright.
The tightrope is very high up.
The musicians in the orchestra look after their own instruments.

3 • Play the recording. Ss listen and follow the lines, then repeat. Present the sentences to Ss by giving examples, synonyms, opposites or by miming.

   e.g. **calm down:** become less angry, excited or upset

   • Ss look at the sentences for two minutes, then close their books and, in teams, try to remember as many sentences as possible. Each correct sentence gets 1 point. The team with the most points is the winner.

   e.g. Team A S1: Calm down.

        Team B S1: Just give me two seconds.   etc

   • Ss should memorise these sentences.

4 Explain the task, then play the recording. Ss listen and match. Check Ss' answers.

ANSWER KEY

Ted: anxious
Angela: annoyed
Thomas: relieved

---

5 a) Read out questions 1 to 6. Allow Ss two to three minutes to do the exercise. Check Ss' answers, then help Ss explain the words/phrases in bold. Ss can look up the words/phrases in their dictionaries.

ANSWER KEY

1 Because he is the referee.
2 She can't decide what to wear.
3 Yes, she really enjoyed it.
4 The people behind Angela chatted constantly.
5 She finds it boring.
6 Because the first concert was sold out.

---

   b) Play the recording for Ex. 4 again. Ss listen and follow the lines, then take roles and read out the dialogues.

(Suggested Homework)

1 **Vocabulary:** Ex. 2 (p. 70), Ex. 3 (p. 71), words in bold in dialogues in Ex. 5a (p. 71)
2 **Dictation:** any five sentences from Ex. 3 (p. 71) and six words from Ex. 2 (p. 70) & Ex. 5a (p. 71) with definition or example.
3 **Reading aloud:** dialogues A-C (p. 71) (Point out that Ss practise *reading aloud* using the S's audio CD.)
4 **Speaking:** Ex. 1b (p. 70)
5 **Project:** Ask Ss to cut pictures from magazines/ newspapers showing various types of entertainment, stick them on paper and label them accordingly.

Listening & Reading

3 🔊 **Listen and repeat. Then close your books and try to remember as many sentences as possible.**

- Calm down.
- I won't be long.
- Do you think it's going to be hot?
- Just give me two seconds.
- I'll have to leave without you.
- Did that make any difference?
- What am I going to do?
- You're in luck, sir.

4 🔊 **Listen to the dialogues and match the people to how they feel.**

Ted	relieved
Angela	anxious
Thomas	annoyed

5 **a) Read the dialogues and answer the questions. Then explain the phrases in bold.**

1 Why can't Ted be late?
2 What is Beth's problem?
3 Did Angela like the concert?
4 What happened during the performance?
5 What does Chloe think of classical music?
6 Why is there going to be a second rock concert?

A Ted: Come on! If you don't **hurry up**, the match will start before we get there. You know that I have to be there **in time** for **the kickoff**.

Beth: Calm down, Ted! I won't be long. I just can't decide what to wear. Do you think it's going to be hot?

Ted: Wear whatever you want – just hurry up!

Beth: OK, here I am. What do you think?

Ted: You can't wear that! We're going to a football match!

Beth: OK, I'll change. Just give me two seconds.

Ted: Hurry up! If you're not ready in ten minutes, I'll have to leave without you. You know I can't be late. I am the **referee**, after all!

6 football match

B Chloe: How was the concert last night, Angela?

Angela: Well, the music was great. I've never heard Vivaldi played so well. The orchestra really was fantastic.

Chloe: I'm glad you liked it, although I don't really enjoy classical music myself. I think it's rather boring.

Angela: So did the people who sat behind me last night! They **chatted constantly** throughout the performance.

Chloe: Oh no! What did you do?

Angela: Well, I couldn't really do anything without making it worse. So I just turned around a couple of times and **glared** at them.

Chloe: Did that make any difference?

Angela: No, they just continued talking **regardless**. People like that shouldn't be allowed to go to concerts.

C Operator: Hello, **Central Booking Office**. Can I help you?

Thomas: Yes. I'd like to book two tickets for the Savage Garden concert on Saturday.

Operator: I'm sorry, sir. I'm afraid that Saturday's concert is **sold out**.

Thomas: Oh, no! What am I going to do? I promised my brother we'd go. I have to **get hold of** some tickets.

Operator: Well, you're in luck, sir. Due to **popular demand**, there's going to be a second concert on Sunday.

Thomas: That's great! You're a **lifesaver**! Can I book two tickets for Sunday, then?

Operator: Certainly, sir. Could I have your name, please?

Thomas: It's Thomas Martin.

Operator: Right then, Mr Martin. Now, the tickets have to be paid for and **picked up** from the ticket office 24 hours **in advance**.

Thomas: That's fine.

b) In pairs, read out the dialogues.

6

Vocabulary

• Social Life

6 a) Which of the following do you do in your free time?

b) Which of these do you prefer doing if you want: to have a relaxing evening; to have a lot of fun; be around a lot of people?

If I want a relaxing evening, I prefer listening to CDs.

- go to a football match
- surf the net
- go to a rock concert
- go to the cinema
- go to the theatre
- listen to CDs
- chat on the phone
- have dinner with friends
- go for a walk/a coffee/a swim
- drive to the beach
- read a book
- go to the gym

7 Work in pairs. Ask and answer as in the example.

A: *Do you fancy going to the theatre?*
B: *No, I'd rather not. I'd prefer to go to the cinema.*

8 Make sentences using *must/mustn't* as in the example.

1 Formal dress only!

2 No pets allowed!

3 Late arrivals not admitted!

4 Show tickets at door!

5 Payment by credit card only!

6 Wait here to be seated!

1 *You must dress formally.*

• Music and Mood

9 Look at the different types of music. How do they make you feel? In pairs, use the adjectives in the table to act out dialogues, as in the example.

rock	excited	aggressive
heavy metal	relaxed	happy
jazz	depressed	lively
classical	moved	sad
country	cheerful	lonely
pop	romantic	annoyed
opera	bored	

A: *What makes you feel excited?*
B: *Listening to rock music.*
A: *Really? What else apart from listening to rock music makes you feel excited?*
B: *Watching an adventure film. What about you? What makes you feel excited?*

Listening

10 Listen and complete the advertisement.

WESTLIFE

Four Corners Tour Extra Dates

Birmingham NEC
Wednesday 12th - Saturday
1) .... April
Tel. 0121 780 4133

Sheffield Arena
Thursday 26th - Friday 27th
2) ....
Tel. 0114 2565256

Wembley Arena
3) ....11th - Monday 14th
4) .... Tel. 0208 795 9570

Tickets £ 5) .... from Box Offices
www.ticketsrus.co.uk

Lesson 2 (pp. 72 - 73)

* Check Ss' HW (10').

6 a) Read out the list and explain any unknown words. Ask Ss to add to the list, then ask them what they do in their free time.

> **SUGGESTED ANSWER KEY**
>
> *I like going to football matches. etc*

b) Allow Ss two minutes to prepare their answers. Check Ss' answers.

> **SUGGESTED ANSWER KEY**
>
> - **relaxing evening:** *surf the net; go to the cinema; go to the theatre; listen to CDs; have dinner with friends; chat on the phone; go for a walk/coffee/ swim; drive to the beach; read a book*
> - **a lot of fun:** *go to a football match; go to a rock concert; have dinner with friends*
> - **be around a lot of people:** *go to a football match; go to a rock concert; have dinner with friends; go to the gym*

> **SUGGESTED ANSWER KEY**
>
> *If I want to have a lot of fun, I prefer to go to a football match.*
> *If I want to be around a lot of people, I prefer to go to a rock concert. etc*

7 Read out the example. Point out that *fancy* is followed by an *-ing* form, whereas *I'd prefer* is followed by a *to-infinitive*. Ss work in closed pairs. Check Ss' answers around the class, then choose some pairs to report back to the class.

> **ANSWER KEY**
>
> A: *Do you fancy going to a football match?*
> B: *No, I'd rather not. I'd prefer to drive to the beach.*

8 Elicit from Ss where they might expect to see these notices e.g. in a theatre, concert hall, restaurant etc. Explain the task, then Ss make sentences.

> **SUGGESTED ANSWER KEY**
>
> 2 *You mustn't bring pets in here.*
> 3 *You mustn't be late. / You must be on time.*
> 4 *You must show your ticket at the door.*
> 5 *You must pay by credit card.*
> 6 *You must wait here to be seated.*

9 Read and explain the task. Elicit/Explain any unknown words. Ss use the prompts to act out dialogues in closed pairs, as in the example. Check Ss' answers, then ask some pairs to act out their dialogue to the class.

> **SUGGESTED ANSWER KEY**
>
> A: *Listening to jazz music.*
> B: *Really? What makes you feel relaxed?*
> A: *Reading a book or going for a walk. What about you? What makes you feel depressed? etc*

10 Ss read the advertisement. Play the recording. Ss fill in the missing words. Check Ss' answers on the board.

> **ANSWER KEY**
>
> | | | |
> |---|---|---|
> | 1 15th | 3 Friday | 5 18.50 |
> | 2 April | 4 May | |

TAPESCRIPT

Don't miss your chance to see Westlife perform all their hit songs, as well as some new tracks, live around the country over the next couple of months. Tickets are selling out fast, so the boys have added some extra dates at the following venues:

- Birmingham NEC – Extra dates are from Wednesday 12th to Saturday 15th April. Call 0121 780 4133.
- Sheffield Arena – The 2 extra dates here are Thursday 26th and Friday 27th April. Call 0114 256 5656.
- Wembley Arena – The boys have added four extra nights at Wembley to satisfy their London fans from Friday 11th to Monday 14th May. Call 0208 795 9570.
  All tickets cost £18.50 and are available from box offices or online at www.ticketsrus.co.uk.
  Don't wait or you may be too late!

6

11 a) Explain that the following are comments made by people who have attended sth. Read out the items, one at a time. Ss decide what each person is talking about. Explain any unknown words. Then, Ss make sentences.

> **ANSWER KEY**
>
> 2 play,   3 circus,   4 opera/concert,
> 5 football/rugby/ ice hockey/etc match, 6 art gallery
>
> 2 The characters were very **realistic**.
>   I was **impressed** with the special effects.
> 3 The lion tamer was **fantastic**.
>   I was **afraid** that the tigers would attack their tamer.
> 4 The music was **uplifting**.
>   I was **moved** by the music.
> 5 The game was very **slow**.
>   The match was **action packed**.
> 6 The paintings were **first rate**.
>   That is a very **imaginative** sculpture.

b) • Point out that **-ing participles** e.g. *uninteresting* say what sth is like, whereas **-ed participles** say how sb feels.
   • Ss work in closed pairs. Check Ss' answers around the class, then choose some pairs to report back to the class.

> **SUGGESTED ANSWER KEY**
>
> • It was a very interesting documentary.
>   They were very interested in the documentary.
> • We were impressed by the acting.
>   The performance was impressive.
> • They were bored to tears.
>   It was such a boring film that we left before it ended.
> • She was moved by the solos.
>   The last scene of the film was very moving.
> • The children were very excited by the performance.
>   The clown's tricks were very exciting.

c) • Read out and explain the task. Explain that there are three parts to the task and that Ss must negotiate to find a solution. Ask Ss to suggest reasons for seeing each type of film – write these on the board.
   • Elicit/Explain useful language. Write on board: (As for Ex. 9). Ss, in closed pairs, do the task. Walk round and help Ss where necessary. Choose some pairs to act out their negotiation in front of the class.

> **SUGGESTED ANSWER KEY**
>
> SA: I think we should see that new comedy. Everyone says that it's very funny and I love funny films.
> SB: No, I don't feel like seeing a comedy. I prefer adventure films so I'd like to see that new adventure film. My brother says that it's really exciting and the special effects are very impressive.
> SA: Well, alright. I think we should watch the adventure film tonight and the comedy tomorrow.
> SB: That's a great idea.

Project (p. 73)

Choose a film Ss have watched. Write the heading on the board. Elicit information to complete the table. Ss copy it into their notebooks, then talk about it. After Ss have done the task orally in class, assign it as written HW. See Writing Project 6 for the Answer Key.

12 a) Go through the list of words and, with Ss, match them to the people.

> **ANSWER KEY**
>
> hat: Mark & Mrs Smith - top hat: Mr Smith - striped tie: Mark & John - riding hat: John - beret: Pete - long jacket: Mr Smith - flat shoes: Mark & Mr Smith - shawl: Lyn - gloves: Mr Smith - sandals: Pete - slippers: Tony - riding boots: John - jodhpurs: John - long dress: Lyn & Mrs Smith - whip: John - waistcoat: Mr Smith - parasol: Mrs Smith - jeans: Pete - bonnet: Lyn - checked trousers: Mr Smith - smock: Pete - suit: Mark - cane: Mr Smith - cotton pyjamas: Tony - cravat: Mr Smith

b) Allow Ss some time to prepare their descriptions. Check Ss' answers. As an extension, Ss can describe each person's facial features. Then Ss describe the costume they would like to wear.

> **ANSWER KEY**
>
> – Lyn is wearing a long blue dress, a pink shawl and a dark blue bonnet.
> – John is wearing a black riding hat, black jodhpurs, riding boots and a white shirt with a striped tie. He is also carrying a whip.
> – Tony is wearing yellow cotton pyjamas and black-and-white slippers.
> – Mark is wearing a dark blue suit and hat, and a striped tie.
> – Mr Smith is wearing checked trousers, a long grey coat and a waistcoat. He is also wearing grey gloves, a top hat and a red silk cravat. He is carrying a cane. Mrs Smith is wearing a long blue dress and a small hat. She is carrying a parasol.
> – Pete is wearing jeans under a smock, sandals and a red beret.
> – Ss' own answers

Suggested Homework

1 **Vocabulary:** words in Exs 6, 8 & 9 (p. 72), Exs 11c & 12 (p. 73)
2 **Dictation:** any ten words from Vocabulary with definition or example
3 **Speaking:** Ex. 9 (p. 72) and Ex. 12b (p. 73) (Ss can also find pictures of famous people and describe what the person looks like.)
4 **Project:** (p. 73)

* Check Ss' HW (10').

23 a) • Ss look at the picture and the title of the article. Discuss the questions in class.

SUGGESTED ANSWER KEY

The picture shows a woman who is pretending to be a statue. I haven't seen anything like that before. I think it's a very difficult job because she needs to stand there without moving at all.

• Ss then discuss items 1 to 7. Any answers are acceptable provided they can be justified.

b) Play the recording. Ss listen and check their answers.

ANSWER KEY

| 1 Yes | 3 Yes | 5 Yes | 7 No |
| 2 Yes | 4 No | 6 Yes | |

24 a) Explain the task. Point out that Ss should skim the text quickly to get the main idea. Ss then read the questions. Allow Ss three to four minutes to read the article and circle the correct answers. Check Ss' answers by asking Ss to read sentences from the text that give the answer. Help Ss explain the highlighted words. Ss can give a synonym, an opposite or an example for each word/phrase.

ANSWER KEY

| 1 C | 2 C | 3 D | 4 A |

b) Write the headings **PROS** and **CONS** on the board. Elicit answers from Ss to complete the table. Ss copy the table into their notebooks, then use the notes to talk about living statues. Ss then discuss the rest of the questions.

ANSWER KEY

PROS	CONS
• earn lots of money	• spend hours practising their movements
• people admire them	• have to stand still for hours in all kinds of situations
• make people feel happy	• take a long time to put on make-up and get dressed

Being a living statue isn't an easy job. They need to spend hours practising their movements and they have to stand still for hours in all kinds of situations. Another drawback is that it takes a long time to put on their make-up and get dressed every day.

On the other hand there are certain advantages to this job. Firstly, they can earn lots of money. What's more, people admire them. The most important thing, though, is the fact that they make people feel happy.

There are living statues in my country. They usually dress as Egyptian mummies, Greek statues, beggars, knights, etc.

25 Allow Ss two minutes to do the exercise. Check Ss' answers. Ss then make sentences using the completed phrases. Ss should memorise these phrases.

> *ANSWER KEY*
>
> | | | | | | |
> |---|---|---|---|---|---|
> | *1* | *demand* | *5* | *crowd* | *9* | *public* |
> | *2* | *stand* | *6* | *spare* | *10* | *believe* |
> | *3* | *extra* | *7* | *tourist* | *11* | *street* |
> | *4* | *form* | *8* | *have* | *12* | *look* |

26 Allow Ss two minutes to do the exercise. Check Ss' answers, then Ss make sentences using the completed phrases. Ss should memorise these phrases.

> *ANSWER KEY*
>
> | | | | | | |
> |---|---|---|---|---|---|
> | *1* | *in, for* | *5* | *in* | *8* | *for* |
> | *2* | *at* | *6* | *of* | *9* | *of* |
> | *3* | *of* | *7* | *of* | *10* | *in* |
> | *4* | *to* | | | | |

Vocabulary Revision Game

Write the following words/phrases on the board. Ss, in teams, make sentences using them. Each correct sentence gets 1 point. The team with the most points is the winner.

Suggested list: makes a difference, chatted constantly, sold out, get cramped, boiling hot, pull a crowd, real challenge, novelty, lack of movement

27 Go through the table with Ss, then Ss do the exercise. Check Ss' answers, then Ss can make sentences using the phrasal verbs in the box. Ss should memorise these phrasal verbs.

> *ANSWER KEY*
>
> | | | | | | |
> |---|---|---|---|---|---|
> | *1* | *up* | *3* | *back* | *5* | *aside* |
> | *2* | *off* | *4* | *up* | | |

28 Go through the table, then Ss do the exercise. Check Ss' answers on the board.

> *ANSWER KEY*
>
> | | | | | | |
> |---|---|---|---|---|---|
> | *1* | *removal* | *3* | *assistance* | *5* | *reference* |
> | *2* | *actions* | *4* | *discovery* | *6* | *information* |

Further practice

After Ss have done Ex. 24, ask them to visit:
http://www.elephantart.com/press/mia_report.htm
read the information, then write an article about painting elephants.

> ### Suggested Homework
>
> **1** **Vocabulary:** highlighted words in text Ex. 24 (p. 76), Exs 25 - 28 (p. 77)
> **2** **Dictation:** any ten words from Vocabulary with definition and example
> **3** **Speaking:** Ex. 24b (p. 76)
> **4** **Writing:** a short paragraph about the pros and cons of working as a living statue. Ss can use their notes from Ex. 24b.

1   How does Paula Burns feel about her job?
    A   She thinks it takes too much preparation.
    B   She only does it for the money.
    C   She is proud of what she does.
    D   She thinks anyone can do it.

2   What does Paula say about the audience?
    A   They think she's a nuisance.
    B   She likes to frighten them.
    C   They are entertained by her sudden movements.
    D   They believe she is a real statue.

3   Why does Mark Sorby talk about an Egyptian mummy?
    A   Because it was the best living statue he had ever seen.
    B   Because it was the first living statue he had ever seen.
    C   Because he earned a lot of money.
    D   To explain how convincing living statues can be.

4   What does Toni Moreno say about children?
    A   They think she's a real statue.
    B   They always want to touch her.
    C   She doesn't want them to touch her.
    D   They make it difficult for her to stand still.

Vocabulary Practice

25   **Fill in the correct word from the list, then make sentences using the completed phrases.**

- have • spare • extra • crowd • street
- public • form • believe • tourist
- demand • look • stand

1   popular ....
2   to .... still
3   .... cash
4   art ....
5   .... pleaser
6   .... time

7   .... attraction
8   to ... an experience
9   .... nuisance
10 to .... one's eyes
11 .... performer
12 second ....

26   **Fill in: *at*, *for*, *in*, *of*, then make sentences using the completed phrases.**

1 to be .... time .... sth; 2 to glare ....
sb; 3 to get hold .... sth; 4 due .... sth;
5 .... advance; 6 to think .... sb as sth;
7 to be made .... marble; 8 to do sth .... a
living; 9 fan .... sb; 10 .... my spare time

Phrasal Verbs

27   **Study the table, then underline the correct particle.**

> **set about** - to begin to do
> **set aside** - to save for a special purpose
> **set back** - to delay
> **set off/out** - to start a journey
> **set up** - 1) to build/erect sth, 2) to start sth (e.g. a business), 3) to arrange sth (e.g. a meeting)

1   Setting **about/up** your own business involves a lot of hard work.
2   The Pattersons loaded up their car, locked the house up and set **up/off**.
3   The earthquake has set **back/about** the construction of the new Olympic Stadium.
4   We need to set **aside/up** a meeting with the client to discuss costs.
5   Fred is very busy, but he always manages to set **back/aside** a little time to spend with his kids.

Word Formation
(forming nouns from verbs)

28   **Study the table, then complete the sentences with the correct form of the word in bold.**

> We can form nouns from verbs by adding *-ance*, *-al*, *-ion*, *-ence*, *-ery*, *-ation* to the verb.
> e.g.   resist - resist**ance**   persist - persist**ence**
>   refuse - refus**al**   cook - cook**ery**
>   react - react**ion**   alter - alter**ation**

1   The doctor said that the ....   REMOVE
    of the lump would be a simple
    operation.
2   Mrs Taylor is sure to have a good   ACT
    reason for her ....
3   With your .... , I'll be   ASSIST
    able to finish the report by Friday.
4   "I've made an incredible ....   DISCOVER
    ....," shouted the scientist.
5   The Prime Minister made a ....   REFER
    .... to the new law in his speech.
6   Ben refused to give her any ....   INFORM
    .... about his new invention.

Communication

• Making Suggestions

29 Fill in the missing words, then listen and check. In pairs, use the prompts to act out similar dialogues.

A: Hi, Angie! It's 1) ....!
B: Oh. Hi, Brett.
A: Listen, are you free tonight?
B: I don't know 2) .... Why?
A: Well, do you 3) .... coming to a barbecue at Graham's house with me?
B: I'm not sure. Can I call you 4) ....?
A: Yeah, but can you 5) .... me know before 6:00?
B: I'll try.
A: 6) ...., bye!

• Veronica/Leo/on Saturday evening/exhibition – art gallery/7:00
• Mary/Craig/on Sunday afternoon/hockey game – ice rink/5:30

Pronunciation (rising intonation in polite requests)

30 Listen and repeat.

Could I have your telephone number?
Can I take a message?
Could I use your pen?
Can I leave early?

Writing (a letter to the editor)

We write letters to the editor of a newspaper/magazine when we want to express our opinion about a topic/article which has been published in the newspaper/magazine. We usually write our letter to express our agreement or disagreement using formal language. We start our letter with "Dear Sir/Madam,". Then, in the **introduction**, we state the reason for writing and our opinion about the topic. If our letter is a reply to another letter or article, we also write where and when we read it, as well as the name of the person who wrote it. In the **main body**, we present our viewpoints giving reasons/examples. We write each viewpoint in separate paragraphs. In the **last paragraph**, we summarise our opinion and state what action we expect to be taken. We end our letter with "Yours faithfully," and our full name.

31 a) Read the extracts from the article, then look at the comments made. How does the person who wrote the notes feel? Why?

Silver Moon

...The venue didn't open its doors until half an hour before the concert started. As a result, we missed twenty minutes of the first performance. ... — *not true! opened two hours before*

...The support group *Silver Moon* was not the one advertised and were a poor substitute for *Black Mud*. ... — *well-known entertainers — no one complained*

...The sound quality was so poor that only those in front of the stage could hear the music. ... — *temporary problem — lasted ten minutes*

b) Read the letter and replace the phrases in bold with those in the list, then answer the questions.

• I feel I have to express my disagreement ...
• I am opposed to ... • In addition ...
• In conclusion ... • Firstly ...

Dear Sir,
   I am writing with regard to your recent review of The Friends of Forest Hill charity rock concert. **I wish to disagree** with several of your comments as follows.
   To begin with, the venue opened its doors two hours before the event began. The writer must have been a latecomer who arrived after the performance had begun.
   I strongly disagree with your comment regarding *Silver Moon*. Although it is true that *Black Mud* did not play as advertised, their replacement, *Silver Moon*, are equally well-known entertainers. No one felt disappointed by the change.
   Furthermore, regarding the problem with the sound quality, this was only a temporary problem and lasted no more than ten minutes. Technicians quickly repaired the fault and we were all able to enjoy the music again.
   To sum up, I believe the whole event was well organised and an overall success. I hope, therefore, that you will print this letter together with an apology to the performers, fans and event organisers like myself, who are looking forward to a similar event in the near future.
Yours faithfully,
T Fuller
Timothy Fuller

Lesson 5 (pp. 78 - 79)

* Check Ss' HW (10').

29 • Ss read the dialogues. Play the recording. Ss listen and fill in the missing words. Check Ss' answers. Then Ss, in closed pairs, read out the completed dialogue.
• Ss, in closed pairs, use the prompts to act out similar dialogues. Check Ss' answers round the class, then ask some pairs to report back to the class.

ANSWER KEY

1 Brett   3 fancy   5 let
2 yet   4 later   6 OK

A: Hi, **Veronica**! It's **Leo**!
B: Oh. Hi, **Leo**.
A: Listen, are you free on **Saturday evening**?
B: I don't know yet. Why?
A: Well, do you fancy coming to **an exhibition at the art gallery** with me?
B: I'm not sure. Can I call you later?
A: Yeah, but can you let me know before **7:00**?
B: I'll try.
A: OK, bye!

A: Hi, **Mary**! It's **Craig**!
B: Oh. Hi, **Craig**.
A: Listen, are you free on **Sunday afternoon**?
B: I don't know yet. Why?
A: Well, do you fancy coming to **a hockey game at the ice rink** with me?
B: I'm not sure. Can I call you later?
A: Yeah, but can you let me know before **5:30**?
B: I'll try.
A: OK, bye!

---

30 Play the recording. Ss listen and follow the lines. Play the recording again, pausing after every sentence. Ss listen and repeat individually.

Writing (p. 78)

• Elicit what an editor is *(person who is in charge of a newspaper or magazine and who decides what will be published in each edition).* Elicit what kind of letter sb would send to an editor and what the letter could be about *(formal letter – letter expressing our opinion about a topic/ article which has been discussed in the newspaper/ magazine).*
• Go through the theory with Ss discussing the points mentioned.

31 a) • Explain that Ss are going to read extracts from an article and comments sb made while reading it. Explain these words: **venue, substitute** by giving examples.
• Allow Ss three minutes to read the extracts and notes and say how the person feels and why.

ANSWER KEY

The person seems to be very angry/furious because there are inaccuracies in the article. We can tell how he feels from the way he has written his notes (e.g. not true!)

---

b) • Explain that this is the letter the person who wrote the notes sent to the editor of the newspaper. Ask: *Who wrote the letter? (Mr Timothy Fuller.) Why does he start with **Dear Sir**? (Because he does not know the editor's name.)*
• Allow Ss three minutes to read the letter silently and do the exercise. Check Ss' answers.

ANSWER KEY

I wish to disagree → I feel I have to express my disagreement.
To begin with → Firstly
I strongly disagree with → I am opposed to
Furthermore → In addition
To sum up → In conclusion

---

32 Explain that sentences 1 - 4 contain informal language which is not appropriate for a letter to the editor. Do item 1 with Ss, then Ss do the rest of the items in closed pairs. Explain that Ss can use phrases from the letter in Ex. 31b. Check Ss' answers.

33 • Go through the plan. Discuss the points Ss will include in their letter.
   e.g T: How should the letter start?
       S1: Dear Sir/Madam.
       T: What is the reason for writing?
       S2: To disagree with some points made in an article.
       T: What is the writer complaining about?
       S3: The tickets were expensive.
       S4: It rained.
       S5: You couldn't see the stage from the sides.
       T: What action do you think the writer might ask to be taken?
       S6: He might want another article written.
       T: How should the letter finish?
       S7: Yours faithfully and your full name.
   • Ss do the task orally in class, then assign it as written HW.

34 Read the sentences and elicit/explain the meanings of the sentences.

Suggested Homework

1   **Vocabulary:** Ex. 31b (p. 78), Ex. 32 (p.79)
2   **Act out:** Ex. 29 (p. 78)
3   **Writing:** Ex. 33 (p. 79)

Lesson 6

Workbook Unit 6
   Click on Grammar 6

1 Why has the writer written the letter? Is it a friendly or formal letter?

2 Who is going to read this letter?

3 What are the writer's objections? Has he included all his points in the letter?

4 What does the writer expect the editor to do?

32 Replace the informal language in bold, with phrases from the letter in Ex. 31b keeping the same meaning.

1 **I would like to say a few things about** your recent article on last Sunday's book exhibition at Greenbury Town Hall.

....

....

2 **I hate to read** articles that make criminals look like heroes.

....

....

3 **One more thing,** it is our responsibility to keep our town clean.

....

....

4 **Well, that's all, so** I believe that we should take action before it is too late.

....

....

33 You recently attended an outdoor theatre performance which you found very disappointing. However, while you were reading your local newspaper, The Morpeth Daily, you came across the following article. Read the article and your notes, then write a letter to the editor expressing your opinion (120-150 words).

Use the plan and the letter in Ex. 31b as a model.

This year's *Theatre in the Park* at Whitby Park was another spectacular success. All three performances were crowded with theatre-goers of all ages. The audience, seated outdoors on blankets and chairs, enjoyed every moment of the performances.

The set looked wonderful, as did the costumes. The whole effect was truly magical.

The highlight of the performance was, without doubt, Charles Grey, whose energetic acting made the audience cheer whenever he was on stage.

not true — tickets expensive — no special offers for senior citizens or young children

it rained twice — two performances cut short!

couldn't see the stage from the sides

Plan

Dear Sir/Madam,
Introduction
(Para 1)   *reason for writing und opinion*
Main Body
(Paras 2-4) *viewpoints and reasons/examples*
Conclusion
(Para 5)   *restate your opinion/state action you expect to be taken*

Yours faithfully,
signature
(your full name)

34 Read the sentences. What do they mean?

What's in a word?

- Art is long and life is short.
- Beauty is in the eye of the beholder.
- They that dance must pay the fiddler.

THE ADVENTURES OF HUCKLEBERRY FINN

Travelling with Royalty

Huck and Jim floated past Cairo in the fog and then a steamboat hit their raft.

There — it's fixed now. Still, we can't go back *up* the river on a raft.

I know, Huck, but it's dangerous to stay here. Let's go down the river until we get some money, and then come back in a steamboat.

Listen! What's that?

WOOF! WOOF!

Help! Help!

Get us out of here — please!

Who are you running away from?

The people in the town near here found out I was trying to cheat them.

Me too — I was pretending to be a priest.

Why are you two hiding? Is this man a runaway slave?

A runaway?! Going *SOUTH*?! No, Jim's mine — I'm just afraid somebody will take him away from me.

Let me introduce myself — I am really the Duke of Bridgewater.

Oh, yes? Well, I'm the son of Louis XVI — *I am* really the King of France!

Huck … they aren't like any royalty *I've* ever met!

They're just a pair of liars, Jim — but I don't know how to get rid of them.

Well, Duke — any idea how we can get money out of the fools in all the little riverside towns we come to?

We can act scenes from Shakespeare! I'll teach you …

O Romeo, Romeo …

Boo! Boo!

They always had to leave town in a hurry.

Pre-Reading Activities

1 Look at the pictures (p. 80). Which shows somebody:

1 introducing themselves? 5
2 fixing the raft? 1
3 acting part of a play? 8
4 walking through the river? 3
5 on the bank of the river? 2
6 talking behind his hand? 6

2 Describe the men in picture 5, using words from the list.
(See Suggested Answers section)

- bad haircut
- bald
- beard
- bow tie
- elderly
- grey hair
- moustache
- old suit

Listening and Reading Activities

3 Listen and fill in the missing words.

1 "Get us out of h e r e, please!"
2 "Is this man a runaway s l a v e?"
3 "They're just a p a i r of liars, Jim."

4 Read the episode on p. 80 and answer the questions.
(See Suggested Answers section)

1 What plan does Jim suggest?
2 Who is chasing the two men in picture 2? Why?
3 Why does Jim look frightened in picture 4?
4 Did the two men know each other before they got on the raft? How do you know?
5 What is happening in picture 8?

5 Read the episode and find the words in the episode which match the definitions.

1 kind of ship = steamboat
2 escaped = runaway
3 behave dishonestly = cheat
4 the members of royal families = royalty
5 couple = pair

Grammar

- *must - can't* (assumptions)

6 Study the grammar box. Then, make as many speculations about the pictures as possible, using *must* or *can't*, as in the examples. *(See Suggested Answers section)*

We make **assumptions** when we are sure about something but we don't know this as a fact. We use ***must*** for positive assumptions and ***can't*** for negative assumptions.

Present

I'm sure these men **are** liars. > These men **must be** liars.	I'm sure they **are lying**. > They **must be lying**.
I'm sure this man **isn't** a king. > This man **can't be** a king.	I'm sure he **isn't telling** the truth. > He **can't be telling** the truth.

Perfect

I'm sure they **did/have done** something wrong. > They **must have done** something wrong.	I'm sure they **were trying/have been trying** to cheat people. > They **must have been trying** to cheat people.
I'm sure they **didn't go/haven't been** to Drama school. > They **can't have been** to Drama school.	I'm sure they **weren't doing/haven't been doing** honest jobs. > They **can't have been doing** honest jobs.

She **must be waiting** for an interview.
They **can't be** friends.
They **must have been waiting** for a long time.

7 Listen to the episode, then read it aloud.

8 Read the summary and underline the correct word in bold.

Huck and Jim fixed the raft, but they couldn't use it to go back up to Cairo. Jim 1) told/suggested going down the river, getting some money and coming back on a steamboat. Then Huck 2) heard/listened two men 3) telling/calling for help. The men 4) admitted/lied they were running from some people they had tried to cheat. One of the men 5) asked/said if Jim was a runaway slave. Huck 6) disagreed/denied this, pretending he was afraid somebody would steal Jim. The younger man 7) said/introduced himself as a duke, so the older man 8) claimed/told he was really the King of France. Huck 9) told/said Jim they were both liars. The 'King' 10) questioned/asked how they could get money in small towns along the river, and the 'Duke' suggested that they could act scenes from Shakespeare. Unfortunately, they were terrible actors, and they always had to leave town in a hurry.

Vocabulary & Grammar

1 Fill in the correct word.

1 How would you like your steak; medium, rare or well done?

2 It was such nice weather that we went to the beach.

3 "I'd like a glass of water, please!" "Still or sparkling, sir?"

4 Hurry up or else we'll be late for the performance.

5 What shall we have for dessert: fruit salad or ice cream?

6 Actors spend hours practising their roles.

7 "Something smells good! What is it, Ann?" "Roast lamb."

8 They've set up their business in Spain.

9 Are there any sandwiches left?

10 Have you decided on the menu for the party yet?

11 Do you fancy going to the opera tomorrow?

12 Put the iron down. You'll burn yourself.

13 It was so cold that we turned the heater on.

14 There is a man glaring at you. Do you know him?

15 Watch out! You're going to fall.

16 Can you please let me know the date in advance?

17 "May I use the telephone?" "Yes, of course."

18 John is allergic to seafood.

19 Statues are made of marble.

20 We won't go to the party unless you come with us.

21 There's going to be a second concert due to public demand.

22 Vitamin C is good for our bones and teeth.

23 Could you get hold of some tickets?

24 I'd love to come to your party.

25 We also need a tube of toothpaste.

26 If you work hard, you'll get a promotion.

27 I'm afraid I can't make it to your party. Sorry.

28 "Shall we go to the cinema instead?" "I'd love to."

29 The lights are on. Sally must be at home.

30 Broccoli is rich in Vitamin C.

(30 marks)

2 Circle the correct item.

1 John likes pizza with lots of .... cheese.
   A mashed (B) grated   C diced D scrambled

2 He finally gave .... and let her drive the car.
   (A) in   B up   C away   D out

3 The .... cheered when Barcelona won.
   A visitors   C guests
   B audience   (D) spectators

4 You can use olive oil to treat .... wounds.
   A fewer   B lesser   C major   (D) minor

5 I'll never forget .... Venice. It was like a dream to me.
   A to visiting B to visit   (C) visiting D visit

6 Could I have .... cherries, please?
   (A) a few   B a little   C any   D lot of

7 You .... enter restricted areas.
   A don't have to   C needn't
   (B) mustn't   D aren't allowed

8 Ben's mum always makes him .... to bed early.
   A to going (B) go   C going   D to go

9 Let's make lasagne with cheese ....
   A bake B ingredients C flakes (D) sauce

10 There's very .... sugar left.
   A a few   B a little   (C) little   D few

(20 marks)

Communication

3 Put the dialogue in the correct order.

1 May I take your order, sir?

4 Prawn cocktail would be fine.

7 And what would you like to drink?

2 Yes, please.

5 Excellent choice, sir. And what would you like to follow?

3 What would you like to start with?

8 I'll have a glass of sparkling water, please.

6 Sirloin steak and a baked potato, please.

9 Thank you, sir.

(15 marks)

Reading

4 Read the text and choose the best heading for each paragraph. There is one heading which you do not need to use.

A New food types
B Possible dangers
C The future is here
D Towards a healthier life
E Added goodness
F The easy way

(15 marks)

Functional Foods

1 **A** For most of us, the idea of soup which stops us getting ill, or crisps which relax us seems like something from a science-fiction film. However, these are not foods of the future. In fact, they are part of a new group of food products known as 'functional foods', and they may already be on your supermarket's shelves.

2 **D** In today's world, we all know that our diet affects our health and more people are watching what they eat. Food companies are taking advantage of this fact. They have already started to use ingredients in their products which will offer extra health benefits to their customers. For example, orange juice already contains vitamin C, but now you can buy orange juice with added calcium to strengthen your bones and teeth, so it's even better for you than ever before.

3 **E** However, food companies are not only producing foods which improve our health. They are also adding ingredients to their products which are designed to make our daily lives easier. For instance, there is now a chewing gum which can improve your memory and help your brain to process information more quickly. Also, if you lead a busy life, try St John's Wort crisps. They make you feel relaxed and less stressed!

4 **B** Of course, there are people who believe that functional foods are a bad idea. They claim that products such as these can be dangerous, as people may end up taking more vitamins than they need and may damage their bodies as a result. Health experts recommend that people check the labels on these products carefully to ensure that they do not take more than the recommended doses of vitamins and minerals.

5 **C** Nevertheless, functional foods are becoming increasingly popular and supporters feel that it won't be long before there are foods which prevent cancer, protect eyesight and much more. With hundreds of different products already available, it looks as though we will all soon be eating the food of the future.

Writing (a letter to the editor)

5 You read an article about a proposal to build a shopping centre in your town. Write a letter to the editor expressing your disagreement (120-180 words).

Plan

(See Suggested Answers section)

Introduction
Dear Sir,
(Para 1) *I am writing/recent article/proposed shopping centre*

Main Body
(Para 2) *provide new jobs but increase traffic and noise; roads dangerous/children*
(Para 3) *town appearance change for worse – tear down beautiful old buildings, replaced by centre*

Conclusion
(Para 4) *I am opposed to – I hope – print letter – shopping centre not built*

(20 marks)

(Total = 100 marks)

Let's sing!

6 Listen and fill in. Listen again and sing.

I love music!

When I'm feeling lonely
When I'm feeling **1)** *sad*
I turn on my stereo
And **2)** *things* don't seem so bad.

CHORUS: I love music
Fast or **3)** *slow*
It's great to know
Music makes me
4) *happy*
And my sadness goes
I love music, music, music.

How can I feel lonely
When music is such
5) *fun*?
When I hear it on my radio

I want to **6)** *jump* up and down
I want to dance all
7) *around*
And sing to everyone.

My **8)** *friends* think I am crazy
But that's alright with me
When I've got a problem
I play my favourite
9) *song*
I feel that nothing is wrong
The music sets me
10) *free*.
I love music, music, music

Environmental & Social Issues

◆ Before you start …

What is your favourite dish? How often do you eat it?
Which is the most popular restaurant for teenagers in your town?
Where do you usually buy your clothes? What kind of clothes do you like wearing?
Which is your most favourite place of entertainment?

◆ Listen, read and talk about …

Nature's Warning

UNIT 7

- the environment
- global warming
- ways to protect the environment
- recycling

One Good Turn Deserves Another

UNIT 8

- public services
- parts of the body
- aches & pains
- symptoms
- charitable organisations

◆ **Learn how to ...**

- make suggestions about a better environment
- give advice
- make offers & requests
- apply for volunteer work
- join an organisation
- ask for information on volunteer work

◆ **Practise ...**

- the passive
- shall (offers/suggestions)
- will/would (requests)
- question tags
- echo questions
- reported speech (statements)
- could/was able to
- used to

◆ **Phrasal verbs**

- carry
- hold
- make
- put

◆ **Write ...**

- a letter to a friend about changes in a place
- an article providing solutions to a problem
- a letter to the editor suggesting ways to help out
- a letter giving advice
- a transactional letter asking for information

NATURE'S WARNING

1

2

3

4

Lead-in

1 **a) Which of the following can you see in the pictures?**
Use your dictionary to explain any new words.

- acid rain
- industrial waste
- deforestation
- overfishing
- famine
- flood
- volcanic eruption
- rising water levels
- hole in ozone layer

- typhoon
- earthquake
- rubbish
- oil spills
- air pollution
- water pollution
- noise pollution
- land pollution
- ultraviolet radiation

b) Which of these problems is your country facing?
Can you list them in order from most to least serious?

2 Look at the table and make true sentences about the
problems our planet faces.

The air Fish stocks Seas and oceans Forests Crops	is being are being	contaminated polluted reduced wiped out destroyed	by due to as a result of because of	oil spills frequent flooding deforestation smoke and gases from factories overfishing

The air is being polluted by smoke and gases from factories.

5

6

* Check Ss' HW (10').

6 • Ask Ss to look at the picture, and say what they can see (*factories, the sun, a thermometer, trees, cows, a volcano, aerosols*). Explain that all these can cause problems to the environment.
 • Read out the words in the list, then Ss complete the sentences. Ss then use the sentences to talk about global warming.

ANSWER KEY

 • The ozone layer ... **radiation** ...
 • Aerosol ... **chemicals** ... **cause**
 • Factories ... **carbon** ...
 • Volcanoes ... **natural** ...
 • This dioxide ... **traps** ... **greenhouse** ...

Global warming refers to the rise in the Earth's temperature caused by the increase in greenhouse gases. These gases act like a blanket around the Earth, trapping the heat in the atmosphere. This problem is being made worse by the hole in the ozone layer. This hole, caused by the use of aerosol sprays and chemicals, is allowing ultraviolet radiation from the sun to to enter Earth's atmosphere making it even warmer.

7 a) Go through the CAUSE column. Explain any unknown vocabulary by giving examples, then Ss work in closed pairs to match the prompts. Check Ss' answers round the class.

ANSWER KEY

Smog and factory smoke cause air pollution. As a result, greenhouse gases are produced.
Industrial waste causes water pollution. Therefore, fish die.
Sewage causes water pollution. As a result, diseases are spread.
The use of aerosols causes damage to the ozone layer. As a result, the Earth is not protected from ultraviolet radiation.

b) • Read and explain the task. Remind Ss that there are three parts to the task and that Ss must negotiate to find a solution. Ask Ss to suggest reasons for using the car and not using the car. Write these on board:
 e.g. **reasons for using the car**
 • travel faster
 • not have to queue for public transport
 • comfortable journey compared to that of public transport   etc
 reasons for not using the car
 • pollutes the environment (exhaust fumes)
 • parking can be difficult
 • more expensive than public transport
 • get stuck in traffic jams   etc

• Present useful language for giving arguments: I don't think it's a good idea; You should(n't); You'd better; Let's; What about ... ?; I think you should; A good idea would be ... etc
• Ss, in closed pairs, do the task. Walk around and help Ss where necessary. Choose some pairs to act out their negotiation in front of the class.

SUGGESTED ANSWER KEY

A: I think you should stop using your car. It pollutes the environment.
B: But it's quick and easy, not to mention comfortable.
A: What about using public transport instead? It's quite cheap and you don't need to worry about finding a parking space.
B: I see your point, still I can't stand being on a bus. It makes me feel stressed.
A: Well, why don't you try the underground then? If you don't like it, you can start using your car again. How about giving it a try?

Further practice

After Ss have done Ex. 6, ask them to visit http://www.epa.gov/globalwarming/kids/gw.html (We can make a difference) read the information, then write a short article about what we can do to make a difference.`

TAPESCRIPT (for Ex. 10b)

Only when all the rivers have run dry
and all the fish in the sea have died
only when all the rainforests have been burnt down
and there is no food for the animals
only when all the blue skies have been filled with smoke
and the cities of the world have choked
will the white man understand
that it's too late to save the earth

8 a) • Set the scene. Ss read out the prompts. Explain unknown vocabulary giving examples, synonyms or opposites. Ss, in pairs discuss the possible effects of global warming.
• Play the recording. Ss listen and check their answers.

ANSWER KEY:
items to be ticked: 1, 2, 4, 6, 8, 9, 11

TAPESCRIPT

Interviewer: Now, Professor, what can you tell our listeners about the effects of global warming?
Prof. Watson: Well, the most noticeable effect is that our weather patterns are changing. Did you know that it only takes a rise of a few degrees in temperature to seriously affect life on Earth?
Interviewer: No, I didn't. That's terrible.
Prof. Watson: Some countries are already becoming hotter while others are becoming much colder.
Interviewer: But that won't affect everyone - only the far north and south?
Prof. Watson: No, that's where you're wrong! All parts of the world will be affected but in different ways. There will be droughts in some parts of the world and bad storms and floods in others. The rise in temperature will also cause the Polar ice caps to melt and so the sea levels will rise. Actually, this is already happening and it will soon get much worse.
Interviewer: Really? I didn't know that.
Prof. Watson: Yes and throughout the world many low-lying areas are in danger of flooding. Think about how often there have been reports of floods lately in places like Holland and Bangladesh.
Interviewer: I suppose you're right. And what about wildlife?
Prof. Watson: Well, many plants and animals won't be able to adapt to the new climate and they may die. Some animals are already losing their homes and many plants are disappearing too. If we don't do something soon ... (fade)

b) Ss go through the suggestions and make sentences as in the examples. Ss, then in closed pairs think of other suggestions. Check Ss' answers.

ANSWER KEY

*Laws must be passed to make people recycle rubbish.
A good idea would be to ride bicycles more.
We could plant more trees.
Something must be done to encourage people to use unleaded petrol.
One way to stop global warming is to use less aerosols.
Laws must be passed to make factory owners put filters on factory chimneys.*

c) Explain the task, then allow Ss three to five minutes, to prepare their monologue. Check Ss' performance, in open pairs, in class.

ANSWER KEY

*Factories are burning rubbish oil and coal which produces carbon dioxide. Volcanoes, trees and animals produce natural greenhouse gases. These gases trap heat in the atmosphere, and the earth becomes warmer. This is called global warming.
As a result of global warming, weather patterns are changing. Temperatures are rising in many parts of the world. The polar ice caps are melting, and this causes the sea levels to rise. Many plants and animals are in danger.*

9 a) • Read through the prompts and elicit/explain any unknown words. Read and explain the task. Ss make sentences, as in the example.

SUGGESTED ANSWER KEY

• *Don't throw away plastic bottles, they can be recycled to make plant pots and vases.*
• *Don't throw away aluminium cans, they can be recycled to make new cans.*

• *Don't throw away glass bottles, they can be returned to the shop or taken to a bottle bank.*
• *Don't throw away plastic bags, they can be used to take out the rubbish at home.*
• *Don't waste rain water, it can be reused to water the garden or your plants.*

b) Individual Ss answer the questions.

SUGGESTED ANSWER KEY

In my town, there is a recycling scheme. We separate our rubbish into glass, plastic, aluminium and paper. These are collected on different days and taken away to be recycled. I think recycling is very important because it decreases pollution and makes our towns nicer places to live in. It is also helping to protect the environment.

10 a) • Explain the task, then allow Ss three minutes to read out the five questions and possible answers.
• Play the recording. Ss listen and do the exercise. Check Ss' answers.

ANSWER KEY: *1 B, 2 A, 3 A, 4 C, 5 B*

TAPESCRIPT

1 Woman: Can you do something for me? It's just that the town council has started a recycling scheme and we have to separate our rubbish. So, when you throw something out, can you put it in the right bin, please? See, I've got one for plastics, one for bottles, and one for cans. Oh, and there's a box here for newspapers. Um, I hope that's alright.
2 A: What are you doing with all those empty cans, Clive?
B: I'm taking them down to the recycling centre.
A: Where did you get them all from?
B: From schools, parks, cafés, football grounds – anywhere really!
A: Oh! Are you on some sort of clean-up campaign?
B: Yes and no. It's kind of a hobby of mine. The centre pays a penny for every aluminium can I give them and then they give the money to charity.
A: Good for you! Do you need a hand?
B: I thought you'd never ask!
3 A: Lunch was lovely. Thanks very much, Jean. Let me help you tidy up. I'll put this rubbish in the bin.
B: Wait a minute. I'd better tell you which one.
A: Oh! How come you've got all these different bins?
B: Well, this one's for glass, that one's for paper, the blue one is for plastic and the end one is for other waste, like food.
A: That's really efficient! I suppose you recycle everything?
B: Well, not me, personally! The local council collects the different bins on different days.
A: Really? Maybe I should check if my council does, too.
B: Why not? We should all do our bit.
4 Woman: Look at this! I saw it yesterday in the news agency and I just had to buy it. It's great. See, it's full of articles about the environment. You know, endangered animals and recycling - things like that. Look at this one about the Bengal tiger - the photos are fantastic. It's going to come out every month and I think I might subscribe to it.
5 Man: Now, Mr Willis. This is Peter Johnson from heating services. I'm just calling to check all the details for our appointment. Now let me see, we're coming on Tuesday at 3pm, that's the 23rd, and we'll be putting in a new low pollutant heating system. Is that right? Now just let me confirm the model number ...

b) • Read the task and elicit/explain any unknown words. Play the recording. [See p. 86(T)]
• Ss write a poem of their own. Walk around and help where necessary. Choose some Ss to read out their poem in front of the class.

Suggested Homework

1 **Vocabulary:** words in Ex. 6 (p. 86), Ex. 8 (p. 87)
2 **Dictation:** any ten words from Vocabulary
3 **Speaking:** Exs. 8c & 9a (p. 87)
4 **Writing:** a short article on global warming. Use the information in Ex. 6 (p. 86) and Ex. 9 (p. 87).

Listening

8 a) **Which of the following do you think the possible effects of global warming are? Listen and tick (✔) accordingly.**

1 ☐	changing weather patterns
2 ☐	a shortage of water
3 ☐	flooding of the entire planet
4 ☐	melting of polar ice caps
5 ☐	a decrease in the population of the planet
6 ☐	rising sea levels
7 ☐	a decrease in food supplies
8 ☐	flooding of low-lying areas
9 ☐	extinction of many species
10 ☐	depletion of natural resources
11 ☐	loss of plant life

Speaking

b) How can we stop global warming? Use the prompts below to make suggestions, as in the example.

> **Useful language:** We could, A good idea would be, One way is to, Laws must be passed to, Something must be done to, People should be required to

- use less fuel
- use public transport
- recycle rubbish
- ride bicycles more
- plant more trees
- use unleaded petrol
- use less aerosol sprays
- put filters on factory chimneys

People should be required to use less fuel.

A good idea would be to use public transport instead of driving your car.

c) Use your answers from Exs. 6, 7 and 8 to give a one-minute talk about global warming. Explain its causes and effects, then suggest possible solutions.

Speaking

9 a) **What can we do with: old newspapers/magazines? plastic bottles? aluminium cans? empty glass bottles? plastic bags? rainwater? Discuss with a partner. Use some of the ideas below to make sentences, as in the example.**

- recycle/make/greeting cards/writing paper
- recycle/make/plant pots/vases
- recycle/make/new cans
- return/shop/take/bottle bank
- reuse/take out/rubbish/at home
- reuse/water/garden/plants

Don't throw away old newspapers and magazines, they can be recycled to make greeting cards and writing paper.

b) Are there any recycling schemes in your town/city? Do you think recycling is important? Why?

Listening

10 a) **You will hear people talking in five different situations. Listen, then choose the correct answer to the questions below.**

1 You are staying at a friend's house. What does she ask you to do?
  A start recycling   B separate the rubbish
  C take out the rubbish

2 You overhear two people talking on the street. What is Clive talking about?
  A his clean-up campaign   B his free-time activity
  C his work for charity

3 Listen to these two women. How many recycling bins has Jean got?
  A Four.   B Three.   C Two.

4 Listen to this woman talking to a friend. What is she talking about?
  A a new film   B a new newspaper
  C a new magazine

5 Listen to the businessman phoning a client. Why has he phoned?
  A to make an appointment   B to check some details
  C to change their meeting

b) Listen to the poem, then use some of these words to make a poem of your own about the environment.

- rivers • fish • sea die • rainforests • burn down • animals
- blue skies • smoke • save the earth

Speaking

11 **a) Look at the pictures and the table, then talk about**

- various ways of keeping towns clean
- what makes a town a pleasant/unpleasant place to live in
- how we can make towns better places to live in

PROBLEMS	TOWARDS A BETTER ENVIRONMENT
• no parks • lots of traffic • air pollution • rubbish • factories • crowded • no bike paths • not enough public transport	

b) What are you doing to keep your town/city clean?

Grammar

- The Passive

12 **Fill in:** *be, is/are, has/have, was/were.* **In which of the sentences, active or passive, is the action more important than the agent (i.e. the person/thing doing the action)?**

	Active	Passive
Present Simple	People **use** alternative fuels for heating.	Alternative fuels .... used for heating.
Present Continuous	Industrial waste **is polluting** lakes and rivers.	Lakes and rivers .... being polluted by industrial waste.
Past Simple	They **built** this factory more than eighty years ago.	This factory .... built more than eighty years ago.
Past Continuous	They **were cutting down** the trees.	The trees .... being cut down.
Present Perfect	They **have dumped** rubbish in the lake.	Rubbish .... been dumped in the lake.
Future Simple	They **will plant** new forests.	New forests will .... planted.

13 **Put the verbs in brackets into the correct passive tense.**

1 A: .... your house ....
      .... (decorate)?
   B: Yes. That's why I'm staying with my parents.
2 A: When .... the health warning........................ (issue)?
   B: Yesterday.
3 A: Why is the river such an awful colour?
   B: Industrial waste ....
      ....
      (pump) into the river for over a year now.
4 A: .... the posters for the campaign ....
      .... (deliver) yet?
   B: No, not yet.
5 A: What makes this new car go?
   B: It ....
      (power) by both petrol and an electric motor.
6 A: Did you see the eco-warriors on TV last night?
   B: Yes, they ....
      .... (interview) about their latest campaign.
7 A: Oh no! I think I've thrown away my homework by mistake!
   B: Well, you can't get it back now. The bins ....
      ....
      .... (already/empty).
8 A: Are the brochures ready, Mrs Davis?
   B: Not yet. They ....
      ....
      (print) when I arrived.
9 A: Why do you want to buy a bicycle?
   B: Because cars ....
      ....
      (recently/ban) from the city centre so I can't drive to work.
10 A: Who won the competition?
    B: We don't know yet. The winner...........................
       .... (not/announce) until tomorrow morning.

Lesson 3 (pp. 88 - 89)

* Check Ss' HW (10').

11 **a)** Ask Ss to look at the pictures and identify the activities in each picture and how they relate to the title (e.g. planting a tree; recycling; rubbish bins waiting for collection; having a picnic in a park – all ways to create and enjoy a better environment). Ask Ss to look at the table. Elicit/Explain any unknown words. Explain the task. Write the discussion points on the board. Elicit Ss' ideas to answer the questions.

SUGGESTED ANSWER KEY

* There should be litter bins.
  It would be a good idea to recycle our rubbish.
  We should definitely sweep the streets.
* A town is pleasant if there are clean parks, no rubbish.
  A town is unpleasant if there is lots of rubbish on the streets or lots of traffic; if there are factories which cause air pollution, etc.
* We should have more clean parks, enough bike paths, frequent public transport, etc.

b) Read the questions. Individual Ss read their answers aloud.

SUGGESTED ANSWER KEY

I always throw my rubbish in the rubbish bin.
I always recycle my rubbish. I go to work by bike. etc

12 * Go through the table. Do item 1 with Ss. Revise how the passive is formed (to be + past participle of main verb). Complete the table with Ss. Refer Ss to the Grammar Reference Section for more detail.

ANSWER KEY

Present Simple: are
Present Continuous: are
Past Simple: was
Past Continuous: were
Present Perfect: has
Future Simple: be
The action is more important than the agent in the sentences containing passive forms.

* Ss look at the sentences containing passive forms. Ask: *How is the agent introduced? (With "by".) Why do most sentences not contain the agent? (Because the agent is unimportant or understood from the context.)*

13 Explain the task, then Ss fill in the correct passive forms. Check Ss' answers.

ANSWER KEY

1 Is ... being decorated
2 was ... issued
3 has been pumped
4 Have ... been delivered
5 is powered
6 were being interviewed
7 have already been emptied
8 were being printed
9 have recently been banned
10 won't be announced

14 Explain the task. Do item 1 with Ss, then Ss work in pairs to do the exercise. Check Ss' answers.

ANSWER KEY

1 It has been polluted by the local factory.
2 It hasn't been picked up for ages.
3 Yes, the invitations were sent last week.
4 Yes, it is being built right now.
5 Yes, it will be finished (by) tomorrow.
6 It is collected twice a week.

15 Explain the theory table. Check that Ss understand what instrument/material/ingredient is by asking them to identify the following: *knife (instrument); wood (material); rice (ingredient)*. Ss do the exercise. Check Ss' answers.

ANSWER KEY

1 by	3 by	5 with	7 with
2 with	4 by	6 with	8 by

16 Explain what a Green Day is (an event which tries to encourage people to care about the environment). Do items 1, 2 in class, then Ss, in closed pairs, do the rest. Check Ss' answers round the class, then ask some pairs to report back to the class.

ANSWER KEY

3 A: Has the bicycle course been set up yet?
  B: Yes. It was set up this morning.
4 A: Have the tables and chairs been delivered yet?
  B: No. They will be delivered tomorrow morning.
5 A: Has the craft tent been put up yet?
  B: No. It will be put up tomorrow.
6 A: Has the catering company been booked yet?
  B: Yes. It was booked three weeks ago.
7 A: Has the competition been organised yet?
  B: Yes. It was organised yesterday.
8 A: Have the speakers been booked yet?
  B: Yes. They were booked last week.

17 • Ask Ss to look at picture A and describe it. (There's an old factory, lots of rubbish, a broken fence, a big hole etc). Ss look at picture B. Ask: Is this the same area? (Yes. There are the same skyscrapers in the background.) What has happened to the area? (It has been turned into a park.) What can you see? (Park benches, lamps, play area, recycling bins, sunshades etc.)
   • Read out the prompts, then Ss use them to make sentences in the passive.

ANSWER KEY

The factory has been torn down.
A path has been laid.
Trees have been planted.
A play area is being built at the moment.
Park benches are being set up at the moment.
The fence has been fixed.
Sunshades are being set up at the moment.
Lights are being put in at the moment.
A sign was put up yesterday.
Recycling bins have been delivered.

Project (p. 89)

Explain that Ss are going to write a letter to a friend. Elicit appropriate beginnings (How are you?; Sorry I haven't written for so long; Thanks for your letter. etc) and endings (Well, that's all for now; Write soon; I'd better go now. etc). Ask Ss to suggest an appropriate topic sentence for the main body paragraph. (e.g. The work is almost finished. You won't believe your eyes. etc) Ask: Why are you writing the letter? (To tell my friend about the park.) Elicit the main body from Ss. Ss use the prompts in Ex. 17. After Ss have done the exercise orally, assign it as written HW. See Writing Project 7 for the Answer Key.

Suggested Homework

1 Vocabulary: Ex. 17 (p. 89)
2 Dictation: table Ex. 12 (p. 88)
3 Speaking: Ex. 11 (p. 88), Ex. 17 (p. 89)
4 Project: (p. 89)

14 Use the prompts to respond in the passive.

1 A: Why is the river so dirty?
   B: It (pollute/local factory) ....
   ....

2 A: There's litter everywhere!
   B: I know. (it/not pick up/for ages). ....
   ....

3 A: Have they organised the party yet?
   B: Yes, (the invitations/send/last week). ....
   ....

4 A: I heard that there will be a recycling centre in
      the city.
   B: Yes, (it/build/right now)..........................
   ....

5 A: Are you working on that report?
   B: Yes, (it finish/tomorrow) ....
   ....

6 A: How often do they collect the rubbish?
   B: It (collect/twice a week)..........................
   ....

15 Study the table, then fill in *by* or *with*.

> **by + agent** e.g. *Twenty Thousand Leagues under the
> Sea was written* **by** *Jules Verne.*
> **with + tool/material/ingredient** e.g. *He was shot* **with**
> *a pistol.*

1 The rivers are being polluted .... industrial
   waste.
2 The fish were caught .... a net.
3 A smog warning was issued .... the
   Health Department.
4 Heat is trapped .... greenhouse gases.
5 He was cut .... a knife.
6 This dish is delicious when served ....
   rice.
7 John's house has been constructed ....
   imported timber.
8 The campaign was started .... students
   at our school.

16 Your class is organising a Green Day. Use the
prompts to ask and answer, as in the examples.

1 the bins/deliver? (yes – yesterday)
   A: Have the bins been delivered?
   B: Yes. They were delivered yesterday.
2 posters/put up? (no – tomorrow)
   A: Have the posters been put up?
   B: No, they will be put up tomorrow.
3 bicycle course/set up? (yes - this morning)
4 tables and chairs/deliver? (no - tomorrow morning)

5 craft tent/put up? (no - tomorrow)
6 catering company/book? (yes - two weeks ago)
7 competition/organise? (yes - yesterday)
8 speakers/book? (yes - last week)

17 The council has decided to turn an old
abandoned factory into a park. Look at the
pictures and use the prompts to make
sentences in the passive, as in the example.

the rubbish/remove; factory/tear down; path/
lay; trees/plant; play area/build/at the moment;
park benches/set up/at the moment; fence/fix;
sunshades/set up/at the moment; lights/put in/at
the moment; sign/put up/yesterday; recycling
bins/deliver

The rubbish has been removed.

• Project

Write a letter to your friend, telling him/her
about the changes above. Use the ideas in
Ex. 17 to help you.

Listening & Reading

18 a) Have you ever been to a zoo? What do you think about animals being imprisoned in cages? What can grow inside a greenhouse? What do you think greenhouses are used for?
b) Look at the pictures. Which shows: people looking at animals? tropical plants; birds; insects & reptiles?

TiP Read the questions and underline the key words. Skim read the texts and try to find phrases with the same meaning as the key words. Don't be discouraged by unfamiliar vocabulary. Concentrate on specific information required from the text.

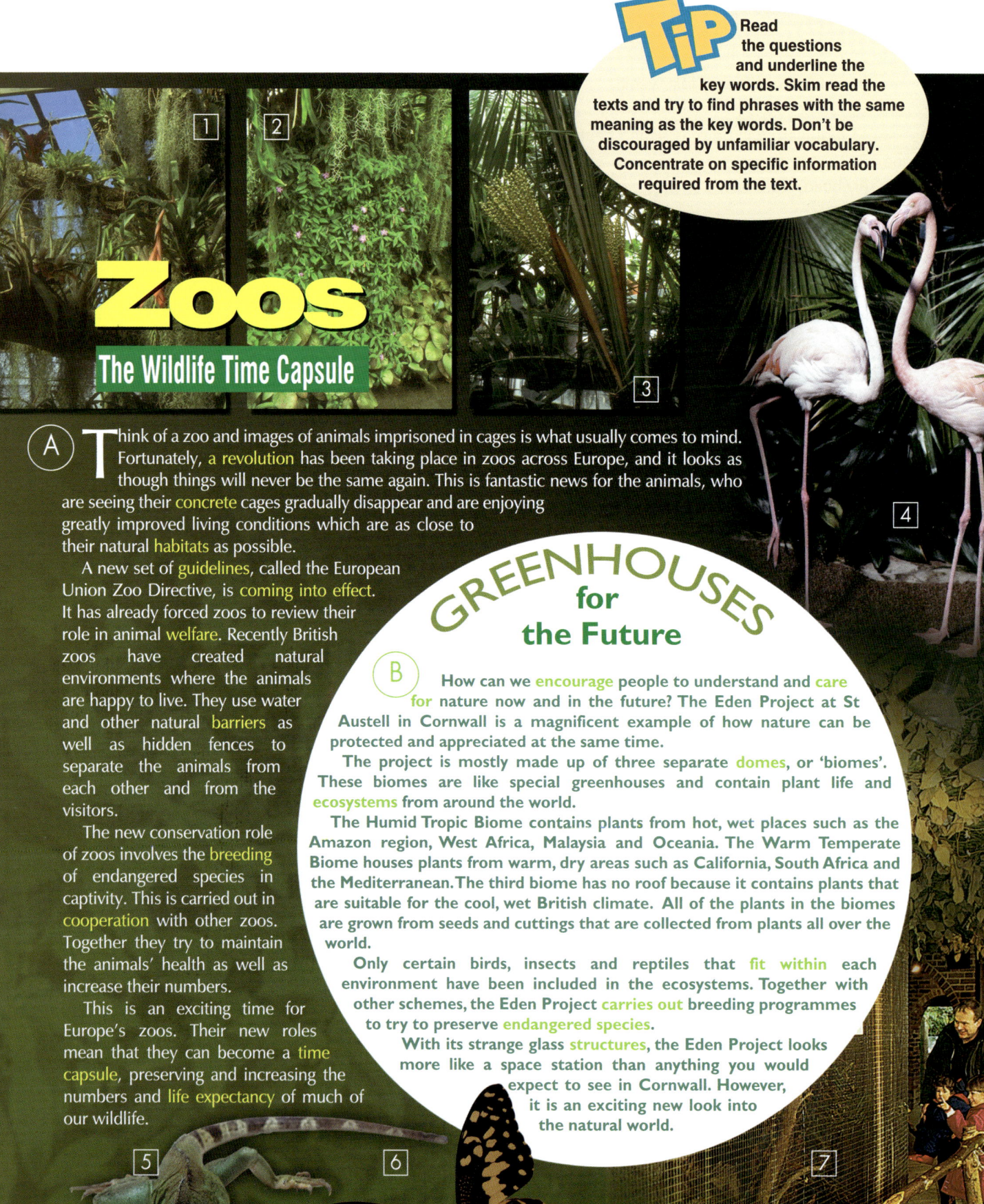

Zoos
The Wildlife Time Capsule

A Think of a zoo and images of animals imprisoned in cages is what usually comes to mind. Fortunately, a revolution has been taking place in zoos across Europe, and it looks as though things will never be the same again. This is fantastic news for the animals, who are seeing their concrete cages gradually disappear and are enjoying greatly improved living conditions which are as close to their natural habitats as possible.

A new set of guidelines, called the European Union Zoo Directive, is coming into effect. It has already forced zoos to review their role in animal welfare. Recently British zoos have created natural environments where the animals are happy to live. They use water and other natural barriers as well as hidden fences to separate the animals from each other and from the visitors.

The new conservation role of zoos involves the breeding of endangered species in captivity. This is carried out in cooperation with other zoos. Together they try to maintain the animals' health as well as increase their numbers.

This is an exciting time for Europe's zoos. Their new roles mean that they can become a time capsule, preserving and increasing the numbers and life expectancy of much of our wildlife.

GREENHOUSES for the Future

B How can we encourage people to understand and care for nature now and in the future? The Eden Project at St Austell in Cornwall is a magnificent example of how nature can be protected and appreciated at the same time.

The project is mostly made up of three separate domes, or 'biomes'. These biomes are like special greenhouses and contain plant life and ecosystems from around the world.

The Humid Tropic Biome contains plants from hot, wet places such as the Amazon region, West Africa, Malaysia and Oceania. The Warm Temperate Biome houses plants from warm, dry areas such as California, South Africa and the Mediterranean. The third biome has no roof because it contains plants that are suitable for the cool, wet British climate. All of the plants in the biomes are grown from seeds and cuttings that are collected from plants all over the world.

Only certain birds, insects and reptiles that fit within each environment have been included in the ecosystems. Together with other schemes, the Eden Project carries out breeding programmes to try to preserve endangered species.

With its strange glass structures, the Eden Project looks more like a space station than anything you would expect to see in Cornwall. However, it is an exciting new look into the natural world.

Lesson 4 (pp. 90 - 91)

* Check Ss' HW. (10')

18 a) Ask Ss to look at the pictures and headlines and guess what the texts are about. Ss then discuss the questions in Ex. 18a.

SUGGESTED ANSWER KEY

Yes, I've been twice. I don't really like the idea of animals being imprisoned in cages. I think that we should let them live in their natural habitats.
We can grow plants, vegetables, flowers etc inside a greenhouse. Greenhouses are used to protect plants, such as vegetables, from the weather. Also, people can see plants and flowers in greenhouses all year round.

---

b) Ss look at the pictures and do the exercise.

ANSWER KEY

people looking at animals; picture 7
tropical plants; pictures 1, 2, 3, 4
birds; picture 4
insects and reptiles; pictures 5, 6

---

19 Ask Ss to read the sentences. Elicit/Explain any unknown words. Play the recording. Ss do the exercise. Check Ss' answers.

ANSWER KEY

1 Yes	3 Yes	5 No	7 No
2 Yes	4 Yes	6 Yes	

20 a) Explain the task. Ss read the questions first, then read the texts and do the exercise. Check Ss' answers.

ANSWER KEY

1 B	3 Both	5 B
2 A	4 Both	6 A

b) Ss read the texts again and try to explain the highlighted words using the context and their dictionaries.

21 Allow Ss two minutes to do the exercise. Check Ss' answers.

ANSWER KEY

article A: 1 gradually
2 close to
3 guidelines
4 increase/ increasing

article B: 1 be appreciated
2 ecosystem
3 suitable for
4 preserve

22 Allow Ss two minutes to do the exercise. Check Ss' answers, then Ss make sentences using the phrases. Ss should memorise the phrases.

ANSWER KEY

1 build	6 plant
2 thick	7 programme
3 breathing	8 species
4 industrial	9 capsule
5 dump	10 expectancy

23 Allow Ss two minutes to do the exercise. Check Ss' answers. Ss, then, make sentences using the phrases. Ss should memorise these phrases.

ANSWER KEY

1 in	6 of	11 for/about
2 for	7 in	12 from
3 on	8 on	13 in
4 for	9 in	
5 in	10 in	

24 • Ss read the dialogue. Play the recording. Ss do the exercise. Check Ss' answers.
• Ss, in closed pairs, use the prompts to act out dialogues. Check Ss' answers, then ask some pairs to act out their dialogue to the class.

ANSWER KEY

1 try 2 should 3 ought 4 can 5 Why

A: I'd like to ask your advice.
B: OK. I'll try to help. What is it?
A: How can I cut down on my **shopping** bills and still do my bit for the environment?
B: Well, you should try to **buy things with less packaging**. You ought to **keep the container and buy refills**.
A: That's a good idea!
B: Also, you can **reuse your carrier bags** by taking your own shopping bags with you.
A: I never thought of that!
B: Why don't you concentrate on simple things like **buying food in recyclable containers**?
A: Thanks. You've been really helpful.

25 Explain the task. Play the recording. Ss do the exercise. Play the recording again for Ss to check their answers. Check Ss' answers then play the recording again with pauses between sentences for Ss to repeat individually.

ANSWER KEY

1 **Where** can I repair my car?
Where can my car be **repaired**?
2 **Who** took these photograph?
Who were these photographs **taken** by?
3 **Who** is decorating the living room?
Who is the living room being **decorated** by?
4 **Who** broke the window?
Who was the window **broken** by?

Suggested Homework

1 **Vocabulary:** highlighted words in texts Ex. 18 (p. 90), Exs 22 & 23 (p. 91)
2 **Dictation:** any ten words from Vocabulary
3 **Act out:** Ex. 24 (p. 91)
4 **Writing:** a short summary of any of the articles in Ex. 18 (p.90)

19 Listen and mark the sentences *Yes* or *No*.

1 European zoos have been using concrete cages for animals. ....
2 Zoos now have to obey new rules. ....
3 Zoos try to stop species from becoming extinct. ....
4 The Eden Project consists of three greenhouses. ....
5 The biomes all have the same temperature. ....
6 The plants in the biomes come from various countries. ....
7 The Eden Project is in a space station. ....

20 a) Read the articles and tick (✓) the correct box.

Which article:	A	B	Both
1 is mainly concerned with plant life?			
2 is mainly concerned with animal life?			
3 mentions preserving endangered species?			
4 mentions the breeding of various species?			
5 mentions the controlled selection of animals?			
6 mentions new rules introduced?			

b) Explain the highlighted words.

21 Read the articles again and find the words/phrases which mean:

article A
1 little by little (adv)
2 similar to (adj)
3 rules (n)
4 make sth bigger (v)
article B
1 to have one's good qualities recognised (v)
2 all the plants and animals that live in a particular area together with the complex relationship which exists between them and their environment
3 appropriate for (adj)
4 to keep sth as it is (v)

Vocabulary Practice

22 Fill in the correct words, then make sentences.

• industrial • thick • plant • build • species • capsule
• dump • breathing • expectancy • programme

1 to .... a road
2 .... cloud
3 .... difficulties
4 .... waste
5 to .... rubbish
6 .... life
7 breeding ....
8 endangered ....
9 time ....
10 life.....................

23 Fill in *on*, *for*, *in*, *of*, *about* or *from*, then make sentences.

1 animals .... captivity; 2 suitable .... sth; 3 .... the front page; 4 do sth .... the environment; 5 to live .... a tree; 6 a new set .... guidelines; 7 .... Cornwall; 8 hear sth .... the radio; 9 to be .... trouble; 10 imprisoned .... cages; 11 to care .... sth; 12 to separate sth .... sth else; 13 .... cooperation with

Communication

• giving advice

24 Listen and fill in, then use the prompts to act out similar dialogues.

A: I'd like your advice.
B: Okay. I'll 1) .... to help. What is it?
A: How can I cut down on my **household** bills and still do my bit for the environment?
B: Well, you 2) .... try to **use less electricity**. You 3) .... to **use the washing machine at night when** it's cheaper.
A: That's a good idea!
B: Also, you 4) .... **use less water** by taking **a shower instead of having a bath**.
A: I never thought of that!
B: 5) .... don't you concentrate on simple things like **turning taps off tight to save water**?
A: Thanks. You've been really helpful.

• shopping
• buy things with less packaging
• keep the container and buy refills
• reuse your carrier bags
• your own shopping bags with you
• buying food in recyclable containers

Pronunciation

• sentence stress

25 Listen and underline the stressed words. Listen again and repeat.

1 Where can I repair my car?
   Where can my car be repaired?
2 Who took these photographs?
   Who were these photographs taken by?
3 Who is decorating the living room?
   Who is the living room being decorated by?
4 Who broke the window?
   Who was the window broken by?

Word Formation

• compound nouns

26 Study the theory box and the example, then form the compound nouns.

We can form a compound noun from two nouns or an adjective & a noun. A compound noun is usually written as two words.
e.g. *post office, coffee table*

1 a gadget that is used to **open tins**. tin opener
2 a device that is used to **dry hair**. ....
3 a machine that is used to **wash dishes**. ....
4 a device that is used to **squeeze lemons**. ....
5 a utensil that is used to **peel vegetables**. ....
6 a utensil that is used to **grate cheese**. ....
7 a machine that is used to **make coffee**. ....
8 a utensil that is used to **crack nuts**. ....

Phrasal Verbs

27 Read the table, then underline the correct particle.

be/get carried away - to be very excited
carry off - to handle a difficult situation
carry on - to continue doing sth
carry out - to act according to instructions, orders etc
carry over - to let sth continue into a new situation
carry through - to complete sth successfully
hold on - to wait for a short time
hold up - 1) to make sb wait or delay sb, 2) to rob a bank

1 The actors carried **away/on** with the play after the lights went out.
2 The fans really got carried **on/away** when the *Red Hot Chilli Peppers* walked onto the stage.
3 If she manages to carry **on/off** this project, she will probably be promoted.
4 I expect my instructions to be carried **out/over**.
5 John's courage carried **on/over** into all parts of his life.
6 She carried **away/through** her plan and became president of the company.
7 Traffic was held **on/up** due to the accident.
8 The operator asked me to hold **on/up** while she dialled the number.

Writing (an article providing solutions to a problem)

An article providing solutions to a problem usually presents the problem and its causes as well as our suggestions and their expected results.

We usually write four paragraphs. In the **first paragraph**, we state the problem and what has caused it. In the **second** and **third paragraphs**, we write our suggestions and their results. We write a separate paragraph for each suggestion and its result. In the **fourth paragraph**, we summarise our suggestions and give our opinion.

We use appropriate linking words to list our suggestions (firstly, in addition, etc). We can find such pieces of writing in newspapers, magazines, etc.

28 Your local newspaper has asked its readers to submit articles entitled **"How we can protect endangered species."** Write your article suggesting ways to help endangered species survive.

Read the article below and answer the questions.

1 *"Every individual can make a difference... if we continue to leave decision-making to the so-called decision-makers, things will never change,"* said Jane Goodall, British chimpanzee researcher. *Today, the danger to our natural world is increasing and many species are becoming extinct. We need to do something soon or else many creatures won't survive.*

2 *First of all, we need to make sure that there are stricter laws that protect endangered species. If long prison sentences for illegal hunters were introduced, then people would be discouraged from harming these animals.*

3 *Secondly, it would be a good idea to educate people about the dangers of extinction. As a result, more people might do voluntary work protecting endangered species. Individuals may also think twice before using or buying products made from, or tested on, these animals such as fur coats and skin creams.*

4 *All in all, there are many solutions to this problem. The sooner we take action, the better the future will be for all endangered species.*

Lesson 5 (pp. 92 - 93)

* Check Ss' HW (10').

26 Explain what a compound noun is (a noun which is made up of two or more words). Go through the theory table, then do item 1 with Ss. Explain that Ss need to focus on the words in bold. Ss do the exercise. Check Ss' answers on the board.

ANSWER KEY

2	hair dryer	6	cheese grater
3	dish washer	7	coffee maker
4	lemon squeezer	8	nut cracker
5	vegetable peeler		

27 Read out the table, then Ss do the exercise. Check Ss' answers. Ss should memorise these phrasal verbs.

ANSWER KEY

1	on	4	out	7	up
2	away	5	over	8	on
3	off	6	through		

Writing (p. 92)

Go through the table and explain the theory. Ask Ss: *What kind of problems could we read about in an article like this? (A problem which is of interest to the public e.g. an environmental problem, a social problem etc)*

28 Allow Ss two to three minutes to read the article, then discuss the questions.

ANSWER KEY

1 endangered species
2 a Stricter laws that protect endangered species → people would be discouraged from harming these animals
   b educate people about the dangers of extinction → people might do voluntary work protecting endangered species
      Linking words: First of all, Secondly, All in all, (Firstly, In addition, Lastly)
3 By using a quotation. Alternative beginning → What will our planet be like when all species have become extinct?
4 **Suggested Answer:**
   para 1: A major problem in the world today is the alarming rate at which endangered species are becoming extinct.
   para 4: We must do something soon to protect endangered species or our whole natural world will be at risk.

29 Explain the task, then go through the prompts with Ss. Ss work in closed pairs to make supporting sentences. Check Ss' answers orally in class.

ANSWER KEY

1 We could introduce long-term prison sentences to stop people from hunting. In addition, we could hire more park rangers to patrol the parks and protect the animals.
2 We could all buy non-aerosol sprays and products without harmful chemicals, to protect the ozone layer. Furthermore, we can help to reduce traffic pollution by using public transport instead of cars, so there will be less smog.

30 Go through the tables and explain any unknown words. Ss, in closed pairs, match the suggestions to the results. Check Ss' answers, then Ss discuss the questions.

ANSWER KEY

1 b   2 c   3 a

SUGGESTED ANSWER KEY

Put up posters around the town showing different ways of recycling - this could encourage people to try different ways of recycling.

31 • Go through the rubric, then ask Ss questions to make sure they have understood the task.
e.g. T: What problem should you write about?
S1: Why people find it difficult to recycle.
T: What is your first suggestion?
S2: To place recycling bins in most places around the town.
T: What will be the result of this?
S3: People will find it easier and more convenient to recycle their rubbish.   etc
• Present the plan, then assign the exercise as written HW.

SUGGESTED ANSWER KEY

Recycling is an important issue today. The problem is that not enough people actually take the time or make the effort to recycle. What, then, can be done to encourage more people to start recycling?

To begin with, more recycling bins could be placed in more places around the town. If this is done, people will find it easier and more convenient to recycle their rubbish. In this way, the situation will certainly improve.

Secondly, we could start a reward scheme to pay people for recycling. If people were paid a penny for every bottle or can they recycled, they would be encouraged to recycle their bottles and cans.

People are not going to learn about recycling by themselves. I believe that we need to take action and encourage people to recycle now, before it is too late. If we all help to recycle, we can make our town a cleaner and nicer place to live in.

32 • Read the sentences. Elicit/Explain any unknown words. Ask Ss what they think these sentences mean.

SUGGESTED ANSWER KEY

• If you haven't helped to find an answer to a problem, you have probably helped to create the problem. (Explain that Malcolm Bradbury was the first person to say this.)
• If you don't waste anything, you will always have something in reserve.
• If you really want something you will find a way to achieve it..

Suggested Homework

1 **Vocabulary:** Exs 26 & 27 (p. 92)
2 **Dictation:** any ten words from Vocabulary
3 **Writing:** Ex. 31 (p. 93)

Lesson 6

Workbook Unit 7
   Click on Grammar 7

1 What problem is the writer talking about?

2 What are the writer's suggestions? What are their results? What linking words does the writer use to introduce each suggestion? Can you suggest other appropriate words?

3 Does the writer start the article by asking a rhetorical question, by a quotation or by addressing the reader directly? Suggest an introduction using a technique which hasn't been applied.

4 Replace the topic sentences in paragraphs 1 and 4 with other appropriate ones.

29 Expand the prompts to write appropriate supporting sentences for the topic sentences below. Use appropriate linking words.

1 To begin with, steps should be taken to stop people from hunting and killing endangered species.

- introduce/long-term prison sentences/stop people from hunting
- hire/more park rangers/ patrol the parks/protect the animals

2 In addition, we can all help to reduce the hole in the ozone layer.

- buy/non-aerosol sprays/ and products without harmful chemicals/protect the ozone layer
- help/reduce/traffic pollution/use public transport/instead of cars/ less smog

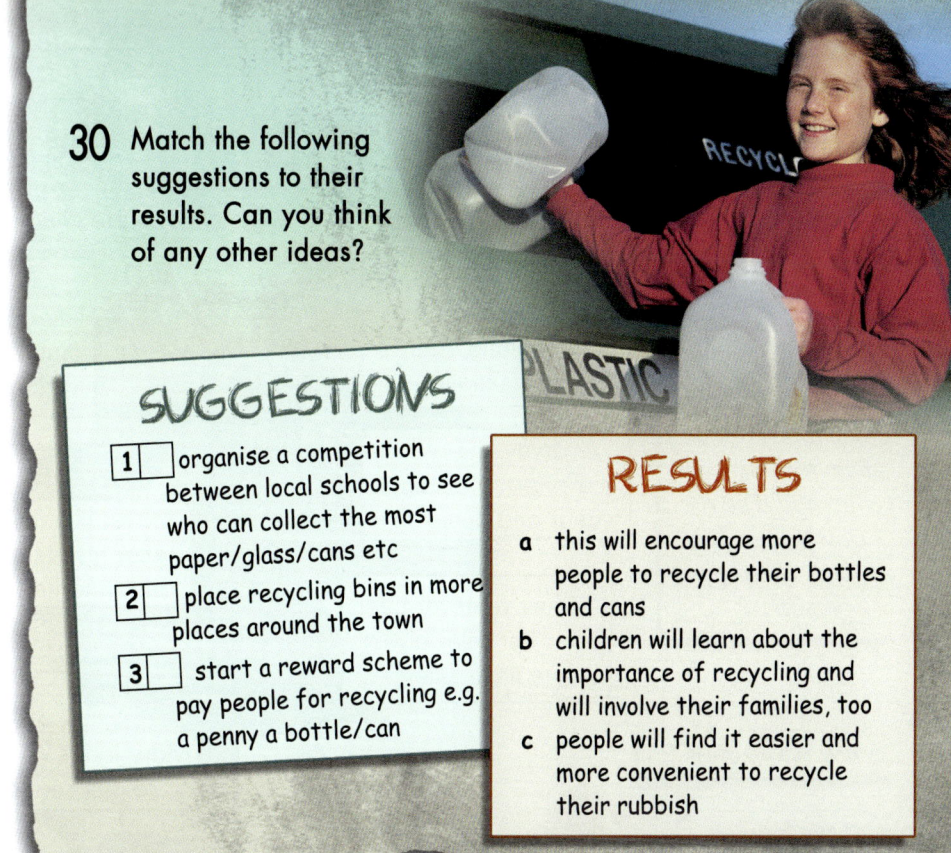

30 Match the following suggestions to their results. Can you think of any other ideas?

SUGGESTIONS

1 organise a competition between local schools to see who can collect the most paper/glass/cans etc

2 place recycling bins in more places around the town

3 start a reward scheme to pay people for recycling e.g. a penny a bottle/can

RESULTS

a this will encourage more people to recycle their bottles and cans

b children will learn about the importance of recycling and will involve their families, too

c people will find it easier and more convenient to recycle their rubbish

31 Your school magazine has asked its readers to write an article suggesting ways to encourage people to start recycling. Write your article for the school magazine (100-150 words).

Use the plan below as well as two of the ideas in Ex. 30. You can use the article in Ex. 28 as a model. Start like this:

Recycling is an important issue today. The problem is that not enough people actually take the time or make the effort to recycle. What, then, can be done to encourage more people to start recycling?

Plan

Introduction
(Para 1) *state problem and its cause*
Main Body
(Para 2) *1st suggestion and result*
(Para 3) *2nd suggestion and result*
Conclusion
(Para 4) *summarise and give your opinion*

32 Read the sentences. What do they mean?

What's in a word?

- If you're not part of the solution, you're part of the problem. (Malcolm Bradbury)
- Waste not, want not.
- Where there's a will there's a way.

THE ADVENTURES OF HUCKLEBERRY FINN

The Wilks Brothers

Huck and Jim continue down the Mississippi with two men who are cheats and liars.

One day, they met a man waiting for a boat to New Orleans. He told them about a rich man from his town who had died the day before. The 'King' asked him all about it …

①

Peter Wilks' brothers are on the way here from England. They'll get all his money …

… Peter left a letter behind for Harvey, saying where his gold is hidden …

… Harvey, the oldest, is a priest. William is deaf and dumb …

… for Harvey to look after his niece, Mary Jane, and her sisters …

… they've never been here, but Peter always wrote them letters …

A FEW HOURS LATER …

②

I am Harvey Wilks, this is my brother William, and our servant Adolphus. Could you show us the way to our brother Peter's house, please?

Mary Jane! William says he's *so* pleased to meet you.

Uncle Harvey! Poor Uncle Peter asked me to give you this letter.

Goo goo goo

③

④

$6,000 in gold! Wait! If we give this to the girls, everyone will trust us …

Yes — and then we can steal *ALL* of their money!

⑤

Don't trust them, Mary Jane! They aren't who they say they are!

We want *you* to have this gold …

Dr Robinson! Of *course* I trust them! Uncle Harvey, will you look after all our money for us?

That doctor knows we aren't the real Wilks brothers. Let's take the gold and run, tonight!

No! We'll wait, sell the house and the slaves, and take everything. Let's hide the gold here until then.

⑥

⑦

I can't let them rob those poor girls! I'll hide the gold where no-one will find it. When Jim and I are safe and far away, I'll write and tell Mary Jane where it is …

94

c) Where could you read these articles? How do they make you feel? Why do you think the writer has written these articles?

d) Suggest appropriate headings for each article.

e) Are there any charitable organisations like these in your country? How do they help people?

Speaking

27 In pairs, ask and answer questions, as in the example.

S1: *What is Oxfam?*
S2: *A charitable organisation. What does it do?*
S3: *It helps save millions of lives every day. How does ...? etc*

TiP Read the preceding sentence carefully to see what the pronoun refers to.

C Queen Elizabeth's Foundation for Disabled People is a charity that is **dedicated** to helping people with **physical disabilities**. It provides many different services such as employment, training and housing as well as advice and **support** through its eight **specialist** disability centres.

The foundation has been helping disabled people since 1934. Although it relies heavily on **donations** and volunteers, it manages to support over 100,000 disabled people every year. Its main **priority** is to help people with disabilities to live a normal life. It does this through the Development Centre where it teaches the life skills disabled people need to achieve as much independence as they are capable of.

The centre is home to 52 young people who all have the ability and determination to stand on their own two feet. Recently, work was completed on 16 new **self-contained** independent living flats for residents, which contain all the special equipment they need.

Communication

• Applying for volunteer work

28 a) Listen and fill in. Then, in pairs, read out the dialogue.

A: Hello. You must be Timothy Leigh.
B: That's 1) ....
A: I see you want to become a **volunteer**.
B: Yes, I do.
A: So, 2) .... did you hear about our volunteer programme, Mr Leigh?
B: I saw an advertisement in the local paper.
A: I see. 3) .... would you be able to start?
B: Anytime after the beginning of September.
A: Great. 4) .... you fill in this form, please, Mr Leigh?
B: Of course.

b) Use the prompts below to act out similar dialogues.

• Tina Johnson / reading tutor / reading club / heard an announcement / on the radio / next week

Vocabulary Practice

29 Fill in the correct word from the list, then make sentences using the completed phrases.

• medical • charitable • relief • physical • water
• developing • minimum • life • main • local

1	.... skills	6	.... disabilities
2	.... distribution	7	.... worker
3	.... period	8	.... people
4	.... supplies	9	.... organisation
5	.... world	10	.... priority

Speaking

30 Make notes under the headings, then talk about each organisation.

• Name • Target • History • Form of help

103

31 Fill in: *of*, *for*, *to* or *on*, then make sentences using the completed phrases.

1 to be a member .... the community; 2 people .... all ages; 3 quality .... life; 4 to provide sth .... sb; 5 to give advice .... sth; 6 thanks .... sth or sb; 7 to be dedicated .... sth; 8 to rely .... sth; 9 apply .... a job; 10 to pay attention .... sb/sth

32 Look up the organisations in a dictionary/on the Internet to find the missing words, then read out the abbreviations. What do you think each organisation does?

BBC - .... Broadcasting Corporation
NHS - National .... Service
WHO - .... Health Organisation
UN - .... Nations
UNESCO - United Nations Educational, Scientific and Cultural ....
RSPCA - Royal Society for the Prevention of Cruelty to ....

Word Formation

33 Study the table, then fill in *re*, *over*, *mis*, *un* or *under* before the verbs.

> We can use certain prefixes before verbs. These are:
> **re-** (again), **over-** (too much), **mis-** (badly/incorrectly)
> **un-** (to reverse), **under-** (not enough)
> e.g.   do - **re**do (do again)
>   eat - **over**eat (eat too much)
>   read - **mis**read (read incorrectly)
>   pack - **un**pack (reverse the packing action)
>   cook - **under**cook (not cook long enough)

1 John .... heard the flight announcement and went to the wrong gate.
2 I left my bag inside! I'll have to .... lock the door and get it.
3 Tom thinks Trudy is .... paid. She never does any work but she gets a high salary.
4 Many children in poor countries are .... fed. They don't get enough to eat.
5 She spilt coffee on her homework so she had to .... write it.
6 Joe .... understood the teacher and read the wrong book.

Phrasal Verbs

34 Study the table, then underline the correct particle.

> make out - to see sth with difficulty
> make up - to invent
> make up my mind - to decide
> put on - to wear
> put off - to postpone
> put out - to extinguish
> put through - to connect sb by phone
> put sb up - to offer sb accommodation

1 Diane can't make **up/out** her mind about which dress to wear.
2 Can you put my sister **out/up** for a couple of nights?
3 Make sure you put **off/on** something warm when you go out.
4 I'm sure Sid made **out/up** that story about losing his wallet.
5 We have to put **out/off** our holidays until next year.
6 I can't make **up/out** what that sign says. It's too far away.

Writing (transactional letter - asking for information)

> We usually write a transactional letter in response to written information such as advertisements, notes, maps and drawings. When we write a transactional letter asking for information, we usually write three paragraphs.
> In the **first paragraph**, we write our opening remarks and state the reasons for writing.
> In the **second paragraph**, we ask our questions. It is important to include **all** the factual information in complete sentences, using **our own words** as much as possible.
> In the **last paragraph**, we write our closing remarks.

35 You are thinking of doing some voluntary work and you have seen the advertisment below. Read the rubric, the advertisement and the notes, then, answer the questions you made after reading the advertisment. Then write a letter to **Learn for Life** asking for information (120-180 words).

Pre-Reading Activities

1 **Look at the pictures on p. 106. Which show(s):**

1 Dr Robinson holding two men?
3
2 Peter Wilks' funeral? 2
3 a flash of lightning? 5 - 6
4 Huck in a graveyard, running away? 5
5 The 'King' and the 'Duke' in a rowing boat? 6

Listening and Reading Activities

2 **Listen and underline the correct word.**

1 "I saw the **slaves**/fools coming out of there yesterday."
2 "Look — a bag of gold in the room/**coffin**."
3 "Quick, Jim! Untie the raft/**rope** and let's go."

3 **Read the episode on p. 106 and answer the questions.**
(See Suggested Answers section)

1 What does the 'Duke' think has happened to the gold?
2 What does the man say he knows about Peter Wilks that proves he is Peter's brother?
3 Why do they decide to dig up Peter Wilks' coffin? What do they find?
4 What happens when Huck wakes up one morning?

4 **Replace the words in bold with appropriate ones from the episode.**

1 Huck hid **something** in Peter Wilks' coffin. a bag of gold
2 Has Peter Wilks got **anything** on his chest? a small blue mark
3 They've buried **someone**.
Peter Wilks
4 Jim is asked to untie **something**.
the rope

Grammar

- could/was able to (past ability)
  used to (past habits/states)

5 **Look at the grammar box, then complete the sentences with *could/couldn't* or *was/wasn't able to*.**

- *could/couldn't* shows general **ability in the past**:
  He **could** run five miles a day when he was young.
- *was/wasn't able to* means "managed/didn't manage to" — i.e. it usually refers to **ability on one occasion in the past**: Couldn't can be used instead of **wasn't able to**.
  They were all looking at the bag of gold, so Huck **was able to** escape. It was raining hard so they **weren't able to/couldn't** drive back to Plymouth.
- *used to/didn't use to* shows **past habits/states**:
  People in the South **used to** own slaves. (NOT "were owning")

1 I couldn't drive a car when I was three years old.
2 When Huck's father went to town, Huck was able to get out of the cabin and run away.
3 Because there weren't many roads, people from Huck's town could only get to New Orleans by travelling down the river.
4 Huck was able to reach the raft within minutes.
5 The people couldn't see the bag of gold so the man had to hold it up.

6 **a) What could you/couldn't you do when you were five?**

I could ride a bike but I couldn't drive a car.

b) What did you/didn't you use to do at the weekends when you were five?

I used to play in the garden. I didn't use to wake up early.

7 **Listen to the episode, then read it aloud.**

8 **Put the sentences into the correct order. Then, close your books and tell the story of the episode.**

1 The 'King' and 'Duke' discovered the gold was missing. Huck made them think the slaves had taken it.
7 Huck ran to the raft and they all went on down the river like before.
6 They forgot about Huck, so he was able to escape.
4 The Englishman said he could prove he was Peter Wilks' brother.
2 When Peter Wilks was buried, Huck believed the gold was safe.
8 When Huck woke up one morning the 'Duke' told him the 'King' had taken Jim to sell him.
5 They dug up the coffin and found the bag of gold coins inside.
3 Two Englishmen arrived claiming to be Harvey and William Wilks.

Vocabulary & Grammar

1 **Fill in the correct word.**

1 Are we going to the theatre tonight?
2 I'm fed up with the situation. We must do something.
3 He slipped on the wet floor and broke his leg.
4 Sorry, I won't do it. I think it's a waste of time.
5 Deforestation is one of the environmental issues under discussion today.
6 The room was filled with smoke.
7 You'd better pay attention to what he says.
8 Jim's got blond hair, hasn't he?
9 You have to wait your turn like everyone else.
10 The air quality is below recommended levels.
11 If you swim in here, you are sure to catch a disease.
12 Tina used to run three miles a day when she was younger.
13 This door must be kept locked.
14 Ultraviolet radiation can cause cancer.
15 Smog and factory smoke cause air pollution.
16 "Al called an hour ago." "Did he? I'll call him then."
17 The organisation is committed to helping those in need.
18 The booklet was produced in cooperation with the government.
19 The robber was caught by the police.
20 She couldn't make up her mind which dress to buy.
21 "My feet hurt." "You should soak them in warm water."
22 I hate seeing animals living in captivity.
23 "This is difficult." "Is it? I'll help you, then."
24 She didn't call, did she?
25 The ozone layer is being destroyed by aerosol sprays and other chemicals.
26 Tony said that he would be back in an hour.
27 Have the posters been delivered yet?
28 Look at your room. It's a total mess.
29 There are special programmes which try to preserve endangered species from extinction.
30 Why don't you put on your red skirt and T-shirt? They look nice on you.

(30 marks)

2 **Circle the correct item.**

1 Hold on a minute! I'll put you .... to the manager.
   A off   **B** through   C out   D in
2 I've got a(n) .... nose. I think I've got a cold.
   A runny   B blurred   C itchy   D aching
3 The volcanic .... killed thousands of people.
   A waste B explosion C radiation **D** eruption
4 People have been .... their rubbish in the lake for years.
   A picking   C pumping
   B dumping   D polluting
5 The council has published a new set of .... on recycling.
   A guidelines   C solutions
   B schemes   D suggestions
6 The air is .... polluted by exhaust fumes.
   A to be   B been   C be   **D** being
7 Our rivers are being .... by industrial waste.
   A wiped out   C flooded
   B contaminated   D dumped
8 They are .... a road near the forest.
   A moving B producing **C** building D creating
9 You need to call the surgery for a(n) ....
   A cast B date **C** appointment D location
10 Everyone got carried .... with the celebration.
   A away   B off   C on   D over

(20 marks)

Communication

3 **Use the table to ask for and give advice on the following situations.** *(See Suggested Answers section)*

• Your friend has a cold.
• Your friend has got a headache.
• Your friend can't see very well.
• Your friend has got stomach ache.

asking:	Could/Can you give/offer me some advice?; What would you do in my place?
giving:	Why don't you ...?; You should ...; How about ...?; The best thing you can do is (to) ...; What you really need to do is (to) ...; If I were you, I'd ...; My advice is to ...; Have you thought of ...?
accepting:	Yes, that's a good idea.; I'll take your advice.; Thanks for your advice.; I'll do as you say.

(20 marks)

Reading

4 Read the article and match the headings. There is one extra heading which you do not need.

A World of Difference

0 | **E**

Health, wealth and happiness are what we all aim for in our lives. Unfortunately, many of us are lucky if we achieve one or two out of the three. Worse still, there are many more people around the world who have little chance of achieving any, but there are some things we can do to change this.

1 | **C**

One of the things we can do is sponsor a child who is poor or hungry. Sponsoring a child helps to break the cycle of poverty, despair and hopelessness they and many other children in the Third World face today. If just one person decides to help another person, he or she can make a world of difference. For as little as £16 a month (that's 50p a day) we can give a child a future full of hope. This money helps provide food, clean water, medical care and education for boys and girls who really need it.

2 | **D**

Investing in a child's life in this way will not only help the child, but also the family and the community in which they live. It's obvious that clean water, decent healthcare and educational opportunities will benefit everyone in the area.

3 | **A**

Child sponsorship is different from other kinds of aid programmes because it focuses on the personal relationship between the giver and the receiver. They exchange letters, gifts, photos and more. The journey to see your adopted child is certainly worth the effort.

4 | **F**

World poverty and hunger are huge problems that will not go away by themselves. Many things will have to happen to make any changes, but I believe that if each of us starts now by doing something to help, then these changes will start to take place.
Sponsoring a child is an easy and cheap way for each of us to make a difference in the life of a poor and hungry child.

A Make a new friend.
B The lucky ones.
C Every little helps.
D A little goes a long way.
E Three wishes.
F Make a difference.

(15 marks)

Writing (an article providing solutions to a problem)

5 A local newspaper has asked its readers to send in an article discussing air pollution in cities and suggesting ways to solve this problem. Use the plan below to write your article. (120-180 words)

> ### Plan
> *(See Suggested Answers section)*
> **Introduction**
> (Para 1) *surrounded by smog – exhaust fumes from cars and gases from factories*
> **Main Body**
> (Para 2) *encourage people to use public transport – fewer cars and exhaust fumes*
> (Para 3) *factories moved out of cities – cleaner air*
> **Conclusion**
> (Para 4) *air pollution – work together – levels come down – cleaner and safer places*

(15 marks)

(Total: 100 marks)

Let's sing!

6 Listen and fill in. Listen again and sing.

Help them to Live

Think of all the children in the world
How many are as fortunate as you?
You have food to eat and somewhere **1)** safe to live
You have clothes to wear and water to **2)** drink too.
We have to fight to save the children
We all have so much to give.
We have to try to save the children
Help them to live.

There are children in the world who have no **3)** homes.
Who live all alone out on the city street.
There are children with no **4)** money to survive
Who can't afford to buy a single thing to eat.

There are children who live under cloudless skies
Where the crops may never see a drop of **5)** rain.
There are children who need medicine and care
But no **6)** doctors are around to heal their pain.

We have money, we have **7)** food and we have love
We have enough of everything and much to spare.
It's our duty to the children of the world
To offer **8)** help and show them that we care.

Changing Ways

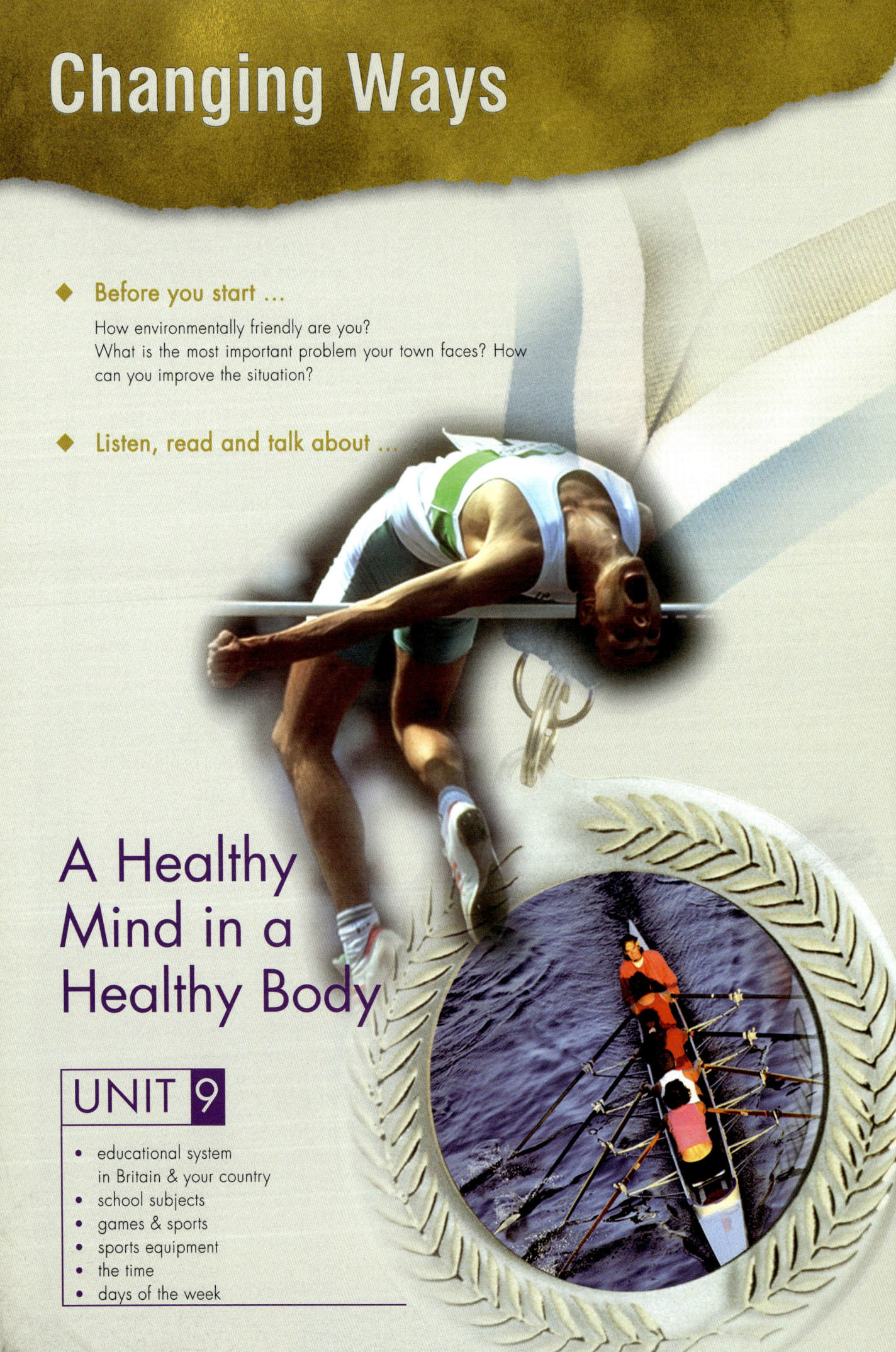

◆ **Before you start ...**

How environmentally friendly are you?
What is the most important problem your town faces? How
can you improve the situation?

◆ **Listen, read and talk about ...**

A Healthy
Mind in a
Healthy Body

UNIT 9

- educational system
  in Britain & your country
- school subjects
- games & sports
- sports equipment
- the time
- days of the week

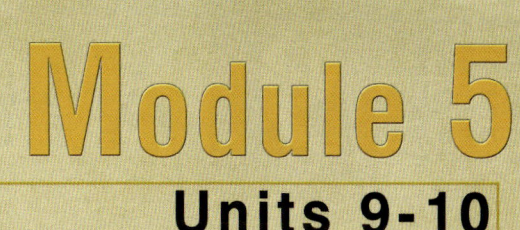

Module 5
Units 9-10

Our Changing World

UNIT 10

- inventors & inventions
- technology
- ambitions & regrets
- people's characters

◆ **Learn how to ...**

- ask & anwer about school timetables
- buy tickets for a sporting event
- persuade sb to buy you sth
- express regrets
- talk about famous people
- describe characters

◆ **Practise ...**

- reported questions
- the imperative
- reported commands
- exclamations
- conditionals Type 2/3
- wishes
- so, neither - nor/either - or
- both/neither - all/none

◆ **Phrasal Verbs**

- take
- come
- run

◆ **Write ...**

- an article about the education system in your country
- an opinion essay
- an essay about the three most important inventions of the 20th century
- a letter of application for a part-time job

9 A Healthy Mind in a Healthy Body

Lead-in

1 a) **Name as many sports as possible.**

b) **Match the words to the pictures, then make sentences.**

- players, referee, rink, helmet, sticks, hit the puck
- rowers, cox, boat, coach, oars, river
- coach, players, court, time out, give instructions
- skiers, slope, goggles, ski suit, skis, poles

Picture 1 shows some rowers and their cox in a boat. The rowers have two oars each. They are rowing down a river.

1 rowing

2 basketball

2 a) **Match the orders to each picture.**

A [ ] "Work as a team."
B [ ] "Put your backs into it."
C [ ] "Bend your knees."
D [ ] "Wait until I blow my whistle."

b) **Complete the sentences, as in the example.**

1 The instructor told the skiers to bend their knees.
2 The cox asked the rowing team ....
3 The coach told the boys ....
4 The referee told the players ....

c) **Do as your teacher says, then report his/her orders.**

Listening and Reading

3 Listen and repeat, then close your books and try to remember as many sentences as possible.

- I wouldn't worry.
- Look out!
- We're fighting a losing battle.
- Spread out!

- That's the spirit!
- That'll be a first!
- So will winning a race.

3 skiing

Objectives

Vocabulary: education; school subjects; sports and games; sports equipment
Reading: reading for specific information/detailed understanding; multiple matching
Listening: listening for specific information; gap filling; multiple matching
Speaking: describing the education system in your country; comparing education in your country to that in Britain; talking about games/sports/activities; persuading sb to join a gym
Punctuation: capital letters; commas; full stops; exclamation marks; inverted commas
Communication: buying tickets for a sporting event
Pronunciation: stressed syllables in exclamations
Grammar: reported questions; reported commands
Phrasal verb: take
Project: an article about the education system in your country
Writing: an opinion essay

Lesson 1 (pp. 110 - 111)

1 a) Ask Ss to name as many sports as possible.

SUGGESTED ANSWER KEY

rowing, basketball, skiing, ice hockey, archery, snooker, badminton, ten-pin bowling, baseball, football, tennis, golf, cricket etc

b) Ask Ss to look at the words and match them to the pictures. Then, ask Ss to use the words to make sentences.

SUGGESTED ANSWER KEY

- Picture 2 shows a **coach** and some **players** on a **court**. The coach has called **time out** so that he can give the players some new **instructions**.
- Picture 3 shows two **skiers** skiing down a **slope**. Each skier is wearing **goggles** and a **ski suit**, and is using **skis** and **poles**.
- Picture 4 shows two **players** and a **referee** on a **rink**. They are wearing **helmets**, and holding **sticks**. They are ready to **hit the puck**.

2 a) Read the orders aloud and elicit/explain the meaning of each order. Ss match the orders to the pictures. Check Ss' answers by asking individual Ss to read their answers aloud.

ANSWER KEY

A 1/2   B 1   C 3   D 4

b) • Elicit from/Explain to Ss that the orders in 2a are in direct speech (the exact words someone says in inverted commas) and that the task in 2b is to change the orders into reported speech. Elicit/Explain the rules of reported commands. (To report commands, we use an appropriate introductory verb e.g. ask/order/tell and the to-infinitive.)
   • Allow Ss two or three minutes to complete the sentences, then check Ss' answers by asking individual Ss to read their completed sentences aloud.

ANSWER KEY

2   The cox asked the rowing team to put their backs into it.
3   The coach told the boys to work as a team.
4   The referee told the players to wait until he blew his whistle.

c) Give orders - Ss carry them out. Each time, write them on the board. Ss then, report back your orders.
   Suggested list: Sit down! Stand up! Open/Close your books. Look at the board. etc

SUGGESTED ANSWER KEY

The teacher told us/the class to sit down.
The teacher told us/the class to stand up.
The teacher told us/the class to open/close our books.
The teacher told us/the class to look at the board. etc

3 • Play the recording. Ss listen and repeat, either chorally or individually.
   • Present these sentences by giving examples, miming or using Ss' L1.
      e.g. **I wouldn't worry.** Mime being very worried. Then mime someone comforting someone else and say: I wouldn't worry.
   • Ss close their books. Ask individual Ss to say one of the sentences. Alternatively, Ss can form two teams and take turns to say sentences. The team which remembers the most sentences is the winner.
      e.g. Team A S1: I wouldn't worry.
            T: Good. One point for Team A!   etc

4 Read the sentences aloud and elicit/explain the meaning of any unknown words. Play the recording. Ss listen and circle the correct words. Check Ss' answers by asking individual Ss to read the correct sentences aloud.

ANSWER KEY

1	soft	4	win
2	faster	5	pace
3	concentrate		

---

5 a) Read the questions and the options aloud. Allow Ss five minutes to read the dialogues silently and circle the correct answers. Check Ss' answers by asking individual Ss to read their answers aloud. Then, help Ss explain the words in bold by giving examples or synonyms.

e.g. **poles:** sticks

ANSWER KEY

1 B   2 C   3 B

---

b) Allow Ss two minutes to do the exercise. Check Ss' answers.

ANSWER KEY

difficult: hard/challenging
set off: set out/start
look out: be careful
tired: weary/exhausted
put your backs into it: try harder

---

c) Play the recording for Ex. 4 again. Ss listen and follow the lines, then Ss take roles and act out the dialogues.

(Suggested Homework)

1 **Vocabulary:** Ex. 3 (p. 110), words in bold in dialogues A-C
2 **Reading aloud:** dialogues A-C (p. 111) (Point out that Ss practise *reading aloud* using the Ss' audio CD.)
3 **Dictation:** sentences from Ex. 3 (p.110)
4 **Writing:** write any five orders about how children should behave at school

---

4 🎧 **Listen to the dialogues and circle the correct words.**

1 The snow is rather **soft / hard**.
2 Bending your knees makes you ski **faster / slower**.
3 The coach wants the team to **fight / concentrate**.
4 The coach wants them to **win / lose** the match.
5 The cox wants the girls to keep up the **race / pace**.

5 **a) Read the dialogues and circle the correct answer, then explain the words in bold.**

1 How do you think Skier 1 feels?
   A confident   B unsure   C scared

2 What do the players think of Greenmont High?
   A They can't play as well as them.
   B They are as good as them.
   C They are better players than them.

3 What is the rowing team doing?
   A Losing a race.
   B Practising for a race.
   C Winning a race.

b) Look up the highlighted words in your dictionary.

A Skier 1: This is more <mark>difficult</mark> than I thought it would be.
  Skier 2: I know what you mean. There are too many things to remember.
  Skier 1: I know. Skis together, **heels apart**, **poles** in front ... I'm sure I'll **fall flat** on my face as soon as we <mark>set off</mark>.
  Skier 2: Oh well, I wouldn't worry. The snow doesn't look too hard, so at least we'll have a soft **landing**.
  Skier 1: You're right. I just hope I can remember enough of the instructor's **tips** to stay **upright**.
  Skier 2: Well, the instructor told us to bend our knees, so that's what I'm going to do.
  Skier 1: Yes, but I think that makes you go faster. <mark>Look out</mark>!
  Skier 2: Aaagh!

B Coach: Now, come on, **lads**! We can win this match if you just **concentrate**!
  Player 1: We're trying Coach, but we're **fighting a losing battle**.
  Player 2: Yeah, Greenmont High are much better than us.
  Coach: Rubbish! You're good enough to **beat** them. Work as a team! **Spread out**! Pass the ball around the court!
  Player 2: We'll try Coach! Come on guys! It's not too late to **even** the score.
  Player 1: That's the **spirit**! Coach told us to work as a team so let's show him what team work is!

C Cox: Come on! Can't you row any faster?
  Rower 1: We're rowing as fast as we can.
  Cox: I know you're all <mark>tired</mark> but **keep up the pace**. A few more strokes and we'll be at the finish line. Then you can all have a nice hot shower and I might let you go home early.
  Rower 2: That'll be a **first**!
  Cox: So will winning a race! Come on! Just, a few more **sessions** like this and you'll be ready to **compete with** the best – so <mark>put your backs into it</mark>, girls.
  Rower 3: Yes, let's do it!

c) Take roles and read out the dialogues.

4 | ice hockey

Vocabulary

• Education

6 a) Look at Mike's timetable. Do you have the same words for school subjects in your language?

TIME	MONDAY	TUESDAY	WEDNESDAY	THURSDAY	FRIDAY
9:00-9:50	MATHS	INFORMATION TECHNOLOGY	GEOGRAPHY	BIOLOGY	HISTORY
10:00-10:50	MATHS	MUSIC	GEOGRAPHY	FRENCH	HISTORY
11:00-11:20	BREAK				
11:30-12:20	ENGLISH	FRENCH	INFORMATION TECHNOLOGY	ENGLISH	CHEMISTRY
12:30-1:20	LUNCH BREAK				
1:30- 2:20	PE	PHYSICS	ENGLISH	MATHS	DESIGN AND TECHNOLOGY
2:30-3:20	PE	HISTORY	ENGLISH	MATHS	ART AND DESIGN

b) In pairs, ask and answer, as in the example.

S1: *What does Mike have at 10 am on Mondays?*
S2: *Maths. What does Mike have at 1:30 pm on Fridays?*
S1: *Design and Technology. etc*

NOTE: Words like physics, maths, politics, police, news, etc, take singular verb forms.

Physics is my favourite subject.

Speaking

7 A new student from abroad has just started at your school. He does not know anything about your education system. Explain to him:

• what subjects are on the curriculum
• the school timetable

8 a) Listen and fill in the gaps, then talk about education in England.

Age	Education in England
....	nursery school
....	primary school
11	secondary school
....	• leave school { go to college for job training / get a job • stay at school for .... more years
....	• go to university • get a job

Speaking

b) Is the education system in your country the same as in England? Make a similar table for your country, then talk about it.

Pre-Reading Activities

1 **Look at the pictures on p. 120. Which shows:**

1 a shed with a locked door? 5
2 Jim wearing chains? 6
3 snakes and rats? 7
4 a farmhouse? 2
5 Huck and Tom Sawyer walking along a country road? 4

Listening and Reading Activities

2 **Listen and correct the word(s) in bold.**

1 Silas Phelps' farm is ~~twelve~~ miles away. two
2 Huck met Tom on the way to ~~the village~~. town
3 Tom says he'll help Huck rescue ~~Sid~~. Jim
4 Tom says real prisoners have snakes and ~~cats~~ for pets. rats
5 Uncle Silas' friends are ~~inside~~ with guns. outside

3 **Read the episode on p. 120 and answer the questions.**
(See Suggested Answers section)

1 Why does Huck go to Silas Phelps' farm?
2 Why does Aunt Sally think that Huck is Tom Sawyer?
3 What plan does Huck suggest to rescue Jim?
4 Who are the "real prisoners" Tom talks about?
5 What do you think was Tom's reason for sending the letter?

Grammar

• Order of Adverbs

4 **Study the table, then put the adverbs in the correct order.**

Adverbs can be one word (*carefully*) or a phrase (*at work*). **Adverbs of manner** (*carefully, slowly, etc*) tell us how something happens. **Adverbs of place** (*here, in the house etc*) tell us where something happens. **Adverbs of time** (*now, at night etc*) tell us when something happens. Note the position: verb + direct object + adverb *He left **the house quickly**.* verb + adverb *He lives here.*
verb + manner + place + time *They **walked carefully towards the school yesterday**.*
We can put some adverbs of manner, place and time at the beginning of a clause to give emphasis. ***Tomorrow** I'm seeing the president.*

1 She worked ... (last night³/late¹/in the office²)
2 The children are playing football ... (now²/in the street¹)
3 He slammed the door (angrily¹/at the end³ of the meeting/after him².)
4 Huck run (towards¹ the raft/in a² hurry.)

• Exclamations

5 **Look at the grammar box, then rewrite the exclamations (1-10) using the word in brackets.** (See Suggested Answers section)

Exclamations show surprise, admiration, anger, etc.
• *how* + adj *How lovely! How pretty she is!*
• *so* + adj *It's so lovely! She's so pretty!*
• *what* (+ a/an) + adj + noun *What a lovely day! What a pretty girl! What lovely weather! What pretty girls!*
• *such* (+ a/an) + adj + noun *It's such a lovely day! She's such a pretty girl! It's such lovely weather! They're such pretty girls!*
• *negative questions* *Isn't it (a) lovely (day)! Isn't she (a) pretty (girl)! Isn't it lovely weather! Aren't they pretty girls!*

1 It's such an exciting film! **(what)**
2 Isn't it hot in here! **(so)**
3 It's so kind of you to say that! **(how)**
4 What a good song! **(isn't)**
5 How smart you look in those clothes! **(so)**

6 **Listen to the episode, then read it aloud.**

7 **Read the summary and fill in *and*, *but* or *so*. Where do you think Huck, Tom and Jim will go? Why?** (Ss' own answers)

Huck asked about Jim in the nearest town, **1)** and learned that a farmer called Silas Phelps had bought him, **2)** so Huck went to the Phelps farm. Mrs Phelps thought he was Tom Sawyer, her nephew, whom she was expecting. Huck met Tom on the road **3)** and told him everything. Tom's aunt had never met Tom or his brother Sid, **4)** so Huck pretended to be Tom **5)** and Tom said he was Sid. When they found where Jim was, Huck wanted to steal the key, rescue Jim **6)** and escape that night, **7)** but Tom had another idea. Tom said Jim must be a prisoner for at least a week, keep snakes and rats as pets **8)** and escape wearing Aunt Sally's dress. A week later, they helped Jim escape — **9)** but Tom had written a letter warning Uncle Silas that someone was going to steal Jim, **10)** so Uncle Silas' friends were waiting with guns.

10 Our Changing World

Lead-in

1 **a) Look at the pictures. Who …**

has got a huge credit card bill?

has got a parking ticket?

has been ill?

is late for work?

has got a job interview?

is rich?

b) How do you think each person feels? *Sean is annoyed because he is late for work.*

Ellen

Ann

Tony

2 **What would you do if you were in these situations? Make sentences, as in the example.**

If I had a huge credit card bill, I would try to pay it off as soon as possible.

Listening and Reading

3 Listen and repeat, then close your books and try to remember as many sentences as possible.

- Good grief!
- How will you cope in the future?
- What do you mean?
- If that happens, I'll be broke.
- If only it was as easy as it sounds.
- I take it you got the job?
- Isn't it wonderful?
- That's really up to me.
- I wish I had a job like that.
- It's never too late.
- I'm fed up.
- I wish I felt better.

4 Listen to the dialogues A-C and complete the sentences.

1 If you'd kept a list of everything you bought, your bill …

2 If you'd taken that Information Technology course, you …

3 If I hadn't been ill, I …

5 **a) Read the dialogues (A-C) and answer the questions.**

1 Why doesn't Ellen like credit cards?

2 What's Ellen's problem with money?

3 When does Tony start his new job?

4 Why doesn't Tony have to go to the office very often?

5 Does Tony want to work from home?

6 What are the advantages of working from home?

7 How can Ann join in Paul's party?

b) How do Ellen, Steve, Lisa, Tony and Ann feel? Who makes wishes for the present/future? Who expresses regret about the past?

18 Make sentences, as in the examples.

- The computer has crashed.
- I lost the information.
- I can't finish my report.
- I feel stressed.
- I don't have enough time.
- My boss won't understand.

If only the computer hadn't crashed.
I wish the computer hadn't crashed.

19 Match the prompts in column A with those in column B, then make sentences, as in the example.

A	B
owned a mobile phone had a computer had satellite TV had done a computer course were better at maths had a lot of money	• watch films from all over the world • buy a sports car • ring you anytime • become a scientist • use the Internet • find a better job

I wish I owned a mobile phone.
If I owned a mobile phone, I could ring you anytime.

Listening

20 🎧 Listen and match the speakers to what they regret. One regret does not match. Then make sentences, as in the example.

Speaker 1	A	not getting a degree
Speaker 2	B	forgetting his/her mobile phone
Speaker 3	C	saying the wrong thing to his/her boss
Speaker 4	D	not learning to use a computer
Speaker 5	E	booking a cheap holiday on the net
	F	borrowing his/her father's car

If only I had got a degree. If I had got a degree, I would have had a different life.

21 What do you regret in your life? Why?

Speaking

22 You have been offered a summer job at your local Internet café. Your parents think you should go to summer camp instead. Persuade your parents to let you take the job.

- tell them why you want to take the job
- present your arguments in favour of working and your arguments against going to camp
- come to an agreement/make another suggestion

23 Use the prompts to ask and answer as in the example.

- have a car • own a big house • can speak Spanish • have more time • play the guitar

A: *If only I had a car.*
B: *Why? What would you do?*
A: *If I had a car, I'd drive to work.*

Word Formation

24 Fill in the correct form of the word in bold.

1 If you eat too much junk food, you will put on .... **weigh**
2 John is as tall as Mark. They are the same .... **high**
3 The .... of a football pitch is 90-120 metres. **long**
4 Being a builder requires a certain amount of physical .... **strong**
5 Remember to measure the .... of the windows before you buy new curtains. **wide**

Phrasal Verbs

25 Study the table, then fill in the correct particle.

> come across - to find by chance
> come down with - to become ill
> come into - to inherit
> come round - 1) to visit sb, 2) to regain consciousness
> come up - 1) to be mentioned , 2) to arise; occur

1 Why don't you come .... for dinner later on?
2 Sandra came .... some money when her grandfather died.
3 The subject of holidays came .... over coffee.
4 Paul came .... the flu, so he took the day off work.
5 Ted came .... his old diaries while he was cleaning the attic.

Listening & Reading

26 Look at the pictures. Who is/are famous for: revolutionising personal computers; the theory of relativity; scientific research and experiments; developing atomic energy; founding Apple; being a strong believer in world peace; surviving lift-off, re-entry and weightlessness in space? How do you think these people changed the world?

27 Listen and write *G* (Gagarin), *E* (Einstein) or *J* (Jobs) next to the adjectives that describe each person's character.

1	outspoken		5	confident
2	calm		6	charming
3	demanding		7	gifted
4	talented		8	visionary

28 **a)** Read the article and write *G*, *E* or *J* in the correct box.

Who ...

- was disappointed with how his work was used? [1]
- made something that could be used by the average person? [2]
- developed something new? [3] [4]
- became famous overnight? [5]
- paved the way for others? [6] [7]
- did something that could have been dangerous for him? [8]
- received an important award? [9]
- achieved his dream? [10]

b) Circle the correct meaning.

1 experimental
  a new and being tested
  b used in a test

2 epic
  a dangerous
  b impressive

3 venture
  a sth done for the first time
  b sth new, exciting and difficult

4 data
  a collection
  b information

5 revolutionised
  a caused great changes
  b started something

6 lift-off
  a when a rocket leaves the ground
  b when a rocket leaves the atmosphere

People who Changed the World

A Yuri Gagarin

"I see Earth. It's so beautiful!" These are the first words ever spoken by a human in space. The speaker was 27-year-old Soviet cosmonaut Yuri Gagarin.

Yuri Gagarin was born on 9 March 1934, in Smolensk, Russia. When he left school, Yuri decided to train as an engineer, so he **enrolled** at a technical college on the **outskirts** of Moscow. While he was a student, he became interested in aircraft and took lessons at a local flying school. Soon it became obvious he was a talented pilot, so when he finished his studies in 1955, he joined the Soviet Air Force. This proved to be a **turning point** in his life. He was chosen to be a test-pilot, flying new and experimental aircraft. Yuri was selected to join a special group of the country's best test pilots and went on to further training to be a cosmonaut. His instructors described him as very calm and **confident** with very **quick reactions**.

Yuri's epic one-hundred-and-eight-minute flight into space on 12 April 1961, made headline news all over the world. It was man's first venture into space and the beginning of his journey to the stars. As the pilot of the spaceship, Gagarin proved that a human could survive lift-off, **re-entry** and weightlessness and return safely to Earth. What's more, he was able to record important data which future astronauts would use.

Yuri Gagarin became a national hero. Unfortunately, he was tragically killed seven years later in a plane crash. He was thirty-four years old.

B Albert Einstein

Albert Einstein is one of the most **gifted** scientists of all time. He is best known for his theory of **relativity**, which he developed when he was only twenty-six and which changed the way scientists looked at space and time.

Einstein was born on 14 March 1874, in Ulm, Württemberg,

c) Use the prompts below to make sentences, as in the example.

- Yuri Gagarin/not be/talented pilot → he/not become/cosmonaut
- Albert Einstein/not be/dedicated scientist → he/ not develop/theory/change the world
- Steve Jobs/not drop out/college → he/not become/ computer designer

If Yuri Gagarin hadn't been a talented pilot, he would not have become a cosmonaut.

d) Explain the words in bold. Then, use your dictionary to find synonyms for the highlighted words.

Lesson 4 (pp. 128 - 129)

* Check Ss' HW (10').

26 Ask Ss to look at the pictures and try to identify the people shown in each picture. Read the questions aloud and elicit/explain the meaning of any unknown words. Help Ss to answer the questions.

> *ANSWER KEY*
>
> *revolutionising personal computers – Steve Jobs*
> *the theory of relativity – Albert Einstein*
> *scientific research and experiments – Albert Einstein*
> *developing atomic energy – Albert Einstein*
> *founding Apple – Steve Jobs*
> *being a strong believer in world peace – Albert Einstein*
> *surviving lift-off, re-entry and weightlessness in space*
> *– Yuri Gagarin*
> *Ss' own answers*

27 • Read the adjectives aloud and elicit/explain the meaning of any unknown words.
  • Explain the task to Ss. Play the recording. Ss listen and decide which person each adjective describes. Check Ss' answers around the class.

> *ANSWER KEY*
>
> | | | |
> |---|---|---|
> | *1 E* | *4 G* | *7 E* |
> | *2 G* | *5 G* | *8 J* |
> | *3 J* | *6 J* | |

28 a) Read the questions aloud and elicit/explain the meaning of any unknown words. Explain the task to Ss. Ss read the article silently and write the correct letters in the boxes. Check Ss' answers around the class.

> *ANSWER KEY*
>
> | | | |
> |---|---|---|
> | *1 E* | *5 G* | *8 G* |
> | *2 J* | *6 G* | *9 E* |
> | *3 E* | *7 E* | *10 J* |
> | *4 J* | | |

b) • Read aloud the words (1-6) and ask Ss to find and underline the words in the text.
  • Allow Ss one minute to look at the texts and decide what each word means. Check Ss' answers.

> *ANSWER KEY*
>
> | | | |
> |---|---|---|
> | *1 a* | *3 b* | *5 a* |
> | *2 b* | *4 b* | *6 a* |

c) Read the first set of prompts and the example aloud. Allow Ss two minutes to use the prompts to make similar sentences. Check Ss' answers by asking individual Ss to read their sentences aloud.

> *ANSWER KEY*
>
> • *If Albert Einstein hadn't been a dedicated scientist, he would not have developed a theory that changed the world.*
> • *If Steve Jobs hadn't dropped out of college, he wouldn't have become a computer designer.*

d) • Ss use their dictionaries to help them explain the words in bold.
    Ss' own answers
  • Ss use their dictionaries to find synonyms for the highlighted words.

> *ANSWER KEY*
>
> *instructors: trainers/teachers*
> *proved: established/confirmed*
> *force: power/influence*
> *outcome: result/consequence*
> *dedicated: committed/devoted*
> *dropped out of: abandoned/quit*
> *pair: two/couple*
> *ordinary: average/common*
> *develop: make/create*

29 a) • Allow Ss two minutes to complete the phrases. Check Ss' answers. Ss should memorise these phrases.

ANSWER KEY

1	important	6	turning
2	personal	7	scientific
3	exploration	8	ordinary
4	national	9	job
5	weather	10	smart

• Ss use the completed phrases to make sentences. Check Ss' answers by asking individual Ss to read their sentences aloud.
  e.g. You can store **important data** on a computer.
  Buzz Aldrin feels regret about his **personal problems**.

b) • Allow Ss two minutes to complete the phrases with the correct prepositions. Check Ss' answers. Ss should memorise these phrases.

ANSWER KEY

1	of	5	of	8	of
2	with	6	over/on	9	of
3	in	7	in, with	10	in
4	from				

• Ss use the completed phrases to make sentences. Check Ss' answers by asking individual Ss to read their sentences aloud.

30 a) • Play the recording. Ss listen and complete the dialogue. Check Ss' answers.

ANSWER KEY

1	horror	2	Why	3	had

• Ss, in pairs, read out the dialogue.

b) Allow Ss one minute to match the problems to the reasons. Check Ss' answers. Ss then use the prompts in the table to make similar dialogues. Check Ss' answers by asking pairs of Ss to perform their dialogues in front of the class.

ANSWER KEY

a - 3   b - 4   c - 5   d - 1   e - 2

A: I wish I hadn't eaten so much chocolate.
B: Really? Why?
A: If I hadn't eaten it, I wouldn't have put on weight.

A: I wish I hadn't left my umbrella at home.
B: Really? Why?
A: If I hadn't left it at home, I wouldn't have got wet.

A: I wish I hadn't forgotten to put sun cream on.
B: Really? Why?
A: If I hadn't forgotten to put sun cream on, I wouldn't have gotten sunburnt.

A: I wish I hadn't gone out without a coat.
B: Really? Why?
A: If I hadn't gone out without a coat, I wouldn't have caught a cold.

A: I wish I hadn't forgotten to set the alarm clock.
B: Really? Why?
A: If I hadn't forgotten to set the alarm clock, I wouldn't have woken up late.

31 a) • Play the recording. Ss listen and complete the dialogue. Check Ss' answers.

ANSWER KEY

1	that	2	keep	3	pay

• Ss, in pairs, read the dialogue aloud.

b) Ss use the prompts to make a similar dialogue. Check Ss' answers by asking pairs of Ss to perform their dialogue in front of the class.

ANSWER KEY

• A: I wish I had a holiday cottage.
  B: Really! Why's that?
  A: Well, If I had a holiday cottage, I could go there at weekends.
  A: Well, I wish I didn't have a holiday cottage.
  B: Oh! Why?
  A: Because If I didn't have a holiday cottage, all my friends wouldn't come to stay.

(Suggested Homework)

1 **Vocabulary:** Ex. 28 b (p. 128), Ex. 29 (p.129)
2 **Reading aloud:** any text in Ex. 28a (p. 128)
3 **Act out:** dialogues Exs 30 & 31 (p.129)

9 Match the notes (A-E) to the characters, then use the notes to describe the characters, as in the example.

A: Huck
- not always truthful, but not really dishonest — tells "white lies" which don't hurt anyone
- quick-thinking (e.g. his story about his "sick family" saves Jim)
- loyal — protects Jim, and helps rescue him
- kind — hides bag of gold to stop Mary Jane being robbed

Although Huck isn't always truthful, he isn't really dishonest. When he tells lies, they are "white lies" which don't hurt anyone ...

B: Tom Sawyer
- loves excitement and adventure
- has a strong imagination, but isn't practical (e.g. strange plans for Jim's "escape")
- risks unnecessary danger (e.g. letter to Uncle Silas leads to being shot)

C: Jim
- loyal and caring (e.g. helps Tom instead of running)
- loves his family — plans to free his wife and children

D: The 'Duke' and the 'King'
- liars and cheats
- dishonest and selfish — don't care about hurting Mary Jane, Huck, etc by stealing from them
- greedy — want to sell Mary Jane's house, etc and steal everything

E: Huck's father, Pap
- filthy, mean and cruel (e.g. keeps beating Huck all the time)
- greedy — tries to get Huck's money
- jealous because Huck has a good life

10 Find the missing word in each of the sentences, then write it in the spaces below, as in the example.

1	T W A I N	16	P H E L P S
2	H U C K	17	D U K E
3	N E W	18	U N C L E
4	P A P	19	K I N G
5	W I D O W	20	W I L K S
6	S L A V E	21	C L E M E N S
7	P E T E R	22	B O Y
8	H A N N I B A L	23	O R L E A N S
9	W A T S O N	24	S A R A H
10	S A M U E L	25	M A R Y
11	C A I R O	26	S A W Y E R
12	F R E E	27	R A F T
13	M I S S O U R I	28	J I M
14	O H I O	29	A U N T
15	F I N N	30	E N D

1 Mark Twain wrote *Huckleberry Finn*.
2 His name is Huckleberry, but everyone just calls him Huck.
3 Miss Watson was going to sell Jim in New Orleans.
4 Huck calls his father "Pap".
5 Huck goes to live with the widow Douglas.
6 Jim was Miss Watson's slave.
7 A rich man called Peter Wilks has just died.
8 Mark Twain grew up in Hannibal, Missouri.
9 Miss Watson is Widow Douglas' sister.
10 Mark Twain's real name was Samuel Clemens.
11 Huck and Jim go past Cairo in the fog.
12 Jim isn't a slave anymore — he's a free man.
13 Mark Twain was born in Missouri.
14 Jim plans to go up the Ohio River on a steamboat to reach freedom in the North.
15 Huck's surname is Finn.
16 A farmer called Silas Phelps has bought Jim.
17 One character says he is the Duke of Bridgewater.
18 Silas Phelps is Tom's uncle.
19 One character says he is really the King of France.
20 William Wilks is deaf and dumb.
21 Mark Twain's real name was Samuel Clemens.
22 Huck isn't a man, he's a boy.
23 Miss Watson was going to sell Jim in New Orleans.
24 Huck, dressed up as a girl, tells Mrs Loftus his name is Sarah Williams.
25 Peter Wilks' niece is called Mary Jane.
26 Huck's best friend is Tom Sawyer.
27 Huck and Jim go down the Mississippi on a raft.
28 Huck and Tom "rescue" Jim.
29 Mrs Phelps is Tom's aunt Sally.
30 The story has a happy end.

Units 9 - 10

Vocabulary & Grammar

1 Fill in the correct word.

1 The news came as a shock to them.
2 Tim is not very good at board games. He prefers team sports.
3 If you had been more careful, you wouldn't have caused such a problem.
4 Satellites send signals all over the world.
5 If I were you, I'd talk to him.
6 I think it's too late for Arsenal to even the score.
7 What a noisy car!
8 His invention changed the course of history.
9 You look very tired. You'd better have a rest.
10 We play ten-pin bowling in a bowling alley.
11 Jane goes to the gym to keep in shape.
12 If I had enough money, I would move to a bigger house.
13 "I've missed the bus."
   "So have I."
14 He told us not to miss the target.
15 She asked him if he had ever been to York.
16 If only I hadn't missed the last bus home.
17 Columbus discovered America.
18 I wish I hadn't failed my exams.
19 Jenny came across this ring as she was tidying up the attic.
20 The team is ready to compete with the best.
21 What do you do for a living?
22 Peter is jealous of Jonathan's talent.
23 How fresh these flowers are!
24 Joining the army proved to be a turning point in his life.
25 She is dedicated to her studies.
26 He achieved success beyond his wildest dreams.
27 The plane had already taken off when we arrived at the airport.
28 Alexander Fleming discovered penicillin.
29 "I've never failed a test."
   "Neither have I."
30 We've run out of sugar. Can you buy some?

(30 marks)

2 Circle the correct item.

1 John .... into lots of money when his uncle died.
   A ran   B turned   C came   D brought
2 The gym has got highly .... staff.
   A equipped B qualified C latest   D lively
3 I think we're .... a losing battle.
   A practising B fighting   C arguing D facing
4 .... Tom and John are here.
   A Both   B None   C Neither D Either
5 Mozart was a .... composer.
   A visionary B gifted   C genius D confident
6 Competition always .... out the best in me.
   A comes   B finds   C takes   D brings
7 Have you got .... muscles? Go to 'Relax Zone'.
   A tired   B painful   C hurt   D aching
8 Keep .... the pace, will you?
   A off   B up   C on   D out
9 Sarah takes .... her father. They are very much alike.
   A out   B in   C after   D up
10 .... you work hard, you'll be fired.
   A If   B When   C Unless D Only

(20 marks)

Communication

3 Put the dialogue into the correct order.

6 Could I please leave a message with you?

1 Microcomputer Co, Steven speaking. How can I help you?

4 Jeremy Philips.

8 Thank you very much.

5 I'm really sorry Mr Philips, but the line is engaged at the moment.

2 Could I speak to Mrs Peters, please?

7 Certainly Mr Philips. Oh, Mrs Peters is free now. Hold on a minute and I'll put you through.

3 Could I ask who is calling?

(20 marks)

136(T)

Reading

4 Read the article and choose the correct answer.

Reach for the stars

What is success? It could be many things and often means different things to different people. For example, money, fame, academic achievement, overcoming a physical disability or discovering the secrets of the universe. A person who has achieved any of these could be considered successful, so if one person has accomplished all of them, what word would you use to describe him? Well, there are two actually — Stephen Hawking.

Stephen Hawking is a theoretical physicist. This means that he works on the basic laws that rule the universe. He has made some remarkable discoveries and has published his findings in books and magazines. Stephen has received numerous awards and medals and is a member of many Royal Societies. He is highly educated and has twelve honourary degrees. He even holds the post of Lucasian Professor of Mathematics which previously belonged to Isaac Newton. All this by someone who has motor neuron disease, is confined to a wheelchair and can't speak without the aid of a computer!

When talking about his illness, Stephen describes it as little more than an inconvenience. Recently, when asked if he would still have been involved in Physics if he hadn't been disabled, he simply said that the only difference would be that he would have worked more with numbers and equations.

When we consider how one man has excelled in all areas of life despite being severely disabled, we learn that we can overcome almost any difficulty to achieve our goals. Success is within our reach, we just have to go for it!

1 What is the writer trying to do in this text?
  A explain what success is
  B show how disabled people can live a full life
  C show how people can overcome misfortune with determination
  D show how Hawking's illness has destroyed his life

2 Why would somebody read this text?
  A to learn about what can be achieved
  B to learn about physics
  C to learn about disabled people
  D to learn about success

3 What does the writer think of Hawking?
  A he pities him
  B he admires him
  C he doesn't understand him
  D he envies him

(15 marks)

Writing (an article advertising a holiday)

5 You have just returned from a holiday with Sun Adventures, which you enjoyed very much. Your teacher asked you to write an article advertising the holiday. Use the plan to you help you. (120-180 words)

Plan

(See Suggested Answers section

Introduction

(Para 1) *enjoy water sports/wide open spaces – Sun Adventures/action-packed – ages 16-60*

(Para 2) *–one week – summer – surfing – kayaking – scuba diving – beach barbecue – boat trip – local island – visit sea turtle reserve/go whale watching*

(Para 3) *the holiday of a lifetime – website www.sunadventures.com*

(15 marks)

(Total = 100 marks)

Let's sing!

6 Listen and fill in. Listen again and sing.

I wish …

I wish I were a millionaire
With lots of cash to
1) spend
Everyone I ever met
Would want to be my friend
I wish I were a
2) film star
Living in Hollywood
I'd be seen on the silver screen
3) Life would be so good.

If only, if only
My 4) wishes would come true
I wish, I wish they would
It's a shame they never do

If only I were famous
I'd be a household name
All my 5) friends and neighbours
Would be jealous of my fame.
If only I were
6) wealthy,
As famous people are
I'd buy a 7) house in the country
And a shiny racing car.

I wish my life were different
I wish I were a
8) star
I've got so much ambition
I really should go far
I wish I knew for
9) certain
Just what I'm going to be
But I can't be told what the 10) future holds
So I'll have to wait and see.

137(T)

Grammar Reference Section

(REVISION) WORD ORDER IN SENTENCES

- The normal word order in **simple sentences** is:

Subject	Modal/ Auxiliary	Verb	Object	Complement/ Object 2*
Jack		is		13 years old.
He		likes	Jill.	
Jack	is	having	a party	next week.
He	has	sent	her	an invitation.*

or:

"There"	Verb	Subject	Complement
There	is	a mouse	under my bed.

- **Negative sentences**

Subject	Modal/ Auxiliary	Verb	Object
Jill	doesn't	like	Jack.
She	hasn't	answered	his invitation.

- **Yes/No Questions**

Modal/ Auxiliary	Subject	Verb	Object
Does	Jack	like	Jill?
Does	Jill	like	Jack?
Has	she	answered	his invitation?

- **Wh- Questions**

Wh-	Modal/ Auxiliary	Subject	Verb	Object
When	is	Jack	having	a party?
What	has	he	sent	Jill?

- **Compound sentences** join simple sentences with conjunctions (*and, but, so, because* etc).

Jack likes Jill, <u>but</u> she doesn't like him.
...   S   V   O   ...   S   M/A   V   O
<u>Although</u>   Jack likes Jill,   she doesn't like him.

PRESENT SIMPLE

Form

Affirmative:	I like, you like, he likes, she likes etc
Negative:	I **don't** like, you **don't** like, he **doesn't** like etc
Interrogative:	**Do** I like...?, **Do** you like...?, **Does** he like?, **Does** she like...?etc
Short answers:	Do I/you/we ...? Yes, I/you/we do. / No, I/you/we don't.
	Does he/She/it ...? Yes, he/she/it does. / No, he/she/it doesn't.
	Do they ...? Yes, they do. / No, they don't.

Use

The **present simple** is used:
- for permanent states, repeated actions and daily routines.
  *They **live** in London.* (permanent state)
  *He **gets up** at 8:00 am every day.* (repeated action, daily routine)
- for general truths and laws of nature.
  *Summers **are** usually hot.*
- for timetables (buses, trains, etc) and programmes.
  *The train to York **leaves** at 5:30 pm.*
- for sports commentaries, reviews and narration.
  *Beckham **passes** the ball to Briggs.* (sports commentary)
  *Tom Hanks **acts** wonderfully in the film.* (review)
  *There **is** a girl called Cinderella.* (narration)

Time expressions used with the present simple: *always, usually, etc, every day/week/month/year etc, on Mondays/Tuesdays etc, in the morning/afternoon/evening, at night/the weekend, etc.*

PRESENT CONTINUOUS

Form

Affirmative:	I'm talking, you're talking, he's talking, she's talking, etc
Negative:	I'm not talking, you're not talking, he's not talking, she's not talking, etc
Interrogative:	**Am** I talking?, **Are** you talking?, **Is** he talking?, **Is** she talking? etc
Short answers:	Are you talking? Yes, I am./Yes, we are. / No, I'm not./No, we aren't.
	Is he/she/it talking? Yes, he/she/it is. / No, he/she/it isn't.
	Are they talking? Yes, they are. / No, they aren't.

Use

The **present continuous** is used:

- for actions taking place now, at the moment of speaking, or for temporary actions – that is, actions that are going on around now, but not at the actual moment of speaking.
  *Tom **is working** hard these days. Right now he's **watching** a film.* (He's not working at the moment of speaking.)
- with **always**, when we want to express irritation, for actions which happen too often.
  *You're **always watching** TV.*
- for actions that we have already arranged to do in the near future, especially when the time and place have been decided.
  *Ross **is flying** to Oslo at 8:00 in the evening.* (The destination and departure have been arranged.)
- for changing or developing situations.
  *The Earth's climate **is changing** rapidly.*

Time expressions used with the present continuous: *now, at the moment, these days, at present, tonight, tomorrow, next week/ month etc, still, at present etc.*

ADVERBS OF FREQUENCY

- Adverbs of frequency *(always, usually, often, sometimes, rarely/seldom, never)* tell us how often something happens. They answer the question **How often …?** .
  How often do you visit your grandparents?
  *I **usually** visit my grandparents on Sundays.*

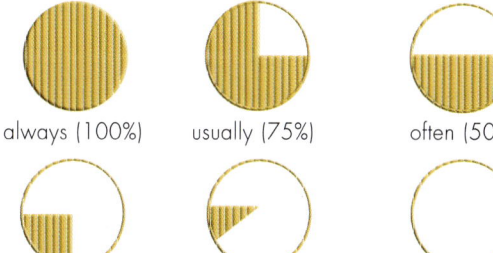

always (100%)   usually (75%)   often (50%)

sometimes (25%)   rarely/seldom (10%)   never (0%)

- Adverbs of frequency come before the main verb (walk, fly etc), but after the verb **to be** and auxiliary or modal verbs such as **do, can, must** etc. The adverbs *rarely, seldom* and *never* have a negative meaning and are never used with the word **not**.
  *Emma **always walks** to school.*
  *You **should always** wear your seat belt when you drive.*
  ***Do** you **often go** out with your friends?*
- Adverbs of frequency go before the auxiliary verb in short answers.
  *Do you read newspapers? Yes, I **sometimes do**.*

RELATIVES

Relative Pronouns

Relative pronouns *(who, whom, which, whose, that)* introduce relative clauses. A relative clause tells us which person or thing the speaker means.

*The man **who is wearing a grey coat** is Joe's father.*

relative clause

The relative identifies which man the speaker is talking about.

- We use **who/that** to refer to people.
- We use **which/that** to refer to objects or animals.
- Who/Which/That **cannot be omitted** if it is the **subject** of the relative clause; that is, when there is not a noun or subject pronoun between the relative pronoun and the verb.
  a) *I know a girl. She is from India.*

  *I know a girl **who/that** is from India.*
  (The relative pronoun is the subject.)

  b) *The dog – it has got grey fur – is mine.*

  *The dog **which/that** has got grey fur is mine.*
  (The relative pronoun is the subject.)
- Who/Which/That **can be omitted** when it is the **object** of the relative clause; that is, when there is a noun or subject pronoun between the relative pronoun and the verb. We can use **whom** instead of **who** when it is the object of the relative clause. *Whom* is not often used in everyday English.
  a) *I saw a woman. I had met her last summer.*

  *I saw a woman (**whom/who/that**) I had met last summer.*
  (The relative pronoun is the object.)

  b) *That's the movie. I saw it last night.*

  *That's the movie (**which/that**) I saw last night.*
  (The relative pronoun is the object.)
- We use **whose** instead of possessive adjectives (my, your, his, etc) with people, objects and animals in order to show possession.
  a) *That's the man – his car got stolen last night.*

  *That's the man **whose** car got stolen last night.*

  b) *That's the car – its window is broken.*

  *That's the car **whose** window is broken.*
- We usually avoid using prepositions before relative pronouns.
  a) *The helicopter **in which** the patient was carried was struck by lightening (formal English – unusual structure).*
  b) *The room **which/that** we keep our tools **in** is in the back yard (usual structure).*
  c) *The room we keep our tools **in** is in the back yard (everyday English).*
- We can use *which* to refer back to a whole clause.
  My brother lent me some money. This was very kind of him.

  *My brother lent me some money, **which** was very kind of him.*
  (**which** refers to the fact that he lent the speaker some money. That is, it refers back to the whole clause.)

- A relative pronoun is not used with another pronoun (I, you, me, him, etc).
  - a) *I know a doctor **who** works in this hospital.*
    (NOT: *I know a doctor who ~~she~~ works in this hospital.*)
  - b) *The people we met are from Brazil.*
    (NOT: *The people we met ~~them~~ are from Brazil.*)

Note: *who's = who is or who has*
who's = *who is or who has*
whose = *possessive*
***Who's** (who is) your favourite rock star?*
***Who's** (who has) got a new car?*
*Richard is the teacher **whose** father is from Spain.*

The Relative Adverb "where"

- **Where** is a relative adverb that introduces relative clauses. It is used to refer to **place**, usually after nouns like *place, house, street, town* and *country*.
  It can be replaced by *which/that + preposition* and, in this case, *which/that* can be omitted.
  *The restaurant **where** we used to eat caught fire.*
  *The restaurant (**which/that**) we used to eat **in** caught fire.*

DEFINING/NON DEFINING CLAUSES

There are two types of relative clause: defining relative clauses and non-defining relative clauses.

- A **defining relative clause** gives necessary information and is essential to the meaning of the main sentence. The relative pronouns can be omitted when they are the object of the relative clause. The relative clause is not put in commas.
  The jeans are too tight. (Which jeans? We don't know. The meaning of the sentence is not clear.)
  *The jeans (**which/that**) I bought yesterday are too tight. (Which jeans? The ones I bought yesterday.)*
- A **non-defining relative clause** gives extra information and is not essential to the meaning of the main sentence. In non-defining relative clauses, the relative pronouns cannot be omitted and cannot be replaced by *that*. The relative clause is put in commas.
  My dog is very friendly. (The meaning of the sentence is clear.)
  *My dog, **whose name is Blacky**, is very friendly. (The relative clause gives extra information.)*

AS - LIKE

We use **as** or **like** to say that things are similar.

- We use *as* to express a **role** or **function**.
  *Simon uses his sofa **as** his bed. (It is his bed.)*
- We use *like* to express **similarity**.
  *My father looks **like** Anthony Hopkins.*

UNIT 2

PAST SIMPLE

Regular verbs

Affirmative:	I walked, you walked, he walked, she walked, etc
Negative:	I **didn't** walk, you **didn't** walk, he **didn't** walk, she **didn't** walk, etc
Interrogative:	**Did** I walk?, **Did** you walk?, **Did** he walk?, **Did** she walk?, etc

Irregular verbs

Affirmative:	I slept, you slept, he slept, she slept, etc	
Negative:	I **didn't** sleep, you **didn't** sleep, he **didn't** sleep, she **didn't** sleep, etc	
Interrogative:	**Did** I sleep?, **Did** you sleep?, **Did** he sleep?, **Did** she sleep?, etc	
Short Answers:	Did I/you/he etc leave?	Yes, I/you/he etc did. No, I/you/he etc didn't.

Use

The **past simple** is used:

- for an action which happened at a definite time in the past. The time is stated, already known or implied.
  *They **travelled** to India **last summer**. (When? Last summer. The time is stated.)*
  *They **had** a great time. (The time is already known.)*
- for actions which happened immediately one after the other in the past.
  *First, he **had** a shower. Then he **had** breakfast.*
- for past habits or states which are now finished. In such cases we can also the expression **used to**.
  *Paul **walked/used to walk** to school every day last year.*

Time expressions used with the past simple: *yesterday, last night/week/month etc, two days/weeks etc ago, in 1979 etc.*

PAST CONTINUOUS

Form

- We form the past continuous with the past tense of the verb **to be** and the **main verb + ing**.
  *I **was walking** down the street when I saw her.*

Affirmative	Interrogative	Negative
I **was** walking	**Was** I walking?	I **wasn't** walking
you **were** walking	**Were** you walking?	you **weren't** walking
he **was** walking	**Was** he walking?	he **wasn't** walking
she **was** walking	**Was** she walking?	she **wasn't** walking
it **was** walking	**Was** it walking?	it **wasn't** walking
we **were** walking	**Were** we walking?	we **weren't** walking
you **were** walking	**Were** you walking?	you **weren't** walking
they **were** walking	**Were** they walking?	they **weren't** walking

Short Answers:	Was I/he/she/it walking?	Yes, I/he/she/it was.
		No, I/he/she/it wasn't.
	Were you/we/they walking?	Yes, you/we/they were.
		No, you/we/they weren't.

Use

The **past continuous** is used:

- for an action which was in progress at a stated time in the past. We do not mention when the action started or finished.
  *At eleven o'clock last night we **were watching** a film.* (We don't know when the film started or finished.)
- for an action which was in progress when another action interrupted it. We use the **past continuous** for the action in progress (longer action) and the **past simple** for the action which interrupted it (shorter action).
  *She **was cooking** dinner when the phone **rang**.*
- for two or more simultaneous past actions.
  *She **was talking** on the phone while he **was taking** a shower.*
- to describe the atmosphere, the setting etc in the introduction to a story, before we describe the main events.
  *Alex **was driving** to work. It **was raining** heavily.*

Time expressions used with the past continuous: *when, while, as, all day/night/morning etc.*

TIME WORDS

- We express **time** with the words: **when, while, before, after, until**, etc. We do not use future tenses with these words.
  *I'll have breakfast **before** I **go** to school.*
  (NOT: ...before I ~~will~~ go to school.)
- When the time word comes at the beginning of a sentence, we use a comma.
  ***Before** you leave, please call me.*
- When the time word comes in the middle of a sentence, we don't use a comma.
  *Please call me **before** you leave.*

POSSESSIVES

Possessive Adjectives	Possessive Pronouns
my	mine
your	yours
his	his
her	hers
its	–
our	ours
your	yours
their	theirs

- **its** = possessive adjective
  *When I washed my shirt **its** colour faded.*
- **it's** = it is or it has
  ***It's** (it is) near my house.*
  ***It's** (it has) got good reviews.*

Possessive Case

- Possessive case is used to talk about:
  - ownership   *This is John's bike.* or:
  - the relationship between people
    Donald is Mickey's friend.
- Possessive case is formed with:
  - **'s** (or **'**) for people/animals   *the girl's book/the girls' books*
    the dog's teeth
  - **of** for objects   *the top **of** the mountain*
    *the back **of** the book*
- Singular nouns and proper nouns take **'s** in the possessive
  - *the boy's bike   John's bike*
  but proper nouns ending in -s take **'** or **'s**
  - *Dickens' novels/Dickens's novels*
- Plural nouns ending in -s take **'** in the possessive
  - *the boys' bikes* (belonging to several boys)
  but other plural nouns take **'s**
  - *the men's shoes   the children's toys*

Possessive Adjectives/Pronouns

- **Possessive adjectives** are followed by nouns, whereas **possessive pronouns** are not.
  *This is **my** car. It's **mine**.*

UNIT 3

PRESENT PERFECT

Regular Verbs

Affirmative:	I've played, you've played, he's played, she's played etc
Negative:	I **haven't** played, you **haven't** played, he **hasn't** played, she **hasn't** played, etc
Interrogative:	**Have** I played?, **Have** you played?, **Has** he played?, **Has** she played?, etc
Short answers:	Have I/you/we/they played? / Yes, I/you/we/they have. No, I/you/we/they haven't.
	Has he/she/it played? / Yes, he/she/it has. No, he/she/it hasn't.

Use

The **present perfect** is used:

- to describe an action which started in the past and continues up to the present, especially with *state verbs* such as **have, like, know, be,** etc. In this case, we often use *for* and *since*.
  They **have been** married since 1995. (They got married in 1995 and they are still married.)
- for an action which has recently finished and whose result is visible in the present.
  Pete **has put** on weight.
- for an action which happened at an unstated time in the past. The exact time is not important, so it is not mentioned. The emphasis is on the action.
  Eric **has visited** Paris three times. (The exact time of his visits is not mentioned. What is important is that he has been to Paris three times.)
- for an action which has happened within a specific time period, which is not over at the moment of speaking, such as *today, this morning/afternoon/week/month/year,* etc.
  We **have watched** two films this afternoon. (The action has been repeated twice up to now and may happen again because the time period (this afternoon) is not over yet.

Time expressions used with the present perfect:	
• *already:*	We **have already been** to the supermarket.
	Have you **been** to the supermarket **already**?
• *yet:*	**Has** Mary **finished** her homework **yet**?
	She **hasn't finished** her homework **yet**.
• *just:*	Mark **has just phoned**.
• *always:*	He **has always wanted** to travel abroad.
• *ever:*	**Have** you **ever been** to Spain?
• *never:*	She **has never been** to Spain.
• *so far:*	I **have received** four e-mails **so far**.
	What **have** you **done so far**?

PRESENT PERFECT CONTINUOUS

Form

We form the **present perfect continuous** with the auxiliary verb **have/has**, the past participle of the verb **to be** and the **main verb + ing**.

Affirmative	
Long form	Short form
I have been playing	I've been playing
you have been playing	you've been playing
he has been playing	he's been playing
she has been playing	she's been playing
it has been playing	it's been playing
we have been playing	we've been playing
you have been playing	you've been playing
they have been playing	they've been playing

Negative	
Long form	Short form
I have not been playing	I haven't been playing
you have not been playing	you haven't been playing
he has not been playing	he hasn't been playing
she has not been playing	she hasn't been playing
it has not been playing	it hasn't been playing
we have not been playing	we haven't been playing
you have not been playing	you haven't been playing
they have not been playing	they haven't been playing

Interrogative	
Have I been playing?	Has it been playing?
Have you been playing?	Have we been playing?
Has he been playing?	Have you been playing?
Has she been playing?	Have they been playing?

Short answers:		
Have I/you/we/they been playing?	Yes, I/you/we/they have.	No, I/you/we/they haven't.
Has he/she/it been playing?	Yes, he/she/it has.	No, he/she/it hasn't.

Use

The **present perfect continuous** is used:

- to emphasise the duration of an action which started in the past and continues up to the present, especially with time expressions such as *all morning/day/night, for, since* etc.
  I **have been writing** letters all morning. (I started writing letters early in the morning and I'm still writing them now.)
- for an action which started and finished in the past and lasted for some time. The result of the action is visible in the present.
  John's clothes are dirty. He **has been playing** in the garden.
- to express anger, annoyance or irritation.
  Who **has been using** my computer? (The speaker is irritated.)

Time expressions used with the present perfect and the present continuous:	
• *how long:*	**How long have** you **known** Alison?
	How long have you been working in this company?
• *for (duration):*	I **have known** Alison **for** ten years.
	I **have been working** here **for** ten months.
• *since (starting point):*	The Johnsons **have lived** in Manchester **since** 1990.
	The Johnsons **have been living** in Manchester **since** 1990.
• *lately/recently:*	**Have** you **been** to the theatre **lately/recently**?
	Have you **been living** abroad **lately/recently**?

- Some verbs/expressions form question tags differently:
  I am – aren't I?
  *I'm late again, **aren't I**?*
  Imperative – will you/won't you?
  *Help me move the sofa, **will you**?*
  Don't – will you?
  *Don't interrupt me, **will you**?*
  Let's – shall we?
  *Let's go swimming, **shall we**?*
  I have (got) – haven't I?
  *They have (got) a yacht, **haven't they**?*
  I have (other meanings) – don't I?
  *He has tennis lessons once a week – **doesn't he**?*
  There is – isn't there?
  *There are classes in the summer, **aren't there**?*
  This/That is – isn't it?
  *That is your shirt, **isn't it**?*

Intonation

- When we are sure of the answer, the voice goes down in the question tag. (↘)
  Lou is only three, she can't read or write, can she? (↘)
- When we are not sure of the answer and want to check information, the voice goes up in the question tag. (↗)
  He doesn't like Indonesian food, does he? (↗)

REPORTED SPEECH - STATEMENTS

Reported speech is the exact meaning of what someone said, but not the exact words. We do not use quotation marks. The word **that** can either be used or omitted after the introductory verb (say, tell, suggest, etc).
*She said **(that)** she wouldn't be back until 10 o'clock.*

Say - Tell

- say + no personal object
  *He **said** he was very tired.*
- say + to + personal object
  *He **said to us** he was very tired.*
- tell + personal object
  *He **told us** he was very tired.*

Expressions with *say* and *tell:*

say: good morning/afternoon etc, something/nothing, one's prayers, so, a few words
tell: the truth, a lie, a secret, a story, the time, the difference, sb one's name, sb the way, one from another, one's fortune

REPORTED STATEMENTS

- In reported speech, personal/possessive pronouns and possessive adjectives change according to the meaning of the sentence.
  Ben said, "I'm having my car repaired."
  *Ben said (that) **he** was having **his** car repaired.*

- We can report someone's words either a long time after they were said (out-of-date reporting) or a short time after they were said (up-to-date reporting).

Up-to-date reporting
The tenses can either change or remain the same in reported speech.
Direct speech: *Ben said, "I still **haven't seen** this film."*
Reported speech: *Ben said (that) he still **hasn't/hadn't seen** this film.*

Out-of-date reporting
The introductory verb is in the past simple and the tenses change as follows:

Direct Speech	Reported Speech
Present Simple *He said, "I **try** to be a good student."*	Past Simple *He said (that) he **tried** to be a good student.*
Present Continuous *He said, "**She's talking** on the phone."*	Past Continuous *He said (that) she **was talking** on the phone.*
Present Perfect *He said, "They **have moved** house."*	Past Perfect *He said (that) **they had moved** house.*
Past Simple *He said, "I **had** lunch earlier."*	Past Perfect *He said (that) he **had had** lunch earlier.*
Past Continuous *He said "I **was thinking** of travelling abroad."*	Past Perf. Cont. *He said (that) he **had been thinking** of travelling abroad.*
Future (will) *He said, "She **will be** back soon."*	Conditional (would) *He said (that) she **would be** back soon.*

- Certain words and time expressions change according to the meaning as follows:

now	→	then, immediately
today	→	that day
yesterday	→	the day before, the previous day
tomorrow	→	the next/following day
this week	→	that week
last week	→	the week before, the previous week
next week	→	the week after, the following week
ago	→	before
here	→	there
come	→	go
bring	→	take

- The verb tenses remain the same in reported speech when the introductory verb is in the present, future or present perfect.
  *Mum **has said**, "Dinner **is** ready."*
  *Mum **has said** (that) dinner **is** ready.*
- The verb tenses can either change or remain the same in reported speech when reporting a general truth or law of nature.
  *The teacher said "Iceland **is** an island."*
  *The teacher said (that) Iceland **is/was** an island.*

Grammar Reference Section

COULD(N'T) - WAS (NOT) ABLE TO

We use the modal verb **could** to show that someone had the ability to do something repeatedly in the past (past repeated action).
When I was young, I could run very fast. (I had the ability to do it repeatedly in the past.)

We use **was/were able to** (= managed to do) to show that someone had the ability to do something in a particular situation in the past (past single action).
He was able to win the race. (= He managed to win the race.)

We use the negative form **couldn't** for both cases:
Ben couldn't drive a few years ago. (past repeated action)
She couldn't/wasn't able to win the race. (past single action)

USED TO

- We use **used to + infinitive** to refer to past habits or states. In such cases, *used to* can be replaced by the past simple with no difference in meaning.
  She used to go/went to work by bus. (She doesn't anymore.)
- We use the past simple, and not *used to*, for actions which happened at a definite time in the past.
  He went to a rock concert last week. (NOT: He used to go to a rock concert last week.)

UNIT 9

REPORTED QUESTIONS

- Reported questions are usually introduced with the verbs **ask, inquire, wonder** or the expression **want to know.**
- When the direct question begins with a **question word** (who, where, how, when, what, etc), the reported question is introduced with the same question word.
  What is the time, please? (direct question)
  She asked me what the time was. (reported question)
- When the direct question begins with an **auxiliary** (be, do, have), or a **modal verb** (can, may, etc), then the reported question is introduced with **if** or **whether.**
  Are there any apples left? (direct question)
  He asked me if/whether there were any apples left. (reported question)
- In reported questions, the verb is in the affirmative. The question mark and words/expressions such as *please, well, oh,* etc are omitted. The verb tenses, pronouns and time expressions change as in statements.
  Can you tell me when the next train to London is, please? (direct question)
  She asked me when the next train to London was. (reported question)

THE IMPERATIVE

- We use the imperative to give orders/instructions, make suggestions, etc. We form the imperative from the **bare infinitive** without a subject; the **negative imperative** is **don't + bare infinitive** without a subject.

Orders: *Come here! Don't touch that!*
Instructions: *Chop the onions and fry them in hot oil.*
Suggestions: *Don't go to school if you feel unwell. Stay in bed.*
Warnings: *Look out! Be careful!*
Invitations: *Come to the cinema with us tomorrow.*
Requests: *Open the window, please.*

REPORTED ORDERS

- To report **orders** in reported speech, we use the introductory verbs **order** or **tell + sb + (not) to-infinitive.**
  Put the gun down! (direct order)
  He ordered him to put the gun down. (reported order)
  Leave me alone! (direct order)
  She told me to leave her alone. (reported order)

TOO - ENOUGH

- **too** goes **before adjectives or adverbs.** It has a negative meaning and shows that something is more than enough, more than necessary or more than wanted.
  too + adjective/adverb + to-infinitive
  Sam is too young to drive. (He mustn't drive.)
  John speaks too quickly for me to understand.
- too... + to-infinitive (negative meaning)
  She's too irresponsible to keep a pet.
- too... for somebody/something + to-infinitive (negative meaning)
  It's too late for Sue to be awake.
- **enough** goes **before nouns** but **after adjectives or adverbs.** It has a positive meaning and shows that there is as much of something as is wanted or needed.
  Kevin is tall enough to reach the top shelf.
  We've got enough money to buy a new car.
- ... enough... + to-infinitive (positive meaning)
  She's clever enough to go to university.
- not ... enough... + to-infinitive (negative meaning)
  We don't have enough flour to make a cake.

EXCLAMATIONS

Exclamations are words or sentences used to express admiration, surprise, etc. To form exclamatory sentences we can use *what (a/an)* and *how.*
- what (+ adjective) + uncountable/plural noun
  What delicious food! (NOT: What a delicious food!)
  What comfortable chairs!
- what + a/an (+ adjective) + singular countable noun
  What a beautiful dress!
  What an unlucky man!
  What a holiday!
- how + adjective/adverb
  How brave you are!
  How beautifully she sings!

UNIT 10

CONDITIONALS – TYPE 2/TYPE 3

Form – Conditional Type 2

If clause		main clause	
If + past simple or past continuous	→	would/could/might + bare infinitive	Type 2
If I *were* you,	→	I *would go* to the police.	

Use – Conditional Type 2

We use **conditional type 2**:
- to talk about an imaginary situation contrary to facts in the present.
  *If I **had** enough money, I **would buy** a new car. (I don't have enough money at present.)*
- to give advice.
  *If I **were** you, I **would send** her a letter.*

Form – Conditional Type 3

If clause		main clause	
If + past perfect	→	would/could/might + have + past participle	Type 3
If I *had woken up* earlier,	→	I *wouldn't have missed* my flight.	

Use – Conditional Type 3

We use **conditional type 3**:
- to talk about an imaginary situation contrary to facts in the past.
  *If he **had apologised**, I **would have forgiven** him.*
- to express regrets or criticism.
  *If you **had been driving** carefully, you **wouldn't have had** an accident.*

Note: We can use **were** instead of **was** for all persons in the if-clause of Type 2 conditionals.
*If she **was/were** here, she would be very upset.*

WISHES

We use the verb **wish** and the expression **if only** to express a wish. *If only* is more emphatic than *I wish*.
- We use **wish/If only + past simple** when we want to say that we would like something to be different in the **present**.
  *I **wish/If only** I **had** lots of money.*
- We use **wish/If only + past perfect** to express regret that something happened or did not happen in the **past**.
  *I **wish** I **hadn't had** this accident.*
  *If only I **had known** the truth.*

Note: We can use **were** instead of was after *wish* or *if only*.
*I wish he **was/were** more careful.*

SO – BOTH – NEITHER ... NOR – EITHER ... OR – ALL/NONE

- We use **so** to express the **cause** or **reason** of an action.
  *She was late, **so** she took a taxi.*
- We use **both** to refer to **two** people/things etc; **both** has a *positive meaning*.
  Both Kim and Mike are clever children.
  They are both clever children.
  Both of them are clever children. } positive meaning
- We use **neither ... nor** to refer to **two** people/things etc; **neither ... nor** has a *negative meaning*.
  Neither Rob nor Paula are coming to the party.
  Neither of them is coming to the party.
- We use **either ... or** to refer to **one or the other of two** people/things.
  Either Ken or Danny will probably win the race.
  Either of them could win.
  My burger's disappeared! Either the cat or the dog must have eaten it. } positive meaning

  It has a positive meaning, but can form a negative with **not**.
  I didn't see either Rob or Paula at the party.
  I didn't see either of them. } negative meaning
- We use **all** and **none** to refer to **more than two** people/things etc; **all** has a *positive meaning*, and **none** has a *negative meaning*.
  Bob, Mary, Jane and Nick are very friendly.
  They are all very friendly.
  All of them are very friendly. } positive meaning

  Bob doesn't have a car. Nor does Mary.
  Nor does Jane. Nor does Nick.
  None of them has a car. } negative meaning

Irregular Verbs

Infinitive	Past	Past Participle	Infinitive	Past	Past Participle
be	was	been	lie	lay	lain
bear	bore	born(e)	light	lit	lit
beat	beat	beaten	lose	lost	lost
become	became	become	make	made	made
begin	began	begun	mean	meant	meant
bite	bit	bitten	meet	met	met
blow	blew	blown	pay	paid	paid
break	broke	broken	put	put	put
bring	brought	brought	read	read	read
build	built	built	ride	rode	ridden
burn	burnt (burned)	burnt (burned)	ring	rang	rung
burst	burst	burst	rise	rose	risen
buy	bought	bought	run	ran	run
can	could	(been able to)	say	said	said
catch	caught	caught	see	saw	seen
choose	chose	chosen	seek	sought	sought
come	came	come	sell	sold	sold
cost	cost	cost	send	sent	sent
cut	cut	cut	set	set	set
deal	dealt	dealt	sew	sewed	sewn (sewed)
dig	dug	dug	shake	shook	shaken
do	did	done	shine	shone	shone
dream	dreamt (dreamed)	dreamt (dreamed)	shoot	shot	shot
drink	drank	drunk	show	showed	shown
drive	drove	driven	shut	shut	shut
eat	ate	eaten	sing	sang	sung
fall	fell	fallen	sit	sat	sat
feed	fed	fed	sleep	slept	slept
feel	felt	felt	smell	smelt (smelled)	smelt (smelled)
fight	fought	fought	speak	spoke	spoken
find	found	found	spell	spelt (spelled)	spelt (spelled)
flee	fled	fled	spend	spent	spent
fly	flew	flown	split	split	split
forbid	forbade	forbidden	spread	spread	spread
forget	forgot	forgotten	spring	sprang	sprung
forgive	forgave	forgiven	stand	stood	stood
freeze	froze	frozen	steal	stole	stolen
get	got	got	stick	stuck	stuck
give	gave	given	sting	stung	stung
go	went	gone	stink	stank	stunk
grow	grew	grown	strike	struck	struck
hang	hung (hanged)	hung (hanged)	swear	swore	sworn
have	had	had	sweep	swept	swept
hear	heard	heard	swim	swam	swum
hide	hid	hidden	take	took	taken
hit	hit	hit	teach	taught	taught
hold	held	held	tear	tore	torn
hurt	hurt	hurt	tell	told	told
keep	kept	kept	think	thought	thought
know	knew	known	throw	threw	thrown
lay	laid	laid	understand	understood	understood
lead	led	led	wake	woke	woken
learn	learnt (learned)	learnt (learned)	wear	wore	worn
leave	left	left	win	won	won
lend	lent	lent	write	wrote	written
let	let	let			

wear out /weəʳ aʊt/
well done /wel dʌn/
well-trained /wel treɪnd/
wound /wuːnd/
yogurt /jɒgəʳt/

Episode 5

awfully /ɔːfʊli/
float /floʊt/
fog /fɒg/
Free States /friː steɪts/
go up /goʊ ʌp/
past /pɑːst/
reach /riːtʃ/
runaway /rʌnəweɪ/
sell /sel/
steamboat /stiːmboʊt/

UNIT 6

action packed /ækʃən pækt/
aggressive /əgresɪv/
alteration /ɔːltəreɪʃən/
annoyed /ənɔɪd/
apology /əpɒlədʒi/
band /bænd/
bother /bʌðəʳ/
cash /kæʃ/
challenge /tʃælɪndʒ/
chatted /tʃætəd/
cheerful /tʃɪəʳfʊl/
conductor /kəndʌktəʳ/
consider /kənsɪdəʳ/
constantly /kɒnstəntli/
convincing /kənvɪnsɪŋ/
cookery /kʊkəri/
cramp /kræmp/
crowd pleasers /kraʊd
   pliːzəʳz/
culture /kʌltʃəʳ/
deck /dek/
depressed /dɪprest/
deserve /dɪzɜːʳv/
entertainer /entəʳteɪnəʳ/
entertainment
   /entəʳteɪnmənt/
exhibits /ɪgzɪbɪts/
fault /fɔːlt/
first rate /fɜːʳst reɪt/

fold /foʊld/
force /fɔːʳs/
functions /fʌŋkʃəns/
get hold of /get hoʊld əv/
glare /gleəʳ/
guide /gaɪd/
half-time /hɑːf taɪm/
highlight /haɪlaɪt/
hurry up /hʌri ʌp/
ID badge /aɪdiː bædʒ/
in advance /ɪn ædvɑːns/
incredibly /ɪnkredɪbəli/
instruments /ɪnstrəmənts/
lengths of time /leŋθs əv
   taɪm/
lifesaver /laɪfseɪvəʳ/
lump /lʌmp/
marble /mɑːʳbl/
motionless /moʊʃənləs/
moved /muːvd/
novelty /novəlti/
nuisance /njuːsəns/
operation /ɒpəreɪʃən/
opposed to /əpoʊzd tʊ/
overall /oʊvəʳɔːl/
patience /peɪʃəns/
pedestal /pedɪstəl/
persistence /pəʳsɪstəns/
person /pɜːʳsən/
picked up /pɪkt ʌp/
plot /plɒt/
reactions /rɪækʃəns/
referee /refəriː/
refusal /rɪfjuːzəl/
resistance /rɪzɪstəns/
restricted areas /rɪstrɪktɪd
   eəriəz/
rope /roʊp/
safety net /seɪfti net/
screen /skriːn/
sculpture /skʌlptʃəʳ/
senior citizens /siːnjəʳ
   sɪtɪzəns/
set back /set bæk/
set about /set əbaʊt/
set aside /set əsaɪd/
set off/out /set ɒf/aʊt/
set up /set ʌp/
skill /skɪl/
sold out /soʊld aʊt/
solos /soʊloʊz/

spectacular /spektækjʊləʳ/
spectator /spekteɪtəʳ/
stage /steɪdʒ/
street performers /striːt
   pəʳfɔːʳməʳz/
substitute /sʌbstɪjuːt/
support group /səpɔːʳt
   grʊp/
surrounded by /səraʊndɪd
   baɪ/
tear /teəʳ/
temporary /tempərəri/
theatre-goers /θɪətəʳ goʊəʳz/
tight rope /taɪt roʊp/
uplifting /ʌplɪftɪŋ/
venue /venjuː/
whale trainer /ʰweɪl treɪnəʳ/

Episode 6

act scenes /ækt siːnz/
admit /ədmɪt/
bald /bɔːld/
bow tie /boʊ taɪ/
cheat /tʃiːt/
claim /kleɪm/
Duke /djuːk/
elderly /eldəʳli/
fixed /fɪkst/
get rid of /get rɪd ɒv/
go back /goʊ bæk/
in a hurry /ɪn ə hʌri/
introduce myself /ɪntrədjuːs
   maɪself/
King /kɪŋ/
liar /laɪəʳ/
pretend /prɪtend/
priest /priːst/
question /kwestʃən/
riverside /rɪvəʳsaɪd/
royalty /rɔɪəlti/
runaway /rʌnəweɪ/
steamboat /stiːmboʊt/
suggest /sədʒest/

UNIT 7

acid rain /æsɪd reɪn/
air pollution /eəʳ pəluːʃən/
air quality /eəʳ kwɒlɪti/
announce /ənaʊns/

appreciate /əpriːʃieɪt/
ban /bæn/
barriers /bæriəʳ/
be/get carried away
   /biː/get kærid əweɪ/
bicycle course /baɪsɪkəl
   kɔːʳs/
bottle bank /bɒtəl bæŋk/
breathing difficulties
   /briːðɪŋ dɪfɪkəltiz/
breeding /briːdɪŋ/
breeding programmes
   /briːdɪŋ proʊgræmz/
brochure /broʊʃəʳ/
campaign /kæmpeɪn/
cancer /kænsəʳ/
captivity /kæptɪvɪti/
care about /keəʳ əbaʊt/
care for /keəʳ fɔːʳ/
carry off /kæri ɒf/
carry on /kæri ɒn/
carry out /kæri aʊt/
carry over /kæri oʊvəʳ/
carry through /kæri θruː/
catering company /keɪtərɪŋ
   kʌmpəni/
chimney /tʃɪmni/
coal /koʊl/
competition /kɒmpɪtɪʃən/
concrete /kɒnkriːt/
conservation role
   /kɒnsəʳveɪʃən roʊl/
construct /kənstrʌkt/
contain /kənteɪn/
contaminate /kəntæmɪneɪt/
craft tent /krɑːft tent/
decrease /dɪkriːs/
deforestation /diːfɒrɪsteɪʃən/
depletion /dɪpliːʃən/
destroy /dɪstrɔɪ/
developer /dɪveləpəʳ/
device /dɪvaɪs/
dioxide /daɪɒksaɪd/
domes /doʊmz/
dump /dʌmp/
earthquake /ɜːʳθkweɪk/
ecosystem /iːkoʊsɪstəm/
eco-warrior /iːkoʊ wɒriəʳ/
elderly /eldəʳli/
electric motor /ɪlektrɪk
   moʊtəʳ/

Word List

encourage /ɪnkʌrɪdʒ/
endangered species /ɪndeɪndʒəʳəd spiːʃiz/
entire /ɪntaɪəʳ/
exhaust fumes /ɪgzɔːst fjuːmz/
extinction /ɪkstɪŋkʃən/
famine /fæmɪn/
fed up with /fed ʌp wɪð/
fish stocks /fɪʃ stɒks/
fit within /fɪt wɪðɪn/
flood /flʌd/
food supplies /fuːd səplaɪz/
force /fɔːʳs/
form /fɔːʳm/
fortunately /fɔːʳtʃʊnɪtli/
frequent flooding /friːkwənt flʌdɪŋ/
gadget /gædʒɪt/
gas /gæs/
glass structure /glɑːs strʌktʃəʳ/
gradually /grædʒuəli/
green day /griːn deɪ/
greenhouse /griːnhaʊs/
greenhouse effect /griːnhaʊs ɪfekt/
guidelines /gaɪdlaɪnz/
household bills /haʊshoʊld bɪlz/
imported timber /ɪmpɔːʳtɪd tɪmbəʳ/
improve /ɪmpruːv/
industrial waste /ɪndʌstriəl weɪst/
insect /ɪnsekt/
land pollution /lænd pəluːʃən/
lay /leɪ/
life expectancy /laɪf ɪkspektənsi/
look /lʊk/
low-lying areas /loʊ-laɪɪŋ eəriəz/
maintain /meɪnteɪn/
melt /melt/
natural habitat /nætʃərəl hæbɪtæt/
natural resources /nætʃərəl rɪzɔːʳsɪz/
noise pollution /nɔɪz pəluːʃən/
oil /ɔɪl/

oil spills /ɔɪl spɪlz/
overfishing /oʊvəʳfɪʃɪŋ/
ozone layer /oʊzoʊn leɪəʳ/
paper /peɪpəʳ/
park bench /pɑːʳk bentʃ/
path /pɑːθ/
plant life /plɑːnt laɪf/
polar ice caps /poʊləʳ aɪs kæps/
pollute /pəluːt/
polluted gas /pəluːtɪd gæs/
population /pɒpjʊleɪʃən/
preserve /prɪzɜːʳv/
pump /pʌmp/
put up /pʊt ʌp/
recommend /rekəmend/
recommended levels /rekəmendɪd levəlz/
reduce /rɪdjuːs/
revolution /revəluːʃən/
rubbish /rʌbɪʃ/
seed /siːd/
sewage /suːɪdʒ/
shortage /ʃɔːʳtɪdʒ/
smoke /smoʊk/
sort of /sɔːʳt əv/
species /spiːʃiz/
spot /spɒt/
sunshade /sʌnʃeɪd/
supporters /səpɔːʳtəʳz/
tear down /teəʳ daʊn/
thing /θɪŋ/
throw away /θroʊ əweɪ/
time capsule /taɪm kæpsjuːl/
typhoon /taɪfuːn/
ultraviolet radiation /ʌltrəvaɪələt reɪdieɪʃən/
unleaded petrol /ʌnledɪd petrəl/
utensil /juːtensəl/
volcanic eruption /vɒlkænɪk ɪrʌpʃən/
water pollution /wɔːtəʳ pəluːʃən/
weather patterns /weðəʳ pætəʳnz/
welfare /welfeəʳ/
wildlife /waɪldlaɪf/
wipe out /waɪp aʊt/
woods /wʊdz/

Episode 7

bald /bɔːld/
bun /bʌn/
cheat /tʃiːt/
deaf /def/
dumb /dʌm/
on the way /ɒn ðə weɪ/
possession /pəzeʃən/
priest /priːst/
servant /sɜːʳvənt/
trust /trʌst/

UNIT 8

ache /eɪk/
aching joints /eɪkɪŋ dʒɔɪnts/
ankle /æŋkəl/
announcement /ənaʊnsmənt/
appointment /əpɔɪntmənt/
appreciate /əpriːʃieɪt/
assistance /əsɪstəns/
background /bækgraʊnd/
basic /beɪsɪk/
blurred vision /blɜːʳd vɪʒən/
broken arm /broʊkən ɑːʳm/
bruised /bruːzd/
capable of /keɪpəbəl ɒv/
careers advisor /kərɪəʳz ædvaɪzəʳ/
cast /kɑːst/
charitable /tʃærɪtəbəl/
check-in desk /tʃek ɪn desk/
chest /tʃest/
committed to /kəmɪtɪd tʊ/
communities /kəmjuːnɪtiz/
contract /kɒntrækt/
curator /kjʊreɪtər/
dedicated to /dedɪkeɪtɪd tʊ/
depressing /dɪpresɪŋ/
determination /dɪtɜːʳmɪneɪʃən/
development /dɪveləpmənt/
dig wells /dɪg welz/
disabled /dɪseɪbəld/
distress /dɪstres/
donation /doʊneɪʃən/
emergency /ɪmɜːʳdʒənsi/
establish /ɪstæblɪʃ/
expert /ekspɜːʳt/

find out /faɪnd aʊt/
flight attendant /flaɪt atendənt/
form /fɔːʳm/
fortunate /fɔːʳtʃunɪt/
foundation /faʊndeɪʃən/
frustrated /frʌstreɪtɪd/
hayfever /heɪfiːvəʳ/
hurt /hɜːʳt/
itchy /ɪtʃi/
knee /niː/
lasting /lɑːstɪŋ/
life skills /laɪf skɪlz/
lifeguard /laɪfgɑːʳd/
local /loʊkəl/
location /loʊkeɪʃən/
long-term /lɒŋ tɜːʳm/
measles /miːzəlz/
migraine /miːgreɪn/
nature reserve /neɪtʃəʳ rɪzɜːʳv/
nausea /nɔːziə/
needy /niːdi/
overseas /oʊvəʳsiːz/
patient /peɪʃənt/
physical /fɪzɪkəl/
plaster /plɑːstəʳ/
priority /praɪɒrɪti/
qualified /kwɒlɪfaɪd/
queue /kjuː/
rash /ræʃ/
reading tutor /riːdɪŋ tjuːtəʳ/
refugee camp /refjuːdʒiː kæmp/
refugee /refjuːdʒiː/
relief /rɪliːf/
relief worker /rɪliːf wɜːʳkəʳ/
rescue /reskjuː/
role /roʊl/
runny nose /rʌni noʊz/
self-contained /self kənteɪnd/
send for /send fɔːʳ/
send in /send ɪn/
send off /send ɒf/
send out /send aʊt/
send up /send ʌp/
serve /sɜːʳv/
session /seʃən/
share skill /ʃeəʳ skɪl/

signal /sɪgnəl/
slipped over /slɪpt oʊvəʳ/
slippery surfaces /slɪpəri
    sɜːʳfɪsɪz/
soak /soʊk/
sore /sɔːʳ/
specialist /speʃəlɪst/
sprain /spreɪn/
starving /stɑːʳvɪŋ/
support /səpɔːʳt/
surgery /sɜːʳdʒəri/
take care of /teɪk keəʳ ɒv/
target /tɑːʳgɪt/
the developing world /ðə
    dɪveləpɪŋ wɜːʳld/
the elderly /ði: eldəʳli/
ticket inspector /tɪkɪt
    ɪnspektəʳ/
twist /twɪst/
uniform /juːnɪfɔːʳm/
volunteer work /vɒləntɪəʳ
    wɜːʳk/
wait one's turn /weɪt wʌnz
    tɜːʳn/
warden /wɔːʳdən/
worry /wʌri/
wrist /rɪst/

Episode 8

bury /beri/
coffin /kɒfɪn/
funeral /fjuːnərəl/
lie /laɪ/
mark /mɑːʳk/
old fool /oʊld fuːl/
prove /pruːv/
rope /roʊp/

UNIT 9

aching muscles /eɪkɪŋ
    mʌsəlz/
adult /ædʌlt/
alley /æli/
archery /ɑːʳtʃəri/
athletics championship
    /æθletɪks tʃæmpiənʃɪp/
attend /ətend/
back /bæk/

badminton /bædmɪntən/
ban /bæn/
baseball /beɪsbɔːl/
be influenced /bi ɪnfluənst/
bend /bend/
beneficial for /benɪfɪʃəl fəʳ/
blow /bloʊ/
brain damage /breɪn
    dæmɪdʒ/
bring out /brɪŋ aʊt/
bubbling /bʌbəlɪŋ/
burn off /bɜːʳn ɒf/
challenge /tʃælɪndʒ/
coach /koʊtʃ/
compete with /kəmpiːt wɪθ/
concentrate /kɒnsəntreɪt/
course /kɔːʳs/
court /kɔːʳt/
cox /kɒks/
curriculum /kərɪkjʊləm/
dedicated /dedɪkeɪtɪd/
discus /dɪskəs/
efficient /ɪfɪʃənt/
energetic /enəʳdʒetɪk/
fall flat /fɔːl flæt/
field /fiːld/
figure /fɪgəʳ/
first /fɜːʳst/
fitness levels /fɪtnəs levəls/
get fit /get fɪt/
golf /gɒlf/
harmful /hɑːʳmfʊl/
heels apart /hiːlz əpɑːʳt/
high jump /haɪ dʒʌmp/
hurdles /hɜːʳdəls/
ice hockey /aɪs hɒki/
ice rink /aɪs rɪŋk/
inconvenience
    /ɪnkənviːniəns/
individual /ɪndɪvɪdʒuəl/
indoor /ɪndɔːʳ/
injury /ɪndʒəri/
instructor /ɪnstrʌktəʳ/
interests /ɪntrəsts/
jacuzzi /dʒəkuːzi/
javelin /dʒævlɪn/
job training /dʒɒb treɪnɪŋ/
keep up /kiːp ʌp/
knees /niːz/
lad /læd/

landing /lændɪŋ/
long jump /lɒŋ dʒʌmp/
men's hurdles /menz
    hɜːʳdəls/
motivated /moʊtɪveɪtɪd/
nil-nil /nɪl-nɪl/
nursery school /nɜːʳsəri
    skuːl/
on hand /ɒn hænd/
on his own /ɒn hɪz oʊn/
pace /peɪs/
participants /pɑːʳtɪsɪpənts/
playmate /pleɪmeɪt/
plenty of /plenti əv/
pole /poʊl/
pole vault /poʊl vɔːlt/
premier league /premɪəʳ
    liːg/
primary school /praɪməri
    skuːl/
promote /prəmoʊt/
punch /pʌntʃ/
range /reɪndʒ/
referee /refəriː/
regulation /regjʊleɪʃən/
release /rɪliːs/
rewarding /rɪwɔːʳdɪŋ/
row /roʊ/
sauna /sɔːnə/
secondary school
    /sekəndri skuːl/
semi-final /semi-faɪnəl/
session /seʃən/
set off /set ɒf/
shed /ʃed/
snooker /snuːkəʳ/
stay fit /steɪ fɪt/
stay upright /steɪ ʌpraɪt/
steamy /stiːmi/
take after /teɪk ɑːftəʳ/
take in /teɪk ɪn/
take on /teɪk ɒn/
take out /teɪk aʊt/
take over /teɪk oʊvəʳ/
take up /teɪk ʌp/
team /tiːm/
team skills /tiːm skɪlz/
team sports /tiːm spɔːʳts/
ten-pin bowling /ten pɪn
    boʊlɪŋ/

term /tɜːʳm/
tip /tɪp/
trainers /treɪnəʳz/
under control /ʌndəʳ
    kəntroʊl/
violent sport /vaɪələnt
    spɔːʳt/
whistle /ʰwɪsəl/
wind down /waɪnd daʊn/
workout /wɜːʳkaʊt/

Episode 9

chain /tʃeɪn/
Master /mɑːstəʳ/
nephew /nefjuː/
prisoner /prɪzənəʳ/
rat /ræt/
rescue /reskjuː/
run away /rʌn əweɪ/
steal /stiːl/
style /staɪl/
unlock /ʌnlɒk/

UNIT 10

achieve /ətʃiːv/
atomic energy /ətɒmɪk
    enəʳdʒi/
average person /ævərɪdʒ
    pɜːʳsən/
award /əwɔːʳd/
believe /bɪliːv/
bill /bɪl/
broke /broʊk/
by accident /baɪ æksɪdənt/
calm /kɑːm/
camp cousellor /kæmp
    kaʊnsələʳ/
cash /kæʃ/
charming /tʃɑːʳmɪŋ/
come across /kʌm əkrɒs/

come down with /kʌm
    daʊn wɪð/
come into /kʌm ɪntuː/
come round /kʌm raʊnd/
come up /kʌm ʌp/
communication skills
    /kəmjuːnɪkeɪʃən skɪlz/

Word List

competition /kɒmpɪˈtɪʃən/
conference /ˈkɒnfrəns/
confident /ˈkɒnfɪdənt/
contact /ˈkɒntækt/
convenient /kənˈviːniənt/
cosmonaut /ˈkɒzmənɔːt/
course /kɔːʳs/
course of history /kɔːʳs əv
  ˈhɪstəri/
crossword /ˈkrɒswɜːʳd/
currently /ˈkʌrəntli/
data /ˈdeɪtə/
dedicated to /ˈdedɪkeɪtɪd tuː/
degree /dɪˈgriː/
demanding /dɪˈmɑːndɪŋ/
design /dɪˈzaɪn/
develop /dɪˈveləp/
discover /dɪsˈkʌvəʳ/
drop out of /drɒp aʊt əv/
energetic /enəʳˈdʒetɪk/
enrol /ɪnˈrəʊl/
enter /ˈentəʳ/
epic /ˈepɪk/
experiment /ɪkˈsperɪmənt/
experimental /ɪkˌsperɪˈmentəl/
fed up /fed ʌp/
force /fɔːʳs/
found /faʊnd/
gifted /ˈgɪftɪd/
grateful /ˈgreɪtfʊl/

improve /ɪmˈpruːv/
industry /ˈɪndəstri/
instructor /ɪnˈstrʌktəʳ/
invented /ɪnˈventɪd/
jealous /ˈdʒeləs/
join in /dʒɔɪn ɪn/
junk food /dʒʌŋk fuːd/
launch /lɔːntʃ/
lift-off /ˈlɪft-ɒf/
lose temper /luːz ˈtempəʳ/
map /mæp/
martial arts /ˈmɑːʳʃəl ɑːʳts/
navigation /nævɪˈgeɪʃən/
orbit /ˈɔːʳbɪt/
ordinary /ˈɔːʳdɪnri/
organised /ˈɔːʳgənaɪzd/
our changing world /aʊəʳ
  ˈtʃeɪndʒɪŋ wɜːʳld/
outcome /ˈaʊtkʌm/
outskirts /ˈaʊtskɜːʳts/
outspoken /aʊtˈspəʊkən/
overnight /ˈəʊvəʳnaɪt/
parking ticket /ˈpɑːʳkɪŋ tɪkɪt/
pave /peɪv/
pay it off /peɪ ɪt ɒf/
physically fit /ˈfɪzɪkəli fɪt/
pitch /pɪtʃ/
plane crash /pleɪn kræʃ/
plug it /plʌg ɪt/
practical /ˈpræktɪkəl/

process /ˈprəʊses/
prove /pruːv/
quick reactions /kwɪk
  riˈækʃənz/
radar /ˈreɪdɑːʳ/
re-entry /riːˈentri/
relativity /reləˈtɪvɪti/
reliable /rɪˈlaɪəbəl/
revolutionise /revəˈluːʃənaɪz/
rockets /ˈrɒkɪts/
run across /rʌn əˈkrɒs/
run away /rʌn əˈweɪ/
run into /rʌn ˈɪntuː/
run out of /rʌn aʊt əv/
satellite TV /ˈsætəlaɪt tiː viː/
scientific research
  /saɪənˈtɪfɪk rɪˈsɜːʳtʃ/
smart card /smɑːʳt kɑːʳd/
survive /səʳˈvaɪv/
talented /ˈtæləntɪd/
transmit /trænzˈmɪt/
turning point /ˈtɜːʳnɪŋ pɔɪnt/
up to me /ʌp tə miː/
user-friendly /ˈjuːzəʳ frendli/
vacancy /ˈveɪkənsi/
venture /ˈventʃəʳ/
visionary /ˈvɪʒənri/
watchmaker /ˈwɒtʃmeɪkəʳ/
weather patterns /ˈweðəʳ
  pætəʳnz/

webcam /ˈwebkæm/
weightlessness /ˈweɪtləsnəs/
with regard to /wɪθ rɪˈgɑːʳd
  tuː/
world peace /wɜːʳld piːs/
wrist /rɪst/

Episode 10

adventure /ædˈventʃəʳ/
care about /keəʳ əˈbaʊt/
caring /ˈkeərɪŋ/
catch /kætʃ/
cruel /kruːəl/
filthy /ˈfɪlθi/
greedy /ˈgriːdi/
honest /ˈɒnɪst/
kind /kaɪnd/
loyal /ˈlɔɪəl/
mean /miːn/
orphan /ˈɔːʳfən/
practical /ˈpræktɪkəl/
quick-thinking /kwɪk-ˈθɪŋkɪŋ/
rescue /ˈreskjuː/
selfish /ˈselfɪʃ/
shoot /ʃuːt/
treat /triːt/
truthful /ˈtruːθfʊl/
white lies /ʰwaɪt laɪz/

Rules for Punctuation

Capital Letters

A capital letter is used:
- to begin a sentence.
  Here we are.
- for days of the week, months and public holidays.
  Friday, August, Christmas
- for names of people and places.
  My teacher's name is Sally and she's from York, England.
- for people's titles. *Mr and Mrs Parker; Dr Mortimer; Professor Riggs; etc.*
- for nationalities and languages.
  They are Chilean.
  He's fluent in German and Russian.
  Note: The personal pronoun I is always a capital letter. *Gus and I are going on holiday together.*

Full Stop (.)

A full stop is used:
- to end a sentence that is not a question or an exclamation.
  We're having a great time. You can never get bored here in Rio.

Comma (,)

A comma is used:
- to separate words in a list.
  We need sugar, milk, tomatoes and apple juice.
- to separate a non-identifying relative clause (i.e. a clause giving extra information which is not essential to the meaning of the main clause) from the main clause.
  Tony, who is a doctor, lives in Africa.
- after certain linking words/phrases (e.g. in addition to this, moreover, for example, however, in conclusion, etc).
  Moreover, Jenny is very patient with children.
- when if-clauses begin sentences.
  If you have any questions, don't hesitate to ask.
  Note: No comma is used, however, when the if-clause follows the main clause.
- to separate question tags from the rest of the sentence.
  Mr Stevens is your maths teacher, isn't he?

Question Mark (?)

A question mark is used:
- to end a direct question. *Where are the children?*

Exclamation Mark (!)

An exclamation mark is used:
- to end an exclamatory sentence, i.e. a sentence showing admiration, surprise, joy, anger, etc.
  That's a lie!   What horrible weather!

Quotation Marks (' ' " ")

Quotation marks are used:
- in direct speech to report the exact words someone said.
  'The train leaves at 10:45am,' said John.
  "What's your name?" she asked him.

Colon (;)

A colon is used:
- to introduce a list.
  There were three of us on the boat : my brother, my cousin Lynn and me.

Brackets ( )

Brackets are used:
- to separate extra information from the rest of the sentence.
  The most popular newspapers (i.e. The New York Times, The Observer, etc) can be found almost anywhere in the world.

Apostrophe (')

An apostrophe is used:
- in short forms to show that one or more letters or numbers have been left out.
  I'm (= I am) writing to complain about ...
  She left for Italy in the winter of '98. (=1998)
- before or after the possessive -s to show ownership or the relationship between people.
  Tom's car, my friend's husband (singular noun + 's)
  my parents' friends (plural noun + ')
  women's dresses (irregular plural + 's)

Listening Practice 1

Questions 1 - 6

Look at the questions for this part. You will hear a working mum talking about her family. Put a tick (✓) in the correct box for each question.

1 The woman's family
   A ☐ are all big.
   B ☐ play soccer.
   C ☐ all eat together.
   D ✓ are very noisy.

2 Cindy is
   A ☐ a small baby.
   B ✓ about four.
   C ☐ about ten.
   D ☐ an adult.

3 Cindy
   A ☐ doesn't like eating.
   B ✓ can't stop talking.
   C ☐ hates painting.
   D ☐ never stops shouting.

4 Brian
   A ☐ lives in the US.
   B ☐ goes to university.
   C ☐ studies all the time.
   D ✓ has many friends.

5 Bob
   A ☐ plays sports.
   B ☐ eats well on trips.
   C ✓ doesn't see his children much.
   D ☐ often plays with the children.

6 Lacey is
   A ☐ a tortoise.
   B ✓ a cat.
   C ☐ a dog.
   D ☐ a canary.

Listening Practice 2

You will hear a woman being interviewed for an opinion survey about how people spend their leisure time in and around the town of Newsbourne. For questions 1-10, fill in the questionnaire.

Age range	1	30-39
Occupation	2	housewife
How much time available for leisure activities?	3	weekends only
Preferred type of activity?	4	evening classes
What facilities could be provided in the town?	5	computing courses
What about the parkland and forest outside?	6	a cafeteria/ refreshments
Transport around town?	7	not too bad
Transport out of town?	8	unreliable
Train versus bus?	9	train
What could the Committee do to encourage other leisure pursuits?	10	provide cycle paths

Listening Practice 3

Look at the advertisement for a food festival. Some information is missing. You will hear somebody talking on the radio about the festival. For each question, fill in the missing information in the numbered space.

Vegetarian's Delight Food Festival

Dates:	5th to 31st **(1)** December
Place:	Health and Fitness Hall
Festival Highlights:	• stalls with food from around the **(2)** world • food preparation demonstrations • an exciting pie-eating contest • try the worlds largest **(3)** vegetarian-pizza
Opening Hours:	10.00 am - 6.00 pm weekdays 9.00 am - 5.00 pm **(4)** weekends
Tickets:	£10 or £15 for **(5)** families

Reserve tickets by phoning **(6)** 764 6611

Listening Practice 4

You will hear five people talking about the environment. For questions [1-5] choose from the list A-F which environmental problem each speaker is describing. Use the letters only once. There is one extra letter which you do not need to use.

Speaker 1	D	A	global warming
Speaker 2	F	B	destruction of ozone layer
Speaker 3	A	C	overfishing
Speaker 4	E	D	air pollution
Speaker 5	B	E	recycling
		F	deforestation

Listening Practice 5

Look at the six statements for this part. You will hear a conversation between a male sports commentator, Howard, and a female sports commentator, Barbara. They are working on a broadcast of a skating competition. Listen and decide whether each statement is correct or incorrect. If you think it is correct, put a tick in the box under A for YES. If you think it is not correct, put a tick in the box under B for NO.

		A YES	B NO
1	This is the first time Howard has had a partner.	✓	
2	Barbara has won two gold medals.		✓
3	Barbara started her career quite young.	✓	
4	Peter isn't nervous at all.		✓
5	Barbara still competes in skating.		✓
6	Barbara and Howard are on television.	✓	

Tapescripts for Listening Practice

Listening Practice 1

Woman:

My family? Well now… let's see. Even though we're not a big family, there is always a lot of noise in our house and sometimes it feels like there is a whole soccer team living in here! At supper everyone wants to be the first to tell the others about what they did that day, so, as you can imagine, meal times can be quite loud! The loudest voice at the table is Cindy's.

Cindy is very energetic and talks quite a bit. She doesn't go to school yet, so she's always quite excited when we all come home. She's smart and beautiful, with long blonde hair. She has lovely green eyes just like a cat's. When she is happy or doing something she enjoys, like painting or singing, her eyes shine like diamonds. She's quite thin for two reasons. First, because she never sits still for even a moment and second because at meal times, she is too busy talking to eat what is on her plate! Right now she is in the living-room watching television. Our family doesn't watch a lot of TV but we let Cindy watch it for an hour each evening. As you can hear, Cindy likes to watch her show with the sound turned up *very* loud… That's why Brian is shouting at her!

Don't get the wrong idea! Brian doesn't usually shout but he is trying to study at the moment. Actually, he's a very good boy and he studies very hard. He's in his last year of school now and next year he is going to the United States to go to university. He's very handsome and quite tall for his age. When he isn't busy doing schoolwork, he loves playing basketball or going to the cinema. Sometimes I worry about him going away but he makes friends very easily and I'm sure he'll be fine. I will miss him, though, terribly.

Bob, my husband, is very kind to both our children. He's a hard-working estate agent so he doesn't get to spend much time with them. Right now he is travelling to Scotland on business. I must say he is a bit fat! He says that's because he doesn't get much exercise! I say it's because of all the terrible food he eats when he's away from home!

Last but not least, I couldn't talk about my family without talking about Lacey. He is very lazy now and isn't as playful as when we first got him. I imagine that at this moment he is sleeping upstairs under Cindy's bed. He is a lovely colour but he is rather overweight because we all feed him too much. He especially loves fish! No, even though he's not as fun as he used to be, our family just wouldn't be complete without Lacey!

Listening Practice 2

Interviewer:	Good afternoon. I'm a member of the Amenities Committee for the Town Council. Would you mind if I asked you a few questions about how you spend your leisure time?
Housewife:	Well I'm in rather a hurry right now, I have to collect my boys from school at four o'clock. Will it take long?
Interviewer:	No, not long. First of all, I need a few personal details for our records. Could you tell me what age group you are in? 20-29, 30-39, other.
Housewife:	I'm 36, so I suppose I am in the second group. Why do you need to know?
Interviewer:	The Council is looking for ways to make the town better for people of all ages. What is your occupation?
Housewife:	I'm a full-time housewife and a mother of two sons. That's plenty enough occupation for me!
Interviewer:	Do you find, with your obviously busy schedule, you have much time for leisure activities?
Housewife:	No, not really except at weekends when we try to get away to the countryside for days out.
Interviewer:	What about during the week? Do you have some time for yourself?
Housewife:	Only in the evenings. Once a week I manage to go to an art class at the local college which I enjoy a great deal.
Interviewer:	What other sorts of activities would you like to do if the facilities were available?
Housewife:	I'd like to learn how to use a computer because my children are both whizz kids and I'd like to be able to keep up with them at least! The trouble is, there is absolutely nowhere in this town for me to learn about computers.
Interviewer:	So would you say that the Council should have computer training classes for people like you?
Housewife:	Definitely. Evening classes in this subject would be brilliant!
Interviewer:	What about Newsbourne Park and the forest, do you think there is anything the Council can do to improve things for visitors there?
Housewife:	Oh yes, there is. The park is beautiful and the forest is a safe place for wild animals but unfortunately that's not enough. Children soon become bored and keeping them entertained is a full-time job. Even a cafeteria or somewhere to buy an ice cream would be a great improvement. The pathways in the woods could be a bit better as well!
Interviewer:	Coming back to the town, what do you think about the transport in and around the town?
Housewife:	Well it's OK, I suppose. A few more buses to the new shopping centre on Lakesbank would improve things but really it isn't too bad – certainly no worse than any other place I know of.
Interviewer:	How do you normally get to the park at weekends? Do you use the train service or the new bus route?
Housewife:	Are you serious? What bus and train service? As far as I'm concerned, there isn't one! Waiting for a bus or train that might or might not turn up is not my idea of fun. No thank you! Until the Council improves public transport in and out of town, I'll continue to use our old car.
Interviewer:	If we could improve either service, which would you choose – the train or the bus?
Housewife:	I'd like to see some more money being spent on the train service. It's a much more pleasant way to travel than the bus, and the boys get so bored on long bus journeys. I know it isn't that far, but it takes such a long time, because of the traffic.
Interviewer:	What else can you suggest to encourage people to take up leisure activities both in and out of town?
Housewife:	I don't know really. The kids complain that there is very little for them to do. I know there are organised activities such as youth clubs and so on, but a lot of young people who live here don't want to be 'organised'. They need to be able to do things by themselves. They need somewhere they can safely ride their bikes, so a few cycle paths would help.
Interviewer:	Thank you for your help. I am sure that some of your useful suggestions will be brought up at our next committee meeting.

Listening Practice 3

Man:

We all know how important it is for us to eat the right foods. If you're confused about what's good for you and what isn't, you should plan a visit to the Vegetarian Delight Food Festival being held later this month. This *tasty* festival is being held from December 15th to December 31st at the Health and Fitness Hall. If you want to learn more about healthy vegetarian eating, or you're just hungry for something delicious, this is one event that you mustn't miss. This year's festival will offer a wide variety of stalls cooking up veggie dishes from around the world. The Chinese and Mexican stalls should be very interesting, especially for those of us who enjoy a little spice in our lives. There will also be demonstrations of how to prepare many vegetarian dishes, including potato cakes, tofu salads and fresh vegetable bake. On the last day of the festival, show how big your appetite is by taking part in the messy but fun pie-eating contest. Remember to bring your apron, because you mustn't use your hands at any time during the contest! If your stomach is still growling after that, make sure you visit the Italian stall where they will be dishing out slices from the world's largest vegetarian pizza. The festival is a great way to find out about how to make healthy food, and an even better way to try out some great new dishes. The festival is open between 10 and 6 on weekdays and from 9 to 5 on weekends. Tickets are 10 pounds for adults or 15 pounds for families. Remember you can book your tickets by phone. The phone number is 764-6611. Your ticket includes the cost of everything at the festival, so at that price, it really is a bargain. Keep the dates in mind, and we hope to see you there.

Listening Practice 4

Speaker 1: Oh, the new job's great; it's getting there in the mornings I hate. Getting some exercise and helping to lower traffic congestion is all very well, but the price I pay for leaving the car at home and riding the bike is pretty high. My eyes are streaming by the time I reach the office and I can hardly breathe. My skin, hair and clothes smell awful, too!

Speaker 2: I can't believe what they've done! Last month I took the whole family there for a picnic; now look at it. There's nothing left - just a great big empty space full of bulldozers. And what for? Yet another out-of town shopping complex! A shopping complex! All those beautiful trees! It's terrible! It was such a special place; it supported so much wildlife … and those wonderful old oaks … all destroyed in a few weeks.

Speaker 3: Well, I don't think that snorkelling will be much fun any more. I may not even bring my gear with me this year. My favourite reef has been ruined. Dad said that it's all because green-house gases affect the ocean. What a shame! No more colourful corals and fish. And the summers are so much hotter now, too!

Speaker 4: I'd never even thought about it before; it was my daughter Jenny's idea. We'd just returned from our weekly visit to the supermarket. She suggested we make a pile of all the useless packaging we'd brought home … you know, plastic bags, trays, boxes and bottles and so on along with the goods we actually wanted. I was amazed! I had no idea we ended up with so much waste every week. And to think we just threw it away.

Speaker 5: At least my kids don't sit in front of computers all day like some. They'd much rather be outside in the sunshine. Mind you, that's a worry in itself these days, isn't it? I sometimes wonder if it's dangerous for them to spend so much time outdoors in the summer, running around with just their shorts on. They cost me a fortune in sunblock, I know that!

Listening Practice 5

Howard: Welcome ladies and gentlemen to the World Figure Skating Championships. We are broadcasting the event live from beautiful Calgary, Canada. I'm Howard Costner and for years you've seen me hosting this competition alone, but this year I'm lucky to have a partner you all recognize. Barbara, what a great pleasure to be working with you.

Barbara: Thank you, Howard. Hello, everyone. I'm really looking forward to the next three days when we'll be watching the top skaters of the world performing in such an exciting competition.

Howard: Well, you know all about winning. During your Olympic career you won 2 silver medals and one gold medal too.

Barbara: That's right, Howard. I took up skating as a hobby when I was only 6 years old and I started training when I was 11. It was difficult to cope with my studies and skating, but my parents supported me a lot. So did my fantastic coach. If they hadn't encouraged me, I wouldn't have succeeded.

Howard: How old were you at your first international competition?

Barbara: I must have been 16.

Howard: Well, you probably understand how tonight's youngest skater feels. Peter Bordovich is only 17 years old and he's competing in his first international competition.

Barbara: I suppose he's a little nervous but he's looking forward to competing too.

Howard: That's what he told me earlier this afternoon. He said that he didn't care about winning any medals. He was going to have fun skating for himself and for the audience.

Barbara: He's certainly got the right attitude. Good luck Peter!

Howard: You competed for over 10 years. Do you miss it?

Barbara: Mmm. Sometimes. I love skating and I will always love it. Maybe I'll coach one day. For now, I'm very happy to sit back and enjoy watching others compete.

Howard: Well, as all of you in TV Land can see, the skaters have just stopped practising and are getting off the ice. This means that the competition is going to start in just a few minutes… (fade).

Suggested Answers Section

The Adventures of Huckleberry Finn - Episode 4 - Sarah Williams

Ex. 4b p. 55(T)

pict. 1: Huck got dressed up as a girl in case somebody recognised him.
pict. 6: Huck went back to the island to tell Jim the news.
pict. 7: Huck woke Jim up so that they would leave the island on time.
pict. 8: Huck and Jim left the island in case Mrs Loftus' husband arrived.

The Adventures of Huckleberry Finn - Episode 5 - Down the Mississippi

Ex. 4 p. 69(T)

1 To sell the raft and go to the Free States.
2 He'll help to free his family.
3 Because they don't want anyone to see them.
4 To protect Jim.
5 Last night. Because it was foggy.
6 Because a steamboat was going to hit them.

Ex. 5 p. 69(T)

2 They are such nice people that everybody likes them.
3 It was such a noisy party that the neighbours complained.
4 It was so dark that the steamboat didn't see their raft.
5 The news was so good that we could hardly believe it.

Ex. 6 p. 69(T)

It was so late that they decided to leave the next morning.
There was so much fog that Huck couldn't see.
It was such nice weather that they went on an excursion.
It was such a long way that they hired a car.
He is such a clever boy that he always gets the best marks in his class.
She was so tired that she went to bed early.
They had so little money that they couldn't afford a holiday.

The Adventures of Huckleberry Finn - Episode 6 - Travelling with Royalty

Ex. 2 p. 81(T)

The first man has a bad haircut and a moustache. He is wearing an old suit and a bow tie.
The second man is elderly. He is bald, with grey hair and a beard.

Ex. 4 p. 81(T)

1 Jim suggests going down the river until they get some money, then coming back in a steamboat.
2 The people in the town near there are chasing the two men in picture 2 because they found out that the men were trying to cheat them.
3 Jim looks frightened in picture 4 because he thinks the men will capture him.
4 No. Because they introduce themselves.
5 The two men are acting a scene from Shakespeare's Romeo and Juliet.

Ex. 6 p. 81(T)

If Ss have difficulty with the exercise write these prompts on the board [be friends, talk to a friend, be at work, plan sth, be anxious, wait for a long time, be busy, talk about their studies, go to a lecture, read an interesting article, be at the doctor's surgery, work hard all day, etc].
Alternatively ask questions to elicit answers.
e.g.   T: Are they friends?
        S1: No, they can't be friends.
        T: Have they been waiting long?
        S2: Yes, they must have been waiting for a long time. etc

1 They can't be friends.
   They must have been waiting for a long time.
   She must be reading an interesting article.
   They must be at the doctor's surgery.
   They must be anxious.
2 She can't be talking to a friend.
   They must be at work.
   They must be busy.
   They must have been working hard all day.
3 They must be friends.
   They must be planning something.
   They must be anxious.
   They must be talking about their studies.
   They must have been to a lecture.

The Adventures of Huckleberry Finn - Episode 7 - The Wilks Brothers

Ex. 9 p. 95(T)

1 Huck and Jim continued down the river with the 'King' and the 'Duke'.
2 One day, a man told them about a rich man from his town who had died the day before. The 'King' asked him a lot of questions.
3 They arrived at the town, and the 'King' said that he was Harvey Wilks. The 'Duke' pretended to be deaf and dumb.
4 Mary Jane gave the 'King' a letter from Peter Wilks, saying where his gold was hidden. They found $6,000 in gold.
5 Doctor Robinson warned Mary Jane not to trust them, but she asked the 'King' to look after all their money.
6 Huck watched them hide the gold under a mattress. He took the gold and hid it in Peter Wilks' coffin.
7 He planned to write and tell Mary Jane where it was.

The Adventures of Huckleberry Finn - Episode 8 - Peter Wilks' Funeral

Ex. 3 p. 107(T)

1 He thinks the slaves have got the gold.
2 The man says he knows that Peter Wilks has a small blue mark on his chest.
3 They dig up Peter's coffin to see if he has a blue mark on his chest. They find a bag of gold.
4 He finds that the 'King' has taken Jim away to sell him.

Ex. 8 p. 107(T)

Two Englishmen arrived claiming to be Harvey and William Wilks.
The 'King' and 'Duke' discovered the gold was missing. Huck made them think the slaves had taken it.
When Huck woke up one morning the 'Duke' told him the 'King' had taken Jim to sell him.
The Englishman said he could prove he was Peter Wilks' brother.
When Peter Wilks was buried, Huck believed the gold was safe.
Huck ran to the raft and they all went on down the river like before.
They dug up the coffin and found the bag of gold coins inside.
They forgot about Huck, so he was able to escape.

The Adventures of Huckleberry Finn - Episode 9 - Looking for Jim

Ex. 3 p. 121(T)

1 To see if Jim is there.
2 Because she doesn't know what Tom looks like.
3 Steal the key, rescue him and escape on the raft.
4 Those in prisons (criminals).
5 To make their escape more adventurous.

Ex. 5 p. 121(T)

1 What an exciting film!
2 It's so hot in here!
3 How kind of you to say that!
4 Isn't it a good song!
5 You look so smart in those clothes!

The Adventures of Huckleberry Finn - Episode 10 - A Happy End

Ex. 3 p. 133(T)

1 When they get to the raft.
2 He wants Jim to take the raft and leave so he doesn't get caught.
3 Because he doesn't want to leave Tom alone.
4 He went and told aunt Sally what had happened.
5 He stayed and helped the doctor.
6 Because she felt so bad about wanting to sell him.
7 Because he wanted to have an adventure.
8 He was running from his father. His father is dead so Huck doesn't have to run anymore.
9 No, because he hated living with the widow Douglas.
10 He is going to go somewhere new for more adventures.

Self-Assessment Module 1 (Units 1 - 2)

Ex. 3 p. 30(T)

A: Hello? Can I speak to Bob?
B: Who is calling?
A: It is Steve.
B: Can you hang on a second?
A: OK.
B: Sorry, Bob has gone out.
A: Shall I call back?
B: Sure. Do you want to leave a message?
A: No, that's OK. I'll call later.
B: Bye.
A: Bye.

Ex. 5 p. 31(T)

Tony felt very excited as he boarded the train. It was the first time he had travelled alone and he was looking forward to the journey. He was going to visit his brother in Leeds.

He found a seat in a comfortable carriage and sat down. The train set off and soon they were in the English countryside. Tony gazed out of the window feeling relaxed and happy. Half an hour into the journey, he heard a loud explosion. The train suddenly stopped and people began to cough and crawl towards the door to get out.

Suddenly, there was a loud bang from outside and someone broke the door open. Firefighters were soon helping people out of the train.

After a while, Tony was standing outside next to the train. He felt shocked, but happy to be safe at last. "Travelling alone really is exciting!" he thought.

Self-Assessment Module 2 (Units 3 - 4)

Ex. 5 p. 57(T)

Dear Sir,

I am writing to complain about a Pacific Island cruise I went on from the 4 - 18 August.

The cabin was so small that there was no space for my suitcase. I had to keep it on my bunk during the day and at night, put it on the floor.

To make matters worse I had no bathroom. I was forced to share one with 4 other cabins. This was a terrible inconvenience and it really annoyed me.

As for the meals – they were really a great disappointment. The food was not fresh and a number of dishes were tasteless.

I expect an apology from the company for subjecting me to this awful ordeal, as well as a refund – the holiday I had was not the package I had paid for.

Yours faithfully,
(Ms) E. Simons

Self-Assessment Module 3 (Units 5 - 6)

Ex. 5 p. 83(T)

Dear Sir,

I am writing in response to the recent article in your newspaper which discussed the council's proposal to build a new Shopping Centre in town. I believe that this would have many negative effects on the town and I hope that the council will reconsider its decision.

The new Shopping Centre would provide important new jobs for this area. However, it would also result in a large increase in traffic in the town centre. Obviously, this would increase noise and air pollution and also make the road much more dangerous for children from the nearby school.

Furthermore, the Shopping Centre would change the appearance of the town for the worse. They will have to tear down some beautiful old buildings in order to make the new centre and this will spoil the atmosphere of our beautiful town.

To sum up, I am strongly opposed to this proposal. I hope you will print this letter so that more people will tell the council that the new Shopping Centre should not be built. I'm sure that this proposal would be a mistake for our town.

Yours faithfully,
Jennifer Mills
Jennifer Mills

Test 2 A (Units 3, 4)

A

1	C	7	D	13	C	19	C	25	C
2	A	8	C	14	A	20	D	26	D
3	B	9	C	15	B	21	C	27	A
4	C	10	B	16	A	22	A	28	A
5	D	11	D	17	C	23	D	29	B
6	D	12	D	18	A	24	A	30	A

B

1 for 5 than 8 on
2 suit 6 Go 9 long
3 yet 7 get 10 in
4 off

C (Suggested answer)

1 can I help 4 you like a single or a double
2 room are you in 5 I take your name
3 like to book

D 1 I 2 C 3 C 4 I 5 I 6 C

E 1 no 3 yes 5 no
2 yes 4 no 6 yes

F (Suggested answer)

Dear Rachel,

How are you? Thanks for your last letter. I've just come back from a two-week holiday in Montreal with my family.

Montreal is a beautiful city in Canada. It is a modern North American city, but it also has European style. It is very easy to travel around Montreal, because it has a good transportation system.

We did a lot of sightseeing and shopping and we even had the chance to go to the Grand Prix car race. We also spent a lot of time in Old Montreal, which is the historical part of the city. It is very beautiful, full of narrow streets and old buildings. Unfortunately, one evening I had a mishap. As I was walking to a restaurant with my family I stopped to look at a shop window and I lost the others. I panicked because I only knew the name of the restaurant and I had no idea how to get there! Luckily it was a well known place so I found a woman who gave me directions and I was able to find it.

Well, that's all my news. Write back soon.

Love,
Monica

Test 2 B (Units 3, 4)

A

1	B	7	C	13	A	19	C	25	C
2	D	8	D	14	B	20	B	26	B
3	A	9	B	15	D	21	A	27	C
4	A	10	A	16	C	22	D	28	D
5	A	11	C	17	C	23	D	29	B
6	B	12	C	18	D	24	B	30	D

B

1 with 5 had 9 since
2 more 6 been 10 as
3 on 7 up 11 the
4 the 8 so

C

1 a single or a double
2 much does it
3 have to pay a
4 can I help you
5 like to order

D 1 C 2 C 3 I 4 I 5 C

E 1 A 3 A 5 D 7 C
2 B 4 C 6 A

F (Suggested answer)

Dear Anna,

I hope you and your family are fine. I've just come back from a week's holiday in beautiful Florence with my brother.

Florence is an amazing city located in central Italy. It is full of history and art. Florence is very easy to explore on foot, so you can do a lot of sightseeing.

Florence has many attractions. We spent a lot of time in the Uffizi Gallery, which is one of the oldest museums in the world. We also went to the famous cathedral of Florence. Unfortunately, I had a mishap there. We wanted to visit the dome of the cathedral, which was very high, so we climbed more than 400 steps to reach it. I was exhausted and as it was very narrow in there I bumped my head on the stone steps. I felt dizzy for some time and I thought I wouldn't be able to make it! However, in the end the view from the top was great!

Well, that's all for now. Write soon. Take care.

Love,
Michael

Test 3 A (Units 5,6)

A

1	A	7	B	13	A	19	D	25	A
2	B	8	B	14	B	20	B	26	D
3	C	9	B	15	A	21	A	27	D
4	C	10	D	16	B	22	B	28	A
5	A	11	C	17	D	23	D	29	B
6	D	12	D	18	C	24	C	30	B

B

1	some	5	is	9	squeaky
2	to	6	in	10	to
3	away	7	main	11	take
4	take	8	to		

C (Suggested answer)

1	can I help	4	many people
2	to book a table	5	time would you like
3	name		

D 1 F 2 A 3 E 4 B 5 C

E

1	C	3	B	5	A	7	A
2	A	4	A	6	C		

F (Suggested answer)

To: Brian Perry, Manager, Portsmouth Hotel
From: Sarah Clough, Assistant Manager
Date: 25th June, 20 …
Subject: Attracting guests to the Portsmouth Hotel

Purpose

The purpose of this report is to suggest ways to attract more guests to the Portsmouth Hotel.

Prices

At present, the prices at the Portsmouth Hotel are not very competitive. We should offer lower prices, special offers and weekend deals in order to attract more guests.

Service

There are very few staff at the Portsmouth Hotel, so the service is quite restricted. If we hired more staff, we could offer room service, more efficient restaurant service and a porter.

Decoration

The decoration at the Portsmouth Hotel is rather old-fashioned and is not very welcoming to guests. We should definitely redecorate in elegant colours and materials in order to make it more popular with guests.

Conclusion

In conclusion, it is my opinion that the Portsmouth Hotel will attract more guests if it has better prices, more efficient service and more elegant decoration.

Test 3 B (Units 5,6)

A

1	A	7	B	13	A	19	D	25	C
2	A	8	B	14	A	20	A	26	A
3	D	9	D	15	A	21	C	27	A
4	B	10	D	16	A	22	A	28	D
5	B	11	C	17	C	23	D	29	D
6	D	12	B	18	B	24	B	30	A

B

1	to	4	of	7	to
2	up	5	have	8	on
3	lot	6	stand	9	to

C (Suggested answer)

1	to be the	4	would you
2	terribly sorry	5	I'll have
3	I'd rather have		

D 1 A 2 D 3 C 4 B 5 F

E

1	B	3	C	5	B	7	C
2	C	4	B	6	C	8	C

F (Suggested answer)

Dear Sir/Madam,

I am writing with regard to your recent review of Benji's Restaurant. I wish to disagree with several of your comments as follows.

To begin with, I visit Benji's Restaurant regularly and the food is always delicious. The dishes are well-prepared and perfectly cooked. Moreover, I find the prices at Benji's very reasonable.

I strongly disagree with your comment that the staff were rude and inattentive. When I visit Benji's, the staff are always extremely pleasant and cheerful, and they work hard to provide customers with an enjoyable eating experience.

Furthermore, the atmosphere at Benji's is very friendly and the decoration is homely and comfortable.

To sum up, I believe that Benji's is a wonderful restaurant which is certainly worth a visit. I hope you will print this letter together with an apology to the manager and staff of Benji's restaurant.

Yours faithfully,
Kirk Taylor

Test 4 A (Units 7, 8)

A
1	B	7	D	13	A	19	C	25	A
2	B	8	B	14	B	20	B	26	A
3	B	9	C	15	A	21	C	27	C
4	C	10	C	16	D	22	B	28	A
5	C	11	D	17	C	23	A	29	D
6	A	12	C	18	A	24	C	30	C

B
1	being	5	with	9	on	
2	will	6	been	10	put	
3	up	7	for			
4	to	8	in			

C (Suggested answer)
1 must be
2 to become
3 did you hear
4 heard an announcement
5 you be able
6 Could you fill in
7 need some

D
1	B	3	A	5	F
2	C	4	D		

E
1	B	3	B	5	C	7	C
2	A	4	B	6	B	8	A

F (Suggested answer)
Dear Sir/Madam,
   I am interested in becoming a volunteer for Easthampton Council and I would appreciate it if you could give me some further information.
   First of all, I would like to know how much spare time volunteers would need to have in order to help clean up our parks. For example, will we be required to work in the parks on working days or at weekends and for how long? Furthermore, could you let me know how old volunteers should be? I would also like to know how many volunteers will be in each team. I am also interested in finding out which parks volunteers will be working in. Finally, could you tell me what exactly 'cleaning up our parks' will involve.
   Thank you in advance for your assistance. I look forward to your reply.
Yours faithfully,
Paul Hewett

Test 4 B (Units 7, 8)

A
1	B	7	D	13	A	19	A	25	D
2	D	8	C	14	B	20	A	26	B
3	C	9	B	15	C	21	B	27	A
4	D	10	C	16	D	22	A	28	B
5	A	11	C	17	D	23	B	29	A
6	B	12	B	18	C	24	C	30	B

B
1	will	4	on	7	through	
2	of	5	away	8	on	
3	shall	6	of	9	mind	

C (Suggested answer)
1	How can I	5	don't you
2	you should	6	been
3	's a good	7	did you hear
4	thought of		

D
1	D	3	A	5	C
2	E	4	B		

E
1	A	3	B	5	C
2	C	4	C	6	B

F (Suggested answer)
Dear Sir/Madam,
   I am interested in becoming a volunteer for Easthampton Council and I would appreciate it if you would send me some further information.
   First of all, I would like to know exactly where volunteers will be working, as Easthampton is quite a large area. Could you also let me know what kind of vehicle volunteers should have? I am also interested in finding out how old volunteers should be. Furthermore, could you tell me what other volunteer programmes Easthampton Council organises. Finally, I would be grateful if you could tell me how often volunteers will have to deliver meals.
   Thank you in advance for your assistance. I look forward to your reply.
Yours faithfully,
Andrew Athow

Test 5 A (Units 9, 10)

A

1	B	7	B	13	D	19	D	25	A
2	C	8	A	14	B	20	B	26	D
3	D	9	D	15	A	21	A	27	B
4	D	10	B	16	C	22	B	28	B
5	C	11	A	17	B	23	C	29	D
6	A	12	C	18	A	24	B	30	B

B

1	had	5	get	9	for
2	only	6	point	10	would
3	not	7	have	11	burn
4	in	8	into	12	would

C (Suggested answer)

1 I help
2 tickets for the
3 for the morning
4 want to watch
5 I have the
6 are your
7 I wouldn't have caught

D 1 C 2 A 3 D 4 B

E

1	B	3	D	5	C
2	D	4	A	6	C

F (Suggested answer)

Can you imagine a world without computers? In the last few years, technology has advanced so much that we rely on computers in almost every area of our lives. I strongly believe that computers have made our lives a lot easier.

First of all, computers allow us to shop in the comfort of our own homes. Using the Internet, we can visit millions of online shops and find a huge variety of products. In this way, we can save valuable time and avoid long queues in busy high street shops.

Moreover, computers make it possible to communicate quickly, cheaply and easily with people all around the world. We can send emails and even talk face to face with friends and family over the Internet. This means that we don't have to pay expensive phone bills or rely on the old-fashioned postal service.

On the other hand, there are people who would argue that computers make people anti-social, as they hardly need to leave their houses any more. People can shop, work and socialise without moving from their computer screen, so they don't have to socialise with people at all.

All in all, it seems to me that the advantages of computers outweigh the disadvantages. Without computers, our lives would be much more difficult.

Test 5 B (Units 9, 10)

A

1	D	7	B	13	B	19	A	25	B
2	A	8	A	14	D	20	D	26	A
3	C	9	D	15	A	21	B	27	A
4	B	10	C	16	C	22	A	28	B
5	A	11	D	17	A	23	C	29	D
6	C	12	A	18	A	24	A	30	C

B

1	with	6	for	11	down
2	been	7	of	12	from
3	in	8	take	13	Neither
4	to	9	only	14	cards
5	up	10	have		

C (Suggested answer)

1 I hadn't eaten
2 hadn't eaten it, I wouldn't have
3 Why is
4 I had a holiday cottage, I would
5 why
6 I didn't have a holiday cottage
7 wish I hadn't watched

D 1 B 2 C 3 D 4 A

E 1 D 2 A 3 E 4 F 5 C

F (Suggested answer)

Can you imagine a world without mobile phones? In the last few years, mobile phones have become extremely popular and now almost everyone owns one. I strongly believe that mobile phones have made our lives a lot easier.

First of all, mobile phones allow us to keep in touch with friends and family wherever we are. With a mobile phone, we can contact people at any time of the day or night, and we never have to worry about missing important calls.

Moreover, mobile phones are extremely useful in emergency situations, as they make it possible for us to call for help, wherever we are. We don't have to worry about finding a phonebox or making sure we have a phonecard with us. Mobile phones can even save lives.

On the other hand, there are people who would argue that mobile phones are annoying, as people use them for unimportant calls and at inconvenient times. Some people play with their mobile phones constantly and for no reason, which can irritate people around them.

All in all, it seems to me that the advantages of mobile phones outweigh the disadvantages. Without mobile phones, our lives would be much more difficult.

EXIT TEST

A
1	D	6	C	11	A	16	A
2	D	7	D	12	D	17	D
3	D	8	B	13	B	18	B
4	A	9	C	14	A	19	A
5	B	10	B	15	C	20	D

B
1	D	6	D	11	A	16	B
2	D	7	A	12	D	17	D
3	D	8	C	13	C	18	C
4	A	9	B	14	A	19	A
5	C	10	C	15	C	20	B

C
1	with	5	on	9	up
2	out	6	on	10	across
3	in	7	to		
4	for	8	out		

D
1	weight	5	displeased	9	illegal
2	cookery/cooking	6	impressive	10	comedian
3	information	7	imagination		
4	national	8	comfortable		

E
1 Could I speak to
2 How long (would you like it)
3 Would you like
4 I'd like to book a table
5 about going

F   1 F   2 E   3 A   4 D   5 B

G   (Suggested answer)

Dear Sir/Madam,

I am writing to complain about the terrible service provided by your rail company when I travelled from London to Glasgow on 25th June.

Firstly, the train was delayed, which caused me great inconvenience as I was travelling to an important business meeting.

In addition, the staff were most unhelpful. They refused to tell me what had caused the delay or how long I would have to wait. Therefore, I was unable to make other arrangements or let my staff know my time of arrival.

Finally, when the train eventually left, the buffet car was closed for most of the journey, so I was unable to buy anything to eat or drink.

As you can imagine, I was extremely angry about the whole experience. I expect a refund of part of the cost of the ticket as well as a written apology from the rail company. I look forward to your immediate reply.

Yours faithfully,
Antony Brookwell

Video Activity Book - Key

Unit 1 – Busy Days!

1 2 A surgeon is someone who operates on people. Surgeons need to be dedicated because they have to study for many years.

3 A receptionist/An operator is someone who answers the phone for a company. Receptionists/Operators have to be polite because they have to talk to people.

4 A nurse is someone who looks after patients. Nurses have to be caring because they have to help sick people.

5 An actor is someone who acts in films, on TV or on the stage. Actors need to be confident because they have to perform in front of an audience.

2 Interviewer:
What qualifications have you got?
What technical skills have you got?
Why did you apply for this job?
Are you fully-qualified?
Why do you want this post?
Would you like to work part time or full time?
Do you have a university degree?

Interviewee:
What is the salary?
Do I need technical skills?
What does this post involve?
Could I work part time?
Do I have to work full time?

3 1 C   3 A   5 C
    2 B   4 A   6 D

4 1 F   3 T   5 F   7 T   9 F
    2 T   4 T   6 F   8 T   10 T

5 A 1 parking   4 tickets   7 car
      2 inspector   5 price   8 parks
      3 patrol   6 machines   9 directions

    B 1 environmental   4 pollution   7 environment
      2 scientist   5 strategies
      3 checking   6 control

6 1 soldier   4 ten   7 13,500
    2 scientist   5 candles   8 sculpture
    3 politician   6 artist

7 1 a   2 b   3 a   4 a   5 a

8 Suggested answer

Name: Tony
Job: mechanic
Before work: have breakfast, go jogging
At work: repair cars
After work: cook dinner, watch TV
Free time: football, surfing the net

Sam's brother Tony is a mechanic. Before he goes to work, he has breakfast and goes jogging. At work, he repairs cars. After work, he cooks dinner and watches TV. In his free time he plays football and surfs the net.

9 Ss' own answers

10 **Name:** Robert
Surname: Elliot
Studies: computer programming
Experience: Administration
Preferred working hours: mornings to early evenings

11 1 programming languages   5 £1,400 per month
     2 computer games   6 Games
     3 youthful   7 Monday
     4 ambitious   8 9 am

12 Suggested answer

Name: Lucy Garner
Qualifications: BA in English
Work Experience: Teaching
Hobbies/Interests: playing guitar, reading

A: Take a seat, please. You must be Lucy Garner.
B: That's right.
A: Now, Lucy. What qualifications do you have?
B: I have a BA in English.
A: That's good. What experience do you have?
B: I have some experience in teaching.
A: Wonderful. Why do you want to work for our company?
B: Because I think you are a very ambitious company.
A: I see. Well, do you have any questions you'd like to ask about the job?
B: Yes. What is the starting salary?
A: We offer a starting salary of £12,500.
B: That sounds fine. What are the working hours?
A: Nine to five, Monday to Friday. Does that suit you?
B: Yes, that's great.
A: Good. Can you start on Monday?
B: Yes, of course. Thank you.

Unit 2 – What a Story!

1 A: When would you use a helmet?
B: You would use it in an earthquake.
A: Why?
B: To protect your head.
A: When would you use a first aid kit?
B: You would use it in an earthquake.
A: Why?
B: To treat a wound.
A: When would you use a life jacket?
B: You would use it in a shipwreck.
A: Why?
B: To prevent yourself from drowning.
A: When would you use a fire extinguisher?
B: You would use it in a fire.
A: Why?
B: To put out the fire.
A: When would you use a mobile phone?
B: You would use it in an earthquake.
A: Why?
B: To call for help.

2 A man was reading a newspaper.
A man was holding a bag of bread.
A man and a woman were sitting in a café.
A man, a woman and a child were waiting for the bus.
A man was walking his dog.
A woman was speeding.
A boy was skateboarding.

3 1 a 2 b 3 b 4 a

A 4a B 2b C 3b D 1a

4 1 c 2 b 3 a 4 a 5 c

5 1 1975 4 1924 7 Six
2 roof 5 Wales 8 fell off
3 film 6 broke

6 (Song)

7 1 This morning an earthquake struck a small village in Portugal. A lot of houses were destroyed and many people were trapped in debris from the collapsed buildings. Some people were injured and were taken to hospital, but no one was killed.
Suggested headline: Earthquake Strikes Village

2 Heavy rain has caused the River Ouse to burst its banks and flood the city of York. Three people were drowned and many houses were washed away.
Suggested headline: City Underwater

3 A hurricane has swept the area of Miami, leaving the coastline completely destroyed. The winds were so strong that they blew away many rooftops. Many buildings were destroyed and 20 people were seriously injured.
Suggested headline: Hurricane Hits Miami

8 1 was coming 4 speeding 7 Stevenson
2 pulled out 5 swerve 8 16, Bridge
3 oncoming 6 smashed

9 Suggested answer

A: Did you see the accident, madam?
B: Yes, I saw everything.
A: Could you tell me what happened, please?
B: Well, the bus was heading down the road when a car pulled out of the car park into the path of the oncoming bus.
A: I see. Was the bus speeding?
B: No, but to avoid the car, the bus driver had to swerve onto the other side of the road into the path of an oncoming lorry.
A: Oh dear. So what happened next?
B: Well, to avoid the lorry, he swerved again, but he lost control of the vehicle and crashed into a tree.
A: Right. Well, you've been very helpful, madam. Can I take your name, please?
B: Yes, it's Helen Robertson.
A: And can you tell me your address, please, Ms Robertson?
B: It's 12, Evermore Road, Bristol.
A: Thank you.

Unit 3 – On the move

1 Suggested answers

Travelling by car is more comfortable than travelling by bus because cars have more comfortable seats.
Travelling by train is more expensive than travelling by bus because the tickets cost more.
Travelling by bus is slower than travelling by car because buses have to make frequent stops.
Travelling by bus is cheaper than travelling by car because running a car costs a lot of money.
Travelling by car is more reliable than travelling by motorbike because motorbikes are difficult to ride in bad weather.
Travelling by bus is more crowded than travelling by train because there is less space on buses.
Travelling by motorbike is more dangerous than travelling by taxi because it is easier to have an accident on a motorbike.
Travelling by car is safer than travelling by motorbike because you have more control over your vehicle.
Travelling by car is more convenient than travelling by train because you can go wherever you like and choose your own route.
Travelling by bicycle is more tiring than travelling by motorbike, because you have to pedal very fast.
Travelling by bicycle is more environmentally friendly than travelling by car because bicycles do not give off dangerous fumes.

2 1 popular 4 reliable 7 tunnels
2 underneath 5 system 8 railway
3 suburbs 6 tube

3 1 F 2 F 3 T 4 F

4 1 a 2 a 3 a

5 1 1911 3 408 5 73,000
2 Two twelve metre 4 112 6 seven

6 1 How long 3 How far 5 What time
2 How often 4 What is 6 How much is

7 Suggested answer

Commuting in: York
Most preferred means of transport: bus
Advantages: cheap, regular service, extensive route
Disadvantages: slow, not many buses late at night
Recommendation: run more buses late at night

8 1 get 3 catch 5 change 7 Many
2 platform 4 comes 6 stops

9 1 Hello, can I help you?
2 Single or return?
3 When's the next train
4 Do you know how long the journey takes?

10 • A: Excuse me. Can you tell me how to get to Warren Street, please?
B: Sure. Take the Circle Line to St Pancras. Then, change to the Northern Line. From there it's two stops to Warren Street.
A: Thank you.

- A: Excuse me. Can you tell me how to get to Hyde Park Corner, please?
  B: Sure. Take the Circle Line to Gloucester Road. Then, change to the Piccadilly Line. From there it's three stops to Hyde Park Corner.
  A: Thank you.

- A: Excuse me. Can you tell me how to get to Liverpool Street, please?
  B: Sure. Take the District Line to Aldgate. Then, change to the Circle Line. From there it's one stop to Liverpool Street.
  A: Thank you.

- A: Excuse me. Can you tell me how to get to Charing Cross, please?
  B: Sure. Take the Circle Line to Embankment. Then, change to the Northern Line. From there it's one stop to Charing Cross.
  A: Thank you.

Unit 4 – Out and About

1 Suggested answer

SA: I prefer to go somewhere picturesque and peaceful for my holidays, so I would like to go to the place in picture 3. It looks much quieter than the city in picture 1.
SB: That's true, but I think it would be more boring as well. I like to go to crowded places where I can meet a lot of new people.
SA: Yes, but the city is probably more polluted. I would rather be somewhere with clean air, like the place in picture 5. Camping holidays are much more fun than city holidays, in my opinion.
SB: I don't agree. The city is more expensive, but there is much more to do there.
SA: Yes, but it is also much more busy and noisy. I can't relax in a place like that. etc

2 Suggested answer

SA: I prefer going on holiday in the winter because I like winter sports like skiing and ice skating.
SB: Going on holiday in autumn is nice, too, because you can walk in the woods and look at the beautiful colours of the autumn leaves.
SA: That's true. I also like going on holiday in spring, because you can do all kinds of extreme sports, like climbing and bungee jumping, without getting too hot!

3 Sheffield

Location: North of England
Population: 800,000
Roads: wide, busy
Transport: trams
Entertainment: department stores, museums, theatres, parks, cathedral

Southwold

Location: East coast of England
Permanent population: 3,000
Summer population: 6,000
Streets: narrow
Accommodation: houses, cottages
Entertainment: restaurants, cafés, beach

Paris
Capital of: France
Famous for: history, architecture
Sights:
The Louvre - more than 30,000 works of art
The Eiffel Tower - 1, 700 steps
The Arc de Triomphe
Shops: open late
Entertainment: cafés, clubs, restaurants

4 A 1 No.   4 Sign the form.
       2 No.   5 The next morning.
       3 The customer's driver's 6 In parking space no. 4.
          license and credit card.

   B 1 The operator.   3 By mail.
      2 Address.   4 In a couple of days.

5 1 c   2 b   3 a

6 (Song)

7 Year: 1873
   Author: Jules Verne
   Title of Novel: Around the world in 80 days
   Plot: a man bets that he will circle the earth in about two and a half months.
   Largest Hotel: Venetia (n)
   Place: Las Vegas
   Type of accommodation: luxury resort
   Cost to build: 2 billion
   Inspired by: Venice
   No. of rooms: 3,036

8 1 of   5 not   9 as   13 best
   2 all   6 almost   10 highest
   3 as   7 best   11 than
   4 which   8 busier   12 many

9 Make: Volkswagen Beetle
   Colour: Blue
   Price: £32, £25
   Insurance: included in the price ✓
   Payment: credit card ✓

10 1 speaking   7 can I confirm
    2 how can I be   8 when did you lose
    3 I'd like to report 9 it was missing
    4 Hold the line   10 I'll cancel
    5 I'll put you through 11 When will I receive
    6 Can you tell me

11 Suggested answer

    A: Good afternoon, can I help you?
    B: I'd like to rent a car, please.
    A: Just a moment, please … we have one Ford Escort free. Would that be OK?
    B: Yes, that would be fine. How much is it?
    A: It's £45 per day for three days, or £38 per day for four days.
    B: I see. And does that include insurance?
    A: Yes. Full insurance is included in the price.
    B: That's great. Can I pay by credit card?
    A: Of course. I'll need to see your driver's license and credit card.
    B: Here you are.

A: Thank you. Here are the keys. It's the red car in parking space 6.

B: Thank you very much.

Make: Ford Escort
Colour: red
Price: £45, £38
Insurance: included in the price ✓
Payment: credit card ✓

Unit 5 – Tasty Treats

---

1 **Pulses:** lentils, chick peas, beans
Fruit & vegetables: courgettes, aubergines, watermelon, kiwi, bananas
Dairy products: cheese, milk, yoghurt
Meat: steak, lamb, mince
Fish & Poultry: turkey, sardines, haddock
Herbs & Spices: basil, parsley, salt and pepper
Desserts: fruit jelly, cheese cake, apple pie, ice cream

A: ... the bananas?
B: In the fruit and vegetable section.
A: Thank you. Could you also tell me where I can find the salt and pepper?
B: In the herbs and spices section. etc.

2 **Suggested answer**
At the butcher's: meat, poultry, game, etc.
At the grocer's: fruit and vegetables, bread, canned goods, etc.
At the greengrocer's: fruit, vegetables, etc.
At the newsagent's: newspapers, magazines, sweets, etc.

A: Another reason why I prefer shopping in big supermarkets is that they often have fresher products. The service is faster, too, so it doesn't take me as long to do my shopping.
B: Oh, I disagree. I don't think the service is faster in big supermarkets. The queues are always much longer than in local shops, because people buy so much more. Anyway, I like the friendly service I get in my local shops.
A: Yes, but in local shops you can't use a credit card or write out a cheque. You have to pay in cash. Supermarkets are much more convenient, because you don't have to carry lots of money with you. etc.

3 1 T   3 T   5 T
   2 F   4 F   6 T

4 The Crown **Restaurant**
Day: this evening
Name: Palmer
No. of people: 5
Time: 8:30 pm

5 1 b   2 b   3 b   4 a   5 a

6 1 olive oil   3 60,000
   2 rose oil   4 £2,000

7 **Suggested answer**

1 A waiter would ask a customer this in a restaurant.
2 A customer might use this in a restaurant, or someone might use it in the home as a joke.

3 Someone might ask this at home (to the person who cooked dinner).
4 A waiter would ask a customer this in a restaurant.
5 A waiter would ask a customer who has ordered steak this.
6 A receptionist in a restaurant would ask a customer this when they called to book a table.
7 A waiter would ask a customer this in a restaurant.
8 A waiter would ask a customer this in a restaurant.
9 Someone would ask this at home if they wanted to help the person preparing dinner.
10 Someone would ask this in a restaurant or at home.
11 Someone who has cooked food at home would ask this.
12 A receptionist in a restaurant would ask a customer this when they called to book a table. An employee at a take away restaurant might also ask this when a customer called to order food.

A: Are you ready to order, sir?
B: I think so, yes.
A: What would you like for starters?
B: I'll have the prawn cocktail, please.
A: Very good, sir. And for your main course?
B: I'll have the steak, please.
A: How would you like it cooked?
B: Medium rare, please.
A: Would you like a dessert?
B: Yes, I'd like the apple tart, please.
A: And to drink?
B: A glass of mineral water, please.
A: Thank you, sir.

8 1 afternoon   6 booking   11 free
   2 speaking   7 to eat   12 alright
   3 How may I help you 8 awfully   13 will be
   4 I'd like to book   9 any tables free 14 wonderful
   5 What name is that 10 Do you have

9 1 I'm in the mood   6 What else
   2 That's a good idea   7 only a little bit, actually
   3 How many have we got   8 that doesn't matter
   4 That's plenty   9 We've got those
   5 very few, I'm afraid   10 Let's get cooking

10 **Suggested answers**

A: Good evening, Angie's restaurant, bookings, Julie speaking. How may I help you?
B: Hello, I'd like to book a table for tomorrow evening, please.
A: OK. What name is that?
B: Stevens.
A: How many people is the booking for?
B: Four.
A: OK. And what time would you like to eat?
B: Around seven o'clock.
A: Oh, I'm awfully sorry, we don't have any tables free until half past seven. Is that OK?
B: Do you have anything earlier?
A: We have a table free at six.
B: Erm ... no, that's alright. Seven thirty will be fine.
A: Wonderful. We'll see you tomorrow, then.
B: Thank you. Goodbye.

Day: tomorrow
Name: Stevens
No. of people: 4
Time: 7.30 pm

11 Suggested Answers

A: Let's make a pizza. I'm in the mood for some Italian food.
B: That's a good idea. Do we need to go shopping?
A: Well, let's see. We need some mushrooms. How many have we got?
B: We've got four or five mushrooms.
A: That's plenty. And we need some flour, too.
B: Let's see. We've got two and a half cups of flour.
A: Good. What about cheese?
B: We've got half a kilo in the fridge.
A: OK, that's great! And we also need some peppers. How many have we got?
B: Very few, I'm afraid. How many do we need?
A: Only two.
B: Oh, that's alright, then. What else?
A: Well, we need some vegetable oil. How much of that have we got?
B: Only a little bit, actually.
A: Well, that doesn't matter. We only need a little bit anyway. And we need a tin of tomatoes.
B: That's alright. We've got those.
A: Great! Let's get cooking!

Unit 6 – All work and no play...

1 a) 2 art gallery   4 orchestra
   3 circus   5 museum

Suggested answers

1 jugglers, fire performers, mime artists, etc.
2 sculptures, statues, etc.
3 jugglers, elephants, tigers, clowns, lions, etc.
4 violinists, musicians, classical music, instruments, etc.
5 antiques, statues, artifacts, etc.

I like listening to orchestras because the musicians are talented and classical music is very relaxing. etc.

b) Suggested answer

A: Would you like to go to an art gallery on Saturday?
B: I'm afraid I can't. I'm working on Saturday. Why don't we go on Friday instead?
A: Great idea!

A: Do you fancy going to the circus this weekend?
B: Yes. Why not?

2 1 war, fighter
  2 art, sculptures
  3 orchestra, concert, classical, conductor

3 1 juggler/fire performer   4 hat
  2 about four   5 £30-50
  3 about twenty minutes

4 1 actor   4 still   7 shorter
  2 living   5 give him money   8 season
  3 Norman   6 three hours   9 most

5 1 F   2 T   3 F   4 T   5 F

6 (Song)

7 1 British   3 1981   5 two
  2 car park   4 back

8 1 T   3 T   5 T   7 F
  2 F   4 F   6 T   8 F

9 2 What are you playing at the moment?
  3 What exactly do you have to do?
  4 How long can you keep the performance going for?
  5 How much money can you make?

10 Friday ✓
   Name: Luke Palmer
   No. of tickets: 2
   Amount per ticket: £30
   Total: £60
   Credit card: ✓
   Card no.: 3278 1302
   Expiry date: 05/04
   Reference no.: 0601

11 1 are you free tonight
   2 What have you got in mind
   3 Do you fancy going
   4 What's on
   5 Can I phone you back
   6 can you let me know before five

12 Suggested answer

1 A: Hi, Joe, it's Luke.
  B: Oh, hi, Luke, how's it going?
  A: Fine. Listen, are you free tonight?
  B: Um, I don't know yet. What have you got in mind?
  A: Well, I was going to go and watch a horror film with Jude, but she can't make it because she's ill, so I've got an extra ticket. Do you fancy going?
  B: Ah, I don't know. What's on?
  A: *Night of Horror*, with David Evans.
  B: Sounds good. I'll have to make sure I'm not working late, though. Can I phone you back?
  A: Sure, but can you let me know before seven?
  B: I'll try.
  A: OK. I'll talk to you later, then.
  B: OK then. Bye!

2 A: Hi, Joe, it's Luke.
  B: Oh, hi, Luke, how's it going?
  A: Fine. Listen, are you free tonight?
  B: Um, I don't know yet. What have you got in mind?
  A: Well, I was going to go and watch a play with Jude, but she can't make it because she's ill, so I've got an extra ticket. Do you fancy going?
  B: Ah, I don't know. What's on?
  A: *Romeo and Juliet*, with Sarah Porter.
  B: Sounds good. I'll have to make sure I'm not working late, though. Can I phone you back?
  A: Sure, but can you let me know before six?
  B: I'll try.
  A: OK. I'll talk to you later, then.
  B: OK then. Bye!

3　A:　Hi, Joe, it's Luke.
　　B:　Oh, hi, Luke, how's it going?
　　A:　Fine. Listen, are you free on Saturday?
　　B:　Um, I don't know yet. What have you got in mind?
　　A:　Well, I was going to go and watch a football match with Jude, but she can't make it because she's ill, so I've got an extra ticket. Do you fancy going?
　　B:　Ah, I don't know. What's on?
　　A:　Sheffield United versus Manchester City.
　　B:　Sounds good. I'll have to make sure I'm not working on Saturday, though. Can I phone you back?
　　A:　Sure, but can you let me know before Friday?
　　B:　I'll try.
　　A:　OK. I'll talk to you later, then.
　　B:　OK then. Bye!

Unit 7 – Nature's Warning

1　a　rising water levels　　d　industrial waste
　　b　oil spills　　　　　　e　exhaust fumes
　　c　deforestation

The earth's coastline is being reduced because of rising water levels. We should plant more trees to help stop the greenhouse effect.
Forests are being wiped out as a result of deforestation. Logging companies should stop cutting down trees.
The air is being polluted by exhaust fumes. We should use unleaded petrol.
Lakes and rivers are being contaminated because of industrial waste. We should stop using products made in factories which damage the environment.

2　a)　1　ozone layer　3　over fishing　5　global warming
　　　　2　oil spills　　4　waste

　　b)　1　b　　2　d　　3　a　　4　c

3　1　B　　2　A, C, D　　3　C, D　　4　A　　5　D

4　1　south west　　3　plastic　　5　all over
　　2　greenhouses　　4　lightweight

5　1　toxins　2　pollutants　3　longest　4　4,000

6　1　is used　　　　　　　4　is released
　　2　has been taken, are cut down,　5　be put on
　　　　have been reduced　　　　6　be banned
　　3　are being designed,
　　　　will be powered

7　1　c　　3　a　　5　b　　7　c
　　2　c　　4　b　　6　c　　8　b

8　1　F　　3　T　　5　F
　　2　T　　4　F　　6　F

9　Ss' own answers

Unit 8 – One Good Turn Deserves Another

1　2　The project in picture 2 involves volunteering to help refugees.
　　3　The project in picture 3 involves volunteering to examine or treat patients.
　　4　The project in picture 4 involves volunteering to look after sick animals.
　　5　The project in picture 5 involves volunteering to plant trees.

2　Ss' own answers

3　1　T　　3　T　　5　F
　　2　F　　4　F　　6　F

4　1　become a volunteer　　3　can't
　　2　in an advertisement　　4　fill in

5　(Song)

6　1　1920s　　3　Christmas Day　5　Save the Children
　　2　radio show　4　293 million　　6　across the world

7　1　b　　3　a　　5　b　　7　b
　　2　c　　4　c　　6　a　　8　a

8　2　She said that there would be a charity drive the following month.
　　3　She said that they had raised money for more than five hundred families the previous year.
　　4　She said that she hoped they would be able to help as many families as possible in the coming years.
　　5　She said that they didn't only raise money, and that everyone could help by sending in clothes, food or toys.
　　6　She said that they were organizing a TV show to raise more money.

9　1　You must be　　　　3　when would you be
　　2　how did you hear about 4　Would you fill in this form

10　Suggested answer
　　A:　Hello. My name is Rachel Taylor.
　　B:　Nice to meet you, Rachel. How can I help you?
　　A:　I want to become a volunteer at the Santa Maria Children's Shelter.
　　B:　I see. So, why do you want to become a volunteer?
　　A:　Because I like helping children and I am good at teaching.
　　B:　Wonderful. When would you be able to start?
　　A:　Anytime after the beginning of June.
　　B:　That's great. Would you fill in this form, please, and we can sign you up to work for us.
　　A:　Of course. Thank you.

Unit 9 – A Healthy Mind in a Healthy Body

1 a) You need a golf club, a golf ball and a tee to play golf. You need a baseball, a mitt and a bat to play baseball. You need a cricket ball and a bat to play cricket.

   b) Suggested answer

      The most popular sport in my country is football. It is our national sport. You need a football and a pair of trainers or football boots to play it. You play football on a football pitch.

2 1 b   2 d   3 a   4 c

3 1 b   3 a   5 b   7 b
   2 b   4 a   6 a

4 Surname: Palmer
   Address: 47 Hammonds Walk
   Payment: cheque ✓
   Facilities offered: swimming pool, squash courts
   Gym membership: £16
   Full membership: £25

5 1 T   2 F   3 T   4 F

6 1 pitch   3 smallest   5 cup
   2 rolled   4 teams

7 Suggested answer

   A: What's your favourite sport?
   B: Well, I really enjoy playing football.
   A: What do you need for it?
   B: A football and a pair of trainers.
   A: What is it you like about football?
   B: It's an exciting game and it keeps you fit.
   A: What is it you don't like about it?
   B: You can get hurt sometimes.

8 1 She asked if/whether the club had a swimming pool.
   2 She asked if/whether she would have to pay cash.
   3 She asked how much it would cost to be a member.
   4 She asked how often she could come to the gym if she bought the full membership.
   5 She asked how long the gym had been open.
   6 She asked when the gym had first opened.

9 Ss' own answers

10 1 Would you like to just join
    2 What does it cost
    3 What do I get
    4 let me take down
    5 How would you like to pay
    6 Can I pay
    7 welcome to the club

11 Suggested answer

    A: Hello! How can I help you?
    B: Hi! I'd like to join the Sports Club, please.
    A: Certainly.
    B: What does it cost?
    A: It's £30 a month for full membership.
    B: What do I get if I buy the full membership?

A: Well, you get to use the tennis and squash courts, the swimming pool, the gym, the basketball courts and the football pitch.
B: Fine. I'll take the full membership then, please.
A: Great. Now, let me just take down your details. What's your name, please?
B: It's Tony. Tony Walsh.
A: And your address?
B: 34, Rich Street, Leeds.
A: That's fine. How would you like to pay?
B: Can I pay by cheque?
A: Sure. Just make it out to Sunshine Sports Club.
B: OK. Here you go.
A: Here's your card and welcome to the club.
B: Thanks.

Name: Tony
Surname: Walsh
Address: 34 Rich Street, York
Payment: cheque ✓

Unit 10 – Our Changing World

1 a) Suggested answer

      SA: I think the most important invention is the mobile phone because it makes it easy to keep in touch with people wherever they are.
      SB: I disagree. I think the most important invention is the television because people can learn about events taking place all over the world.

   b) Suggested answer

      A: Technology has had a very positive influence on our lives. For example, the world has become a smaller place because now we can use the Internet and satellite phones to keep in touch with people all over the world.
      B: I agree. Communication has been made much easier. Also, information can be spread all over the world on the Internet and via satellites.
      A: Office work has become much faster, too, as these days, everyone uses computers in the workplace. People can do more creative jobs because they have computers to help them.
      B: That's true. Nowadays, machines do all the boring mechanized jobs, so people don't have to do them anymore. Technology has also given us cheap means of entertainment. We can download music from the Internet, or watch programmes and films on TV.
      A: Yes, technology has brought about advances in all aspects of life. Scientists have found cures for diseases, because technology has enabled them to do more research. Life has been made much better for everyone.

2 Suggested answer

   I think that the disadvantages of technology are that people have become less sociable. Now that they can chat online and entertain themselves in the home, they do not bother to go out and meet people as much as they used to.

3 1 T   3 F   5 T
   2 F   4 T   6 T

4 1 15   2 dark   3 protested   4 noise

5   1   a   2   a   3   b   4   a

6   (Song)

7   A   2   If I hadn't left my homework at home, the teacher wouldn't have thought I hadn't done it.
          3   If the alarm had gone off, I wouldn't have been late for class.
          4   If I had studied before the exams, I wouldn't have failed.

     B   1   If I hadn't made a study plan, I would have got stressed during the exam period.
          2   If I hadn't studied hard for the exam, I wouldn't have passed it with flying colours.
          3   If I had slept late, I wouldn't have got up early enough to revise for the test.
          4   If I hadn't listened carefully to the teacher, I wouldn't have been able to answer all her questions.

8   A   2   I wish/ If only my sister would lend me some money.
          3   I wish/If only I could afford to buy a new dress.
          4   I wish/If only I didn't have to wear my old dress to the party.

     B   1   I wish/If only I had got a promotion.
          2   I wish/If only I would get a pay rise.
          3   I wish/If only I could go on holiday.
          4   I wish/If only I didn't have to stay here all summer.

9   1   Did you go out   7   would have been
     2   I hadn't   8   ordered
     3   would still have   9   dropped
     4   did you spend   10   didn't go
     5   we'd try out   11   there'll be
     6   wouldn't have had to wait

10   Suggested answer

A: So, tell me. Did you go out with Sarah last night?
B: Yes, I did, and I wish I hadn't.
A: You wish you hadn't? Why?
B: If I hadn't gone out with her, I would still have my leather jacket and Sarah would still be talking to me.
A: Why? What happened?
B: Well, the thing is, I thought we'd go to the cinema to see that new comedy. Anyway, when we got there, I realized I had forgotten my wallet.
A: Oh dear.
B: I know. If I hadn't forgotten my wallet, Sarah wouldn't have had to pay for the tickets. Also, Sarah hadn't eaten any dinner, so she was very hungry. If she hadn't been hungry, she wouldn't have bought popcorn and Coke.
A: What's wrong with popcorn and Coke?
B: Well, the film was very funny. If it hadn't been so funny, Sarah wouldn't have laughed so much. If she hadn't laughed so much, she wouldn't have spilt Coke all over my leather jacket. If she hadn't spilt Coke on my jacket, I wouldn't have got angry and Sarah would still be talking to me.
A: Oh dear. It sounds like you had a bad evening.
B: You could say that.
A: Oh well … better luck next time.
B: I don't think there will be a next time.

The Adventures of Huckleberry Finn

> # Episode 1 — How It All Started

1   1   a   2   d   3   c   4   e   5   b

2   A   3   C   2   E   1
     B   5   D   6   F   4

3   1   C   3   E   5   B
     2   F   4   A   6   D

4   1   Tom Sawyer   4   In the woods
     2   Judge Thatcher   5   Miss Watson
     3   A dollar each   6   He sees a footprint in the snow

5   1   take care of it ≠ look after the money   Tom
     2   forest ≠ woods   Widow Douglas
     3   formal ≠ smart   Huck
     4   footprint ≠ mark   Huck
     5   big ≠ fancy   Pap

6   Suggested answer

Widow Douglas

Huckleberry Finn and his young friend Tom Sawyer found some gold coins. They took the coins to Judge Thatcher so that he could look after the money for them. The Judge is a sensible man and he decided to give them a dollar each, every day for the rest of their lives. I was worried about Huck, though. Everyone thought his father was dead. Huck was all alone in the world. A young boy shouldn't be living in the woods like a wild animal, not going to school and wearing old clothes. I told him to come and live with me, so that I could look after him. I don't think he liked going to school and wearing smart clothes, but he became friends with my sister's slave, Jim, and he seemed to be happy. Then one day, Huck's Pap came back.

Judge Thatcher

Huckleberry Finn and his young friend Tom Sawyer found some gold coins. They brought the coins to me so that I could look after the money for them. I decided to give them a dollar each, every day for the rest of their lives. Widow Douglas came to my home and spoke to Huck. She told him that it wasn't right for him to be living in the woods like a wild animal and not going to school. We all thought the boy's father was dead, so the Widow told Huck to go and live with her. I don't think he liked going to school much, or having to follow rules for the first time in his life, but he became friends with Miss Watson's slave, Jim, and I think he was happy enough, until his Pap came back.

Tom Sawyer

Huck and I found some gold coins! We couldn't believe it – we were rich! We asked Judge Thatcher to look after the money for us and he told us he would give us a dollar each, every day for the rest of our lives! We were very happy. Then the Widow Douglas told Huck that he shouldn't live in the woods like a wild animal and that he should go and live with her and go to school! I don't think he liked the idea very much. We saw each other every day at school and Huck told me Miss Watson made lots of rules. Huck didn't like rules! He liked Miss Watson's slave, Jim, though. Then one day, Huck's Pap came back. We all thought he was dead, but we were wrong. He was a bad man and I think Huck was afraid of him.

Episode 2 — How Huck Was Murdered

1   1 a   2 b   3 b

2   1 F   3 T   5 F   7 F
    2 T   4 T   6 T

3   1   Widow Douglas wants Huck to live with her.
    5   Huck wants to escape and run away from Pap.
    7   Huck thinks Pap won't try to find him.

4
```
            ¹J U D G E
         ²B E A T
            ³C H A N C E
    ⁴L O C K E D
            ⁵S C H O O L
       ⁶W O O D S
              N
              S
          ⁷W I D O W
              I
              S
            ⁸L I F E
            ⁹C A B I N
        ¹⁰R U N ▢ A W A Y
     ¹¹M U R D E R
```

5   A 4 – Huck killed a pig to make it look as though he had
                been murdered.
    B 3 – Huck made it look as though robbers had got into the
                cabin.
    C 2 – Pap locked Huck in the cabin.
    D 1 – Pap took Huck to live in the woods with him.
    E 5 – Huck escaped and went to Jackson's Island.

6   Suggested answer

    I think Huck's father will be very angry when he returns, but I don't
    think he will try to find Huck because he will think that Huck has
    been murdered.

Episode 3 — Jackson's Island

1   1 d   2 c   3 e   4 a   5 b

2   a 3   c 6   e 2
    b 1   d 4   f 5

3   2   Where does Huck hide?
        On Jackson's Island.

    3   Why did Jim run away?
        Because Miss Watson wanted to sell him.

    4   Where do Jim and Huck make camp?
        On Jackson's Island.

    5   What do they find floating down the river?
        A raft/A house.

    6   Why does Huck want to go to town?
        To get the latest news.

7   Why does Huck dress up as a girl?
    So that no one will recognise him.

4
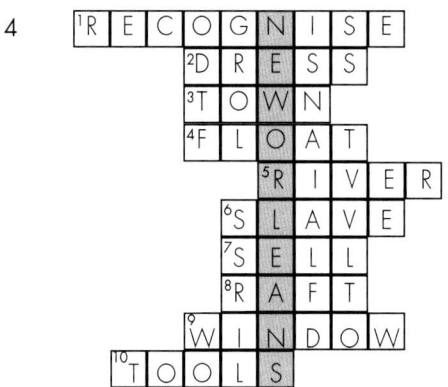
```
¹R E C O G N I S E
  ²D R E S S
  ³T O W N
  ⁴F L O A T
       ⁵R I V E R
  ⁶S L A V E
  ⁷S E L L
  ⁸R A F T
      ⁹W I N D O W
¹⁰T O O L S
```

5   1   we'll ever find   3   will recognise   5   all sorts of
    2   wants to sell me   4   ran away from

6   Suggested answer

    SA: I think that someone will recognise Huck and he will have to
         go back to live with the Widow Douglas.
    SB: I disagree. I think that Huck will hear some exciting news.
         Maybe his Pap has gone away forever and Huck will be
         free. etc.

Episode 4 — Sarah Williams

1   1 a   2 b   3 a   4 b

2   Suggested answer

    I think that Huck tells the woman that he is new in town. I think the
    woman tells Huck that he has been murdered and that Miss
    Watson's slave ran away.

3   1   never met   3   have to go
    2   slave ran away   4   midnight…gun

4   1   To get the latest news.   4 $300
    2   Because she has never met him.   5   Mr Loftus.
    3   They think he has murdered Huck.

5   1   dressed   3   name   5   reward
    2   new   4   murderer   6   husband

6   a 6   c 3   e 4   g 5
    b 1   d 2   f 7

7   Suggested answer

    Jim: Huck! You're back! What happened?
    Huck: I met a woman called Mrs Loftus. She was new in town
           so she had never met me.
    Jim: Did she believe that you were a girl?
    Huck: She did at first. I told her my name was Sarah Williams. She
           told me that I had been murdered, and that you ran away
           the same day. Jim, everyone thinks you are the murderer.
           They think you are hiding here on Jackson's Island. Mr Loftus
           is coming to Jackson's Island at midnight with a gun!
    Jim: Oh no!
    Huck: Yes, and then Mrs Loftus saw that I was a boy and I had
           to go.

Jim: Huck. If they think I am the murderer then I am in trouble. What are we going to do?
Huck: We'll have to use the raft to escape, Jim. Let's go!

Episode 5 — Down the Mississippi

1 1 b   2 a   3 a

2 Suggested answer

If I were in Huck and Jim's position, I would go down the river on the raft and try to get to a new town where nobody knew me. I would start a new life there.

3 A 2   B 1   C 5   D 3   E 4

4 1 a   2 d   3 c   4 e   5 b

5 1 float, joins   4 awfully, taking
   2 reach, sell, steamboat   5 past, fog
   3 stars, lit up

6 Suggested answer

I think that the steamboat is going to hit Huck and Jim's raft, but I don't think they will be hurt. They will have to swim to the shore and find another way of getting to Cairo.

Episode 6 — Travelling with Royalty

1 a) 1 moustache   3 old suit   5 beard
       2 bow tie   4 bald spot

   b) The first man has short brown hair and a moustache. He is wearing an old suit and a bow tie.
       The second man is older. He has got white hair with a bald spot and a beard. He is wearing a black coat.

2 1 B   3 A   5 A, B
   2 C, D   4 C   6 D

3 1 To return in a steamboat.
   2 People found out they were trying to cheat them.
   3 A runaway slave.
   4 He thinks they are liars.
   5 To make money.

4

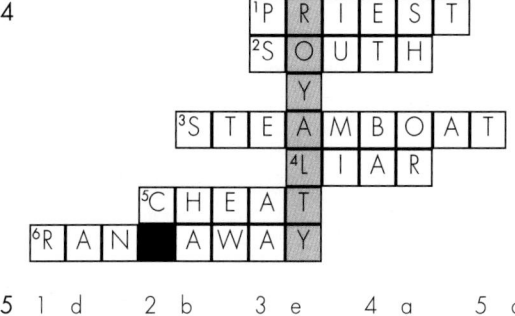

5 1 d   2 b   3 e   4 a   5 c

6 Suggested answer

A man came to my house and knocked on the door. When I opened it, he told me that he was a priest. He said that he needed money to help the poor, so I gave him money, food and clothes.

The next day, I saw him wearing the clothes himself! He played the same trick on everyone in town and took everyone's money and clothes!

Episode 7 — The Wilks Brothers

1 1 f   2 a   3 d   4 b   5 e   6 c

2 1 T   3 T   5 F   7 T
   2 F   4 F   6 F

3 1 It was Peter Wilks' desire that Harvey took care of his niece and her sisters.
   2 Huck plays the role of Harvey Wilks' servant.
   3 The "Duke" and the "King" decide to give the money to the girls.
   4 Mary Jane doesn't think that the men are lying.

4 1 letter   4 deaf and dumb   7 hide
   2 niece   5 servant   8 sell
   3 priest   6 trust   9 gold

5 a 5   c 1   e 2   g 6
   b 4   d 7   f 3

6 Suggested answer

Mary Jane
Two men came to the house and said that they were my Uncles Harvey and William. They had a young servant with them called Adolphus. I gave Uncle Harvey the letter from Uncle Peter, which told them where his gold was hidden. Uncle Harvey gave me the gold. There was $6,000! Dr Robinson told me not to trust Harvey and William, but I told him that I did trust them, and asked Uncle Harvey to look after the money for me and my sisters.

Dr Robinson
Two men arrived in town. They said that they were Peter Wilks' brothers, Harvey and William. Mary Jane gave them a letter from her uncle Peter. The two men found Peter's gold and gave it to Mary Jane. I didn't trust them and I told Mary Jane that they weren't who they said they were, but she didn't listen to me. She gave the gold to the older man and asked him to look after it for her and her sisters.

Episode 8 — Peter Wilks' Funeral

1 1 a   2 a   3 b

2 1 b   2 a   3 a   4 a

3 Ss' own answers

4 2 Harvey Wilks told Dr Robinson that he could prove that he was Peter's brother.
   3 When they dug up Peter Wilks they found the gold in the coffin.
   4 Huck ran back to the raft.
   5 Huck woke up late and the "Duke" told him that the "King" had taken Jim to sell him.

5 1 bought ≠ sold   4 opportunity ≠ chance
   2 hidden ≠ safe   5 think ≠ suppose
   3 show ≠ prove   6 raft ≠ rope

6 Suggested answer

King: Wake up! Let's go!
Jim: What's happening?
King: You're coming with me.
Jim: Where are we going?
King: We're going into town. I need some money and I could get
       a good price for a slave like you.
Jim: But I'm Huck's slave. You can't sell me!
King: Oh yes, I can! Come on!

Episode 9 — Looking for Jim

1 2 In picture 2 Silas and Sally Phelps are standing outside the
      farmhouse.
   3 In picture 3 Jim is wearing chains.
   4 In picture 4 Tom and Huck are holding snakes and rats.
   5 In picture 5 Tom and Huck are walking along a country road.

2 1 expecting, nephew   4 have to, wearing
   2 met, rescue   5 saying, steal
   3 Unlock

3 1 Two miles.
   2 Her nephew (Tom Sawyer). She is expecting him.
   3 He has to get his suitcase.
   4 To find Tom.
   5 His brother, Sid.
   6 To rescue him tonight.
   7 Rescue Jim in style.

4 Suggested answer

Tom – You have to stay here for at least a week, and then escape
wearing Aunt Sally's dress.
Huck – Um, I have to go to town to get my suitcase…
Jim – Unlock my chains and let's go!
Sally – We've been expecting you.

5 1 house   4 town   7 style
   2 nephew   5 keeping   8 escape
   3 expecting   6 rescue   9 guns

6 Ss take roles and act out the episode.

Episode 10 — A Happy End

1 1 b   2 c   3 a   4 d

2 Suggested answer

I think that Tom and Huck will rescue Jim. I don't think that Jim will
get caught, but I think that someone will get hurt. I don't think that
Huck's father will come to get him back.

3 A 2   B 5   C 3   D 4   E 1

4 1 C   2 D   3 A   4 B   5 E

5 Suggested answer

Huck and Tom help Jim escape but Silas and his friends are
waiting with guns. They shoot at Huck, Tom and Jim as they are
running for the raft. Huck, Tom and Jim get away, but Tom has
been shot. Jim says that he won't leave Tom. Huck gets a doctor,
then he goes and tells Aunt Sally the truth. Aunt Sally goes to Tom
and the doctor tells her that Jim helped him instead of running
away, so she shouldn't treat him badly. Tom tells Huck and Jim that
Jim isn't a slave any more because Miss Watson set him free, and
he gives Jim $40 for being a good prisoner. Jim tells Huck that the
dead man in the floating house was his Pap, so he is free too.
Sally and Silas ask Huck if he would like to live with them, but he
doesn't want to because he wants to go somewhere new and
have more adventures.

6 1 free – T   3 set - T
   2 leave – J   4 prisoner – T

7 a) 1 Huck. Huck is wearing a straw hat and a white shirt. He
          has got short blond hair and brown eyes. He is
          adventurous, brave and honest. He is also independent.
          He doesn't like following rules.
       2 Tom. Tom is wearing a white shirt and a sleeveless
          pullover. He has got short black hair and brown eyes. Tom
          is adventurous and cheerful. He is not very sensible,
          though.
       3 Jim is wearing a cream shirt. He has got short black hair,
          a beard and a moustache. Jim is kind and friendly.
       4 The "King". The "King" is wearing a black coat. He has got
          white hair with a bald spot and brown eyes. He has also
          got a beard and moustache. The "King" is dishonest. He
          lies and cheats all the time.
       5 The "Duke". The "Duke" is wearing an old suit and a bow
          tie. He has got black hair and dark eyes. He has also got
          a moustache. The "Duke" is dishonest. He lies and cheats
          all the time.
       6 Pap. Pap is wearing an old brown jacket and an old
          brown hat. He has got long brown hair and brown eyes.
          He is very ugly. Pap is aggressive and treats Huck badly.
          He is bossy and unkind.

   b) Suggested answer

       My name is Huckleberry Finn. I used to live in the woods,
       but one day my best friend Tom and I found some gold coins.
       We took them to Judge Thatcher and asked him to look after
       the money for us. He decided to give us a dollar each, every
       day for the rest of our lives. Then, Widow Douglas told me
       that it wasn't right for me to live in the woods like a wild
       animal and not go to school. Everyone thought my Pap was
       dead, so the widow told me to go and live with her. I had to
       go to school, wear smart clothes and follow all the rules that
       the widow's sister, Miss Watson, made. I liked Miss Watson's
       slave, Jim, though, and we became friends. One day, I saw
       a mark in the snow. It was from Pap's boot, so I knew he
       wasn't dead. That night, he came to get me.
       Pap took me to live with him in a cabin in the woods. He
       locked me in the cabin when he went into town. One day, I
       escaped. I made it look as though robbers had got into the
       cabin and I shot a pig and dragged it to the river so that it
       would look as though I had been murdered. I got in a little
       boat and went to Jackson's Island.
       People from the town thought I was dead. They were
       looking for my body. I stayed on Jackson's Island where I was

safe. One day, I found Jim on the island! He had run away because Miss Watson wanted to sell him. We made camp on the island. We found lots of things floating down the river, like a raft, and even a house! Inside the house were lots of clothes and tools. There was a dead man in there, too, but Jim wouldn't let me look at him. I found a dress in the floating house, so I decided to dress up as a girl and go into town to get the latest news.

I found a woman who was new in town and had never met me. I told her my name was Sarah Williams. She told me that I had been murdered and that everyone thought Jim was the murderer because he ran away on the same day. There was a reward for Jim, and people thought he was hiding on Jackson's Island, so her husband was going there at midnight with a gun. I hurried back to the island and Jim and I escaped on the raft.

We sailed down the Mississippi. We planned to go down the river to Cairo, get some money, then come back up the river on a steamboat. Jim wanted to go to the free states where he would be free, so that he could free his wife and children. But one night, it was very foggy, and we went past Cairo. Then, a steamboat hit our raft and we had to jump into the river!

We fixed the raft and carried on down the river. One day, we heard shouting and two men ran towards the river. They had been trying to cheat the people in the town, and everyone wanted to catch them. They came onto our raft. The older man said that he was the King of France, and the younger man said that he was the Duke of Bridgewater. Jim and I knew that they were liars, but we didn't know how to get rid of them. The "King" and the "Duke" decided to act out scenes from Shakespeare in the riverside towns to make some money, but they were bad actors and no one liked them.

One day, we came to a town and met a traveller. He told the "King" about a man named Peter Wilks who had died. Peter's brothers were coming from England to look after his nieces. Well, the "King" and the "Duke" decided to pretend to be Peter Wilks' brothers and I had to pretend to be their servant, Adolphus. Peter's niece, Mary Jane, gave them a letter from Peter, telling them where his gold was hidden. The "King" and the "Duke" found the gold and decided to give it to Mary Jane so that she would trust them. A man called Dr Robinson, who was a friend of Mary Jane's, didn't trust them at all, but Mary Jane did and she gave them the money to look after. They hid it in their room, but I took it and hid it in Peter's coffin. I planned to write and tell Mary Jane where it was when I had escaped.

The next day was Peter Wilks' funeral. When they put the coffin in the ground, I knew the gold was safe. Then, two men arrived and said that they were the Wilks' brothers! The older man said that he could prove it because Peter had a blue mark on his chest. Dr Robinson said that they would dig Peter up again to find out which of the brothers were lying. They found the gold in the coffin and knew that the "King" and the "Duke" were lying. I ran back to the raft and tried to escape, but I wasn't fast enough. The "King" and the "Duke" caught up with me.

We continued to sail down the river until one morning, I woke up late. Jim was gone! The "Duke" told me that the "King" had taken him into town to sell him, so I decided to go and look for him. A boy in town told me that Silas Phelps had bought the slave, so I went to his farm. When I arrived, a woman called me Tom Sawyer and said that she had been expecting me! The Phelps were Tom's aunt and uncle! I told

them that I had to go back into town to get my suitcase, and I found Tom on the road. He said that I should pretend to be him, and he would pretend to be his brother, Sid.

We found Jim in a shed. I wanted to rescue him that night, but Tom said we should do it in style. We brought Jim snakes and rats to keep as pets like a real prisoner and told him he had to stay there for a week, then escape wearing one of Aunt Sally's dresses. Tom wrote a letter to Silas, telling him that someone was going to steal Jim, then that night, we went into the shed and got Jim. We tried to run to the raft, but Silas and his friends were waiting with guns. Tom got shot, and Jim told me to go and get help while he stayed with Tom. I got a doctor and then I told Aunt Sally the truth. The doctor told her that Jim had helped him instead of running away, so she shouldn't treat him badly. Then Tom said that Jim wasn't a slave any more because Miss Watson had set him free. Tom gave Jim $40 for being such a good prisoner, so Jim was rich and free. I was free too, because Jim told me that the dead man in the floating house had been my Pap. Aunt Sally and Uncle Silas asked me if I wanted to stay with them, but I didn't want to. I wanted to be free to have more adventures!   etc

CLICK ON 3

Virginia Evans - Neil O'Sullivan

AROUND THE
ENGLISH-SPEAKING
WORLD

Express Publishing

1 Clans

Lead-in

Which of the pictures (A-E) shows:

1 Castle Campbell in Scotland?   A
2 an ancient Aborigine rock painting?   D
3 a Scotsman wearing a kilt?   B
4 the tartan of the MacDonald clan?   C
5 an Aborigine elder today?   E

Listening

Listen and circle the correct words.

1 Scottish clans were ruled by a
(chief)/king.
2 Tartan is a **clan surname**/(**type of cloth**).
3 Aborigines have lived in Australia
since 1788/(for 40,000 years).
4 Aborigines believed it was important to
(look after)/fight for the clan's land.

Reading

a) **Read the texts and mark the
sentences *S* (Scotland), *A* (Australia)
or *B* (both), then use your dictionary
to look up the words in bold.**

Scottish Clans

The **Gaelic** word "clan" means "children", but it is also used to describe a large group of families, all **related** to the same **ancestors**.

The Scottish clans began 800-1000 years ago in the Highlands of northern Scotland. Each clan might include several thousand people, and was **ruled** by a chief. All members of a clan were expected to be **loyal** to the chief and to each other. Fighting between clans was common, and powerful clans such as the MacDonalds or the Campbells had wide areas of clan **territory**.

All members of a clan had the same surname, and all wore the same tartan. This is a type of **woollen cloth** with a pattern of coloured checks, and each clan had its own design. In early Scotland, only Highlanders wore kilts — Lowlanders, as Scots from the south are called, saw them as **barbaric**. In those days the kilt was just a long piece of thick tartan cloth **wrapped** around the body and held in place with a belt.

Nowadays, kilts are part of the national dress of Scotland, and are worn with **pride** by Highlanders and Lowlanders **alike**.

Australian Aborigines

Aborigines (*ab origine* is Latin for "from the beginning") were the first **inhabitants** of Australia. When English **colonists** reached Australia in 1788, the Aborigines had been there for at least 40,000 years.

They lived in small **bands** of a few families, moving from place to place to hunt animals and **gather** roots and fruit for food. Each band was part of a clan, made up of other family groups who had the same ancestors. The clan didn't have a chief, but the elders (**respected** older men) usually made any important decisions. The whole clan **shared** a wide territory where they lived and hunted, and they would all get together at certain times of the year for **religious rituals**.

Part of their religious belief was the need to take care of the land and all plants and animals on it. As well as humans, each clan included several species of animals, which were seen as related members of the clan. Songs, dances and painting had religious importance, too. Some **ancient** Aborigine rock paintings can still be seen today.

Sadly, the traditional Aborigine culture has almost completely **disappeared** now, but it has a special place in Australia's history.

1 Families were part of a larger group called a clan. **B**
2 Clans often fought each other. **S**
3 Clans owned wide areas of land. **B**
4 Certain animals were seen as members of the clan. **A**
5 The clansmen's traditional dress is more popular now than in the past. **S**
6 All the members of the clan used to meet from time to time. **A**

b) Read the texts again and find words similar to words in your language.

(Ss' own answers)

Speaking

- Who were the first inhabitants of your country? Where did they come from?
- What do you know about your own ancestors?

(Ss' own answers)

2 By Land and Sea

Lead-in

Which of the pictures (A-C) show(s):

1 a traditional Inuit dog sled?   B
2 a skin boat called a curragh?   C
3 a competitor in a sled dog race? A

Listening

Listen and circle the correct word(s).

1 Early settlers used **snowmobiles/ dog sleds** to get around in Canada.
2 Siberian Huskies are the **fastest/most popular** sled dogs used in racing.
3 Racers in the John Beargrease Marathon carry a **parcel/letter** on their sleds.
4 A curragh is a type of **boat/fisherman**.
5 Today, curraghs are usually made of **wood and canvas/steel and fibreglass**.

Reading

a) **Read the texts and answer the questions, then use your dictionary to look up the words in bold.**

Canadian Dog Sleds

In the freezing winter months, much of Canada is covered with snow and ice. The Inuit people, Canada's first inhabitants, have travelled by dog sled for thousands of years. When **settlers** from Europe arrived, they copied the Inuit means of transport.

Nowadays, **snowmobiles** have replaced dog sleds as the normal way of getting around, but sleds are still used for fun or sport, especially sled dog racing.

Although there are many types of sled dogs used for racing, Siberian Huskies are probably the most **popular**. Each dog wears a **harness** connected to a long rope on the front of the sled. Drivers, who are called 'mushers', don't have any **reins**. Instead, they control the dogs by shouting **commands**, such as "gee" (turn right) and "haw" (turn left).

There are large numbers of **keen** sled dog racers in parts of Canada and Alaska. There are short speed races, as well as races that can last several days, and there is big prize money for top **events**. One such race is the John Beargrease Marathon, named after the man who used a dog sled to deliver the **mail** over a century ago. Today, competitors in the race carry a letter on their sleds in his memory.

Irish Skin Boats

Humans began making boats 50,000 years ago, and one of the earliest types had a wooden **frame** covered in animal skins. The ancient Egyptians, the Vikings, the Inuit and other native Americans all used skin boats. Celts arriving in Ireland around 6000 BC used boats of this kind, which they called **curraghs**, for fishing. The surprising thing, however, is that Irish fishermen still use curraghs today.

Medieval Irish curraghs were made in the traditional way, but many of them also had **sails**. Some were 20 metres long, with a crew of 6-10 people. A curragh built in Cork in 1750 was over 30 metres long, the largest ever made.

Nowadays, the fishermen do not use animal skins, but a tough cloth called **canvas**, which they **stretch** over a light wooden frame. They then paint the canvas with **tar**, which hardens to make the boat **waterproof**.

The results may look **primitive**, but curraghs have one great advantage over other fishing boats. They are as light as a feather and rise high on the waves, so they can **survive** rough, stormy seas and rocky shores, when steel or **fibreglass** boats would crack or **sink**. That's why so many of Ireland's fishermen prefer curraghs, especially on Ireland's beautiful but dangerous west coast.

©

1 What traditional form of transport did the Inuit use to travel over land? dog sleds
2 How do dog sled drivers control the dogs when they are racing? by shouting commands
3 Who was John Beargrease? A man who used a dog sled to deliver the mail a century ago.
4 When were the first skin boats made? 50,000 years ago
5 How are today's curraghs different from those of the past? Canvas is used to cover the wooden frame instead of animal skins.

6 What advantage do curraghs have over other fishing boats? They are very much lighter.

b) **Read the texts again and find words similar to words in your language.**

(Ss' own answers)

Speaking

• What traditional types of transport are still used in your country? What are they used for? Briefly describe one of these.

(Ss' own answers)

3 Home to Royalty

Listening

 Listen and answer the questions.

1 Who was born in Edinburgh Castle?
James I

2 When is the Military Tattoo, and how long does it last? every August - 3 weeks

3 Whose holiday home was Osborne House? Queen Victoria

4 What was the Swiss cottage used for?
a playhouse

Reading

a) **Read the texts and match the headings (A-E) to the paragraphs (1-4) in each text. There is an extra heading you do not need.**

A A lot to see
B Used by the Army
C Home to royalty
D Ancient traditions live on
E A national symbol

Edinburgh Castle

1 C Edinburgh Castle, situated high above the city on Castle Rock, was once the home of the kings and queens of Scotland. The 700-year-old **Crown** of Scotland is still on display there, and the Royal apartments include a tiny room where the future king of England, James I, was born in 1566.

2 E The castle was the site of many battles with the English. Over the centuries it **survived** many attempts to destroy it, which is why many Scots see it as a **symbol** of their own survival.

3 B Visitors to the castle will see a **military guard** at the gate, because the castle is still the **headquarters** of the army's Scottish Division. The famous Military Tattoo is also held here every August. This is a **spectacular** three-week festival of **bagpipe** and band music, **marching** and displays by Scottish **regiments**.

4 A Edinburgh Castle houses exhibitions of Scottish history and a collection of **armour** and **weapons**. As well as what there is to see inside, the castle's hilltop position offers the best views of the city.

Osborne House

1 C Osborne House is located on the Isle of Wight, overlooking the sea. A beautiful Italian-style **stately home**, it was the holiday home of Queen Victoria and her family.

2 E Osborne House has been kept almost exactly as it was when Queen Victoria lived and died there. The rooms are full of the Queen's personal possessions, including pictures and books. Visitors can also see how the Royal Family spent their leisure time. In the grounds there is a Swiss cottage designed as a **playhouse** for the royal children, as well as beautiful gardens open to the public.

3 A One of the **jewels** of Osborne House is the Durbar Room. The beautifully decorated walls and ceiling were made by Indian craftsmen. This room was where Victoria entertained **heads of state**, but it was also where her children used to perform plays for their parents.

4 D Queen Victoria saw Osborne House as her home, and its **privacy** was an escape from the **formal** atmosphere of Buckingham Palace. Today it stands as a **memorial** to Britain's much-loved and longest **reigning** queen.

A A room for official and family occasions
B Playground of the rich and famous
C A holiday home
D A private place
E House and gardens

b) Use your dictionary to look up the words in bold. Then, make notes under each of the headings, and use your notes to talk about each building.

c) Read the texts again and find words similar to words in your language. (Ss' own answers)

Speaking

- Which of the two buildings would you most like to visit? Why?
- Briefly describe a historic building from your country. When and why was it built? What can visitors see and do there?

(Ss' own answers)

4 In Search of a New Life

Lead-in

What is the difference between:

1 an *emigrant* and an *immigrant*?
one who leaves his country to live in another - a settler who arrives in a new country

2 a *passport* and a *visa*?
travel document issued by your country - permission to enter/stay in a country for a limited time

3 *permanent* and *temporary*?
for ever - for a limited period

4 a *close* relative and a *distant* relative?
parents/children, brothers/sisters, grandparents, aunts/uncles and first cousins - second & third cousins etc

Listening

Listen and mark the statements T (true) or F (false).

1 Australian Non-Business Visas are for people who don't need to work.   F

2 You must have a place on a course before you can apply for an Australian student visa.   T

3 It's easy to get a visa to live and work in the US.   F

4 A green card allows you live in the US permanently.   T

Reading

a) **Read the texts and mark each statement *A* (Australia), *U* (USA) or *B* (both), then use your dictionary to look up the words in bold.**

Australia

Thousands of people **emigrate** to Australia every year, leaving their own countries in search of a better life 'Down Under'. It's a huge, brave step and it takes months of **paperwork** before they can be accepted into their new country.

There are two main types of **permanent visas** for a move to Australia. For Class A (Non-Business Visas) there is a points system. The more points you score for things like qualifications and experience, the better your chances of being given a visa. However, the points system **applies** only to younger people, and anyone over 45 must have **close relatives** in Australia in order to get a Class A visa. Class B (Business Visas) are mostly for people who own successful companies and want to **base** them in Australia.

There are several **circumstances** which allow you to get a **temporary** visa. One of the easiest ways to live in Australia for a while is as a student. If you can pay your course fees and living expenses, you can stay in the country for the **duration** of your studies. Naturally, your school, college or university must accept you on the course before you can apply for a visa.

The USA

The United States of America (US) has often been called a nation of immigrants. For **centuries**, people moved to the US in search of the 'American Dream', and millions of people a year still apply for visas to live and work in the US. Nowadays, however, the United States has very **strict** immigration controls.

There are two main types of visa. A non-immigrant visa is given to people visiting the US for a temporary period — for example, as a tourist, or to study at an American university. If you want to live in the US permanently, you need an immigrant visa. (This is known as a "green card", although these days the visas are actually white, pink or **multi-coloured**.)

There are a number of ways in which you can **qualify** for a green card, such as having close relatives who are American **citizens**, or **investing** money to start your own business in the US. There are limited numbers of visas **issued** each year, though, so you will probably be put on a **waiting list**. This means that, even if you meet all the **requirements**, it might be a long time before you can start a new life in the United States.

1 Qualifying for a visa is based on a points system.   A
2 You can get a visa if you have close relatives who already live there.   B
3 If you are under 45, well-qualified and experienced, you have a good chance of getting a visa.   A
4 You can get a permanent visa if you have your own businesss there.   B
5 You may have to wait a long time to get a visa.   U
6 You can get a temporary visa to study at a university there.   B

b) Read the texts again and find words similar to words in your language.

(Ss' own answers)

Speaking

- Would you ever emigrate to another country? Why/Why not? If you had to emigrate, where would you choose to go, and why?
- Does your country have many immigrants? What are the rules concerning visas to visit or live in your country?   (Ss' own answers)

5 Highways to the Sea

Lead-in

Which of the pictures (A-D) shows:

1 Tower Bridge in London? D
2 a Mississippi riverboat? A
3 the Thames Barrier? C
4 the Thames in London at low tide? B

Listening

**Listen and mark the statements
T (true) or *F* (false).**

1 New Orleans is in the heart of
the US. F
2 The French and Spanish explored
North America in the 1800s. F
3 Abraham Lincoln wrote several
books about the Mississippi. F
4 The Thames is the longest river
in the UK. F
5 William Shakespeare's theatre
was next to the Thames. T

Reading

a) **Read the texts and mark each
statement *M* (Mississippi), *T* (Thames)
or *B* (both), then use your dictionary
to look up the words in bold.**

The Mighty Mississippi

Dividing the US from north to south, the mighty Mississippi River flows 3,760 kilometres through the **heart** of the country to New Orleans. Native Americans called it *Mizi-sipi* ("Father of Waters" or "Big River"), and it is the largest river in North America.

Before the days of roads and railways, the river was an important means of travel and **transportation**. The French and Spanish used the river to **explore** North America, and when steamboats began to travel the Mississippi in the 1800s, it became a **major trade route**. The river is still one of the busiest **commercial** waterways in the world.

Passengers today can travel the river on a Mississippi riverboat exactly like the **luxury** steamboats of the 19th century. They enjoy the history and adventure of the past as they admire the beautiful scenery of the river.

The Mississippi has a special place in the history and **literature** of North America. One of the greatest US Presidents, Abraham Lincoln, worked as a boatman on the river. Mark Twain, who grew up in a small town on the banks of the Mississippi and worked as a riverboat pilot, helped make the river famous through works such as *Huckleberry Finn* and *Life on the Mississippi*. Twain loved the Mississippi, and he compared it to a "wonderful book" which has "a new story to tell every day."

Ⓐ

10(T)

London and the River Thames

Only 338 kilometres long, the River Thames is not the longest river in the UK, but it is the most famous and important. Nearly 2,000 years ago, the Romans built a small town called Londinium next to the Thames which grew into what is now London. The river helped to make London one of the world's major **ports**, even though it is 50 kilometres from the sea.

For more than a thousand years, trading ships sailed up the Thames to London. The huge London **docks** built in the 1800s have now been replaced by newer ones at Tilbury, further **downstream**, but the lower part of the Thames is still one of the world's most important commercial waterways.

Visitors to London can enjoy sightseeing cruises along the Thames, past some of the city's most famous **landmarks**, such as Big Ben and Tower Bridge. Some cruises go down as far as the Thames Barrier, built to protect London from **flooding** by the **tide**. (The level of the Thames in London rises and falls 7 metres with the tide in the North Sea.)

London and the Thames have been part of the lives and works of great writers and poets throughout England's history. For instance, William Shakespeare's *Globe* theatre stood on the bank of the Thames, while many of Charles Dickens' great novels are about the city and the river which runs through its heart.

1 It is a busy commercial waterway. B
2 It is the largest river in its country. M
3 It started to carry trade goods in the 1800s. M
4 One of its bridges is a famous landmark. T
5 There are things worth looking at if you travel on the river. B
6 It is mentioned in the literature of its country. B

b) **Read the texts again and find words similar to words in your language.** (Ss' own answers)

Speaking

- Which is the longest/most famous river in your country? What is its history?
- What other famous cities are built on the banks of a river? What do you know about each of these cities/rivers?

(Ss' own answers)

American English–
British English Guide

American English	British English	American English	British English
A		**D**	
account	bill/account	delivery truck	van
band aid	sticking plaster	desk clerk	receptionist
airplane	aeroplane	dessert	pudding/dessert/ sweet
antenna	aerial		
anyplace, anywhere	anywhere	downtown	centre (city/ business)
apartment	flat		
area code	dialling code (phone)	drapes	curtains
		dresser	chest of drawers
B		druggist/pharmacist	chemist
bathrobe	dressing gown	drugstore/ pharmacy	chemist's (shop)
bathtub	bath		
bill	banknote	duplex	semi-detached
billion=thousand million	billion=million million	**E**	
broil	grill	eggplant	aubergine
bureau	chest of drawers	elevator	lift
busy	engaged (phone)	eraser	rubber, eraser
C		**F**	
cab	taxi	fall	autumn
call/phone	ring up/phone	faucet	tap
can	tin	first floor, second floor etc.	ground floor, first floor etc
candy	sweets		
candy store	sweet shop/ confectioner	flashlight	torch
		flat (tire)	flat tyre, puncture
check	bill (restaurant)	freeway/highway	motorway
closet	cupboard	french fries	chips
closet (hanging clothes)	wardrobe	freshman (at university)	1st year undergraduate
connect (telephone)	put through	front desk (hotel)	reception
cookie	biscuit		
corn	sweetcorn, maize		
couch/sofa	sofa		
crazy	mad		

American English–British English

American English	British English	American English	British English
G		**O**	
garbage/trash	rubbish	office (doctor's/	surgery
garbage can/trash	dustbin/bin	dentist's)	
can		one-way (ticket)	single (ticket)
gas	petrol	overalls	dungarees
gas station	petrol station/		
	garage	**P**	
grade	class/form	pants, trousers	trousers
		pantyhose/nylons	tights
I		parka	anorak
intermission	interval	parking lot	car park
intersection	crossroads	pass (vehicle, etc)	overtake/pass
		pavement	road surface
J		pedestrian crossing	zebra crossing
janitor	caretaker/porter	(potato) chips	crisps
jello	jelly	public school	state school
jump rope	skipping rope	purse	handbag
		pocketbook	purse
K			
kerosene	paraffin	**R**	
		railroad	railway
L		restroom	toilet/cloakroom/
lawyer/attorney	lawyer/solicitor/		public convenience
	barrister	round-trip (ticket)	return (ticket)
lost and found	lost property		
		S	
M		salesclerk/	shop assistant
mail	post	salesperson	
mailman	postman	schedule	timetable
make a reservation	book	Scotch tape	Sellotape
motorcycle	motorbike/	shorts (underwear)	pants
	motorcycle	sidewalk	pavement
movie	film	stand in line	queue
movie house/	cinema	store, shop	shop
theater		subway	underground
N			
newsstand	newsagent		

American English–British English

American English	British English	American English	British English
T			
truck	lorry, van		
two weeks	fortnight, two weeks		

Grammar

American English	British English
Do you have a car?/Have you got a car?	Have you got a car?

V

American English	British English
vacation	holiday(s)
vacuum (v.)	hoover
vacuum cleaner	hoover
vest	waistcoat

Spelling

American English	British English
aluminum	aluminium
analyze	analyse
center	centre
check (n)	cheque (n)
color	colour
defense	defence
honor	honour
jewelry	jewellery
labor	labour
practice (n, v)	practice (n)
	practise (v)
program	programme
realize	realise
theater	theatre
tire	tyre
trave(l)ler	traveller

W

American English	British English
with or without (milk/cream in coffee)	black or white

Y

American English	British English
yard	garden

Z

American English	British English
(pronounced "zee")	(pronounced "zed")
zero	nought
zip code	postcode

Grammar

American English	British English
She just went out./She has just gone out.	She has just gone out.
My sister had a baby.	My sister has had a baby.
Did you write the letters yet?	Have you written the letters yet?
Hello, is this Ann?	Hello, is that Ann?

Expressions with prepositions and particles

American English	British English
different from/than	different from/to
live on X street	live in X street
on a team	in a team
on the weekend	at the weekend
Monday through Friday	Monday to Friday